The Forty-Seven Rōnin

The forty-seven rōnin vendetta is one of the most famous incidents in Japanese history, but it is also one of the most misunderstood. John A. Tucker seeks to provide a credible account of the vendetta and its afterlife in history. He suggests that, when considered historically and holistically, the vendetta appears as a site of contested cultural ground, with conflicts, disagreements, and debates characterizing its three-century history far more than cultural unanimity about its values, virtues, and icons. Tucker narrates the incident as the historical event that it was, within the context of Tokugawa social, political, cultural, and spiritual history, before exploring the vendetta as conflicted cultural ground, generating a steady flow of essays, novels, plays, and ideologically driven expressions intrinsic to the course of Japanese history. This engaging, accessible study provides insights into ways in which events and debates from early modern history have continued to inform developments in modern Japan.

John A. Tucker is a professor of history at East Carolina University in Greenville. He has published extensively on Japanese and Chinese history, and his publications include *Critical Readings in Japanese Confucianism*, 4 vols. (2012), and the *Dao Companion to Japanese Confucian Philosophy*, coedited with Chun-chieh Huang (2014).

The Forty-Seven Rōnin

The Vendetta in History

John A. Tucker
East Carolina University

CAMBRIDGE
UNIVERSITY PRESS

CAMBRIDGE
UNIVERSITY PRESS

University Printing House, Cambridge CB2 8BS, United Kingdom

One Liberty Plaza, 20th Floor, New York, NY 10006, USA

477 Williamstown Road, Port Melbourne, VIC 3207, Australia

314–321, 3rd Floor, Plot 3, Splendor Forum, Jasola District Centre, New Delhi – 110025, India

79 Anson Road, #06–04/06, Singapore 079906

Cambridge University Press is part of the University of Cambridge.

It furthers the University's mission by disseminating knowledge in the pursuit of education, learning, and research at the highest international levels of excellence.

www.cambridge.org
Information on this title: www.cambridge.org/9781107096875
DOI: 10.1017/9781316156643

© John A. Tucker 2018

First published 2018

Printed in the United Kingdom by Clays, St Ives plc.

A catalogue record for this publication is available from the British Library.

ISBN 978-1-107-09687-5 Hardback
ISBN 978-1-107-48075-9 Paperback

CONTENTS

FIGURES

PREFACE

This study began with my dissertation, completed through Columbia University's Department of East Asian Languages and Cultures (1990). There, I traced the influence of a late Song Confucian text by Chen Beixi, *The Meanings of Human Nature and Principle,* on seventeenth-century Japanese texts by Yamaga Sokō, Itō Jinsai, Ogyū Sorai, and others. In researching the dissertation, I noticed that many secondary sources claimed that Yamaga taught the forty-seven rōnin, and so influenced their vendetta. My knowledge of the rōnin incident largely derived from an early reading of Maruyama Masao's *Studies in the Intellectual History of Tokugawa Japan,* wherein Maruyama discussed Ogyū's essay on the vendetta, the *Giritsusho,* as one of the decisive pieces shaping the shogunate's verdict for the rōnin. Itō Jinsai, according to other sources, taught Ōishi Yoshio, the leader of the rōnin vendetta, at his school in Kyoto.

Looking for primary sources documenting these claims, I soon realized that there were virtually none, especially none related to the most commonly repeated claim, that Yamaga had taught Ōishi Yoshio and the samurai retainers of Akō domain whence the vendetta arose. This claim I eventually traced back to the vendetta debates, especially essays by Satō Naokata and Dazai Shundai, criticizing the rōnin and blaming their vendetta on the ideas of Yamaga. Eventually, I traced the metamorphosis of those denunciatory allegations into points of pride for later thinkers such as Yoshida Shōin, and then his followers as they embraced the vendetta as a model for anti-shogunal activism. Simply put, then, my interest in the vendetta developed out of my interest in

Tokugawa Confucianism, and over time, Yamaga Sokō in particular. The disagreements, critical allegations, and polemics voiced in the Confucian debates came to shape my perception of the vendetta generally, from its origins through all subsequent outgrowths, leading to my overall assessment of it as a hotly contested cultural site wherein conflict and dissonance rather than consensus and unity ruled.

Articles and paper presentations in conjunction with my translation studies of texts by Yamaga, Itō, and Ogyū regularly discussed the alleged rōnin connections. Ultimately my conclusions were of the debunking variety, arguing that the conventional wisdom was essentially groundless. More careful readings of Beixi's text led me to realize that the pivotal notion in the debates, "loyal and righteous samurai" (chūshin gishi), had appeared in Beixi's text wherein it was explained in relation to individuals who had died, in many cases by their own hands, in their defense of some cause, meriting for them legitimate worship in temples established for them. Knowing that Beixi's text was one of the most well known, widely read among seventeenth-century Confucians, I came to view the vendetta debates as about more than contested questions of loyalty and righteousness, honor and duty. They were admittedly about that, but more significantly they were about whether the rōnin might be legitimately worshipped. This spiritual dimension of the debates soon colored my readings of the vendetta and its aftermath, leading me to develop a somewhat comprehensive framework through which the vendetta in theory and practice might be viewed.

It was only after formulating these ideas that I finally got around to reading Donald Keene's translation of Kanadehon Chūshingura, and then the Japanese text itself. As a result, my vision of that work was very much influenced by my study of Confucianism and the Confucian debates over the vendetta. Also, while a graduate student at Columbia studying classical Japanese with Professor Keene, I read my first Nō play, Shunkan, long before looking at Chūshingura. Interest in Nō led me to the Kanze kaikan in Kyoto for performances, and a vision of Japanese drama as not infrequently spiritual. Seeing torchlit Nō performances at the Heian Shrine in Kyoto and later in Nara at the Kasuga Shrine did nothing to dissuade me from that view.

The route to this project, then, was circuitous, via intellectual rather than military history. Along the way, I accumulated more debts in scholarship than can be meaningfully acknowledged here. However, a few must be recognized. At Cambridge University Press, Lucy

Rhymer's encouragement and patience will always be appreciated. Funding for research directly related to this project came from two sources, Duke University's East Asian Library grant program and Harvard University's Yenching Library grant program. Both helped keep me motivated, with a sense of indebtedness, to bring this project to completion. I hope that readers will find it useful.

INTRODUCTION: VENDETTA OVERVIEW

The forty-seven rōnin vendetta is one of the most famous incidents in Japanese history, but it is also one of the most misunderstood. This book seeks to provide, via critical analyses of relevant documents, a credible account of the vendetta and its afterlife in history. It suggests that when considered historically and holistically, the vendetta appears as a site of contested cultural ground, with conflicts, disagreements, and debates characterizing its three-century history far more than cultural unanimity about its values, virtues, and icons.

The Incident

In the spring of 1701, shogun Tokugawa Tsunayoshi was hosting annual ceremonies at his castle in Edo (modern Tokyo), the center of his samurai regime. At that point, the Tokugawa enjoyed exceptional authority and prestige, having governed the realm on behalf of the imperial line for nearly a century. The ceremonies featured Tsunayoshi welcoming emissaries bearing New Year's greetings from the emperor, Higashiyama, and retired emperor, Reigen, who resided in the imperial capital, Heian (modern Kyoto). Just before the start of the final day, one of the lower-level samurai hosts, Asano Naganori, lord of Akō domain, suddenly drew his sword and attacked, but did not kill, the shogun's master of ceremonies, Kira Yoshinaka.

Asano was promptly restrained and interrogated by shogunal officials. That afternoon, Tsunayoshi decreed that Asano commit seppuku, or ritual suicide, forthwith. Subsequently, the shogun abolished the condemned lord's branch of the Asano line and confiscated Akō domain, which Asano lords had ruled since 1645. Word of Asano's attack and seppuku soon reached Akō, where his former vassals – now rōnin, or masterless men – reacted to the shocking news. Most of the three hundred rōnin soon scattered, resigned to their fate as warriors adrift, tainted by the seemingly disgraceful behavior of their late lord. However, another group, in the end numbering forty-seven and led by Ōishi Yoshio, banded together in a secret league to plot revenge.

In the twelfth month of the following lunar year,[1] after subterfuge and conspiracy, the forty-seven met in Edo, invaded Kira's mansion, tracked him down, and beheaded him. The rōnin then marched across the city, making their way to the Sengakuji, Asano Naganori's family temple in Edo. Following his seppuku, Asano had been buried at the Sengakuji. There the rōnin band presented Kira's head before Asano's grave, reverently conveying that his task was complete. Minus the lowest-ranking member of the group, Terasaka Kichiemon, now mysteriously departed, the rōnin remained at the Sengakuji, awaiting their fate. Earlier, two from their ranks had been sent to inform the shogunate of their vendetta. Rather than an immediate, final verdict, shogunal officials had the rōnin divided into four groups and imprisoned. Nearly two months later, following extended deliberations, Tsunayoshi sentenced the rōnin en masse to death by seppuku. With their demise on the last day of winter 1703, the forty-seven rōnin vendetta, also known to history as the Akō vendetta or Akō incident, came to a gruesome end.

History's drama soon reincarnated in various forms. First a succession of Confucian scholars debated its ethics and implicitly spiritually related issues. Then theatres staged puppet and kabuki performances, accompanied by copious woodblock prints. Temples and shrines established multiple graves and memorial sites. The vendetta quickly found its way into foreign narratives and cultural commentaries. Over time, the vendetta elicited an unprecedented flood of apocrypha, cultural look-alikes, statements, and counterstatements that, rather than replaying the incident with historical fidelity, conveyed more controversy and dissonance than cultural consensus and

---

[1] All months referred to numerically are lunar months. The year, when specified, refers to the Western calendar.

homogeneity. From the start, the vendetta had been born out of conflict: first with Asano's attack on Kira, and later, in Akō domain, with more than two hundred and fifty rōnin turning away from the minority group dedicated to taking direct action. During the following three centuries, the vendetta generated an ever-expanding litany of responses and aftershocks, often volatile and sometimes violent in expression. These belied the harmony and consensual unity implied by its status, touted in the mid-twentieth century, as Japan's national epic.

The vendetta has been called "arguably the most famous event in Japanese history."[2] There are good reasons for its renown: as history, it brimmed with court ritual and rivalries, shogunal pomp and circumstance, samurai intrigue, swordplay, passion, and tragic displays of loyalty, righteousness, and reverence. Yet for precisely those reasons, the historical events of 1701–1703 came to be submerged by three centuries of legend, drama, ideology, religion, philosophy, art, mass media, and popular culture. The multifaceted by-products of its history have entertained generations, making evident its capacity for individual, social, national, and international resonance. In addition to militarism, nationalism, and imperialism, the vendetta has been recast repeatedly to serve the rhetorical ends of civilization, popular rights, Christianity, capitalism, Marxism, pacifism, and contemporary cartoon culture as well.

As one of the first incidents of Japanese history introduced to the outside world, the vendetta became a staple in Western descriptions of the profoundly different culture, ones that warped along the way much of Japan's past, its ethics, values, and patterns of behavior. Compounding matters, some Japanese interpreters hawked the vendetta, claiming to explain thereby their supposedly unique national essence. With enduring appeal, even historical charisma, the vendetta became a cultural obsession, fascinating and disgusting, enchanting and deluding, inspiring and repulsing those trying to come to terms with it. Yet its accrued fame and infamy left few with any historically grounded understanding of what transpired in the first place. This study, by striving to document a credible narrative of the historical events of 1701–1703, seeks to return the integrity of primary sources to the forefront of understandings of the incident.

---

[2] Beatrice Bodart-Bailey, *The Dog Shogun: The Personality and Politics of Tokugawa Tsunayoshi* (Honolulu, HI: University of Hawaii Press, 2006), p. 160.

Out of the culturally rich Genroku period (1688–1704), the vendetta became the immediate sensation, leaving everything else – including masterful poetry, literature, and art – pale by comparison. Novelist Ihara Saikaku, poet Matsuo Bashō, philosopher Ogyū Sorai, and playwright Chikamatsu Monzaemon attained considerable renown. Yet none compares with the leader of the forty-seven rōnin, Ōishi Yoshio, in terms of perennial, national, and international celebrity. Hardly had the rōnin completed their seppuku in 1703 than the incident began to elicit strong responses from erudite Confucians variously constructing vendetta narratives and appraising its ethics. One indication of the incident's sensational nature was the shogunate's ban on dramatic representations of it. Bypassing such efforts and beautifying its horrific dimensions, cultural doubles such as the puppet and kabuki play *Kanadehon Chūshingura* (*Storehouse of Loyal Retainers*, 1748) emerged, looking like history, albeit with aliases and altered spatiotemporal identities, massaged for mass appeal.

Spiritually, the rōnin vendetta occasioned three centuries of worship, remembrance, and veneration in Shinto shrines, Buddhist temples, and memorial sites all over Japan. These dimensions of the vendetta were integrally related to the popularity of its dramatic doubles, as theatre and religiosity inevitably overlapped, much as they had in earlier history with works of Nō drama calming the agitated spirits of those who had fallen tragically to fate. At another level, the spiritual standing of the rōnin had been central to the Confucian debates wherein an individual's ultimate devotion to loyalty and righteousness established his worthiness for sacrificial worship. In debating whether the rōnin were "loyal and righteous samurai" (*chūshin gishi*), Confucians were implicitly debating whether the rōnin merited legitimate temple-based reverence. Tracing and interpreting the vendetta's multiple, contested lives in spiritual culture is another objective of this study.

The vendetta is also one of the most infamous events in Japanese history. Legally, the rōnin and earlier their late master, Asano Naganori, were declared guilty of outrageous acts and sentenced to death by seppuku. Several Confucian scholars soon declared the rōnin lacking in any sense of righteousness and duty, and so denounced them for misguided expressions of homicidal loyalty on behalf of a lord whose ethical compass was, according to some contemporary accounts, equally warped. Vulgar parodies of the incident portrayed the rōnin as monsters or rapists, or with phallic imagery, bawdily caricaturing their vendetta and thus distancing it from any form of respectable nobility and honor. Even though the rōnin were later elevated by the imperial state and its military as exemplars of self-sacrificing loyalty, some government propagandists also criticized the incident for displaying nothing more than a "minor righteous duty" compared to the grand variety worthy of the imperial throne.

In postwar Japan, the U.S. Occupation censored cultural expressions reminiscent of the vendetta, including those in textbooks, public discourse, literature, theatre, and film. In contemporary culture, some interpreters have cast the rōnin as cutthroat assassins who saw their mission exclusively in cold-hearted, strategic terms. Twenty-first-century popular culture, often embracing more positive, life-affirming expressions of heroism, has shunned the vendetta, compromising its standing as the iconic expression of Japanese culture. Internationally, hints of a shift away from rōnin culture came in 2013 when the Hollywood production *47 Ronin*, directed by and starring Keanu Reeves, ended up a monumental box office flop. Earlier, international events such as the September 11, 2001, terrorist attack made the vendetta's modus operandi profoundly problematic and difficult to own, much less revere and celebrate. Deconstructionists and postmodern commentators, in questioning absolute values and ethical icons, have spurned the vendetta as a feudal relic.

Considered comprehensively, the vendetta, in fame and infamy, is best recognized as one of the most contested events in early modern and modern Japanese history. In addressing the historical vendetta and then the debates, controversies, and interpretive tensions it spawned, this study advances an innovative paradigm for understanding the incident, one highlighting its historical capacity as an intellectual lightning rod, attracting if not catalyzing critical polarities and divergences in thought and action over the past three centuries. Along the way, it explores the vendetta's vicissitudes, showing that its standing as an almost universally known historical event, one with multifaceted modern and contemporary expressions, is deeply rooted in the Japanese historical experience and its efforts to invent and reinvent national exemplars.

The vendetta's historical waxing and waning as an iconic cultural expression is also analyzed. This book suggests that modern and contemporary technologies of cultural presentation have given the incident unprecedented levels of broadcast, yet in rendering it as mass entertainment, have emasculated its historical vitality and relevance.

Television, radio, cinema, and the Internet have repeatedly plumbed the vendetta, leaving it little more than a domesticated expression of history that middle-class Japan safely dominates and controls with the click of a remote. The rise in popular culture of myriad super-warriors, male and female, has questioned the dominant masculinity enshrined in the vendetta. As a result, *manga* and *anime* have tended to bypass traditional macho narratives in favor of the elastic possibilities of the historical imagination to recreate the past with newly invented, gender-diverse, and life-affirming cultural heroes and icons. Yet despite marked atrophy, the vendetta remains a versatile and resilient archetype, one that apparently has not and perhaps will not go quietly into the night.

Methodology, Sources, and Interpretation

Studies of the forty-seven rōnin incident sometimes drop the name "Chūshingura" in their titles, with an addendum explaining that they are not actually about the dramatic masterpiece *Kanadehon Chūshingura*, but instead are about the historical incident and its many cultural forms, including the play, that followed it. This approach, while sometimes merely headlining the vendetta's famous dramatic expression, blurs lines between documentable facts and their facsimiles in fiction. Without discounting *Chūshingura*, which made the historical vendetta far more significant than it ever would have been otherwise, this study mentions "Chūshingura" exclusively in reference to the play, or works that otherwise take it as their title. Herein, the historical events of 1701–1703, variously known as "the forty-seven rōnin vendetta," "the Akō incident," or "the Akō vendetta," are typically referred to as "the vendetta."

In grouping everything from Asano's attack on Kira, through the vendetta itself, and then beyond to the rōnin seppuku, together as an incident, this study continues an approach pioneered by Muro Kyūsō in his *Records of the Righteous Men of Akō Domain* (*Akō gijin roku*). The latter is a quasi-historical work that, along with its frequent credulity and pro-rōnin bias, presented the first major study of the events, from Asano's attack through the rōnin seppuku.[3] Muro's study, which preceded *Chūshingura* by four decades, was hardly compromised, in

[3] Muro Kyūsō, *Akō gijin roku*, in Ishii Shirō, ed., *Kinsei buke shisō*, Nihon shisō taikei, vol. 27 (Tokyo: Iwanami shoten, 1974), pp. 271–370.

interpretation or narrative, by the latter work. If anything, *Chūshingura* owes much to Muro regarding important aspects of the incident. For example, Muro early on described Kira as a greedy, vile individual who, when not bribed by Asano, humiliated him, prompting Asano's sword attack.

While extant documents do not substantiate Kira's greed beyond doubt, that interpretation came to be widely repeated as plain truth. Ironically, its broadcast was not due to Muro's text, but to the popularity of *Chūshingura* wherein Muro's interpretation of Kira as a rapacious bully reappeared, there to be seen and believed by theatregoers ever since. The result was a legend sprung from an early quasi-historical work that, in some of its undocumented interpretations, lent scholarly weight to dramatic efforts to make sense of what might have been a senseless, irrational attack that had nothing to do with greed, bribes, or money.

Muro was one of the most unabashed admirers of the rōnin, declaring them, in the title of his work, "righteous men" (*gijin*). This appellation goes well beyond objectivity and so will not be used here, except when quoting or summarizing sources that do use it. Nor will the forty-seven be called samurai. Following Asano's seppuku in the spring of 1701, the men who launched the vendetta were rōnin, or masterless men. Without meaning to disparage the forty-seven, this study differs with Muro by referring to them as such. On another count, while studies of pre-Meiji history often refer to major figures from Tokugawa times by their given names or their studio names (*gō*) instead of their family names, this study, rather than follow that Tokugawa practice and then switch in modern narratives to last names, typically refers to all historical persons by their last names. Thus, Asano Naganori is called Asano, and Kira Yoshinaka is called Kira. However, in discussing Asano family history or the Tokugawa line of shoguns, the given names are used to distinguish one family member from the next.

Another recounting of the vendetta appeared in the *Veritable Records of the Tokugawa House* (*Tokugawa jikki*), an early nineteenth-century work detailing events from the reign of Ieyasu, the founder of the shogunate, through the twelfth shogun, Ieyoshi. Although it offers no comprehensive account of the vendetta, the *Veritable Records* records pertinent events as it traces Tokugawa rule year by year. In 1701, it notes Asano Naganori's appointment as one of the hosts welcoming imperial emissaries bearing New Year's greetings to Tsunayoshi. It also documents Kira Yoshinaka's decades of service to the shogunate as its master of ceremonies, including his ritual work at the imperial palace, the Ise Shrine, and the Nikkō Tōshōgū where Ieyasu was enshrined. Rumors about Kira's greed are mentioned, but they are recorded as just that, rumors.[4] Overall, entries mentioning Kira suggest that he was a man who helped define Tokugawa rule not in terms of battlefield power, but rather in terms of court rituals and high ceremony. The *Veritable Records* was, it must be remembered, an officially sponsored Tokugawa source rather than an unbiased, objective history. Thus, whatever the truth might have been, it would not likely have portrayed Kira as an evil minister who merited the brutal vigilante justice meted out by a band of vengeful rōnin.

Rather than Muro's *The Righteous Men of Akō Domain* or the shogunate's *Veritable Records*, this study relies largely on primary sources recognized by an array of historians as credible and reliable. Most of these sources have been reproduced in two modern compilations, *Documents on the Righteous Men of Akō Domain* (1910) and *Historical Sources on the Righteous Akō Samurai* (1931). While the titles to these two compendiums suggest bias in favor of the rōnin, many of the documents included are widely recognized as authentic, objective, and reliable. Three key sources inform this study's efforts to reconstruct, historically, what happened between 1701 and 1703: *Kajikawa's Diary* (*Kajikawa nikki*), an eyewitness description of Asano's attack on Kira; *Hakumyō's Memoir* (*Hakumyō waroku*), a Buddhist monk's memoir of his encounter with the rōnin at the Sengakuji; and *Accounts of Things Seen and Heard in Edo and Akō* (*Kōseki kenmonki*), a patchwork anthology documenting developments throughout the incident. Even these sources are not beyond reproach, making the project of impeccable historical reconstruction of the vendetta admittedly risky. Nevertheless, at the very least this study lays bare the sources and the events, as possible, hopefully without credulity or intentional fabrication. Other sources such as *Okado Denpachirō's Memoir*, attributed to an Edo Castle inspector, Okado Denpachirō, although widely viewed as a forgery, are also considered for the sake of laying bare apocryphal layers that later passed, in some accounts, into the quasi-historical record.[5]

---

[4] *Tokugawa jikki*, Kokushi taikei, vol. 43 (Tokyo: Yoshikawa kōbunkan, 1999), pp. 427–433, 492–494.

[5] Nabeta Shōzan, ed., *Akō gijin sansho*, 3 vols. (Tokyo: Kokusho kankōkai, 1910). Chūō gishi kai, ed. *Akō gishi shiryō*, 3 vols. (Tokyo: Yūzankaku, 1931). Takeda Izumo and Shuzui Kenji, *Kanadehon Chūshingura* (Tokyo: Iwanami shoten, 1937).

In discussing the Confucian debates, this study follows the annotated modern editions of relevant essays and treatises found in *Early Modern Samurai Thought*, an anthology of sources published as part of the *Compendium of Japanese Thought* (Nihon shisō taikei) by the reputable Iwanami shoten. Discussions of *Chūshingura* are based on the Iwanami bunko text, published in 1937, and available online through the University of Virginia Japanese Text Initiative. Later Tokugawa, Meiji, and twentieth-century developments are analyzed, when possible, through modern, first editions. While notes are kept to a minimum, they are provided as necessary for a documented historical account.

An important secondary source is Shigeno Yasutsugu's *A True Account of the Righteous Akō Samurai* (*Akō gishi jitsuwa*, 1889), the first modern historical study of the vendetta.[6] Shigeno was a professor at Tokyo Imperial University and cofounder of the *Journal of History* and the Japanese Historical Society. A student of Ludwig Riess, who in turn had studied under Leopold von Ranke, Shigeno is known for applying the "scientific" methods of German historiography to traditional Japanese history. Famous for "eliminating" sources he deemed apocryphal, Shigeno, in his *True Account*, sought to distinguish the historical vendetta from *Chūshingura*, legendary fictions, and popular lore. As a first step, Shigeno compiled a list of sources with some classified as credible, others as partially credible, and still others as absurd fabrications. Many of his judgments remain widely accepted among vendetta scholars.

Yet even Shigeno had limitations. As the title to his work reveals, he praised the rōnin by referring to them as righteous samurai. The frontispiece of Shigeno's study is a reproduction of the rescript that the young Meiji emperor had delivered before the grave of the rōnin leader, Ōishi Yoshio, as he, the emperor, approached his new capital, Edo, soon renamed Tokyo. In prefacing his study with the rescript, Shigeno reminded his readers that the emperor – sacred and inviolable under the Meiji constitution, promulgated in 1889 (the year Shigeno's study was published) – had conveyed admiration for the rōnin vendetta. Thus, the father of objective historical research in modern Japan, though critical of dubious sources in other contexts, remained a man of his times regarding the rōnin vendetta. Postwar scholars affirm some

---

[6] Shigeno Yasutsugu, *Akō gishi jitsuwa* (Tokyo: Taiseikan, 1889).

ideals of scientific history, but also acknowledge that pure objectivity is unattainable because interpretive biases, often unrecognized, inevitably come into play. Rather than objective truth, the most realistic goal is an interpretive paradigm that garners credible consensus and lays foundations for future research. Such is the ambition of this book.

While following Shigeno and others in distinguishing *Chūshingura* the play from its historical antecedent, this study recognizes that highly respected historians of the incident such as Henry D. Smith II, without whose major contributions this study would have been impossible, speak of "Chūshingura" in reference to the historical event, the play, and other related cultural productions.[7] Many respected Japanese works, such as the multivolume compendium published by the Akō Municipal Office of Historical Studies, *Chūshingura* (1989–1997), provide ample precedent. Studies labeled "Chūshingura" admittedly garner attention because the dramatic production is better known than the historical event.[8]

Yet Smith also refers to the vendetta using other rubrics, and readily acknowledges that many historians favor "the Akō incident" due to its relative neutrality. Bitō Masahide's essay, translated by Smith as "The Akō Incident of 1701–1703,"[9] endorses this approach. Others such as Tahara Tsuguo, in his study of the Confucian debates, *Discussions of the Forty-Six Samurai of Akō Domain* (1978), have alluded to the titles of the Confucian essays in naming their own works. Miyazawa Seiichi, whose research on the vendetta has been more comprehensive than that

---

[7] Henry D. Smith II, "The Capacity of Chūshingura," *Monumenta Nipponica*, 58/1 (Spring 2003), pp. 1–42; "The Trouble with Terasaka: The Forty-Seventh Rōnin and the Chūshingura Imagination," *Japan Review*, vol. 16 (2004), pp. 3–65; "The Media and Politics of Japanese Popular History: The Case of the Akō Gishi," in James C. Baxter, ed., *Historical Consciousness, Historiography, and Modern Japanese Values* (Kyoto: International Research Center for Japanese Studies, 2006), pp. 75–97; "*Chūshingura* in the 1980s," in Kevin J. Wetmore, Jr., *Revenge Drama in European Renaissance and Japanese Theatre* (New York, NY: Palgrave, 2008), pp. 187–215; Federico Marcon and Henry D. Smith II, "A Chūshingura Palimpsest: Young Motoori Norinaga Hears the Story of the Akō Rōnin from a Buddhist Priest," *Monumenta Nipponica*, 58/4 (Winter 2003), pp. 439–465; Hyōdō Hiromi and Henry D. Smith II, "Singing Tales of the Gishi: *Naniwabushi* and the Forty-seven Rōnin in Late Meiji Japan," *Monumenta Nipponica*, 61/4 (Winter 2006), pp. 459–508.

[8] Akō shi sōmubu shishi hensanshitsu, *Chūshingura*. 7 vols. (Akō: Akō shi, 1987–).

[9] Smith, "*Chūshingura* in the 1980s," pp. 190, 209. Bitō Masahide, "The Akō Incident: 1701–1703," Henry D. Smith II, translator, *Monumenta Nipponica*, 58/2 (Summer 2003), pp. 149–170.

of any active Japanese scholar, and especially invaluable to this study in its coverage of modern developments, straddled the issue with his monograph, *The Masterless Samurai of Akō: Spinning Yarns of Chūshingura*, revealing his primary interest in the historical vendetta, but recognizing its cultural legacy in *Chūshingura* and other artistic, literary, spiritual, and philosophical spin-offs. Miyazawa's extensive studies provide, incidentally, much of the content in the coverage of the vendetta herein, especially in Meiji and post-Meiji modern times. Nevertheless, this study follows Tahara in using a title reminiscent of those in the Confucian debates, highlighting the climactic deeds of the forty-seven rōnin in relation to the entire incident. As noted previously, this study differs from earlier works in not referring to the vendetta as the work of "righteous samurai." Instead, it calls the agents of the vendetta what they were: rōnin, or masterless men.

Still, there is the question of number. Were there forty-six or forty-seven rōnin? Early Confucian essays addressing the vendetta sometimes refer to forty-six rather than forty-seven because in the end, forty-six men, following Kira's murder, were required to commit seppuku. However, one additional rōnin, Terasaka Kichiemon, was listed in the "Declaration of Asano Takumi-no-kami's Retainers" (*Asano Takumi-no-kami kerai kōjō*), an authentic document naming members of the vendetta group. By the latter count, there were forty-seven.[10] Mysteriously, Terasaka vanished after the rōnin arrived at the Sengakuji.[11] Some claimed that Terasaka was sent away to inform Asano's widow, Yōzeiin, and his younger brother, Asano Daigaku, about the vendetta's success.

Others concluded that Terasaka was dismissed by the samurai band because of his low standing as a foot soldier. The thinking was that a foot soldier did not merit the honor of seppuku. Still others speculate that Terasaka was simply a coward and ran rather than face

---

[10] Thomas J. Harper and Henry D. Smith II, "110 Manifesto," *Sengakuji Akō gishi kinenkan shūzōhin mokuroku/Memorial Hall of Akō Loyal Retainers, Sengakuji Temple Catalogue of the Collection* (Tokyo: Sengakuji, 2002), pp. 114–115. Shigeno, *Akō gishi jitsuwa*, pp. 118–122; Bitō, "The Akō Incident," p. 8; Miyazawa, *Akō rōshi*, pp. 175–176; *Akō gishi jiten*, pp. 85–86; Akō-shi, *Chūshingura*, vol. 1, pp. 174–180. Takumi-no-kami was Asano Naganori's court title. Kira Yoshinaka's title was Kozuke-no-suke.

[11] For a full discussion, see Henry D. Smith II, "The Trouble with Terasaka," pp. 3–65. Smith notes that there are several versions of Terasaka's account, but does not dismiss their authenticity.

punishment: certain death by public execution or, with samurai honor, by seppuku. Whatever the case, by the time the rōnin were divided for detention, there were only forty-six. Perhaps overwhelmed with the nearly four dozen men who had just completed a murderous vendetta, the shogunate did not launch a search for the one who disappeared. As things turned out, Terasaka passed away in 1747, nearly forty-five years after the vendetta. Early on, then, there were good reasons for referring to forty-six rather than forty-seven rōnin.

Nevertheless, the vendetta eventually came to be known as the work of forty-seven. Accepting the list of names on the "Declaration," this study refers to the vendetta as that of the forty-seven rōnin. In doing so, however, it acknowledges that the general tendency to accept forty-seven rather than forty-six is not due to early documents, but instead to *Kanadehon Chūshingura*. Donald Keene explains that the word *Kanadehon* alluded to "'a copybook of kana,' a penmanship book for writing the first forty-seven symbols making up the Japanese syllabary. The title calls attention to the coincidence between the number of *kana* and the number of heroes who took part in the vendetta (if we include one man who was only an honorary participant). There are references to this coincidence in the last act."[12]

The "honorary participant" Keene mentions is not, however, Terasaka. Keene's reference is to Kayano Sanpei, a former retainer of Asano Naganori who found himself torn between obligations to his family and his deceased lord. Rather than take sides, Kayano committed suicide on the fourteenth day of the first month, 1702. Because he had earlier pledged himself to the vendetta, an honorary gravestone was later placed alongside the original forty-six for those interred at the Sengakuji, just below that of their master, Asano Naganori. Yet another gravestone was added after Terasaka's death, bringing the total number to forty-eight. Sticking with the number of men listed in the "Declaration" as participants, this study refers to the vendetta as that of the forty-seven rōnin. Most frequently, however, for simplicity's sake, it is called "the vendetta."

Overall, this study analyzes the Akō vendetta as an ongoing, debate-ridden historical event, one giving rise to multifaceted, often provocative, and certainly disputed philosophical, ideological, artistic,

---

[12] Donald Keene, trans., *Chūshingura* (New York, NY: Columbia University Press, 1971), p. ix.

and literary expressions in early modern, modern, and contemporary history. Examining the vendetta's conflicted metamorphoses in cultural history facilitates levels of analysis and understanding that transcend grisly narratives of decapitation and seppuku. Instead, the study highlights seminal issues integral to the debates over warrior honor and duty, especially as they relate to the problem of civil disobedience in service to affirmed ideals of rightness and justice.

Also addressed are spiritual nuances pertinent to the question of whether those who violate laws in serving their ideals should be deemed capital felons, or deities worthy of temple-based sacrificial reverence. Moreover, this study shows how three centuries of vendetta debates have crystalized a crucial nucleus, the vendetta, around which much of early modern, modern, and contemporary Japanese history might be configured. Discussions of this nucleus make evident, in turn, how early modern events and discourse about them remained alive and central to Meiji and twentieth-century struggles over Japan's samurai past and its relevance to future developments of history and culture.

Chapter Overviews

While the vendetta is widely known at one level or another, it is often grasped with little attention to the historical circumstances that spawned it. The first two chapters of this study offer a historically contextualized presentation of the vendetta, situating it vis-à-vis the time, place, and circumstances that the lord of Akō domain somehow became oblivious to. After all, what made the attack so outrageous, as the shogunal verdict stated, was Asano's utter disregard for the time and place, meaning the climactic day of the high ceremonial occasion so important to Tsunayoshi. This study highlights that ritual context and the politics of ceremonial power for understanding relations between the shogun and the emperor, the shogunal master of ceremonies and the distant daimyō, as well as the fate of the latter. Perceptions of the vendetta in later history were undeniably shaped by the fact that it sprang from a murderous attack proximate imperial emissaries hosted by the shogun, and cohosted by the ill-fated would-be assassin, Asano Naganori, lord of Akō domain.

The central theme of Chapters 3 and 4 relates to the contested, conflicted cultural complex from which the rōnin vendetta emerged.

Clearly either Asano Naganori had lost his senses or he found himself in a humiliating, grudge-based conflict with a shogunal official and sought to resolve it with his sword. Perhaps both were factors. More significant, however, was the reaction in Akō among Asano's former retainers. Although the vendetta is typically cast as a foregone conclusion of the rōnin, their writings reveal considerable disagreement, even vehement debate over what should be done. In negotiating this discord to a successful conclusion, the rōnin leader, Ōishi Yoshio, proved to be a shrewd and skillful manager of men, even if – as seems apparent – he did not always know in advance just what the right course might be.

Letters, memoirs, and other documents establish that the rōnin were hardly a homogenous group of single-mindedly loyal and honorable rōnin. Of the more than three hundred, only forty-seven, i.e., just over 15 percent, participated in the vendetta. The majority ended up walking away from the tragic loss of their lord. Even within the core group devoted to doing something, tensions and differences were real, and continued to simmer, to one degree or another, until the vendetta was done, and even thereafter.

One of the most well-documented, but often overlooked reverberations of the vendetta took the form of Confucian ethical discussions and debates over the rōnin and their deeds. Chapters 5 and 6 reveal that in those debates, the contested nature of the incident is again evident. Even in the writings of individual thinkers such as Hayashi Hōkō, a divided mind appears, recognizing on one hand the rōnin as intolerable violators of shogunal law, and yet on the other also acknowledging them as admirable exemplars of loyal and righteous devotion. Other thinkers praised the rōnin without hesitation, as did Muro Kyūsō, declaring unequivocally that they were "righteous samurai." Still others such as Satō Naokata denounced them as dishonorable men who were utterly misguided in their lawless, homicidal fury. In addition to highlighting the parameters of the debates, Chapters 5 and 6 suggest that they were not merely about whether the rōnin should be praised as loyal and righteous samurai, but whether they might merit, due to such recognition, legitimate sacrificial worship at shrines and temples dedicated to their memory. The fate of Yamaga Sokō's Confucian teachings in Edo, a philosophical casualty of the debates, is also explored within this context.

Prompt shogunal decrees meant to silence the Akō incident were, in the end, ineffective. Vendetta-related cultural expressions, the subject of Chapters 7 and 8, surfaced prodigiously throughout the eighteenth century, typically in token disguise with thin aliases and alternative historical settings, but clearly addressing, at one level or another, the rōnin vendetta. Regardless of censorship, more literary, dramatic, and artistic reverberations came forth than from any other single event in early modern history. Of these, the most popular, *Kanadehon Chūshingura*, emerged, ironically, from puppet theatre and kabuki culture often patronized by urban merchants, artisans, and townspeople of early modern Japan. Decades before *Chūshingura*, multiple attempts at drafting suitable dramas were made, and in the decades after, still other attempts sought to rival the popularity of *Chūshingura*. Many were parodies, spoofing through thematic deconstruction *Chūshingura* and the vendetta at multiple levels.

Yet parody and satire hardly compromised the appeal of *Chūshingura*. Soon the play was translated into Chinese, and in often confused, summary form became a staple in Western accounts of Japanese history and culture. High-level woodblock artists tapped the virtually insatiable market for vendetta-related memorabilia, most featuring kabuki actors rather than the presumably less handsome rōnin of history. The late Tokugawa explosion of vendetta-related culture culminated in potent teachings prompting vendetta-inspired political activism. The latter, emerging from newly risen expressions of Yamaga Sokō's Confucian learning in the hinterlands, in turn contributed to the collapse of the Tokugawa and ushered in a new age, the Meiji, in which the historical deeds and their dramatic double, *Chūshingura*, became prominent – but not uncontested – icons of art, drama, philosophy, literature, ideology, and religion.

Chapters 9 and 10 examine the vendetta in modern Japanese history by first highlighting the importance of the Meiji emperor's rescript for pioneering a new, imperially sanctioned regard for Ōishi and the rōnin. Though sometimes noted, this rescript has not previously been assigned much significance. Yet arguably through it, the rōnin were no longer bound by their historical loyalty to their old-regime lord, Asano Naganori, but instead came to be posthumously enlisted by the young emperor as he and those managing his regime brought the rōnin into ideological service to the new imperial order. Thereafter, the vendetta reached new heights. Virtually every movement, from rightwing nationalism to the multifaceted forces of militarism, as well as left-wing ideologies including Marxism, sought to appropriate the iconic rōnin for the sake of advancing their modern agendas. The forces of Taishō (1912–1926) liberalism and democracy equally embraced the vendetta by casting the rōnin as model protesters against corrupt and abusive regimes. Some of the most unfortunate modern reverberations, however, occurred during World War II as young officers time and again launched military pushes meant to realize their ideas regarding direct imperial-military rule.

In postwar Japan, Chapter 11 suggests, the vendetta moved from its wartime past and Occupation-imposed censorship to phenomenal popularity as mass entertainment on the silver screen and TV. By the 1970s, the vendetta had become a domesticated staple of postwar popular culture, entering homes across the land by the millions. By the early twenty-first century, vendetta entertainment had so saturated society that its tercentennial was anticlimactic, leaving observers wondering whether its spirit had finally been laid to rest, perhaps due to an overdose of mass media broadcasts. New perspectives from Japanese animation, especially the life-affirming super girl roles popularized in *Sailor Moon* and *Princess Mononoke*, made the suicide-driven honor ethic of the macho rōnin seem dated. New intellectual currents such as deconstructionism and postmodernism contributed to the relative decline if not demise of the vendetta, at least as traditionally conceptualized. Nevertheless, the cultural resilience of the vendetta over three centuries reflects its formidable capacity for navigating change and meeting if not overcoming the challenges of the future. If debate, discussion, and dialectic are the means to a better grasp of things, the vendetta's contested experience in cultural history has prepared it well to march forward with its new century and beyond.

1 TIME AND PLACE

The forty-seven rōnin vendetta is often traced to a sword attack by a samurai lord on a shogunal official. Little attention, however, has been devoted to the circumstances surrounding the attack. This chapter seeks to address those circumstances in an effort to better contextualize the crucial events that set the whole incident in motion. Overall, it suggests that the attack was not, in and of itself, so outrageously egregious. Rather, it was the samurai lord's complete disregard for the extraordinary circumstances of time and place that made his deed intolerable and subject to immediate judgment and punishment. This chapter identifies the historical players – the shogun, the master of ceremonies, and the samurai lord – central to the unfolding of the tragic events. Rather than provide a facile rehash casting the fight as one between heroes and villains, this chapter tries to lay bare the political, ceremonial, and personal complexities pertinent to all involved, hoping to illuminate the intrinsic historical ambiguities of the incident.

An Insane Attack?

The chain of events climaxing in the vendetta of 1703 began with a shocking act of violence committed just before the start of a high ceremonial occasion in the shogun's castle on the morning of the fourteenth day of the third month, 1701. According to the Western calendar, the date was April 21, 1701. For no apparent reason, one of the hosts, the young daimyō lord of Akō domain, Asano Naganori

(1667–1701), suddenly drew his sword and attacked the shogun's master of court ceremonies, the elderly Kira Yoshinaka (1641–1703). Kira was not killed, only seriously wounded. Yet intent to murder was manifest to all. Also, blood was spilled in the grand corridor bordering the ceremonial chambers. The attack was not, however, unprecedented. In 1684, four years after the reigning shogun, Tsunayoshi, assumed power, one of his grand councilors, Hotta Masatoshi, had been mortally wounded by a junior councilor, Inaba Masayasu, while in attendance at the shogun's castle. Inaba was cut down on the spot by senior councilors. Thereafter, Tsunayoshi distanced himself from his grand and senior councilors, and instead relied on his chamberlain and personal favorite, Yanagisawa Yoshiyasu, to mediate relations with the shogunal bureaucracy.

Hotta's murder helped shape what happened in 1701. When the shogun's verdict came down, it was largely the product of none other than Yanagisawa Yoshiyasu, a man who had risen to power following Hotta's assassination, and was not about to be lenient with another, attempted during an occasion wherein he and the shogun were present. The verdict was quick and severe. Yet rather than appeal to law, the shogunate condemned Asano to death for having forgotten the time and the place, and due to some private grudge, for having "behaved outrageously (*futodoki*)." Instead of highlighting its legal and institutional authority, the shogunate handed down a more subjective, but lethal judgment on Asano's ceremonial behavior. Implied was that while samurai might do such things with their swords, doing them while helping to host a ceremony in Edo Castle including representatives of the emperor and retired emperor was outrageous and intolerable.

With blood spilled in the castle, the site – and the ceremony – had been offensively polluted. In finding Asano guilty of outrageous behavior, Yanagisawa was, perhaps, referring to various breaches – of etiquette, law, and ritual purity – in one fell swoop. None questioned that Asano was in mortal trouble. Some instantly concluded that Asano must have been deranged (*ranshin*) when he committed the violence. Otherwise, its profound untimeliness was inexplicable. In the end, *ranshin*, or madness, might well be the most plausible explanation for Asano's sudden burst of murderous violence. Before examining these issues in detail, however, more needs to be said about the time, place, and people involved in the events of that fateful spring morning in 1701.

The Place

One of the most outrageous aspects of Asano's attack was that it occurred in the shogun's castle, located in Edo, the ultimate center of Tokugawa samurai rule. Edo Castle was the political nucleus of the capital and the entire archipelago, a monumental physical expression of Tokugawa power and authority. Before the Tokugawa, the area consisted of delta-based fishing villages. A castle once stood inland in the mid-fifteenth century, but gave way to a new construction effectively coordinated by the Tokugawa after their rise to power in the early seventeenth century. Until the 1590s, Edo had indeed been a place of no grand consequence. During that decade, however, Tokugawa Ieyasu, then a vassal of the country's overlord, Toyotomi Hideyoshi, made it his base of operations. Thereafter, it grew explosively, becoming the country's largest urban area in just over fifty years.

Following Toyotomi's death in 1598 and Tokugawa Ieyasu's rise to power in 1600 at the Battle of Sekigahara, Edo and the new Tokugawa castle soon emerged as the military, political, and economic center of the realm. Along the way, the Tokugawa ordered their three hundred vassal lords (*daimyō*) to undertake construction projects that transformed the bay area into coveted samurai real estate, making Edo the premier urban site of the island realm. By 1700, it was a full-blown metropolis with nearly a million inhabitants. According to Engelbert Kaempfer, a German physician who resided in the archipelago in the early 1690s, Edo was, among cities, "the largest in the world."[1]

Edo's enormous population growth resulted, in part, from the Tokugawa policy requiring all daimyō to establish a residence in Edo, reside there in alternating years (or every other six months), and leave their families as hostages on a permanent basis. Daimyō residences were assigned in relation to the center of power, Edo Castle, with the more trusted hereditary (*fudai*) daimyō situated proximate the "outer lords" (*tozama*) to establish a residential balance of power within the capital. While in Edo, daimyō rendered various forms of military, civil, and ceremonial service to the shogunate. Along with daimyō came a considerable entourage, in some cases hundreds if not thousands of

---

[1] Beatrice Bodart-Bailey, "Urbanisation and the Nature of the Tokugawa Hegemony," in Nicolas Fieve and Paul Waley, eds., *Japanese Capitals in Historical Perspective: Place, Power and Memory in Kyoto, Edo and Tokyo* (New York: Routledge, 2003), p. 100.

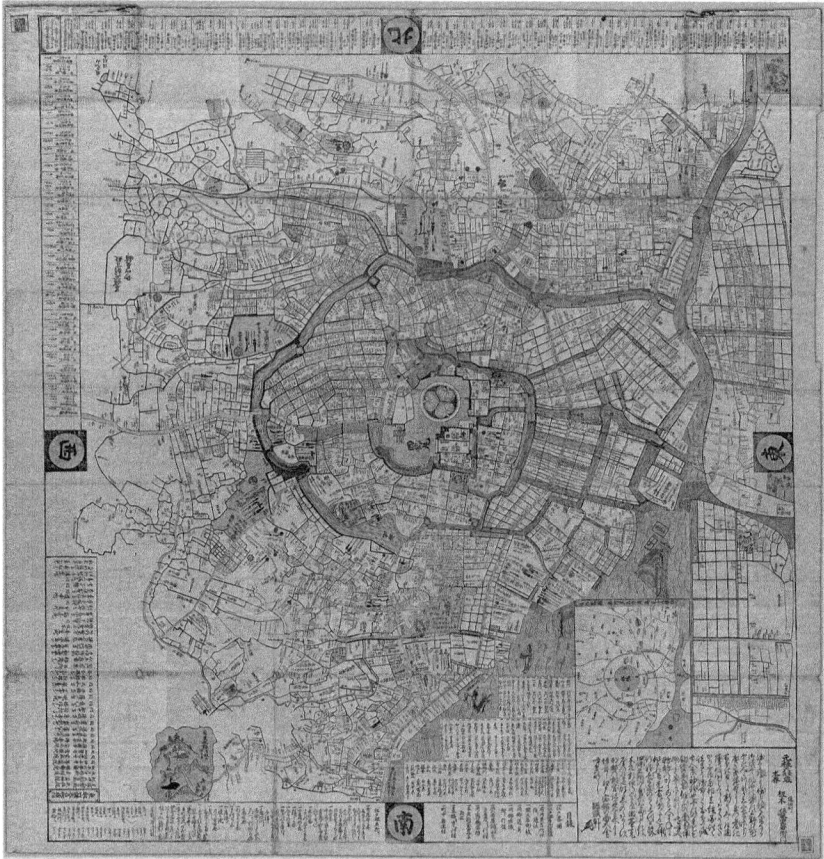

Figure 1.1 Map of Edo, dated 1693. Collection of Japanese Maps of the Tokugawa Era. Rare Books and Special Collections, University of British Columbia Library.

samurai vassals, attendants, artisans, and support staff. Known as the "alternate attendance" requirement, this regulation of daimyō life and resources served primarily as a means for the shogunate to establish control and surveillance of its vassals. If the shogun found a daimyō untrustworthy or offensive, he could confiscate his domain and order him to commit seppuku.

The alternate attendance requirement was also a powerful growth engine for Edo. Daimyō mansions soon surrounded Edo Castle in the inland western foothills. Along with the three hundred daimyō were an additional hundred thousand samurai retainers, plus a sizeable support staff for the daimyō lords and their entourage. Their residential compounds, although constructed with daimyō funds, were controlled by the shogunate and belonged ultimately to it. As a minor outer daimyō, Asano Naganori inhabited a modest mansion located in Teppōzu, a low-lying area well east of Edo Castle, and just west of the banks of the Sumida River. Following his attack on Kira, Asano's wife, relatives, retainers, staff, and attendants – he had no biological heirs – were ordered by the shogunate to vacate that residence. It, along with his tiny fiefdom, Akō domain, was being confiscated. Within Edo, it was not unusual for daimyō and shogunal officials to be assigned a change of residence, depending on circumstances and active service to the shogunate.

Edo's rise to power was coupled with the decline, at least in terms of effective, coercive prestige, of the ancient imperial capital, Heian-kyō (Kyoto). Founded in 794, Kyoto had been the imperial center for eight centuries by the time Tokugawa Ieyasu made Edo his head-quarters in the 1590s. Shogunal capitals such as Kamakura, not far from Edo, had earlier rivaled Kyoto in terms of power, but none had ever surpassed its population, economic vitality, or cultural prominence. By 1700, however, Edo and the Kantō had long since overtaken the old center, even as the shogun Tsunayoshi continued to revere, at least ceremonially, the imperial line.

Tokugawa respect for the imperial capital was evident through-out the seventeenth century with the shogunate contributing to the reconstruction of temples and shrines defining, along with the imperial line and aristocracy, the city's cultural and spiritual character. After having been burned down by the warlord Oda Nobunaga, the Tendai Buddhist temple, Enryakuji, atop Mt. Hiei just northeast of Kyoto, was reconstructed with the support of the early Tokugawa shoguns. Yet because Tokugawa regulations limited daimyō presence in the imperial capital, Kyoto never benefited from the ongoing concentration of human and economic resources that flowed from the alternate atten-dance requirement fueling the exponential growth of Edo. By 1700, Kyoto's population had surpassed half a million, but even so it amounted to only half that of the shogun's capital.

As of 1700, the Tokugawa had presided over six decades of peace. If one overlooks the siege of Osaka Castle (1614–1615) and the Shimabara Uprising (1637–1638), the peace spanned a full century. Compared to the sixteenth century, one of incessant civil war, the seventeenth-century peace was a major achievement by any measure. With it, Edo Castle transformed from an imposing warrior fortification into a low-profile but still powerful compound that, in addition to the

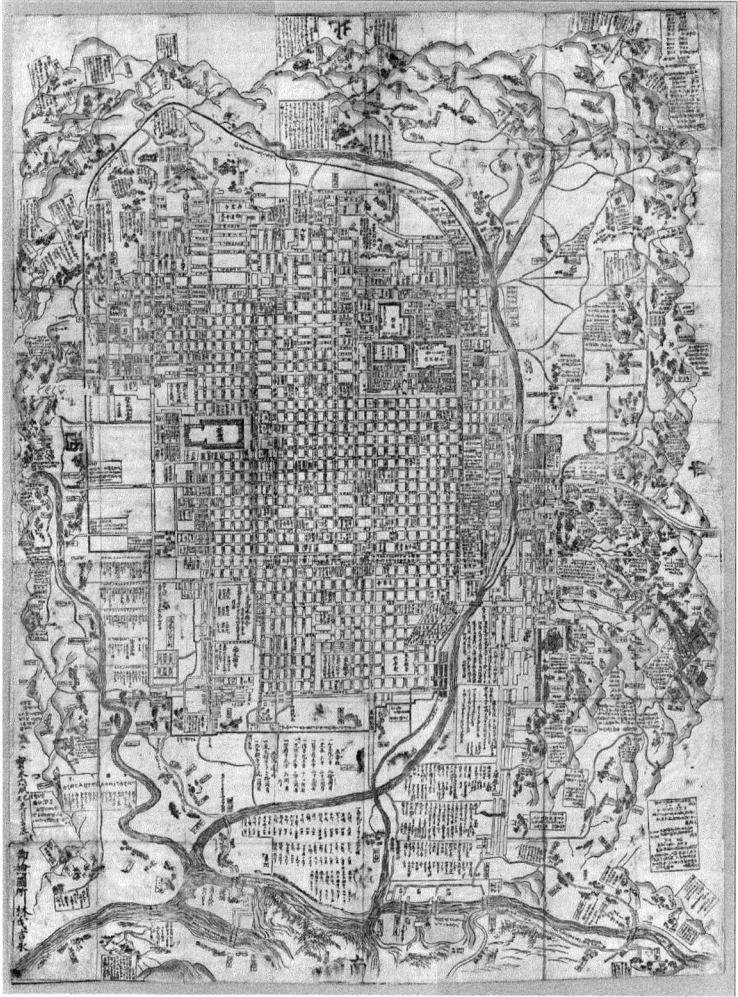

Figure 1.2 Map of Kyoto, dated 1709. Courtesy of the C. V. Starr East Asian Library, University of California, Berkeley. Reprint of the 1696 Map of Kyoto.

halls of power, hosted high rituals and ceremonies, some involving Kyoto aristocrats and imperial emissaries. The shogunate, in keeping with ancient thinking about ceremonial control as an instrumental expression of political power, deemed these ritual functions crucial for right and effective governance of the realm.

Although he was a seasoned military leader who unquestionably dominated the imperial court, Tokugawa Ieyasu revered the trappings of imperial culture, especially the ranks and titles the imperial court conferred. In 1603, Emperor Go-Yōzei thus obliged in appointing him minister of the right and "great barbarian-subduing general," thus making Ieyasu officially the first shogun of the Tokugawa line. In part, Ieyasu's requests for imperial appointments emulated the approach of Minamoto Yoritomo, founder of the Kamakura shogunate in the late twelfth century who had also sought court sanction for himself and his regime. Even as military leaders presiding over a sprawling federation of vassals and domains, later Tokugawa shoguns equally coveted imperial titles and ceremonial relations with the court in Kyoto that they otherwise effectively and undeniably controlled.

The shogunate's interest in imperial culture and its gradual shift away from crude military power is evident in the fate of Edo Castle's main tower located in its central citadel. The tower had a distinguished architectural lineage: Tokugawa Ieyasu initiated its construction; the second shogun, Tokugawa Hidetada, expanded it; and the third shogun, Tokugawa Iemitsu, completed it. However, after the tower burned in the Meireki conflagration of 1657, it was not immediately rebuilt. Two years after its loss, the fourth shogun, Tokugawa Ietsuna, decided to eliminate it altogether. The central citadel area thus evolved from a military bastion into an administrative and residential area that included grand ceremonial facilities for ritual occasions. Among the most important were those related to the exchange of New Year's greetings between the shogun and the emperor. These ceremonies, held annually, were centered in two chambers of the central citadel's main quarters, the White Study Chamber and the Grand Reception Hall. It was in this most ceremonially esteemed part of Edo Castle that, in the spring of 1701, Asano decided to launch his murderous attack on Kira.

The transformation of Edo Castle's central citadel reflected the realm's move away from warring samurai running roughshod over the population into a more peaceful age wherein developments in literature, philosophy, drama, and art flourished. These developments attained a pinnacle between the end of the seventeenth and the beginning of the eighteenth centuries, and so are referred to as expressions of Genroku culture, named after the Genroku period (1688–1704) during which the emperor Higashiyama reigned. Often described as hedonistic, self-indulgent, and extravagant, the Genroku period produced many great works of Japanese culture.

In literature, fiction by Ihara Saikaku such as *The Life of an Amorous Man* and *Five Women Who Loved Love* signaled a shift from the martial to the sensual, even though Saikaku typically concluded his racy works with edifying observations about the futility of fleshly pleasures. Woodblock prints, especially "pictures of spring," illustrated these themes, depicting samurai, monks, geisha, and women in all manner of passion. Artist Ogata Kōrin revived the Rinpa School of painting, catering to the tastes of Kyoto's aristocrats and wealthy merchants with gilt-covered landscapes on folding screens, sliding doors, and hanging scrolls. Kyoto was also home to one of the Genroku period's most important Confucian philosophers, Itō Jinsai, whose *Meanings of Terms in the Analects and Mencius* furthered a genre – the philosophical lexicon – defining the conceptual foundations of a moral, civil society, one quite at odds with the samurai-dominated social and political order of his day.

More than Kyoto, however, Edo was the primary source of cultural innovations, including new forms of drama, most notably kabuki, which thrived during the Genroku period with actor Ichikawa Danjūrō I defining styles that subsequently became standards for the stage. Puppet theatre also flourished in Osaka, with works by playwright Chikamatsu Monzaemon, such as *Love Suicides at Sonezaki*, often dominating. In poetry, the Genroku period was the age of Matsuo Bashō, the masterful pioneer of haiku (then known as *hokku*) who wandered the realm poeticizing early modern time, space, and history.

Within this cultural complex, the Akō vendetta appears as a profound aberration. Yet if the Genroku period is considered an age characterized by peace, hedonism, and secular extravagance, this is somewhat evident in the events of the vendetta too, with its leader, Ōishi Kura-no-suke, allowing a full year for, among other things, visiting the pleasure quarters of Kyoto for rest and relaxation, presumably playing out his passion for life and all its dimensions. Extravagance of a tragic sort was evident at the beginning of the incident with Asano's attack. Then again, with the revenge attack on Kira's mansion, extravagant if not outrageous ambition, translated into astounding success, occurred with the beheading of Kira and the long march, in the early cold of a winter morning, across the peripheral expanse of Edo, to the Sengakuji temple, with Kira's head in tow. And finally, the verdict – that all forty-six of the rōnin would die by seppuku, en masse, one by one, on the same day – was arguably an extravagance in discipline and punishment that in its own macabre manner perhaps matched the grand trends of the age from which it sprang.

The Time

On the fourteenth day of the third month, 1701, imperial representatives sent from Kyoto by the reigning emperor, Higashiyama, and the retired emperor, Reigen, were to convey New Year's greetings to the shogun. The ceremonies, held annually, were staged in the central citadel of Edo Castle. During this, the final day of the rituals, the shogun was to convey his gratitude to the emissaries for their visit. Because of his featured participation, this day was especially important to Tsunayoshi. The agenda included no provisions for an attempted assassination. Rather, the day was to seal, hopefully in a perfect way, the ceremonies, and mark the beginning of a more auspicious year to come. Gift exchanges and banqueting were also scheduled before the envoys embarked upon their return to the emperor's capital. Three days earlier, on the eleventh, they had arrived in Edo and taken up lodging at the emissaries' mansion just outside Edo Castle's main gate. On the twelfth, they were banqueted and welcomed by the shogun before conveying to him the emperor's and retired emperor's formal greetings.

On the thirteenth, the emissaries were entertained in the grand aristocratic manner of Kyoto, with a slate of Nō performances. Unlike the upstart, often gaudy kabuki that was popular among the Edo and Osaka townspeople, Nō drama was a centuries-old form of aristocratic entertainment, infused with spirituality, austere elegance, and cultured allusions. More typically, Nō was performed at Shinto shrines or Buddhist temples rather than in samurai castles, but by the early Tokugawa, shoguns and daimyō had become patrons as well, bringing the refined drama into their fortifications. By far, however, Nō was more associated with Kyoto and imperial culture than the sort of entertainment most lower-level samurai preferred. Tsunayoshi's interests in Nō reflected his fascination, even if from a distance, with the imperial capital and its cultural heritage. His sponsorship of it presumably distinguished him as a sophisticated samurai ruler, one who enjoyed the same forms of entertainment as did his aristocratic guests from Kyoto.

Tsunayoshi, a Nō enthusiast with a solidly Confucian respect for the importance of ritual occasions, was personally and professionally invested in these ceremonies. Their success enhanced not only his ceremonial and cultural prestige, but also his political power over the court and the realm. The Edo Castle events marked the climax of ritual exchanges begun earlier in the year, on the eleventh day of the first month. On that day, Tsunayoshi had sent his senior master of court ceremonies, Kira Yoshinaka, to the imperial capital to convey his, Tsunayoshi's, New Year's greetings to the emperor and retired emperor. That Tsunayoshi initiated the exchanges and provided their climactic, final voice reflected the leading role his regime meant to have throughout the year, in matters august and mundane.

The ceremonies traced back to 1610 when Tokugawa Ieyasu sent New Year's greetings to the imperial court. As an annual practice, shogunal greetings to the court dated from 1616 and marked the consolidation of a new era, one built upon the Tokugawa victory in the siege of Osaka Castle and the final elimination of the Toyotomi family. From 1631, the emperor and retired emperor responded with similar greetings conveyed to Edo. The exchanges opened with the shogunate sending emissaries to the imperial court, followed by the emperor and retired emperor answering through emissaries sent to Edo.

Typically, the shogunate selected lower-level yet affluent outer lords to assist in the hosting of the emissaries. Participation meant a drain on their resources and, given the importance of the occasion, demanded that their behavior be beyond reproach. In effect, this duty amounted to one means of testing and taxing the outer lords, and glorifying the shogunate in the process. While it was undoubtedly a great honor for Asano Naganori and Daté Muneharu, the other outer daimyō chosen to host the emissaries, the assignment was not necessarily cherished. In any event, these ceremonies continued annually until 1863, just five years before the collapse of the Tokugawa shogunate.

By any account, this was the most important annual ceremony linking court and shogunate. In 1701, Tsunayoshi had exceptional cause to be concerned about how it unfolded. Reportedly, he was unusually close to his mother, Keishōin, who held significant sway over him and his decisions. No doubt prompted by Keishōin, Tsunayoshi had asked the emperor to grant her junior-level, first court rank, i.e., imperial standing higher than any living woman in the realm. Keishōin had been granted third court rank just a few years after Tsunayoshi became shogun. None of the previous Tokugawa shoguns had requested such a prestigious honor for their mothers.

Success in the New Year's ceremonies would hardly guarantee anything, but infelicities or gross breaches of the ceremonial order – such as attempted murder of the senior master of ceremonies – would not enhance Keishōin's prospects for elevation. As things turned out, Asano's attack on Kira marred the occasion egregiously. Bloodshed in the central citadel polluted the occasion at its finale. Although Kira survived, the rituals otherwise meant to facilitate auspicious relations were embarrassingly compromised. In the end, despite Keishōin's hopes for elevation, it was only in the following year that she was granted imperial recognition as the highest-ranking woman in the land. The delay was most likely related, at least in part, to the outrageous events of the final day.

The Shogun

Tokugawa Tsunayoshi, the fifth shogun, was born in Edo Castle, the fourth son of the third shogun, Tokugawa Iemitsu. His mother was Iemitsu's consort, Keishōin, who, despite humble birth in Kyoto, had charms that helped catapult her to a position of considerable power within the castle, and thus within the shogunate. Nevertheless, her son, Tsunayoshi, as the younger half-brother of the fourth shogun, Ietsuna, had not initially been considered a successor to the title. However, in 1680, a twist of fate – Ietsuna died at the age of thirty-nine – soon led to that very possibility. A dispute ensued between two shogunal advisors, Sakai Tadakiyo, who favored a successor from the imperial line, and Hotta Masatoshi, who championed Tsunayoshi.

Hotta prevailed and was subsequently named senior counselor, while Sakai was demoted following Tsunayoshi's accession. Shortly after, however, Hotta was assassinated in Edo Castle, leaving the new shogun to rely increasingly on his mother and his favorite, Yanagisawa Yoshiyasu. Yanagisawa had entered Tsunayoshi's service early on, eventually becoming his personal chamberlain. It was Yanagisawa, incidentally, who played a crucial role in negotiating imperial acceptance of Tsunayoshi's request that Keishōin be granted first court rank. Yanagisawa was also responsible for the verdict that condemned Asano to death by suicide on the same day as his attack on Kira.

Figure 1.3 Portrait of Tokugawa Tsunayoshi. Courtesy of the Tokugawa Art Museum © The Tokugawa Art Museum Image Archives/DNPartcom.

Tokugawa Tsunayoshi's early education focused on Confucianism, literary studies, and Nō drama more than martial arts. However, he ruled in an un-Confucian, somewhat Machiavellian manner, ordering vassals to commit suicide due to alleged misgovernment, then confiscating their domains and thus enhancing shogunal revenues. Indeed, he presided over the confiscation of fiefs worth a total of 1.4 million *koku* (one *koku* = approx. 180 liters, or five bushels of rice). His rule was most notorious, however, for his "Decree of Compassion for

Animals." The origins of the decree are disputed, but reportedly a Buddhist priest convinced Keishōin that her son's failure to produce a male heir resulted from his cruelty to animals, especially dogs, in a past life. To atone, Tsunayoshi was persuaded to decree that no dogs or any other living creatures were to be harmed during his reign. Violators, especially in Edo, were dealt with severely, with some reportedly executed for their offenses. Later accounts of the vendetta often cited this peculiar and unpopular decree as evidence of Tsunayoshi's profoundly wrongheaded rule.

In 1701, following Tsunayoshi's New Year's greetings, the reigning emperor, Higashiyama, appointed two emissaries – Yanagiwara Sukekado, an imperial counselor of the first rank, and Takano Yasuharu, a counselor of the second rank – to travel to Edo to offer his greetings. Retired emperor Reigen sent one emissary, Seikanji Hirosada, imperial counselor of the first rank, emeritus. On the fourth day of the second month, just over a month before the ceremonies in Edo Castle were to begin, the shogunate appointed two vassals, both outer daimyō, to assist in the ceremonies as hosts for the emissaries. Asano was given responsibility for entertaining Emperor Higashiyama's emissaries. Daté Muneharu, lord of Yoshida domain in Iyo province (now Ehime Prefecture), was assigned to host Reigen's representative.

Daté was only twenty, and new to this ceremonial responsibility. Also, his resources were more modest than Asano's: his domain was assessed at 30,000 *koku*. Nevertheless, Daté fulfilled his duties without incident. Apparently, he had, for whatever reasons, the good graces of Kira and other functionaries who provided guidance for those hosting the occasion. The 1701 appointment was not, incidentally, Asano's first. In 1683, when he was only seventeen, Asano had participated in the New Year's ceremonies at Edo Castle without incident. On that occasion, Kira had also coordinated the formalities. Round two, however, would be fateful.

The Master of Ceremonies

Kira's role as shogunal master of ceremonies came to him in part because he was a scion of one of the "esteemed families" (*kōke*) recognized by the shogunate. Established in 1608, the "esteemed families" were select descendants of officially acknowledged lineages that had once served, in many cases, as military governors during the earlier Kamakura (1185–1333) or Ashikaga (1336–1573) shogunates. In addition to the Kira, which was one of the less prestigious lines, the esteemed families included the Ōtomo, Hatakeyama, Takeda, Imagawa, Arima, and Kyōgoku lines. Along with coordinating ritual occasions at Edo Castle, members were selected to participate in ceremonies at Nikkō Tōshōgū, the shrine dedicated to Ieyasu, and the Ise Shrine, dedicated to the sun goddess, Amaterasu.

However, the esteemed families received relatively modest stipends. With incomes below the 10,000 *koku* threshold that defined daimyō, the esteemed families were better off, financially at least, than the shogun's lower vassals (*hatamoto*), but they were generally well below the lowest level of the daimyō. Asano Naganori, a small daimyō, had, for example, an income of 53,000 *koku*. Despite their proximity to the shogun's lower vassals in income, members of the esteemed families typically looked down on *hatamoto* as well beneath them. Intimate associations with the shogun, the imperial court, aristocrats, and high-level clergy prompted many in the esteemed families to assume quasi-aristocratic airs, while lower-level vassals were generally, by comparison, considered an unrefined sort. Well-positioned members of the esteemed families such as Kira sometimes regarded small-scale outer daimyō such as Asano as below them as well, despite the differential in income suggesting the opposite.

The Kira family reportedly descended from the Minamoto line that traced its origins to the ninth-century emperor Seiwa and included renowned samurai such as Minamoto Yoritomo, founder of the first shogunate. Kira's father, Yoshifuyu, had inherited his standing from his father, Yoshimitsu, who in turn had been appointed to that rank in the early Tokugawa. Kira's mother was a niece of the powerful daimyō Sakai Tadakatsu, lord of Kawagoe domain in Musashi province. Privileged from the start, Kira was born in his family's Kajibashi mansion near the shogun's castle, and lived there until it was destroyed by fire.

In 1658, Kira married the younger sister of Uesugi Tsunakatsu, lord of Yonezawa domain in Dewa province. Working alongside his father in ceremonial occasions, the young Kira first traveled in 1663 to Kyoto to participate in ceremonies related to the construction of the Sentō palace for retired emperors and on that occasion had an audience with Emperor Go-Sai. Thereafter he participated in the New Year's ceremonies in Kyoto repeatedly, surpassing by far other members of the esteemed families of his day. In 1663, Kira, again participating in the New Year's rites, was elevated in court status to junior fourth rank.

Upon his father's passing in 1668, Kira inherited his status as a representative of one of the esteemed families, along with his father's ceremonial position in service to the shogunate and a meager stipend. When his brother-in-law, Uesugi Tsunakatsu, died without an heir, Kira maneuvered to have his own eldest son recognized as Tsunakatsu's successor so that the Uesugi line might continue. This move also meant that Kira would become the biological father of the daimyō of Yonezawa, a sizable domain. Although it was later rumored that Kira had poisoned Tsunakatsu to arrange for his son's succession, there is no proof of that. No doubt, however, securing an indirect hold on Yonezawa domain by offering his firstborn son to the Uesugi line secured for Kira more clout, financial and military, than ever before.

Evidence of Kira's good graces with the shogunate surfaced shortly after his second son died prematurely in 1685, leaving Kira without an heir. When Kira's first son, now the adopted head of the Uesugi line and the daimyō of Yonezawa domain, fathered a son in 1686, Kira was permitted by the shogunate to adopt the child (his biological grandchild) under the name Kira Sahyōe Yoshimasa. This further strengthened Kira's ties to the Uesugi line and its considerable resources. It also meant that Kira family's standing as an esteemed family would likely continue well into the future. Relative swapping aside, Kira's superior abilities in handling ceremonial occasions prompted Tsunayoshi to treat him as one of his favorites, along with Yanagisawa. In 1680, Kira was assigned the highest rank within the esteemed family hierarchy. Also, with Tsunayoshi's blessings, Kira traveled frequently to Kyoto where, among other things, he befriended the tea master, Yamada Sōhen, a former student of the grandson of the great tea master, Sen no Rikyū. In 1698, when the Kira family mansion in Kajibashi burned, he moved, with shogunal pleasure, to new quarters in Gofukubashi, even closer to Edo Castle, reflecting his relative importance to Tsunayoshi's regime.

According to the *Veritable Records of the Tokugawa*, by the eleventh day of the first month of 1701, Kira had arrived in Kyoto to convey the shogun's New Year's greetings to Emperor Higashiyama. Two weeks later, Kira, accompanied by the Kyoto shogunal deputy, had an audience with the emperor. Shortly after, the shogunate informed

Asano Naganori that he would be assisting Kira and several other members of the esteemed families in hosting emissaries of the emperor and the retired emperor participating in the New Year's rites. Kira, who was to provide ceremonial guidance for the young cohosts, Asano and Daté, was not, however, quick to leave Kyoto. Only at the end of the second month, four weeks later, did he return to Edo.

Thereupon, he had an audience with the shogun to report on the exchanges. Kira then proceeded to arrange, in the week and a half remaining, the reception of the emissaries. The latter, having departed from Kyoto at the end of the second month, arrived in Edo on the eleventh day of the third month, just over ten days after Kira's own arrival. Along with a senior counselor to the shogun and another of the shogunal masters of ceremony, Asano was present at the emissaries' mansion to greet them. That night, Asano assisted in hosting the welcoming banquet, his duties in the ceremonies having thus already begun. The following day, the twelfth of the third month, reportedly rainy, the emissaries entered Edo Castle and conveyed, during ceremonies held in the White Chamber, the greetings of the emperor and retired emperor to Tsunayoshi.

The thirteenth day, cloudy, featured Nō performances, including *Okina*, a spiritual performance staged at New Year's to bring prosperity; *Takasago*, a drama about two pine trees paired forever; *Tamura*, a piece about the founder of the Kiyomizu temple who defended the imperial realm against rebels; *Kasuga ryūjin*, a work about a Buddhist priest's visit to the Kasuga Shrine in Nara; *Tōboku*, a play about the Tōboku temple in Kyoto where the spirit of the poet-immortal Izumi Shikibu appears; and the comic play, *Fuku no kami*, about two yokels worshiping the god of good fortune on New Year's day.[2] The following day, the fourteenth, was to be the final one. Reportedly, the emissaries, apparently ready to be done, had requested, even before the morning ceremonies began, an early start.

The Vengeful Daimyō

Asano Naganori was born on the eleventh day of the eighth month, 1667. Although known to history as the lord of Akō domain, a small

---

[2] *Tokugawa jikki*, Kokushi taikei, vol. 43, pp. 427–432.

marshy, seaside fief due west of Osaka, he was born in Edo at the main
Asano residence in Teppōzu, just west of the Sumida River. That fringe
location, somewhat removed from the shogun's castle, was by no means
one of the more prestigious. Indeed, it arguably reflected the insignificance of the lords of Akō domain within the geopolitical hierarchy of
Tokugawa daimyō power relations in Edo. Nevertheless, Edo was in
many respects Asano Naganori's home. Compared to life in Akō, his
Edo dwelling was grandly situated. During his youth, he apparently
spent little time in his domain.

This remained the case after he lost his father, Asano Nagatomo,
age thirty-three, in 1675. At that time, Asano Naganori was only eight
years old. Nevertheless, as the eldest son, he was promptly recognized as
his father's successor. Administration of the fief was left in the hands of
the Asano senior retainer, Ōishi Yoshishige, while Asano Naganori, still
a boy, remained, for the most part, in Edo. Yet eight years later,
Yoshishige also died, leaving his court title and practical responsibility
for the fief to his nephew, Ōishi Yoshio, then twenty-five. Earlier, in 1673,
Ōishi Yoshio, then only fourteen, had lost his father. As a result, for both
the Akō daimyō and his chief vassal, intergenerational wisdom and
guidance were sadly lacking from the mid-1670s forward.[3]

The Asano were outer daimyō. Generally, these daimyō had
recognized Tokugawa hegemony late, some only after the fateful Battle
of Sekigahara. As a result, as latecomers to the hierarchy of Tokugawa
vassals, they were sometimes treated differently, as outer lords rather
than as the more trusted, long-standing hereditary vassals. These distinctions can be overemphasized, but there seems little room for doubt
that Asano Naganori, as a minor outer daimyō, was not in a favored
position vis-à-vis the shogunate or its officials. At best, his insignificance
as the lord of a small seaside domain might have given him a degree of
security. It is worth noting that he was a relative of the powerful branch
of the Asano family that ruled Hiroshima Castle and an expansive
domain surrounding it in southwestern Japan. However, that line of
the Asano was apparently unwilling to sacrifice its good standing vis-à-
vis the shogunate simply for the sake of minor relations such as the lord
of Akō domain.

[3] "Asano Naganori nenpu," *Akō gishi jiten* (Kobe: Akō gishi jiten kankōkai, 1972),
p. 126.

Asano Naganori's relatives had something of a checkered past within the geopolitical realm of samurai power. His great-great grandfather, Asano Nagamasa, achieved prominence as a brother-in-law and trusted vassal of powerful warlord Toyotomi Hideyoshi. In 1598, during Toyotomi's Korean invasions, Asano Nagamasa oversaw some of the campaigns on the Korean peninsula. After Toyotomi's death the same year, Nagamasa, then fifty-two, went into retirement, but reemerged in 1600 as a vassal of Tokugawa Ieyasu's son, Hidetada. Having fought with the Tokugawa at the decisive Battle of Sekigahara in 1600, the Asano, although outer lords, emerged relatively secure in their standing within the new Tokugawa order. Asano Nagamasa's eldest son, Nagaakira, was enfeoffed in Wakayama domain in Kii province, but later named daimyō of Hiroshima domain. His line, which emerged as the most powerful of all Asano branches, remained in Hiroshima until the beginning of the Meiji period.[4]

Asano Nagamasa's third son, Nagashige, was born in Ōmi province, but in 1599, at age thirteen, moved to Edo at the request of Tokugawa Ieyasu to begin service to his son, Hidetada, as his personal attendant. In 1601, Nagashige was rewarded with the northeastern domain of Mooka, in Shimotsuke province, assessed at 20,000 *koku*. In 1622, Nagashige replaced Honda Masazumi as lord of Utsunomiya Castle, also located in the northeast; the same year, he was further rewarded with nearby Kasama domain in Hitachi province. In 1627, his power in that region expanded even more when he was made lord of Wakamatsu Castle in Mutsu province. Upon his passing at age forty-five in 1632, Asano Nagashige was buried in Makabe, as his father, Asano Nagamasa, had been, at the Denshōji, the Asano family temple there. Nagashige's eldest son, Naganao, inherited his domain in Kasama.[5]

Notably, Asano Naganao enjoyed the favor of the third shogun, Iemitsu, much as his father Nagashige had. In 1634, after having been earlier awarded rank of junior fifth level and a minor court title, Takumi-no-kami, Naganao was designated chamberlain of Sunpu Castle, one of the Tokugawa strongholds and the castle to which Ieyasu retired before his death. In 1636, Naganao assisted in the construction of the western citadel of Edo Castle and was named a supervisor of Osaka Castle. In 1639, he became one of sixteen lesser daimyō recruited to serve in a leadership position in the newly organized

---

[4] "Genroku gikyo no kōgai," *Akō gishi jiten*, p. 3.   [5] Ibid., p. 4.

Figure 1.4 Portrait of Asano Naganori. Kagakuji.

Edo firefighting groups. In that capacity, he became well-known as one of Edo's "firefighting daimyō." In 1645, he was transferred to Akō domain after Ikeda Teruoki, lord of Akō, apparently went insane, murdered his wife, and then reportedly went on a rampage cutting down his consorts as well.[6]

Akō became a place of consequence during Asano Naganao's time as its lord. There had been no castle during Ikeda Teruoki's tenure as daimyō. Asano Naganao promptly petitioned and received permission from the shogunate to build one, a project completed in 1661. He also expanded waterworks projects in the domain. Most significantly, he orchestrated efforts to improve Akō salt production, considerably enhancing the economic wealth and well-being of the small seaside domain. Within decades, Akō's white salt – other domains produced

[6] Ibid., p. 5.

red and black salt – accounted for nearly 10 percent of all salt consumed in the Tokugawa realm. As a result, the real income for Akō grew to approximately 75,000 *koku*,[7] considerably more than its officially assessed rice income of 53,000 *koku*.

Asano Naganao also defined a philosophical identity of sorts for Akō by recruiting Confucian scholar Yamaga Sokō to serve as his instructor of military learning from 1652 until 1660. However, Yamaga resigned his position in 1660, apparently hoping to secure a better one. When the shogunate exiled him from Edo in 1666 for publishing a philosophically offensive work, *Sagely Confucian Teachings*, Yamaga was sent to Akō and placed under house arrest. During his near decade-long exile there, he was treated more as a guest than as a Confucian criminal. And it was during that time that Yamaga had contact with the young Ōishi Yoshio, who delivered vegetables to him. Following his pardon and return to Edo in 1675, Yamaga remained under quasi-house arrest and so had no extensive, ongoing contacts with Akō samurai.

In 1671, one year before his death at age sixty-three, Asano Naganao passed his position on to his eldest son, Nagatomo. The following year, Nagatomo, upon his death, was cremated at the Sengakuji in Edo. His ashes were returned for burial at the Kagakuji, a Sōtō Zen temple and the Asano family place of worship in Akō. Naganao had, incidentally, been a patron of the Sengakuji in Edo, and sponsored construction of the Kagakuji in 1645, shortly after being transferred to Akō. Thus, he contributed significantly to the spiritual identity of the domain as well as the Asano line of daimyō governing it.[8]

Four years after succeeding his father, Asano Nagatomo died in 1675 at age thirty-three. He too was buried at the Kagakuji. Only eight when his father died, Asano Naganori, as the eldest son, became the next daimyō of Akō. Even before his father passed, he had already lost his mother, who died in 1672, the same year as his grandfather Asano Naganao. Despite these tragic losses, there were good moments. In 1680, the year Tsunayoshi began his reign as the fifth shogun, Asano Naganori, age fourteen, was granted junior fifth rank and the

---

[7] Estimates vary, but there was increased income of 50 percent, perhaps more, for the domain. One source claims that the total income, with salt profits, came to between 80,000 and 100,000 *koku*, effectively doubling Akō's income.

[8] "Asano Naganao," *Akō gishi jiten*, pp. 331–332.

court title Takumi-no-kami. In 1682, he assisted in hosting Korean emissaries received by the shogunate.

In 1683, he was selected to host, as part of the New Year's ceremonies, a banquet for two emissaries of the emperor, Reigen. Although Kira led the formalities, Asano Naganori's service went without incident. Nothing suggests that the attack that erupted in 1701 stemmed from anything associated with the 1683 ceremonies. The same year, Naganori, with shogunal permission, married, at the Asano residence in Edo, a young lady named Aguri, the daughter of Asano Nagaharu, lord of Miyoshi Castle in Bingo province. While in Edo the following year, 1684, Asano and his brother Daigaku took an oath as students of Yamaga Sokō's teachings. The very next year, however, Yamaga passed away.[9]

In late 1694, Asano Naganori received his most significant assignment from the Tokugawa shogunate. He was instructed to preside over the confiscation of Matsuyama Castle in Bitchū (now Okayama Prefecture). Its lord, Mizunoya Katsuyoshi, had passed away that year at age thirty-one without an heir. On March 24, Asano Naganori led a samurai force several thousand strong in a march on Matsuyama Castle. A few days later, the elder retainer of the Mizunoya clan surrendered the castle without bloodshed. Shortly after, Asano returned to Akō, leaving his senior retainer, Ōishi Yoshio, in charge of the confiscation. However, the very next year, in 1695, Asano Naganori fell critically ill with what appears to have been smallpox. Apparently fearful for his line, he adopted his younger brother, Daigaku, as his heir. However, Naganori soon recovered from his illness and was appointed once more as fire inspector for Edo's lumber storage facility in Honjo.

In 1698, he was named supervisor of the Kanda Bridge area in Edo, and in 1700, supervisor of Sakurada Gate, one of Edo Castle's more important and central gates. Asano Naganori also served as part of the Edo firefighting corps, but never distinguished himself as his grandfather Asano Naganao had.[10] Still, his service was important. One of the threats Edo faced as a burgeoning metropolis with a population of nearly a million people was fire. In 1657, the Meireki Conflagration destroyed half of the city and reportedly took more than one hundred thousand lives. In the autumn of 1698, a major fire broke out in the Kyōbashi area and spread, destroying thousands of homes, temples, and shrines, and leaving more than three thousand dead.

[9] "Asano Naganori nenpu," *Akō gishi jiten*, p. 126.   [10] Ibid., pp. 126–127.

Among the mansions burned was Kira Yoshinaka's, located near Kajibashi just east of the southeastern corner of Edo Castle.

Two contemporary sources, *Dirty Filth and Thieving Enemies* (1690) and *Admonish, Punish, and Correct* (1701), provide disparaging accounts of Asano Naganori as a man and as a ruler. The title of the first alludes to an ancient Confucian text, the *Mencius*, which observes, "When the ruler regards his ministers as dirty filth, they see him as a thieving enemy."[11] These works were apparently compiled for the shogunate to provide intelligence on the vassals of the realm. Tsunayoshi presumably wanted to know who his daimyō were, how they governed, and the status of their fiefs, as well as their personal strengths and failings. Tsunayoshi's intent, no doubt, was to use this knowledge to ensure his own success and power as a ruler. The circumstances of the compilation of these texts remain a mystery, but they were most likely produced by surveillance teams and government functionaries working confidentially for the shogunate. Some 243 daimyō were written up, without distinguishing hereditary from outer vassals, so there is no reason to suspect that Naganori was targeted simply because he was an outer lord.

The entries about Asano Naganori are not flattering. *Dirty Filth and Thieving Enemies* first admits that Asano Naganori wisely provided for the bounty of his domain. Samurai and commoners thus enjoyed abundance. Yet the text also mentions his obsession with women's charms and his tendency to promote the "corrupt and perverted," who, noting his desires, searched out beauties for his pleasure. Thus, early on he entrusted his domain to senior retainers. *Dirty Filth and Thieving Enemies* adds that he accomplished nothing in the martial arts or scholarly learning. In short, he merited no praise. Presciently, the text warns that rulers must be careful lest excesses, lewdness, and immorality signal ruin for their realms and the end of their family lines.[12]

The second text, *Admonish, Punish, and Correct*, includes a postscript dated 1701, but does not mention Asano's attack on Kira. Presumably it was completed earlier in the same year. It notes that Asano was fond of military studies, but adds that he was not a cultivated scholar. Moreover, he reportedly lacked much in the way

---

[11] *Mencius*, 4B/3. In *Lunyu yinde/Mengzi yinde*. Hong Ye et al., eds. (Shanghai: Shanghai Guji Chubanshe).

[12] Kanai Madoka, ed., *Dokai kōshūki* (Tokyo: Shinjinbutsu ōraisha, 1985), p. 350.

of compassion and was short-tempered. While allowing that he was honest, had not betrayed his duties, and took his responsibilities seriously, it added that in years past he had been involved with his wife's maids. Additionally, his reputation was not, of late, particularly good, and his administrative profile was undistinguished, leaving cause for concern about his prospects for the future.[13]

If Tsunayoshi and his favorites, including Yanagisawa and Kira, relied on these assessments in managing the daimyō of the realm, then Asano Naganori appears to have been something of a marked man. His passions and short temper, if real, could have been the subject of one of Ihara Saikaku's short stories. For the latter, however, there was always a moral message. Here it would have been that when lust and anger are not coupled with wise and distinguished rule, tragedy awaits the vulnerable.

[13] Ibid., p. 350.

2 EYEWITNESSES TO BLOODSHED

Using various Tokugawa period sources, this chapter seeks to reconstruct the Edo Castle altercation and its fateful aftermath for the lord of Akō domain, Asano Naganori. One source, left by an Edo Castle attendant, is authentic and reliable. Another, attributed to a shogunal physician, has been questioned, but not dismissed. A third, often shunned as apocryphal, includes much information that came to inform popular retellings. A fourth, from the Asano house, is credible, but spotty in coverage. The result is a multifaceted reconstruction wherein conflicting, contradictory accounts with varying degrees of reliability leave students of the vendetta with admittedly only a partial knowledge of what happened, along with much speculation and many fabrications. Regarding the long-standing mystery of why Asano attacked Kira, this study finds the fourth source, suggesting that Asano was mentally unstable, most credible. Overall, however, the search for history takes students to the beginnings of legends that dominated later understandings of vendetta.

The Servant to the Inner Chambers

Around 10:00 AM, on the fourteenth day of the third month, with the final round of the New Year's ceremonies about to unfold, one of the daimyō hosts, Asano Naganori, drew his sword, ran down the grand corridor adjacent to Edo Castle's ceremonial chambers, toward the shogunal master of ceremonies, Kira Yoshinaka, and struck him twice.

We know this from an eyewitness, Kajikawa Yosobei, who left an account, known as *Kajikawa's Diary* (*Kajikawa nikki*), recorded shortly after the attack. For three centuries, Kajikawa's account has been considered the most credible description of Asano's attack on Kira.

Kajikawa was a lower-level vassal of the shogun, serving in the castle's inner chambers and therein working closely with Tsunayoshi's mother, his wife, and his concubines. According to Kajikawa's text, on the day of the attack, he had arrived, as usual, at the castle around 8:00 AM. He first stopped by the front entrance to the inner chambers to check on his assignments for the day. There he learned that he was to assist Tsunayoshi's wife in presenting a gift to the imperial envoys. Out of consideration for the emissaries, however, the itinerary had been moved up so that things could begin earlier than previously planned. To confirm this, Kajikawa proceeded toward the central citadel, looking for Kira. Along the way, he reported passing Okado Denpachirō, a shogunal inspector whose name later came to be attached to a variant, suspect account of the attack. Kajikawa's account establishes beyond doubt that Okado was indeed on the scene, even before the attack began. That they crossed paths foreshadowed the crossings that their profoundly different accounts would have.

Kajikawa proceeded through the banquet hall, on to "the grand corridor," possibly referring to the "Pine Tree Corridor" – although he never referred to it as such – where he encountered a group of ritual attendants and members of the esteemed families waiting for the ceremonies to begin. Kajikawa stopped near a column along the grand corridor in front of the White Chamber, where the morning's events were to occur. While maintaining a watch from that point, Kajikawa sent pageboys looking for Kira. One soon reported that Kira was meeting with some of the shogun's senior counselors. In the meantime, seeing Asano, Kajikawa greeted him. Asano was cordial but terse, speaking only briefly. Kajikawa mentioned that he hoped everything would go well. Asano reportedly responded, succinctly but positively, in agreement. The two then parted. Shortly after, Kajikawa noticed Kira coming from the direction of the White Chamber.[1]

---

[1] *Kajikawa shi hikki*, in *Akō gijin sansho*, vol. 2, p. 268. Kajikawa's account is also in Yagi Akihiro, ed., *Chūshingura* (1987), vol. 3, pp. 5–9, as the *Kajikawa shi nikki*, or *Kajikawa's Diary*.

Kajikawa asked a pageboy to summon him. Kira, apparently pleased to see Kajikawa, greeted him six or seven bays down the corridor from where Kajikawa had been standing. At that time, around 10:00 AM, the ceremonies were to begin momentarily. Kajikawa relates that before much had been said, "someone" suddenly ran up from behind Kira. Kajikawa, taken by surprise, did not immediately recognize the person, but remembered hearing the words, "Do you recall my recent grudge?" Kajikawa next reported a sword blow making a loud noise, prompting him to think that the wound would be serious. Kajikawa did not specify, however, whether the first strike was to the forehead or the shoulder. Kajikawa next recognized that the attacker was Asano. According to Kajikawa, Kira's initial response to the attack was "This ... " (*kore wa*).[2] Presumably, Kira meant "this" as a question, as in, "What on earth do you mean by this?"

Kira tried to flee, scrambling toward Kajikawa, but then Asano delivered his second blow. Kajikawa did not specify where the second strike hit, but it was apparently to the forehead, with the blade first hitting a metal strap on Kira's ceremonial cap, blunting the blow and most likely saving Kira from what might have been a lethal cut. Kajikawa noted that Kira then collapsed, face first. Kajikawa and others nearby promptly seized Asano. Kajikawa recalled that he used one hand to seize the guard on Asano's weapon, identified now as a ceremonial short sword,[3] and forced him to the ground with his other hand. Several representatives of the esteemed families, as well as Asano's colleague in hosting the ceremonies, Daté Muneharu, plus a group of pageboys gathered to help Kajikawa restrain Asano. In the meantime, Kira pled for help. Two members of the esteemed families next carried "the elderly" Kira, now wounded, unresponsive, and apparently in shock, to safety, and eventually to care by castle physicians.[4]

---

[2] Ibid., p. 269. Akō shi, *Chūshingura*, vol. 1 (Akō: Akō shi, 1989), p. 2, gives "around 11:00 a.m." Miyazawa, *Akō rōshi: tsumugidasareru Chūshingura* (Tokyo: Sanseidō, 1999), p. 19, also gives "around 11:00 AM."

[3] The ceremonial short sword (*chiisagatana*), not generally considered a weapon of attack, was used by samurai while serving in Edo Castle.

[4] *Kajikawa shi hikki*, p. 269.

The Wound Surgeon's Account

Kurisaki Dōyū, a respected wound surgeon in service to the shogun, reportedly treated Kira. Although of questionable authenticity, a document purportedly by Kurisaki describes his work in tending to the wounded master of shogunal ceremonies. Kurisaki's account reports that the wound to Kira's head was three and a half inches long but deep to the bone. It received six stitches. The wound to Kira's back was relatively shallow, and so required just three.[5] After being carefully treated by Kurisaki, Kira was allowed to return to his home in Gofukubashi that afternoon to recuperate, with wishes for quick recovery being made in the presence of the shogun's chamberlain, Yanagisawa.

As directed by the shogunate's Council of Elders, the inspector general, Sengoku Hisanao, read a version of the shogunal verdict, regarding both Asano and Kira. It stated:

> Asano Naganori, disrespectful of the circumstances within the shogun's castle, acted outrageously (*futodoki*) in attacking, without any reason, Kira Yoshinaka. Asano will be punished.
>
> Kira Yoshinaka, you maintained your sense of decorum and did nothing disgraceful. We wish you the best in your convalescence.[6]

The basics of the verdict were first revealed to Kira. Another, similar version would be read to Asano Naganori, just before his seppuku, later that day.

A shogunal inspector coordinated arrangements for Kira's return home, with the route supposedly proceeding out the Hirakawa gate, "the gate of the unclean." The violence had, in addition to seriously wounding Kira, left that part of the castle, and most especially Kira, in a state of blood pollution, meaning that he would not leave via the closest, most direct gate, the Ōtemon, or "front gate." Moreover,

---

[5] Akō shi, *Chūshingura*, vol. 3, p. 12. For an account of Kurisaki's treatment of Kira, and his later work following the rōnin attack on Kira's mansion, see Thomas Harper, "The Kurisaki School of Sword Wound Surgery: From Sengoku to Genroku; Nagasaki to Edo (Via Manila)," in Anna Beerens and Mark Teeuwen, eds., *Unchartered Waters: Intellectual Life in the Edo Period: Essays in Honour of W. J. Boot* (Leiden: Leiden University Press, 2012), pp. 233–234.

[6] Akō shi, *Chūshingura*, vol. 1, p. 9.

there were fears that departure via the front gate would take Kira past the guest mansion where the imperial emissaries had lodged, and where Asano's retainers were known to have remained over the prior several days. Thinking it best to avoid any encounter with them, a circuitous route was followed. A sizable contingent of shogunal retainers reportedly accompanied the palanquin carrying Kira to his residence. There, it entered through the rear gate. While Kira's recovery was expected to be uneventful, the physician Kurisaki agreed, at the request of Kira's son, Uesugi Tsunanori, to visit Kira daily for the next sixty days to create the illusion that he was in critical condition. With news of the attack spreading rapidly and questions about Kira's fate becoming the talk of the town, Kira and his family wanted to maintain the illusion that his circumstances were dire.[7]

More from the Servant to the Inner Chambers

Kajikawa's account adds that a group of castle attendants led Asano to a room behind the Banquet Hall and then on to the Willow Room. Along the way, Asano repeatedly stated that he had attacked Kira "because of a grudge he had harbored over the last several days." Asano admitted that he regretted attacking Kira in the castle just as the ceremonies were about to begin. Nevertheless, he added, "Without fail, I wanted to cut Kira down." Asano repeated the same over and again, in a loud voice that attracted the attention of several of Kira's colleagues and a crowd of others participating in the rituals. One of the representatives of the esteemed families who was nearby asked Asano why he was so boisterous. He added that Asano's deed was done and so implored him to silence. Thereafter, Asano said nothing more.[8] With this, Kajikawa's report on the attack concluded. Later, in gratitude for his report, Kajikawa was given a 500-*koku* raise to his stipend, bringing his annual income to 1,200 *koku*.

Kajikawa's report is considered the most reliable account of the time just before and after the attack. It explains Asano's blows in terms of a grudge, and implies that Asano had reasons for the grudge, ones

---

[7] Harper, "The Kurisaki School," *Unchartered Waters*, pp. 222–224, 228–236. Akō shi, *Chūshingura*, vol. 3, pp. 13–14.

[8] "Kajikawa shi hikki," *Akō gijin sansho*, vol. 2, pp. 269–270.

that he wanted Kira to recall just before he, Asano, killed him. Yet Kajikawa leaves the precise nature of the grudge and its rationale unexplained. Otherwise, he casts Asano as a somewhat rational, even cunning man who waited patiently until the right moment for his strike, yet was foiled by a castle functionary (himself, i.e., Kajikawa) who restrained him and so aborted his attack. It should be added that Asano's attack failed in part because he used his short ceremonial sword as if it were a powerful long sword. Instead of stabbing, the most effective use of a short sword, Asano brought his blade down on Kira as if it had the weight to make a deep, mortal wound. Later assessments of Asano's abilities lampooned him for not knowing how to use a small weapon effectively. With his bold but botched attack, Asano hardly captured the admiration of Edo samurai. Many pitied him, realizing that regardless of the failed attempt, Asano would pay dearly for it.

Kajikawa's report, although widely deemed the most credible, is not beyond question. For example, it casts Asano as a relatively calm, collected individual, coldly rational in choosing, unprompted, the moment to attack. Other sources, however, suggest that Asano simply lost his senses. Kajikawa's primary duties were in the inner quarters of the castle where he worked under the direction of Tsunayoshi's mother, Keishōin. Kajikawa surely realized that his first and foremost obligation in reporting the altercation was to the Tokugawa, not a minor daimyō from southwestern Japan. Casting Asano as a coldly calculating samurai acting secretly on a personal grudge localized the blame and possibly minimized questions regarding shogunal judgment in the selection of the ceremonial participants.

The shogunate, of course, accepted Kajikawa's account as credible, concluding that Kira, a Tokugawa official and close associate of the shogun, had impeccably maintained decorum. In preventing Kira's murder and in affirming that Kira was neither the cause of nor a participant in the altercation, Kajikawa served the shogun and Keishōin well. His narrative cast the altercation as nothing more than a poorly executed, grudge-driven, lone-wolf attack by an outer lord from the hinterlands, launched against an innocent, much older, non-violent member of one of the esteemed families of the realm. As a by-product, Kajikawa's testimony justified confiscation of yet another domain, not as an act of shogunal greed, but as just punishment for a premeditating but pathetically wayward daimyō. With Kajikawa's account in hand, the shogunate acted, putting Asano to death the same day and thus sealing the matter quickly.

Others, however, including some imperial emissaries, concluded that Asano had simply gone mad (*ranshin*), or that he was deranged (*ranki*). The physician, Kurisaki, for example, notes that even as he was treating Kira, the question of Asano's mental stability arose with some saying that he was "insane" in attacking Kira. Complicating matters, however, was the fact that, as Kurisaki also notes, Asano specifically denied being "crazy."[9] But then again, that denial reflected, arguably, the widespread suspicion that he indeed was. The diary of a shogunal retainer notes that during the attack Asano behaved "in a crazed manner" (*ranshin no yō ni*), for no clear reason. Higashizono Motomasa, a Kyoto aristocrat of high standing who served in the court of Emperor Higashiyama, added in his memoir that Asano's attack on Kira, which soiled the White Chamber with blood, leaving it unclean and forcing a relocation to the Black Chamber, resulted from Asano's "mad energy" (*ranki*). Yanagiwara Sukekado, one of the emissaries Asano hosted, also recorded that Asano's attack resulted from his "mad energy."

Concluding that Asano had lost his mind would have reflected poorly on Tsunayoshi since the shogunate had approved Asano's selection as a host for the important occasion. The question would have arisen of why an unstable, possibly deranged, even crazy daimyō had been chosen in the first place. Regardless of the answer, the question alone would impair imperial respect for the judgment of the shogunate on matters related to court ceremonies. The imperial house might well have wondered whether Tsunayoshi was indeed in full control of his senses. And the shogun was asking, simultaneously, that his mother be elevated imperially to status as the highest-ranking woman in the realm. That aside, even if Kajikawa were correct in depicting Asano Naganori as a sane assailant acting on a personal, hitherto secret grudge, he gives no indication as to what exactly was the nature of the grudge that prompted Asano to forfeit everything.

Things Seen and Heard

The single most valuable text documenting the vendetta from beginning to end is *Things Seen and Heard in Edo and Akō*, attributed to Ochiai

[9] Akō shi, *Chūshingura*, vol. 3, p. 12.

Yozaemon, a chamberlain to Asano Naganori's wife.[10] The Meiji pioneer of modern historiography, Shigeno Yasutsugu, recognized it as authentic and reliable, as have virtually all historians since. Two caveats are in order. First, the source has an obvious pro-Asano bias. Second, the final three volumes, five through seven, include some authentic material, but also much drawn from rumor, lampoon, and popular fabrication. Volumes one through four are often disjointed, with one source being followed by another in a scrapbook-like patchwork of related but often random information. Nevertheless, the text amounts to a mine of largely reliable source material about the incident from Asano's attack through the beheading of Kira, the mass seppuku, and the burial of the rōnin at the Sengakuji. Any well-informed account of the vendetta should take this text into consideration.

Things Seen and Heard offers one of the first explanations of Asano's grudge. Whether it is credible is open to question since matters of the mind and heart – such as the nature of one's anger – are virtually impossible to establish. That aside, there can be no doubt that at least part of the gloss on the grudge presented in *Things Seen and Heard* has been repeated, by far, more than any other. The text opens by recalling that on the fourth day of the second month of 1701, Asano was appointed to serve the shogun as one of the daimyō hosting ceremonies for imperial emissaries attending Edo Castle the following month. The ceremonies were to be coordinated by Kira, the master of court rituals for the shogunate. *Things Seen and Heard* quickly identifies Kira as a man given, ironically, to improper behavior. Most basically, he is described as a "man of deep desires" who expected "presents" from those benefiting from his guidance. Asano, however, is described as a more formal and frugal sort. Kira was apparently not pleased with this and so, more and more, behaved improperly toward Asano, prompting Asano to develop an angry grudge toward him.[11]

Such was the situation, *Things Seen and Heard* relates, in advance of the arrival of the imperial representatives in Edo on the eleventh day of the third month. The next day, the text simply relates, the emissaries met the shogun. Then, on the thirteenth, it adds that there was a banquet followed by Nō plays. The following day, the fourteenth, was the occasion of the imperial response to the shogun. *Things Seen*

---

[10] Ochiai Yozaemon, *Kōseki kenmonki*, in *Akō gijin sansho*, vol. 3, pp. 172–362.
[11] Ibid., p. 172.

and Heard then projects beyond the fated day, noting how the imperial emissaries were to visit the Kan'eiji, a Tendai temple, in Ueno, and the Zōjōji, the Tokugawa family Pure Land temple, on the fifteenth. The sixteenth was to be a day of rest prior to the emissaries' departure on the seventeenth.[12]

However, on the fourteenth, with the imperial guests already in the castle and proceeding toward the White Chamber, Asano overtook Kira in the grand corridor while Kira was speaking with Kajikawa Yosobei. The attack came from behind, with Asano simply asking, "Will you remember now?" before landing his first sword blow to Kira's shoulder. Kira turned, only to face Asano's second blow to his forehead. Because Kira was wearing a ceremonial cap with a forehead strap, the sword blow to his forehead was broken. Nevertheless, Kira collapsed, bleeding. Asano was promptly restrained by Kajikawa. Kira cried out twice for help. Soon a group of attendants from the esteemed families arrived from the adjoining rooms and helped him away. Restrained by four inspectors, Asano was taken from the corridor into the pageboys' room.

Kira was soon excused, but Asano was questioned about the improper disturbance he had caused. For his misconduct, Asano was assigned to the custody of Tamura Takeaki and made to exit the castle via the Hirakawa Gate, reserved for criminals and the polluted, in a palanquin secured by a net, with a horseman leading the way, accompanied by approximately forty samurai guards. Quite significantly, at the Tamura residence, Asano reportedly confessed that he had had "an unfortunate life, one afflicted by illness and suffering. In whatever endeavor, he had been unable to find peace and stability. Therefore, he had not been mindful of the circumstances and so badly behaved in the castle."[13] Asano's remarks, if considered credible, provide stunning

---

[12] "Genroku Akō jiken kankei nenpu," pp. 243–244. And the final day of ceremonies continued with Toda Noto-no-kami Tadazane, lord of Sakura domain in Shimōsa province, serving as an emergency replacement for Asano. The final ceremonies were held in the Black Chamber.

[13] *Kōseki kenmonki*, pp. 172–174. Asano's remarks about "illness and suffering" are discussed in Akō shi, *Chūshingura*, vol. 1, pp. 26–27, vis-à-vis the "sickness theory" explaining Asano's attack. The *Tokugawa jikki* records that on the twenty-sixth day of the sixth month of 1680, Asano's maternal uncle, Naitō Tadakatsu, lord of Toba domain, then twenty-six, suddenly attacked and killed Nagai Naonaga, lord of Miyazu domain, while the two vassals were attending memorial services held at the Zōjō Temple for the recently deceased shogun, Tokugawa Ietsuna. Naitō was

testimony regarding his state of mind. Without doubt, they suggest that Asano was a troubled soul, perhaps even mentally upset.

Witnessing Asano's seppuku at the Tamura residence were a grand inspector, two inspectors, plus an additional ten minor inspectors. The verdict, read by the grand inspector, did not mention madness. Rather, it restated the familiar lines: Asano held a grudge against Kira, ignored the circumstances, and attacked Kira. The verdict was that he had committed "an extremely serious outrage of the utmost degree" (*jūjū futodoki shigoku*). For that, Asano would commit seppuku. After the verdict, Asano positioned himself on the tatami mats arranged in the garden outside the White Chamber of the Tamura mansion and readied his robes for the blow of his second, who was to cut off his head promptly. Unfortunately, *Things Seen and Heard* relates, the second, [Isoda] Takedayū, missed his mark, striking Asano just below his ear. After finally finishing his task, Isoda held Asano's head up with both hands, per the seppuku ceremony, showing it to the grand inspector and witnesses, thus concluding the grisly ritual.

Tamura arranged to turn Asano's remains over to his younger brother, Daigaku, who in turn sent several retainers to receive the corpse. A palanquin transported Asano's coffin to his family temple in Edo, the Sengakuji. There, a posthumous name was soon assigned and a simple service held for the young lord, age thirty-five at death. The following day, Asano Daigaku was placed under house arrest. Asano residences in Edo, including the main compound in Teppozu where Asano's wife had remained throughout the day of Asano's attack, were given notice of imminent confiscation.

Reportedly, the night of Asano's seppuku, his widow, Aguri, cut her hair and resolved to take up life as a Buddhist nun. She later assumed the Buddhist name Yōzeiin and supposedly dedicated herself to praying for her husband's well-being in the afterlife. First, however, on the sixteenth day, two days after her husband's seppuku, she moved into the Edo residence of a relative, Asano Nagazumi, lord of Miyoshi Castle. In the meantime, Asano Naganori's senior retainers in Edo

restrained by Tōyama Masasuke, lord of Yunagaya domain, taken into custody, and sentenced to seppuku the following day at the Shunryōji. Naitō's line was abolished and his fief confiscated. Some have speculated that Naitō suffered from a hereditary mental disorder that resurfaced in Asano who, twenty-one years later, met a similar fate.

were informed that Akō Castle and the surrounding domain would be confiscated.[14] *Things Seen and Heard* thus recognizes, first, Kira's greed and Asano's refusal to cater to it as a remote, possibly contributing factor, but also suggests, quite significantly, that Asano was a mentally troubled, even disturbed individual, one who offered an execution-site confession regarding his "illness and suffering" in what seems to have been his only explanation for his outrageous behavior.

The Castle Inspector's Account

A shogunal inspector on duty in Edo Castle during the attack, Okado Denpachirō, or at least someone writing under his name, left a detailed account, *Okado's Memoir*, beginning with Asano's attack and concluding with his seppuku later that day. In breadth and detail, *Okado's Memoir* offers the fullest account of Asano's fateful day. However, scholars have repeatedly questioned its authenticity because many of its sensational claims lack external corroboration. Meiji historian Shigeno Yasutsugu called *Okado's Memoir* "an apocryphal text full of fabricated explanations." More recently, historian Bitō Masahide noted its "excessively sympathetic attitude towards Asano." Bitō even declared that its words "cannot be trusted as a contemporaneous account," even though he, Bitō, has "no direct evidence" for dismissing it other than its being widely questioned. The leading contemporary authority on the Akō incident, Miyazawa Seiichi, also questions *Okado's Memoir*, noting its numerous discrepancies with Kajikawa's. Miyazawa adds that Okado indulged in "fabrication and forgery of historical facts." Yet Miyazawa acknowledges that Okado's and Kajikawa's accounts "have complementary dimensions" and that "both are necessary for a comprehensive reexamination of the incident." Nevertheless, Miyazawa also raises questions about Kajikawa's account, noting that it is difficult to imagine how Kajikawa, who was reportedly standing beside Kira talking to him, did not notice Asano charging at Kira from behind until after Asano had struck his first blow.[15]

---

[14] Ibid., pp. 174–176, 178–179. Asano retainers near the shogunal guest mansion for imperial emissaries were instructed to disperse without incident following the attack. Also, Akō shi, *Chūshingura*, pp. 42–47.

[15] Shigeno Yasutsugu, *Akō gishi jitsuwa* (Tokyo: Taiseikan, 1889), p. 3. Bitō, "The Akō Incident," p. 151. Miyazawa Seiichi, *Akō rōshi: tsumugidasareru Chūshingura* (Tokyo: Sanseidō, 1999), pp. 33–47.

Of the two accounts, Kajikawa's has generally been deemed more reliable than Okado's, but the latter should not simply be banned from historical analyses of the incident. Even if a forgery, *Okado's Memoir* needs to be considered as one of the sources from which certain features of the vendetta legend originated. One of the historian's tasks is to discern which is which and to analyze why the legendary, mythic, and ideologically exploitive dimensions were generated and what they signify in relation to the historical event and its cultural legacies. The Okado text, regardless of what it purports to be, arguably amounts to one of the first iterations of the vendetta tale as historical fiction, one that came to inform later versions, in early modern and modern popular culture. Henry D. Smith II, the leading authority in contemporary vendetta studies in the West, judges that *Okado's Memoir* "should be used with great caution." However, Smith also acknowledges, "it is really all that survives in the way of an eye-witness account, and as such remains indispensable; it is the basis for the depiction of the palace attack in almost all 20th-century historical novels and films about the Akō incident."[16]

Some, including Smith, have speculated that *Okado's Memoir* was written well after the incident, when public sympathy for the rōnin vendetta was relatively high. Okado, according to this view, presented himself as an on-the-scene champion of Asano's cause, objecting vocally to the shogunate's overly swift and severe decisions at every turn.[17] Yet if *Okado's Memoir* is questionable because it casts Asano as a man deserving of respect and consideration, a similar charge could be directed at Kajikawa for his early, arguably self-serving sympathy for another in-house shogunal functionary, Kira, and his simultaneous disuse for the minor, outer daimyō, Asano. Consequently, despite the two on-the-scene reports, Kajikawa's and Okado's, Asano's attack on Kira remains a puzzle wherein various accounts add insights, yet they also conflict and even contradict one another, and at one level or another are questionable, so that none can be accepted as completely reliable. While the two accounts leave questions unanswered, overlap remains on key issues, suggesting that Okado's text cannot simply be

---

[16] "Talk: Forty-seven Rōnin/HenryDSmith." en.wikipedia.org/wiki/Talk%3AForty-seven_Rōnin/ HenryDSmith. Last accessed September 24, 2016.

[17] Ibid.

deemed across-the-board taboo testimony. At another level, the disagreements evident in these two recountings foreshadow later debates.

Regardless of the veracity of the work bearing his name, Okado
was apparently of good standing in Edo Castle: he was a lower-level
vassal who served the shogunate as an inspector-overseer within the
castle. His annual stipend was, like Kajikawa's (before Kajikawa's
raise), 700 *koku*. Notably, Kajikawa's account mentions that while
looking for Kira just prior to the ceremonies, he passed Okado, establishing that Okado was proximate the assault even though he was not,
like Kajikawa, an eyewitness from the start. Okado had no immediate
business in the central citadel, but upon hearing the commotion, proceeded there, arriving after Asano's blows had been struck. Okado next
served as one of the official interrogators questioning Asano to determine how the incident would be adjudicated. When Asano was sentenced to death, Okado served with two other inspectors as official
witnesses. There is no doubt that Okado was, then, on the scene
throughout much of the day, from shortly after Asano's attack on
Kira, until after Asano's seppuku at the Tamura mansion.

Yet Okado's presence hardly guarantees the credibility of the
text, *Okado's Memoir*. Some of the most questionable portions of
Okado's Memoir pertain to Asano's seppuku. *Okado's Memoir* claims,
for example, that due to Okado's plea for "compassion," one of Asano's
retainers, Kataoka Gengoemon, was allowed silent eye contact with
Asano just before the latter's seppuku. Tamura officials presiding over
the seppuku protocol were not pleased, but did not overrule Okado.
Supposedly surrounded by guards to prevent any breach, Kataoka
cooperated. Thus, master and loyal vassal supposedly shared
a farewell glimpse before Asano mounted the dais for his end.[18]

Later incorporated into novels, movies, and supposed histories,
this detail became a staple in popular accounts of Asano's final hour. Yet
there is no mention of it in the business-like Tamura house report on
Asano's seppuku. Skeptics have concluded that because this poignant
detail lacks corroboration, it was fabricated to provide an embellished,
ultimately apocryphal account of the absolute loyalty that Asano's
retainers supposedly had for him as he went to his death. Without this

---

[18] *Okado hikki, Akō gijin sansho*, vol. 1, p. 312. For an early English translation of
a good portion of this text, see Hiroaki Satō, *Legends of the Samurai* (Woodstock,
NY: The Overlook Press, 1995), pp. 307–321.

touching fabrication, Asano died alone, without retainers, friends, or family anywhere nearby. The fictitious detail of Asano's last visual exchange with a loyal samurai beautified the sad facts about Asano's fate with a moving, emotionally and ethically satisfying alternative version of his last moments.

Another apparent fabrication is Asano's death poem: according to *Okado's Memoir*, just before his seppuku, Asano requested brush, ink, and paper to write his parting poem. The latter supposedly read, "As cherry blossoms are called away by a breeze, what will spring's ending bring next?"[19] No other documents mention this poem. After the Okado text, however, it became a staple in popular tales of Asano's death. Noting that the poem only appears in *Okado's Memoir*, scholars have questioned if not completely dismissed its authenticity and the text recording it. Arguably, the account of Asano's poem was another fabrication meant to provide an alternative narrative beautifying a tragically abrupt and lonely end by casting the ill-fated Asano in the best possible light, as a sensitive, cultured samurai greeting his own demise with a thoughtful verse likening the end of his brief existence to that of cherry blossoms beckoned by a late spring breeze, wondering what lay beyond the floating world.

Generally, *Okado's Memoir* is faulted for its overly sympathetic portrayal of Asano, something evident from the start. The text relates that a "great commotion" occurred within the castle at around 10:00 in the morning. Soon an alert was delivered to the inspectors' offices that an altercation had occurred in the Grand Pine Corridor (*matsu-no-orōka*) – first identified as such by Okado. When Okado arrived on the scene, he came across Kira cradled in the arms of another ceremonial official, disoriented and shouting, "I need a doctor." Kira's blood had stained a section of the Grand Pine Corridor as he fled toward the Cherry Chamber. Nearby was Asano, without sword, his face flushed, being held down by Kajikawa. Docile and unarmed, Asano reportedly said:

> I am not deranged (*ranshin*) ... Please let me go. My attack failed and I am ready to face the consequences. I will not attack him again so please let go of me. I need to put on my ceremonial hat and straighten my crested robe so that I might be judged according to samurai house laws.

[19] Ibid., p. 314.

Kajikawa, however, would not release Asano, prompting the latter to explain that he was the lord of a castle and a domain with an annual stipend of 53,000 *koku*. Asano added apologies for his behavior, which was, admittedly, disrespectful of the circumstances in the castle. He emphasized, however, that his ceremonial robes would be in disarray if he were not released. More importantly, Asano declared, "I have no grudge whatsoever against the shogun and would not raise a hand against him." Asano supposedly added, "I regret that my attack failed, but that is what happened and nothing can be done about it now."[20]

Okado's Memoir relates that Kajikawa kept Asano pinned to the floor in the Grand Pine Corridor until Okado and several other inspectors took him into custody and helped him straighten his hat and robe as they proceeded to the Sago Palm Room for interrogation. There Asano was confined to a corner, given the privacy of a folding screen, and guarded by four men. Reportedly, Kira was later brought into the same room, assigned another corner, also protected by a folding screen and guards. *Okado's Memoir* thus casts its supposed author as an able, experienced inspector, here playing the role of shogunal crime scene investigator and public relations manager. The account thus relates that Okado promptly instructed staff to draft an announcement to preempt rumors. Written in large characters on a pine board, it read, "Asano Naganori wounded Kira Yoshinaka with his sword. Both are being interrogated. Retainers are warned against causing a commotion."[21] This release supposedly quieted the clamor for information about what had transpired, but also surely served to feed myriad rumors circulating from the castle, now the epicenter of Edo talk.

Okado's Memoir presents Asano as a man aware of charges that he had lost his mind, but insistent that he had not. Here again, perhaps the memoir meant to offer an alternative narrative revamping the unpleasant reality that Asano was a mentally unstable, disturbed soul. Asano acknowledged the disrespectful nature of his attack, understood the consequences, and amazingly enough, simply wanted to appear presentably attired before the authorities who would surely condemn him to death. Asano reportedly disavowed any animosity toward the shogun. He only admitted harboring a "personal grudge," or, alternately, a "long-standing grudge," that caused him to forget his surroundings and attack Kira. Asano even vowed to accept punishment

---

[20] Ibid., p. 306.   [21] Ibid., p. 307.

without objection. He added that he greatly regretted failing in his attempt to strike down Kira. Then, Asano asked about Kira's condition, apparently unaware that Kira was, according to *Okado's Memoir*, in another corner of the same room, also under interrogation. When told that Kira's wounds were shallow, but serious for a man of Kira's age, sixty at the time, Asano said no more.[22]

Okado's text also describes the interrogation of Kira. It was in the same room, the Sago Palm Room, that, according to *Okado's Memoir*, Kira was treated by the shogun's physician. Okado first asked Kira about the nature of Asano's grudge, suggesting that he, Kira, must have known the reasons for a hatred so strong as to prompt an attempt on his life. Kira flatly denied knowing anything. He quickly added that in his view, the attack resulted entirely from Asano's insanity (*ranshin*). He noted that he was an old man, and asked why anyone would have a grudge against him. Kira finished his testimony reemphasizing that he had no idea what caused the attack. That, he added, was all he had to say.[23]

The deputy inspectors then submitted their reports. The verdict came down quickly: Asano had failed to recognize the honorable place and circumstances in which he was a participant and instead, acting on a personal grudge, attacked and injured Kira. This, the shogunate declared, was "outrageous." Although Asano's misdeed is often explained in terms of a shogunal law against unsheathing one's sword within the shogun's castle, that violation was not mentioned in the verdict as reported by Okado, nor by other contemporary accounts. Instead, the latter called attention to how Asano's attack was an extreme breach of protocol informing ceremonial relations in the shogun's castle involving the shogun and representatives of the emperor and retired emperor. According to the verdict, Asano's outrage was not disobeying a law so much as blatantly disregarding the ceremonial time and place in his behavior. If a specific infraction were at issue, it was not identified.[24]

Yet rather than concur with the verdict as just, *Okado's Memoir* presents Okado objecting, noting that while Asano confessed to

---

[22] Ibid., p. 307.   [23] Ibid., p. 308.

[24] Ibid., p. 308. Also see *Kōseki kenmonki*, p. 174. The verdict as recorded in the *Akō gishi jiten*, p. 45, notes that Asano's attack polluted the ceremonial occasion and was "outrageous to an extreme and extraordinary degree."

everything, and even allowed that he would accept punishment, Asano was still a daimyō and a relative of the powerful Asano clan of Hiroshima Castle. Okado emphasized that dealing with Asano was of consequence to relations with the outer daimyō of the realm, and so it should not appear that he had been sentenced capriciously. Okado did not, then, object to the verdict so much as to the speed with which it had been handed down, with Asano, a daimyō with powerful family ties, arrested, interrogated, and sentenced to death in a single day. Okado added that even if Asano had attacked because he was deranged (*ranshin*), it seemed doubtful to conclude that Kira had done nothing to provoke him. Okado therefore called on the shogunate to conduct a more thorough investigation to make certain that its decision was beyond reproach. Alternatively, Okado suggested, Asano should first be stripped of his court appointment and his standing as a daimyō. Once reduced to commoner status, Asano could be sentenced as the shogunate saw fit, without the appearance of impropriety.[25]

Okado's objections were promptly reported to the shogunal officials who had decided the verdict, in this case, Yanagisawa Yoshiyasu. Okado was soon told that Yanagisawa had made his decision and that it was final. Just as quickly, Okado reiterated his objections, asking that they be conveyed to Yanagisawa's superior, the shogun. In his view, such a "one-sided" decision would be shameful for outer daimyō, since they might see it as indicative of how they would be treated. Okado added that if the shogun had reviewed the matter previously and issued the verdict, he would stand by it. But, if it reflected only the judgment of Yanagisawa, then he wanted his concerns relayed directly to the shogun.

Again, Okado's objections were supposedly reported. Yanagisawa responded by claiming responsibility for handling the matter. He declared that he found it hard to fathom why Okado would voice his objections once more. To put an end to the matter, Yanagisawa ordered that Okado be confined to his quarters within the castle until further notice. There, Okado remained until late that afternoon. By the time he was released from confinement, Kira had been escorted to his residence, the imperial emissaries had left the castle, and arrangements for Asano's seppuku had been planned. Okado was praised for having spoken so seriously about the matter, but criticized for repeating his

---

[25] Ibid., p. 309.

objections over and again. After being released, Okado prepared to fulfill his next duty as an overseer-inspector, witnessing Asano's death. Accordingly, he met Shōda Yasutoshi, the grand inspector assigned by the shogunate to oversee the arrangements. Okado then prepared to leave Edo Castle with the retinue of inspectors, magistrates, and guards proceeding to the site of the next ceremony, that of Asano's seppuku. The group departed around 5:00 PM.[26]

Earlier, around 1:00 PM, Asano had been turned over to Tamura Tateaki, daimyō of Ichinoseki domain, for punishment that afternoon. He was transported in a secured palanquin, marked as prisoner's transport. It was accompanied by forty men on foot, plus a lead horseman, followed by two more horsemen. The procession departed Edo Castle via the Hirakawa Gate, from which Kira had exited earlier, reportedly in secret. Asano left by this gate, however, because he had egregiously violated a high ceremonial occasion by attempting to slay a shogunal official. At the Tamura residence, Asano was not treated warmly: he was confined to one room, under watch, for the four hours between his arrival, around 2:00 PM, and his seppuku, just after 6:00 PM. He was allowed tea, soup, and vegetables.[27] During this time, Asano's countenance and his "breathing" seemed normal,[28] nothing like the enraged, perhaps momentarily deranged man who had earlier tried to commit murder in the shogun's castle just before a high ceremonial occasion.

Sometime after 5:00 PM, Shōda and Okado arrived at the Tamura mansion.[29] Thereupon Okado inspected the arrangements for Asano's seppuku, found them egregiously lacking, and immediately registered complaints. He found a platform covered with tatami mats and topped with a rug, surrounded by a curtain and oil-treated folding screens. Rather than indoors, the seppuku site was in a garden area outside a small drawing room in the Tamura residence. Lanterns were added to provide lighting in anticipation of nightfall. Okado found the arrangement "extremely austere," but most of all objected to the garden setting, claiming that the *seppuku* should accord with "the way of the samurai" (*bushidō*) which held that a daimyō of Asano's standing be given the dignity of a formal, tatami-covered room, not the grounds of a garden.

---

[26] Ibid., pp. 309–310.   [27] *Chūshingura hyakka*, p. 55.   [28] *Kōseki kenmonki*, p. 174.
[29] The site in Minato-ku, Shinbashi, yon-chōmei has a marker that states, "This is where Asano Takumi-no-kami met his end." The Tamura residence was approximately halfway between Edo Castle and the Sengakuji.

Okado's objections were reportedly so strenuous as to prompt Tamura's anger. Tamura indicated that he had the approval of the grand inspector, Shōda, and if he, Okado, wished to file a complaint, he should do so. But there was simply no time for any changes. Okado then launched yet another diatribe about how Asano, a daimyō with court rank, should be treated with more delicacy, or at least a delay by a day or two in execution. By the time Okado finished, Shōda, angered by the objections, encouraged Okado to file whatever complaint he wished, but added that ultimately, the matter was for him, not Okado, to decide.[30] The Tamura account of the seppuku, incidentally, offers no corroboration for Okado's objections to the garden setting, nor does it record Okado's input on any count before, during, or after the ceremony.

Okado's narrative at this juncture shifts to a previously noted fabrication: the arrival of one of Asano's retainers, Kataoka Gengoemon, and his request for a last exchange with his lord. Upon hearing this, Okado reportedly dropped his objections to the garden setting and took up Kataoka's cause. Okado proposed that Kataoka be stationed along Asano's approach to the seppuku mats, for one final glimpse, but no verbal exchanges, with Asano. Providing this much, Okado claimed, would be an act of compassion. Shōda showed no interest in the matter and permitted Okado to have his way. Thus, *Okado's Memoir* reports that Asano and Kataoka shared final, optical contact in silence as Asano walked toward death.

Okado also recorded that after Shōda had read the shogunate's verdict, Asano expressed his sincere gratitude for being allowed to commit seppuku. Asano also thanked the various inspectors for serving as witnesses for the occasion. Then, Asano asked about Kira. When told that the wounds had been treated and Kira sent home, Asano pressed for more information. Okado volunteered that while the cuts were shallow, Kira was advanced in years and might not be able to recover. Hearing that, Asano reportedly "shed a tear, smiling." Asano then proceeded, in a composed manner, to the tatami mats. He did request, according to *Okado's Memoir*, that his own long sword be used by his second, and then be given to him as a gift. The assembled inspectors agreed. Asano further requested paper, ink, and a brush with which to compose his parting poem. Shortly after Asano had completed the poem, the Okado

[30] *Okado hikki*, pp. 310–312.

account adds, Asano's second, Isoda Takedayū, completed his task, beheading Asano.[31]

According to *Things Seen and Heard*, however, Isoda botched his duties, first striking just below Asano's ear and so failing to decapitate him with one swift blow. After Isoda finally severed the head and held it up in presentation to the inspectors, the ceremony was done.[32] Isoda's missed blow was not reported in *Okado's Memoir*. *Things Seen and Heard*, as an account issuing from the Asano family, had no reason to add this unfortunate bit of information if it were not true. Okado, who was undoubtedly present, would have known about it. That it did not enter "his" account hints that he was not the author of that text. Moreover, if Kataoka had been present in the garden prior to Asano's seppuku and allowed a last glimpse of his lord, a report of this moment would have appeared in *Things Seen and Heard*, but such is not there, much less in the Tamura account of the seppuku.

Nor is there mention in either text, or others apart from *Okado's Memoir*, that Asano requested that his own sword be used in the seppuku, and then given to his second. Nor were his repeated questions about Kira's condition recorded elsewhere. Indeed, nothing in *Okado's Memoir* from the arrival of Kataoka forward appears in *Things Seen and Heard*, not even Asano's supposed death poem. *Things Seen and Heard* only has Kataoka arriving at the Tamura residence well after Asano's seppuku, along with five other retainers, now rōnin, to receive their deceased lord's remains.[33] One account estimates their time of arrival as 10:00 PM, hours after Asano's death.[34] It is worth noting that *Things Seen and Heard* does not register Okado's supposed complaints about the place of execution, though it does describe the garden setting in detail. This, again, suggests that much of *Okado's Memoir* is simply apocryphal.

Whether Okado earlier took issue with the shogunate's verdict, objecting repeatedly, is another matter. Although not corroborated by other documents, there would be no reason for those exchanges, presumably communicated in private, to have appeared in *Things Seen and Heard*. And since Okado's supposed objections to the verdict were overruled, their absence elsewhere was conceivably due to the shogunate refusing to dignify them. But then again, they might well have been

[31] Ibid., pp. 312–314.　[32] *Kōseki kenmonki*, pp. 175–176.　[33] Ibid., p. 176.
[34] Akō shi, *Chūshingura*, vol. 1, p. 40.

simply fabrications meant to portray Okado as a man of outspoken integrity. *Okado's Memoir* is thus an enigmatic, and surely somewhat apocryphal source. Yet even if largely a fabrication, its significance in cultural history is evident in the countless times that Asano's silent encounter with Kataoka and the words of Asano's death poem have been presented in popular retellings as touching, last moments in Asano's tragic life. The legacy of *Okado's Memoir* in the fabricated lore of popular culture and historical fiction has been, in a word, considerable.

The Tamura House Account

The Tamura daimyō left an official statement documenting the brief confinement and ultimate seppuku of Asano Naganori, as well as the final deposition of his body. It stands as yet another valuable source, especially regarding the events of the end of the day. Well after Shōda and the official witnesses – including Okado – had departed, six of Asano Naganori's retainers – including Kataoka – arrived to receive his coffin. Asano Daigaku had sent them, after earlier being informed of the seppuku. The retainers also received Asano's personal effects including his ceremonial hat and his ceremonial short sword, along with his family crest, and handkerchiefs. Earlier, shogunal senior counselors had authorized the return of these items to the Asano family. The Tamura also handed over to the Asano retainers a brief text, authentic by all counts, that the Okado account, tellingly, does not mention. Before being taken to the seppuku garden, Asano asked if he might leave a statement for his retainers. He was allowed to dictate a missive, recorded by a scribe. The contents of the message and its transfer are recorded in the Tamura official report on Asano's seppuku. The terse, enigmatic message read, "I should have made you aware of this matter beforehand. Today, however, things came to an inevitable head. By that point, I could not inform you of anything. You will surely have questions about what has happened."[35]

---

[35] "Tamura Ukyōdaibu dono ni Asano Takumi-no-kami oazukari ikken," in *Akō gijin sansho*, vol. 2, p. 5. Shigeno Yasutsugu and others have deemed this document authentic.

Emphasizing the significance of this puzzling remark, Bitō Masahide notes that "these words, together with the mention of 'my grudge' recorded by Kajikawa, constitute the totality of what we know about the reasons for Asano's attack on Kira."[36] This opaque missive was later delivered to Ōishi Yoshio, Asano's chief retainer, and served as a Zen-like challenge for those retainers who dedicated themselves to completing the intention of their deceased master, incomprehensible in motive though it may have been. That the Tamura account includes this brief note, but makes no mention of the poem that *Okado's Memoir* cites, calls into question, again, the authenticity of Okado's reports about Asano's seppuku.

The group of retainers accompanying the coffin-bearing palanquin left the Tamura residence as they had entered, via the horse stable entrance rather than the front gate. Thereafter, they proceeded southward, to the Asano family temple, the Sengakuji, for burial. The young daimyō's final procession thus went virtually unnoticed in the darkness of the night, around 11:00 PM. A brief service, attended only by the accompanying retainers, was conducted. The head monk soon assigned Asano a lengthy posthumous name, *Reikōinden zenshōfu chōsandaifu suimō genri daikoji*, eighteen characters, alluding to his passing in the spring of life.[37] As of that evening, there were no plans to erect a memorial stone. A month later, however, a gravestone had been completed and a small memorial service held.[38]

In the Tamura account of Asano's seppuku, the verdict was read just before the seppuku. There, Asano's "grudge" is cited as the cause of his unreasonable attack on Kira. Next, the verdict emphasizes the "extraordinarily outrageous" nature of Asano's disregard for the shogun's castle and circumstances of the moment, and then decrees seppuku. The account does add that Asano's behavior was *buchōhō*,[39] which could easily be translated as "illegal" or "not in harmony with the law," but could equally be rendered "impolite," "inconsiderate," and "abnormal." Since the verdict does not cite a law that Asano violated, it is perhaps excessive to interpret the matter legalistically, as if the rule of universal, equitable law prevailed during Tsunayoshi's

---

[36] Bitō, "The Akō Incident," p. 151.
[37] *Kōseki kenmonki*, p. 176. Miyazawa, *Akō rōshi*, p. 45.
[38] "Genroku gikyo nenpu," *Akō gishi jiten*, p. 131.
[39] "Tamura Ukyōdaibu dono ni," in *Akō gijin sansho*, vol. 2, pp. 4–5.

Figure 2.1 Asano Naganori's gravestone, Sengakuji. Photograph by the author.

reign. An exclusively legalistic reading of the shogunate's judgment reflects a Western, perhaps even Orientalist determination to make Tokugawa sensibilities consistent with those of the more legalistically driven West.

According to the shogunate's verdict, Asano's attack was an outrageous violation of etiquette and standards of ritual purity and protocol that demanded nothing less than another ceremonial response, his seppuku. The judgment was arguably not a matter of law, then, so much as shogunal ritual sensibilities, offended in an unforgivable way by Asano's failure to appreciate the exceptional significance of the occasion. Rather than maintaining a respectful demeanor and humble compliance with the occasion hosted by the shogun, and subordinates like himself, for representatives of the emperor and retired emperor, Asano acted "outrageously" (*futodoki*), as though he were encountering Kira in some field. Although *futodoki* was used not infrequently by the shogunate to refer to deeds thoroughly unacceptable, the word has nuances akin to *ranshin* or at least something utterly irrational, suggesting that one had lost one's senses, or as the ancient Confucian work, the *Mencius*, put it speaking of the "lost mind," one had lost one's moral compass. Kira, on the other hand, is praised not for having followed the law but instead for having been cognizant of the circumstances and so not lifting a finger in opposition.

In noting that Asano was an outer daimyō, *Okado's Memoir* highlights a true nuance of the daimyō's vassalage not typically mentioned in accounts of his outrageous attack. Historian Harold Bolitho has argued that distinctions between "long-trusted daimyō lines" (*fudai*) and "outer daimyō lines" (*tozama*) were no longer significant by the early eighteenth century.[40] However, in 1701, it seems that Kira had no reservations about treating Asano badly, perhaps knowing that he was from a small but somewhat lucrative domain led by lords whose loyalties to the Tokugawa were nuanced in terms of distance, as "outer" or fringe vassals. Kira knew that Tsunayoshi had repeatedly confiscated domains without much hesitation, as a means of enforcing discipline, extending power, and replenishing coffers. Kira might have viewed Asano as easy prey to be provoked, trapped, and then handed over to Tsunayoshi for consumption.

Kira targeted an outer lord not because he had issues with outer lords as such, but rather because those were the daimyō with whom he regularly had dealings in the New Year's ceremonies. Though speculation, Kira might have bullied Asano not for petty gifts, but instead because he understood Tsunayoshi's readiness to confiscate entire domains as a means of gaining resources. Kira might also have recognized in Asano a degree of emotional and mental instability that could easily be triggered. Asano fell into the trap, and then into total loss. However, if Kira himself expected to gain by hounding Asano into his tragic end, the plan soon boomeranged.

---

[40] Harold Bolitho, *Treasures among Men: The Fudai Daimyō of Tokugawa Japan* (New Haven, CT: Yale University Press, 1974).

Kira was exonerated on the fourteenth day of the third month, but less than two weeks later, on the twenty-sixth, he resigned his position as master of ceremonies, and his resignation was immediately accepted. On the nineteenth day of the eighth month, Kira was relocated, by the shogunate, from his Gofukubashi residence proximate Edo Castle, to the former residence of a lower-level vassal in Honjo. As a newly developed, eastern suburb of Edo populated by artisans, merchants, and lower vassals, Honjo was home to people well below Kira, at least from his perspective. Kira's new compound, distant from the shogun's castle and in an area bustling with artisans and commercial growth, left him somewhat isolated. On the twelfth day of the twelfth month, Kira offered to step down as head of his family, and again his offer was accepted. Kira's adopted heir, Sahyōe, succeeded him in that position.[41]

Kira's fall from grace might have been a result of his age, sixty, but for whatever reason, the shogunate had decided to distance itself, quite literally, from Kira. Others have speculated that as rumors of probable revenge against Kira circulated, the shogunate relocated Kira, and in so doing, facilitated, wittingly or not, the chances of a successful attack. Kira had once lived in the shadow of Edo Castle, shielded by it and surrounded by trusted daimyō mansions. In Honjo, on the reclaimed outskirts, he became a relatively marginal man, now moved aside, remote, and exposed. In his own way, then, Tsunayoshi dealt with Kira much as he had with other problems, by shunning them through relocation, and then, with time, confiscation.

[41] *Tokugawa jikki*, pp. 436, 457. "Kira Yoshinaka nenpu," *Akō gishi jiten*, p. 129.

3 RŌNIN SCHISMS

Accounts of the Akō vendetta often omit mention of the many rōnin who simply quit the domain in the wake of Asano Naganori's death. Some accounts even suggest that Asano only had forty-seven vassals, and that all took up his cause as a loyal, unified group resolved on revenge. This chapter highlights the varied responses that emerged from the three hundred rōnin of Akō domain following their lord's death, emphasizing the deep divisions even within the minority faction determined to take action. These schisms persisted until just before the attack. The debates and disagreements reveal the degree to which the vendetta was, even among rōnin factions, replete with conflict and animosities. In this context, an often-overlooked source, *Akō Castle League*, is highlighted as a statement harshly vilifying those who abandoned the vendetta. It also casts the vendetta cosmically as an expression of the decree of heaven, an ethical imperative meant to eliminate an evil force in the world, Kira Yoshinaka.

The Rōnin Debate

Asano's seppuku brought no closure to the incident. Well-established channels of communication soon relayed reports of the attack and the swift punishment of Asano into the hinterlands. Tsunayoshi's regime, unable to control word of mouth in a city of nearly a million, must have been infuriated as retellings of the incident spread like wildfire. Edo discussions at the commoner and lower-samurai level, informed only by terse official statements and sensational rumor, were surely as myriad as they were misinformed.

Two sets of messengers – one departing shortly after Asano's attack and the other following his seppuku – traveled approximately 600 kilometers via express palanquin to Akō domain to inform Ōishi and the vassals who served Asano Naganori, numbering more than three hundred, of the events in Edo. Their arrival on the nineteenth, four and a half days later (normally, the trip took more than two weeks) brought disbelief, then shock, but ultimately debate, disagreement, and heated schisms regarding what should be done.

In Edo, the tragedy continued to unfold the day after the attack as Asano Naganori's younger brother and prospective heir, Daigaku, was placed under house arrest. Asano's cousins were forbidden entrance to Edo Castle. Asano's wife and retainers were told to vacate both the main Asano family residence in Teppōzu and the secondary compound in Akasaka. A few days later, a long-standing daimyō, Sakai Tadasono, arrived to take possession of the Teppōzu mansion. On the fifteenth day of the third month, four days after Asano's seppuku, the shogunate appointed two vassals – Ishihara Masauji and Okada Toshinobu – to supervise confiscation of Akō Castle. They entered Akō a month later, on the seventeenth day of the fourth month. The shogunate also appointed two inspectors to oversee the surrender of the domain. The same day, two shogunal vassals were appointed to receive Akō Castle. Later that year, Tsunayoshi named Nagai Naotaka, a long-standing daimyō, the new lord of Akō domain.[1]

At dawn on the nineteenth day of the third month, the first couriers arrived in Akō with a message sent by Asano Naganori's younger brother, Daigaku, explaining that Naganori had attacked and wounded Kira. The messengers in the first group included Hayami Mitsutaka and Kayano Sanpei. Hayami was among the rōnin who ultimately invaded Kira's mansion in 1703. Kayano, however, committed suicide in 1702, well before the attack on Kira. Prior to their unexpected arrival in Akō, the other retainers knew nothing about what had transpired in Edo five days earlier.

The senior retainer, Ōishi Yoshio, was the first to read the communication. He promptly called a meeting of all retainers to convey

[1] *Kōseki kenmonki*, pp. 178–179, 182, 205–207, 211–212, 217, 221. *Chūshingura hyakka*, p. 250.

the news to them. Many of the vassals – technically, at this point, rōnin, or masterless men, although they had yet to realize as much – wanted to know whether Kira was alive or dead. As *Things Seen and Heard* records the unfolding of events, that would remain a mystery until the end of the third month. Early that afternoon, Ōishi sent couriers to Edo to determine Kira's fate. Around 9:00 PM, approximately twelve hours after the first group of messengers, the second wave of couriers arrived to report that Asano had committed seppuku. Still, they could not say whether Kira was alive, nor anything about whether the domain would be confiscated. However, given that their lord had been required to commit seppuku, and the nature of Tsunayoshi's rule, domain confiscation was hardly unlikely.

Ōishi surely realized as much. Knowing that time was of the essence, he immediately put the domain's finances in order, settling accounts as possible, so that financial chaos would not accompany any subsequent round of egregious news. Reports soon filtered in that Asano Daigaku was under house arrest and that the Asano mansion in Edo had been reassigned. But still there was no word about Kira's fate. Once it became clear that Kira was alive, some retainers such as Horibe Yasubei and Okuda Magodayū advocated a direct attack on Kira in the hopes of taking vengeance on their lord's enemy.

Understanding the urgency of the situation, Ōishi had the rōnin meet in the reception hall of the domain's tiny castle over a three-day period. Some advocated immediate seppuku to follow their lord in death; others favored besieging the castle and resisting surrender unto death; still others advocated yielding the castle in the hopes that submission to the shogunate would enhance the chances that the Asano line might continue. On the twenty-eighth, more couriers arrived with word of the appointment of interim governors and a team of shogunal representatives to supervise and witness the surrender of the castle. From the twenty-fifth forward, samurai representatives from surrounding domains, including Hiroshima, had moved on Akō, encouraging Ōishi and the rōnin to acquiesce.[2]

After learning that two *bakufu* retainers would be overseeing the transfer of Akō Castle, Ōishi sent them a petition conveying his assessment of the situation. Ōishi admitted that Asano had "unthinkingly violated the rules of the ceremonial occasion" and so had been

---

[2] *Kōseki kenmonki*, p. 181.

required to commit seppuku. He added that they had heard, from various sources, that Akō Castle was to be confiscated. Ōishi related that at first the rōnin thought that Asano had committed seppuku because he had killed Kira. However, they had come to learn that Kira had not in fact been murdered. Ōishi next warned that the domain's samurai were "brash, rustic men (*bukotsu no mono*)" who thought exclusively of their lord. They were not familiar with the complexities related to ceremonial rules and regulations. They were, however, most distraught knowing that while their lord's enemy lived, Akō Castle and the domain would be confiscated. By the time Ōishi's letter arrived, the shogun's vassals to whom it had been sent had already departed Edo, en route to Akō, and so never saw the communication. It was eventually turned over to a cousin of Asano Naganori, Toda Ujisada, daimyō of Ōgaki domain. Toda promptly wrote Ōishi urging him to calm the vassals, suggesting that their strong feelings were due to their ignorance of circumstances in Edo.[3]

Ōishi's petition made clear that the verdict for Kira was not, in the eyes of Akō samurai, equitable. In a paraphrase, he alluded to the Tokugawa principle that all involved in an altercation be punished equitably. Ōishi did not deny that his daimyō had done wrong, but strongly suggested that the shogunate should provide for fair treatment, i.e., punishment, for Kira. Otherwise, the verdict would be considered one-sided.[4] Ōishi's petition to the *bakufu* inspectors reveals his forthright, but accommodating leadership style. At this point, his primary concern was with seeing equitable justice realized. Otherwise, he implied, the consequences might be the product of Akō's brash, unsophisticated samurai. Ōishi thus hoped to mediate the old-fashioned impulses of samurai vengeance with the emerging order of ceremonial rule presided over by Tsunayoshi, most of his Edo vassals, and the shogunal elite in Edo. It was with the latter that Akō samurai had, for the most part, no real experience whatsoever. For that matter, Ōishi also, having spent relatively little time in the shogun's capital, was only vaguely aware of the nature of the new political sensibilities of the day.

---

[3] This exchange is discussed in Miyazawa, *Akō rōshi*, pp. 57–58. Bitō, "The Akō Incident," p. 158. Ōishi's petition ("Yoshio no chinjōsho") and Toda's response are in Chūō gishi kai, eds., *Akō gishi shiryō* (Tokyo: Yuzankaku, 1931), vol. 1, pp. 66–67.
[4] *Kōseki kenmonki*, 190–191.

Figure 3.1 Akō Castle. Photograph by the author.

Ōishi considered the various alternatives carefully in the hopes of effectively managing the infuriated rōnin of his domain. One option was besieging the castle, as many favored, and challenging shogunal forces to a final, pitched battle. Yet there would be no victory for the rōnin, other than in knowing that they had died defending what had once been their late master's castle. Ōishi also considered prompt seppuku to follow Asano in death. This option also seemed to have support among the rōnin. Contrary to Ōishi, some favored promptly targeting Kira. The most aggressive spokesmen for this were the Edo-based rōnin,

Horibe and Okuda. Two weeks after Asano's seppuku, they had arrived in Akō hoping to recruit a cohort for quick action. However, after conferring with Ōishi and others, they agreed to a compromise of sorts. First, they would surrender the castle rather than die defending it. Then, when circumstances offered hope for success, action would be taken. Even the most radical, attack-now proponents such as Horibe saw no point in dying senselessly. Although Asano had died without completing his task, the rōnin would secure his spiritual repose, as well as his reputation and honor (and their own), by completing his intentions, killing Kira.

With this covert consensus, Ōishi met the shogunal inspectors and the interim supervisors of Akō in the middle of the fourth month. However, even as the castle was being inspected, Ōishi asked the shogunal representatives repeatedly about the possibility of a restoration of the Asano line. Ōishi apparently remained willing to forgo the attack on Kira if the shogunate would recognize Asano Daigaku as the head of a restored Asano line. One of the inspectors, Araki Masahane, agreed to take the matter up with the shogun's council of elders upon his return to Edo. Nothing, however, came of this proposal. On the eighteenth day of the fourth month, the outer daimyō from neighboring Tatsuno domain, Wakizaka Yasuteru, arrived leading a massive force to assist, if needed, in the confiscation of the castle. Maritime forces had also been mobilized from neighboring domains so as to surround Akō on all sides. On the nineteenth, surrender of Akō Castle was finalized without bloodshed.[5] This was surely one of Ōishi's most noteworthy achievements.

One bitter conflict involved Ōno Kurobei, one of Asano's senior-most retainers. Ōno early on advocated peaceful surrender of the castle, but at that juncture encountered opposition from Ōishi who then favored, along with a substantial number of rōnin, dying in defense of it. When the matter of distributing domain funds arose, Ōno, who specialized in domain finances, proposed dividing the balance in proportion to stipends received. Ōishi championed another solution, allotting funds to favor those with lower stipends. Ōishi's approach

---

[5] *Kōseki kenmonki*, pp. 193, 235. "Akōjō hikiwatashi jiken," in *Akō gijin sansho*, vol. 2, pp. 487–576, gives an account of the fate of Akō Castle, beginning shortly after Asano's attack on Kira until the castle's surrender less than two months later. It is widely recognized as authentic and reliable. "Genroku gikyo nenpu," *Akō gishi jiten*, p. 131. *Chūshingura*, vol. 1, p. 84.

prevailed. Ōno also came into conflict with another retainer, Okajima Yasoemon, regarding resolution of issues related to the domain currency. Ōishi eventually concurred with Ōno's position that surrender of Akō Castle was the only reasonable option. Nevertheless, early on Ōno apparently felt isolated from the rōnin leadership and so fled the domain during the night, on the thirteenth day of the fourth month, just before the surrender of Akō Castle. Ōno was subsequently branded an "outrageous villain" who had committed "an outrage beyond anything one would encounter in a thousand or even ten thousand people." Mention was also made of domain resources missing with his exit.[6]

Ōno's departure revealed how, within days, deep divisions emerged within the rōnin. While his case was among the most dramatic, two-thirds of the three hundred Akō retainers eventually quit the domain as well, quietly and on their own, in the days and weeks following news of Asano's death and the prospect of domain confiscation. Of the remaining hundred or so retainers who were initially dedicated to doing something, more than half eventually fell away. Among the most hardcore, disagreements remained until a few months before the vendetta as to whether revenge against Kira or restoration of the Asano line should be the priority. Even the quick revenge faction, led by Horibe, harbored divisions between those who favored prompt and direct action, and others willing to wait for the best moment of attack. Ōishi's approach was not first and foremost revenge, but instead closing out domain business and making every effort to reestablish the Asano line as led by Asano's younger brother and designated heir, Asano Daigaku. From the middle of the fourth month through the end of the fifth as the surrender of Akō Castle was under way, Ōishi based himself at the Enrinji, a Rinzai Zen temple proximate the castle that had served as the Asano prayer hall, working from there to manage the remaining practical affairs of the domain and its rōnin.[7]

Along with trying to channel the frustrations and anger of the rōnin, Ōishi orchestrated spiritual efforts remembering his deceased lord. On the fourteenth day of the fourth month, i.e., one month after Asano's

---

[6] *Kōseki kenmonki*, p. 203, gives the thirteenth as the date of departure; pp. 227–228, 229, 233, gives the night of the twelfth and notes that Ōno was later seen in Kyoto. *Horibe Taketsune hikki*, in Ishii Shirō, ed., *Kinsei buke shisō*, Nihon shisō taikei vol. 27 (Tokyo: Iwanami shoten, 1974), pp. 181–182. Also, in the same volume, Muro Kyūsō, *Akō gijin roku*, pp. 284–285. *Akō gishi jiten*, pp. 354–356. *Akō Castle League* also vilifies Ōno.

[7] *Akō gishi jiten*, p. 734.

death, a gravestone was completed and a small ceremony held at the Sengakuji. The same day, Ōishi coordinated donations of farmland, forests, and money for the initiation of services in perpetuity for the repose of Asano Naganori, to be held at the Kagakuji (Sōtō Zen), the Asano family temple in Akō, as well as the Dairenji (Pure Land), the Manpukuji (True Pure Land), and the Kōkōji (Nichiren) temples in Akō, each with ties to the Asano family. On the fifth day of the following month, Ōishi allotted funds for perpetual services at Mount Kōya, in the holiest burial site there, the Oku-no-rin, honoring four Asano daimyō: Nagashige, Naganao, Nagatomo, and Naganori. Additionally, Ōishi coordinated a donation for a gravestone to be erected there in remembrance of his deceased lord. On the twelfth day of the fifth month, he made a donation to an ancient Buddhist temple in Kyoto, the Rokuhara Mitsuji, for the revival of the Asano line. On the twentieth, he persuaded the Enrinji monk, Yūkai, to travel to Edo to organize a movement for the restoration of the Asano line in Akō, one meant to enlist the support of Tsunayoshi's mother, Keishōin. Finally, on the twenty-fourth day of the sixth month, the hundredth day after Asano's death, memorial services were held at the Sengakuji in Edo, with radicals Horibe and Okuda attending. The same day, memorial services were held at the Kagakuji in Akō, with Ōishi and other samurai in the vicinity attending. The day after, Ōishi departed Akō domain.[8]

Retreat to Yamashina

After first traveling to Osaka, Ōishi moved to rural Yamashina, southeast of Kyoto, where he had relatives and associates who facilitated his relocation. There he reportedly assumed an alias, Ikeda Kyūzaemon. At that time, approximately sixty rōnin of "like mind" had relocated and were living in the Kyoto, Osaka, and Fushimi areas, all under assumed names. Others resided in Edo, many with ties to the attack-now faction led by Horibe and Okuda. Over and again in what became an extensive correspondence,[9] Horibe emphasized that if Kira became

---

[8] *Kōseki kenmonki*, pp. 221–227, 233. "Genroku gikyo nenpu," *Akō gishi jiten*, pp. 131–132, 730, 734, 736, 738, 740. Akō shi bunka shinkō zaidan, *Akō gishi shiseki meguri* (Akō: Akō shi kyōiku kenkyūjo, 1999), p. 26.

[9] Much of this correspondence is in the *Horibe Taketsune hikki*, compiled by Hosoi Kōtaku Tomochika (1658–1735), a Confucian scholar and noted calligrapher serving Yanagisawa Yoshiyasu. Hosoi and Horibe knew each other through sword practice at

sick and died, the rōnin would have lost their chance to complete their lord's task. Moreover, they would end up being branded disloyal retainers. Ōishi and Horibe, despite different strategies, agreed that they had no higher priority than honoring their lord's intentions, and that for that end they would readily discard their lives.

Proximity to Kyoto was advantageous for Ōishi because shogunal power was weaker there than in Edo. The shogunate controlled the imperial capital from its grand fortification, Nijō Castle, where a shogunal deputy and contingent of samurai resided. However, the aristocracy, clergy, and townspeople of Kyoto were not given to armed resistance, making much in the way of coercive power unnecessary. Yamashina, located in the rural southeast, well across town from the shogunal base, was a convenient meeting place. Thus, upon learning, on the eighteenth day of the seventh month, that the Asano line would not be restored and that their lord's younger brother, Asano Daigaku, was to be placed in the custody of the Hiroshima Asano line,[10] Ōishi called a meeting of nearby rōnin dedicated to taking direct action. That meeting, later called the Maruyama Conference, was held at the Anyō temple in Kyoto's eastern hills on the twenty-eighth day of the seventh month, 1702. It climaxed with an agreement by the nineteen rōnin attending that they would take revenge on Kira.[11] Ōishi had opposed making definite plans for revenge while Asano Daigaku's fate remained uncertain. Once termination of the Asano line was definite and Daigaku's prospects for succession nil, Ōishi committed to joining forces with the radical faction.

The aristocratic culture of Kyoto and its well-known entertainment districts appealed to Ōishi, a Genroku samurai who enjoyed life, even while planning the fateful vendetta. Later lore cast Ōishi as feigning debauchery to mislead others into thinking that he had neither courage nor capacity to lead a move against Kira. That characterization, while shrewd and colorful, is surely exaggerated. However, *Things Seen and Heard* does note that Ōishi was a man full of energy who enjoyed going out on "excursions" in Kyoto, "sightseeing and so forth," and even engaged in "inappropriate behavior," carelessly spending money.

---

the Horiuchi *dōjō* in Edo. Just before the vendetta, Horibe sent his correspondence with Ōishi and others to Hosoi, presumably so it would be preserved. Hosoi later had it published. The text is in *Akō gijin sansho*, vol. 3, pp. 1–101.

[10] *Kōseki kenmonki*, pp. 255, 260–261.

[11] "Genroku gikyo nenpu," *Akō gishi jiten*, p. 133.

For this he was reproached by some rōnin. Rumor was that Ōishi, realizing that Kira spied on him, engaged in such behavior to mask his real intentions. Such, at least, *Things Seen and Heard* suggests, was the common gossip.[12]

Yet what can be documented are Ōishi's continued, tireless efforts on behalf of continuing the Asano line, as well as his efforts to have Asano Naganori and the previous Asano lords of Akō domain remembered spiritually. Thus, on the fourteenth day of the eighth month, 1701, Ōishi had a memorial stone erected for Asano Naganori in north-central Kyoto at the Zuikōin, under which he supposedly buried Naganori's court headdress. Later, Ōishi reportedly arranged, well in advance, for the priest of the Zuikōin to collect, when the time came, the severed topknots of each of the rōnin who participated in the vendetta for burial there following their seppuku. Later that same year, on the fourteenth day of the eleventh month, Ōishi, while in Edo to meet with Horibe and others there, attended memorial services held at his lord's grave at the Sengakuji. During the same visit, Ōishi met with the two inspectors who had supervised the confiscation of Akō Castle, Araki and Sakakibara, to reiterate his plea for a restoration of the Asano house.[13]

Not long after Ōishi's relocation to Yamashina, fortuitous events occurred, at least for those advocating attack: Kira was relocated from his mansion in Gofukubashi to the Honjo area across the Sumida River from Edo Castle. The significance of this move was not lost on the rōnin. Also, it is prominently noted in *Things Seen and Heard*. For Kira, this was surely a step down, well away from the power and ceremonial glory of his earlier years. Four months later, Kira yielded his position as head of his family to his adopted heir, Sahyōe. On the twelfth day of the twelfth month, Kira resigned his position as master of court ceremonies.[14]

As the debates over strategy continued, Ōishi and his often-fractured, rump cohort continued to discuss and plan with successive meetings in Edo, Kyoto, and Yamashina, disagreeing, most importantly, on timing. Their discussions show that the vendetta, though sometimes presented as a seamless expression of samurai honor, single-minded consensus, and utter uniformity of will, was the product of ongoing

[12] *Kōseki kenmonki*, p. 263.   [13] "Genroku gikyo nenpu," *Akō gishi jiten*, p. 132.
[14] *Kōseki kenmonki*, p. 258.

clashes of ego, vision, passion, self-interest, and even ethical ideals. While restoration of honor might have provided a modicum of unity to the group, understandings of honor seem to have varied, with some more focused on their own, while others obsessed over that of the Asano line. Also, it is questionable whether honor or a spiritually informed determination to pacify their late lord's angry spirit was the motivating force for most rōnin. Ōishi, at least, persistently advocated patience, hoping that restoration of the Asano family would follow, apparently willing to sacrifice the honor of Asano Naganori and of the rōnin for the sake of the Asano line. Whether this was a self-serving move – since he would have likely remained senior retainer of the restored line – is open to question.

Months earlier, on the fifteenth day of the fourth month, 1702, Ōishi had divorced his pregnant wife, Riku, and broken off relations with his three youngest children, sending them to Toyooka to live with Riku's father. Ōishi's son Chikara, who had barely attained maturity, was allowed to remain with him and participate in the vendetta. Ōishi's divorce was, by all accounts, in preparation for the revenge attack. Punishing family members for a relative's crimes was standard. Some rōnin kin were indeed punished in the wake of the vendetta. By divorcing Riku and sending his younger children away, Ōishi hoped to spare them.

Apparently, Ōishi kept Chikara with him because even if Chikara had been sent away, he would have eventually felt obliged, presumably, as a good Confucian son, to take revenge on his father's enemy. Instead of leaving him in that predicament, Ōishi let Chikara partner with him in the vendetta so that they could meet their fates together. In the seventh month, following their divorce, Riku gave birth to Ōishi's third son. Records do not establish, however, that Ōishi ever saw the boy. The month before his divorce, on the fourteenth day of the third month, 1702, Ōishi participated in memorial services for Asano Naganori at the Asano family temple, the Kagakuji, in Akō. That ceremony, one year after Asano's death, was the last Ōishi observed before the vendetta.[15] On the fifth day of the eleventh month, Ōishi and some of his cohort arrived in Edo and took up lodging at the Oyamaya Inn, located in Nihonbashi. Ōishi remained there until the vendetta. On the second day of the twelfth month, he and his rōnin band visited

---

[15] *Chūshingura hyakka*, p. 258.

the Tomioka Hachiman Shrine, the largest in Edo dedicated to the god of war, surely to pray for success.[16]

Divisions, Desertions, and the Decree of Heaven

Things Seen and Heard reveals that divisions within the rōnin took many sorts. A fair number of the two hundred and fifty rōnin who quit Akō rather than dedicate themselves to the cause, did so not because of cowardice but rather due to their sense of duty to relatives and loved ones. Of them, the most dramatic was Kayano Sanpei. At age twelve, Kayano began service to Asano Naganori as a pageboy, and then continued, as an adult, as one of Asano's close attendants. Kayano was in Edo the day Asano attacked Kira. No sooner had word reached the Akō retainers in Edo that their lord had caused an upheaval in Edo Castle than two of them, Kayano and Hayami Tōzaemon Mitsutaka, traveled by express palanquin from Edo to Akō. Thereafter, Kayano remained in Akō, becoming one of the first to swear loyalty to the rōnin band.

Kayano was soon drawn, however, to his aging parents in Ise, and there took up service to the lord of Ise domain. Subsequently, Kayano was reportedly torn between competing loyalties to his family, the rōnin cause, and his new lord. Overwhelmed by the conflicting demands, Kayano fell short of Ōishi's ideal of "single-minded devotion to one's premier duty." On the fourteenth day of the first month, 1702, a year before the vendetta, Kayano committed suicide, reportedly following his lord belatedly in death. In another, less noble case, Hashimoto Heizaemon, an eighteen-year-old Akō retainer who pledged himself to the rōnin cause early on, later traveled to Osaka, where he fell into a relationship with a geisha at the Awajiya tea house. On the evening of the fifteenth day of the seventh month, Hashimoto, feeling torn between his loyalty to the rōnin cohort and his passion for the geisha, ended up stabbing her to death and then killing himself.[17]

One surviving document, *Akō Castle League (Sekijō meiden)*, completed in the eleventh month of 1702, just one month before the

---

[16] "Genroku gikyo nenpu," *Akō gishi jiten*, p. 135.
[17] *Kōseki kenmonki*, p. 260. *Akō gishi jiten*, pp. 370–371, 418.

vendetta, presents an authentic, philosophical account of the thinking of some of the conspirators. *Akō Castle League* combines two brief texts, Maebara Munefusa's *Domain Hardships* and Kanzaki Noriyasu's *Dissolving the Bonds*, with commentary by Kanzaki and a postscript by Kimura Sadayuki. Prior to the vendetta, Maebara and Kanzaki reportedly operated a rice shop near Kira's mansion to gain intelligence. Their text records that it was completed in Honjo, presumably in their rice shop. Throughout their subterfuge, the men used aliases and, had they been discovered, would have suffered mortal consequences. In the face of hardship and with a determination ultimately to die in taking direct action against Kira, the authors justified their choices and harshly vilified the defectors. Confucian thinking pervades the text. In part a justification for forming a league (*mei*), or less politely, a band of assassins, the text vehemently denounces those retainers who had early on done disservice to Asano, or later turned against the league.[18]

Akō Castle League explains that in advancing good and dis- couraging evil, the greatest good taught in the sagely classics consists of "embracing loyalty and acting righteously." As a means of making this possible, "the way of the league" derives from "the great vessel of heaven and earth," "the standards and measures of human ethical relations" (humaneness, righteousness, propriety, wisdom, and trust- worthiness), "the one thread uniting all things," and, most tellingly, the "iron hammer that destroys difficulties." *Yin* and *yang* work together, as do the five processes (fire, metal, wood, earth, and water), to complete the four seasons; the heavenly bodies (the sun, moon, stars, and con- stellations) cooperate so that the days and months proceed on course. A note adds that "the way of the league" thus combines "rational principle" and "practical function" and expresses "the great ultimate" as formed by the complementary interaction of "the roundness of heaven and the squareness of earth." Ominously, *Akō Castle League* asks where might people turn if they betray a pledged alliance.[19]

More ominously, *Akō Castle League* observes that real-world transformations are not due to an individual's whims. Instead, existence and nonexistence are matters of fate. A note explains that fate is "the decree of heaven" (*tenmei*) as produced through the workings of

---

[18] *Sekijō meiden*, in *Akō gijin sansho*, vol. 1, pp. 172–181. The text, written in Sino-Japanese, is followed by a later colloquial version, *Kokuji sekijō meiden*, pp. 182–195.
[19] Ibid., pp. 172–173.

origination, flourish, advantage, and endurance, i.e., metaphysical modalities informing all change. In citing these modalities, *Akō Castle League* alludes to the *Book of Changes*, where these modalities are explained as the capacities of the first two hexagrams, "heaven" and "earth." In mentioning "the decree of heaven," however, the text alludes to another ancient Chinese classic, the *Book of History*, in announcing its main theme, that those who embody wickedness will face the punishment of heaven. Written just prior to the launch of the vendetta, *Akō Castle League* presumably sought to record the stalwart participants' sense of the divine and cosmically sanctioned ethical purpose, resonating with the workings of heaven and earth. In effect, the text presents the vendetta as an aggressive, fated expression of the ethical justice of the operations of the universe, as effected by them, agents of the will of heaven and earth. The rōnin league thus claimed to have, per *Akō Castle League*, sanction in the natural, cosmic, and ethical spheres.[20]

In recounting Asano's attack on Kira, *Akō Castle League* vilifies the master of court ceremonies, relating that on the fourteenth day of the third month, Kira exuded a deeply rooted wickedness and insincerity. Asano despised this display of evil and so, in anger, attacked him inside the palace. Kira's cowardice and lack of "right passion" became more evident in his attempt to flee from Asano's attack. Although Asano, in anger, failed, his passing was regretted. In addition to seppuku, Asano's family line was abolished, his castle confiscated, and the people he governed left adrift. It notes that of "the three hundred and eight" samurai retainers, many lost their sense of righteousness and duty, but one hundred and eight followed the course of heaven, maintained themselves within the workings of origination, flourish, advantage, and endurance, and sought to attain the virtues of humaneness, righteousness, propriety, and wisdom. These men are described as courageous warriors who never forgot their duty and remained steadfast, stout-hearted, and solid within. *Akō Castle League* promises that when heaven punishes those steeped in evil, it first sends down omens. The dark resentment felt throughout heaven and earth had supposedly been made manifest in spring flooding, cold winds, and even snow and hail storms.[21]

---

[20] Ibid., pp. 172–173.   [21] Ibid., p. 173.

Akō Castle League addresses the shogunate's verdict that Asano had disregarded the ceremonial occasion, literally, the time and place. Rather than concur, admitting that the late lord had erred egregiously, *Akō Castle League* claims that Asano had withheld his anger for more than one morning, patiently waiting until finally he was in a space where his actions would not create a more public disturbance. There, in the shogun's castle, he acted bravely, knowing that he was one man alone, standing up for righteousness in striking out against the evil that was Kira. Nor was this, *Akō Castle League* contends, Asano's first stand for righteousness. His humaneness and compassion for others was well recognized by the four estates of his realm, and even after his death, the people of his old domain, Akō, made pilgrimages to the temples he had frequented, including the Kagakuji, the Dairenji, and the Kōkōji, to honor his goodness, revering him as though he were still the father and mother of their families. In one farm village, even the peasants built a shrine for him.[22]

Akō Castle League paraphrases an ancient saying from the Confucian classic, the *Mencius* (5A/5), "Heaven does not speak; the people express [its intentions]." *Akō Castle League* then adds that virtually everyone in the realm detested Kira, from the various lords, government officials, and aristocratic families, down to the rural people. Indeed, everyone within the four seas hated and was ready to be done with him. Such sentiments were an expression of heaven's order, akin to the commonly shared disgust with putrid odors. Nevertheless, many remained who opposed the league but somehow claimed to have once been Asano retainers. According to *Akō Castle League*, all samurai study humaneness and righteousness and consider them their constant standards. The way of humanity likewise consists of exhausting filial piety and loyalty, honoring one's relatives, and establishing a good name throughout the world below heaven. Those who reject the way of humanity for the sake of hedonism, lewd pleasures, and nepotism are nothing more than "dogs and horses." How, the text asks, could such creatures not end up dying an early death?[23]

Before listing the "shamed" who had abandoned heaven's will for hedonism, thievery, and disloyalty to the league, *Akō Castle League* presents examples of true fidelity. First it notes how Hayami Tōzaemon and Kayano Sanpei had, following Asano's attack on Kira, immediately

[22] Ibid., p. 174.   [23] Ibid., p. 174.

embarked on a journey of hundreds of miles via palanquin to report the incident to the Akō retainers. They were followed by Hara Sōemon and Ōishi Sezaemon, who also made the trip, reporting this time, however, Asano's seppuku. Kataoka Gengoemon and Isogai Jūrōzaemon are cited as two retainers with special bonds to Asano and so favored, from the start, a plan to kill Kira. In Akō, they encountered resistance from hundreds of retainers who wanted to defend the castle to the end, dying a "righteous death" within it.[24]

Akō Castle League next examines the shamed retainers who, despite having enjoyed substantial stipends and positions of responsibility, simply left the domain after Asano's death. Fujii Muneshige, senior retainer in Edo at the time of Asano's attack, is described as one whose physical disposition was advantageous, but who betrayed it for the sake of thievery and hedonism. Although asked to join the league, Fujii declined and took up service to another lord. Yasui Hikoemon, a close associate of Fujii, was asked by Horibe Yasubei Taketsune to lead the radical "attack-now" faction, but declined. *Akō Castle League* describes Yasui as one who was "evil," "wicked," "polluted," and "oblivious to righteousness." Ōno Kurobei is similarly described in the worst of terms, as "evil," a "betrayer of the way of morality," and given to utter self-interest. The text goes on to list many other evil retainers who quit the league, deriding them as shameful, wicked, and despicable men.[25]

Akō Castle League next introduces Ōishi Yoshio as one who had initially hoped for a settlement that was not one-sided, and most especially, one that provided Asano Daigaku with standing as his brother's successor. Still, the Akō retainers wanted to slay Kira, and once the abusive tyrant was dead, to go to their master's grave to die there. Serving their master's family thusly expressed, in their view, "the way of loyalty and empathy." In the end, Ōishi's hope of restoring the Asano line was lost, despite the peaceful surrender of Akō Castle. Along the way, many who once pledged loyalty to the league dropped out. *Akō Castle League* lists sixty such men, including Mōri Koheita. The latter dropped out on the eleventh day of the twelfth month of 1703, three days before the vendetta.[26] Its mention of Mōri Koheita suggests that *Akō Castle League* was completed just after his departure, only days prior to the vendetta.

[24] Ibid., pp. 174–175. [25] Ibid., pp. 175–176. [26] *Sekijō meiden*, pp. 176–178.

Drawing on ancient Confucian correlative thought linking the cosmos to the human arena, *Akō Castle League* next explains some "abstruse cosmic principles" that defined, supposedly, the character of the league. Most basically, the text claims that "an indignant mind can quickly congeal to form a shooting star (*hoshi*)." Just as human nature, generative force, and the actions of all things, including humanity, birds, beasts, and the myriad forms, derive from heaven, within that context generative force resonates with the stars. As generative force transforms, it manifests a star; as generative force flows, it yields brightness, or a shooting star. The generative force of those with the same intentions congeals and forms a shining star in heaven. Flowing downward, it takes the form of an indestructible diamond warrior. *Akō Castle League* adds that as the generative force of the comrades in the league congealed and formed, it resonated in heaven as shining stars that flowed downward to steel their bodies as unstoppable warriors. In other cases, rather than stars, their human energy manifested itself as a "red generative" force of the sort that appeared earlier in the year. A colloquial version of the *Akō Castle League* adds that in the past, it reportedly had taken form as thunder, spirits, and "vengeful spirits."[27]

Akō Castle League lists the forty-seven who were to take part in the vendetta, beginning with Ōishi. It also mentions others such as Kayano Sanpei and Hashimoto Heizaemon, who committed seppuku before the vendetta, and Yatō Chōsuke, who passed away before the vendetta. Even though these men died prior, they were praised for their devotion to loyalty and righteousness and their contempt for death. The text predicts that wise samurai of later generations would admire their sense of righteousness. By recording these accounts, the text preserves a record of loyalty and disloyalty, to be known by posterity, thus encouraging all to consider the consequences of their choices. The postscript by Kimura recasts the tone of the text by noting that the humane man forms one body with the ten thousand things, so that nothing is external to him. When he wishes to establish himself, he first establishes others. When he wants to attain things, he makes sure that others attain them as well. Such a person was Ōishi Kura-no-suke Yoshio, who planned day and night with others to bring the league together against the abusive tyrant, Kira.[28] A powerful testimony to the

---

[27] *Kokuji Sekijō meiden*, p. 192. *Sekijō meiden*, pp. 178–179.
[28] *Sekijō meiden*, p. 180.

text's authenticity is that the authors never mention the success they soon realized.

Undoubtedly, however, *Akō Castle League* establishes that well before the post-vendetta Confucian debates, the rōnin conceptualized themselves philosophically, in distinctly Confucian terms, as cosmic agents of righteousness and loyalty, meting out the justice of heaven as human expressions of its decree.

Edo Rendezvous

After twenty months of debate, division, defection, and determination, there emerged a resolve to join forces in Edo for prompt direct action. On the seventh day of the tenth month of 1702, Ōishi and five other rōnin left Kyoto for Edo.[29] Once in Edo, they met with the others repeatedly to make final plans for the attack on Kira's mansion, with Kira's death as the sole objective. Gaining the element of surprise required that they attack deep in the night. They planned to rendezvous from more than a dozen lodgings in Edo. At each, from one to seven members of the group, all under assumed names, lodged. The lodgings were scattered around the periphery of Edo, in Nihonbashi, Shinkōjimachi (four dwellings), Shiba, (two dwellings), Honmachi, Fukagawa, Hatchōbori, Honjo (three dwellings), and Ryōgoku.[30] The rōnin joined forces, as assigned, at one of three Honjo residences, and from there made their final rendezvous, in the form of front and rear attack forces, at Kira's mansion.

The final group of forty-seven amounted to a small fraction of the samurai who had once counted themselves retainers of Asano Naganori. More than 80 percent of the retainers had gone their separate ways. While early on nearly half had supported the league, by the time Akō Castle was surrendered, approximately one hundred remained committed. During the following twenty months, that number was nearly cut in half. Of the fifty-seven who had once sealed their pledge with blood, an additional ten dropped out, leaving a cohort that included a few elderly rōnin (one, seventy-seven), and many relatively young family members of older participants. Note that these younger relatives had, on their own count, no official position in Akō domain.

---

[29] *Kōseki kenmonki*, p. 264.
[30] "Rōshi no Edo senpukusaki," *Genroku Chūshingura Dētafuairu*, pp. 66–67.

Arguably they were participating, at least in part, out of filial loyalty to their elder kin as much as out of loyalty to their deceased lord.

Ōishi assumed active leadership of the remnant group in the late fall of 1702, approximately six weeks before the vendetta. In that capacity, he reportedly drafted a set of rules governing rōnin behavior going forward. Most importantly, Ōishi emphasized the need for discipline and organization. During the attack, he asked that the rōnin wear black robes, with trousers, protective leggings, and straw sandals. Passwords, to be announced later, would be used. In all matters, he emphasized, there could be no negligence. Participants had to act quickly and effectively, without unnecessary talk. Pilfering was forbidden. Overall, Ōishi stressed the need for courage and a firm resolve once inside Kira's residence. Prior to the attack, the rōnin had to maintain personal discipline, giving the enemy no cause for suspicion. Ōishi emphasized that the enemy was Kira and his son Sahyōe, and that others should not be targeted unnecessarily. However, he added that if anyone attempted to keep them from succeeding, they should be cut down, regardless. Moreover, none should be allowed to escape from any gate.[31]

League participants would be strategically deployed. Unaware of the exact number of Kira's guards, Ōishi added that the enemy might have as many as one hundred warriors defending the residence, while the Akō band totaled fifty or so. Therefore, members must go into the attack "prepared for certain death." Along the way, if each could defeat two to three of the enemy's forces, victory would be secured. Ōishi added that soon comrades would be asked to rededicate themselves to the vendetta by signing a "sacred pledge." He concluded his instructions by noting that these were his thoughts, and that if others had more to add, their contributions were welcome. The exact date of the attack, at that point, remained open. Ōishi's instructions offered no guidance regarding what the rōnin would do following the attack. *Things Seen and Heard*, which includes Ōishi's text, notes, however, that if the attack were successful, some token would be taken to their deceased lord's grave.[32]

After Ōishi's instructions were circulated, a few more dropped out. Tanaka Sadashirō, who along with Kataoka Gengoemon and Isogai Jūrōzaemon had accompanied Asano's coffin from the Tamura residence

---

[31] *Kōseki kenmonki*, pp. 265–266.
[32] Ibid., pp. 266–267. In the end, Sahyōe was only injured (p. 278), not killed. Ōishi's later instructions targeted Kira alone.

to the Sengakuji, reportedly gave himself over to drink, became ill, and ended up deserting. Another, Oyamada Shōzaemon, reportedly stole money from Kataoka Gengoemon and fled. Mōri Koheita, who earlier had provided intelligence about Kira's residence, dropped out shortly before the vendetta, supposedly due to family concerns. Two other rōnin, Seo Magozaemon and Yano Isuke, quit just two days before the vendetta. With these final defections, the rōnin cohort came to number forty-seven.[33] This was the final number entered in *Things Seen and Heard*.

Edo rōnin had been conducting surveillance of Kira's Honjo residence well before the arrival of Ōishi and the others from the Kansai. One of the Edo rōnin, Ōtaka Gengo Tadao, who was proficient in the tea ceremony and somewhat skilled in poetry, used his knowledge of tea to present himself under an assumed name to Yamada Sōhen, a disciple of Sen no Rikyū's grandson and, significantly enough, Kira's tea master. In addition to his alias, Ōtaka claimed to be an Osaka poet visiting Edo. Hoodwinked by Ōtaka's subterfuge, Yamada received him as a student. Over time, Ōtaka came to learn about Kira's activities, including Kira's plan for a tea gathering on the fourteenth day of the twelfth month. Once Ōishi, who had long considered Ōtaka a trusted retainer, learned this, he set the fourteenth as the date for the vendetta.[34]

Things Seen and Heard denies that the rōnin band was disguised as a group of firefighters. However, if stopped en route, they were to claim to be "members of a fire brigade," presumably on patrol. Over their black robes, most wore a jacket, which was discarded outside Kira's residence just before the attack. Ōishi's son Chikara reportedly wore a distinguished outfit with a black exterior and red lining, and wide sleeves with white cords. Many rōnin wore mail armor underneath their robes. Rōnin reportedly wore name tags for identification on their right shoulder. However, one of the rōnin, Kimura Okaemon Sadayuki, wore his tag over his left shoulder, and instead of his real name, had his posthumous name, reportedly given him by a Zen priest, recorded, thus making evident that he was ready for the grave. Overall, the rōnin were a motley group, with one account noting their "various, bizarre clothes."[35]

The passwords, in the event of uncertainty, were "mountain" (*yama*) and "river" (*kawa*): if someone said *yama*, the correct response

---

[33] Ibid., p. 270. *Akō gishi jiten*, pp. 79–80, 398–399.

[34] *Kōseki kenmonki*, pp. 269–270. *Akō gishi jiten*, pp. 206–212.

[35] *Hakumyō waroku*, pp. 108, 120.

was *kawa*. En route to Kira's residence, the rōnin were instructed to proceed at an ordinary pace, in small groups of two or three, heading toward the front or rear gates of Kira's mansion. They had been strategically divvyed up, with half making entry through the front gate, led by Ōishi, and the other half through the rear, led by Ōishi's son Chikara and a senior rōnin, Yoshida Chūzaemon. Ōishi further divided each group into interior attack forces and peripheral guard forces, thus coordinating duties as systematically as possible for military efficiency. Sketches of the compound were reportedly provided to expedite the search. A list of the two groups, with weapons, age, domain positions, and stipends, is provided in what follows. Similar lists appear in *Things Seen and Heard*.[36]

Front Gate/Eastern Group	Domain Position	Stipend	Age
Ōishi Kura-no-suke Yoshio Front gate, commander Spear	senior retainer	1,500 *koku*	45
Hara Sōemon Mototoki Front gate command Spear	commander of foot soldiers	300 *koku*	56
Kataoka Gengoemon Takafusa Front gate, interior invasion Spear	chamberlain	350 *koku*	37
Mase Kyūdayū Masaaki Front gate command Short bow	chief inspector	300 *koku*	63
Horibe Yahei Kanamaru Front gate, flight prevention Spear	retired, Edo attendant	300 *koku*	77
Chikamatsu Kanroku Yukishige Front gate, ground force Spear	mounted guard	250 *koku*	34
Tominomori Suke'emon Masayori Front gate, interior invasion Spear	mounted guard	200 *koku*	34
Hayami Tōzaemon Mitsutaka Front gate, ground force Bow	mounted guard	150 *koku*	42
Okuda Magodayū Shigemori Front gate, interior force Halberd	superintendent of weaponry	150 *koku*	57

[36] *Kōseki kenmonki*, pp. 271, 302–304. *Akō gishi shiseki meguri*, pp. 44–47.

(*cont.*)

Front Gate/Eastern Group	Domain Position	Stipend	Age
Yada Goroemon Suketake Front gate, interior invasion Halberd	mounted guard	150 *koku*	29
Ōtaka Gengo Tadao Front gate, ground force Halberd	treasury minister	20 *koku*	32
Kaiga Yazaemon Tomonobu Front gate, flight prevention Spear	manager of the grain storehouse	10 *ryō*	54
Okano Kinemon Kanehide Front gate, flight prevention Spear	heir, dependent	0	24
Okajima Yasoemon Tsuneki Front gate, interior invasion Battle axe	finance minister	20 *koku*	38
Yoshida Sawaemon Kanesada Front gate, interior invasion Battle axe	storehouse supervisor	13 *ryō*	29
Takebayashi Tadashichi Takashige Front gate, interior invasion Halberd	mounted guard	15 *ryō*	32
Muramatsu Kihei Hidenao Front gate, flight prevention Spear	magistrate	20 *koku*	62
Katsuda Shinzaemon Taketaka Front gate, interior invasion Spear	domain currency supervisor	15 *koku*	24
Onodera Kōemon Hidetomi Front gate, interior force Spear	heir, dependent	0	28
Hazama Jūjirō Mitsuoki Front gate, ground force Spear	heir, dependent	0	26
Yatō Emoshichi Norikane Front gate, ground force Spear	heir, dependent	0	18
Yokogawa Kanpei Munetoshi Front gate, flight prevention Spear	private inspectors	5 *ryō*	37
Kanzaki Yogorō Noriyasu Front gate, ground force Bow	private inspector	5 *ryō*	38

Rear Gate/Western Group	Position	Stipend	Age
Ōishi Chikara Yoshikane Commander, rear gate Spear	heir, dependent	0	16
Yoshida Chūzaemon Kanesuke Rear gate, commander Spear	commander of foot soldiers, district magistrate	200 koku	64
Onodera Jūnai Hidekazu Rear gate, command Spear	Kyoto attendant	150 koku	61
Hazama Kihei Mitsunobu Rear gate, command Spear	auditor	100 koku	69
Isogai Jūrōzaemon Masahisa Rear gate, interior invasion Spear	commander of foot soldiers	150 koku	25
Ushioda Matanojō Takanori Rear gate, ground force Spear	magistrate	200 koku	35
Akabane Genzō Shigekata Rear gate, interior invasion Spear	mounted guard	200 koku	35
Ōishi Sezaemon Nobukiyo Rear gate, interior invasion Spear	mounted guard	150 koku	27
Horibe Yasubei Taketsune Rear gate, interior force Halberd	mounted guard	200 koku	34
Kimura Okaemon Sadayuki Rear gate, ground force Spear	mounted guard, minister of maps and illustrations	150 koku	46
Nakamura Kansuke Masatoki Rear gate, ground force Spear	mounted guard	100 koku	48
Sugaya Hannojō Masatoshi Rear gate, interior force Spear	mounted guard	100 koku	44
Chiba Saburobei Mitsutada Rear gate, ground force Bow	mounted guard	100 koku	51
Fuwa Kazuemon Masatane Rear gate, ground force Halberd	mounted guard	100 koku	34
Kurahashi Densuke Takeyuki Rear gate, interior invasion Halberd	magistrate mid-level attendant	20 koku	34
Sugino Jūheiji Tsugifusa Rear gate, interior invasion Spear	bureaucratic supervisor mid-level attendant	8 ryō	28

(*cont.*)

Rear Gate/Western Group	Position	Stipend	Age
Maebara Isuke Munefusa Rear gate, ground force Spear	treasury manager mid-level attendant	10 *koku*	40
Hazama Shinroku Mitsukaze Rear gate, ground force Bow	rōnin	0	24
Okuda Sadaemon Yukitaka Rear gate, ground force Hand bell (*kane*)	retainer	9 *koku*	26
Muramatsu Sandayū Takanao Rear gate, interior invasion Spear	heir, dependent	0	27
Mase Magokurō Masatoki Rear gate, ground force Spear	heir, dependent	0	23
Kayano Wasuke Tsunenari Rear gate, ground force Bow	administrative inspector	5 *ryō*	37
Mimura Jirozaemon Kanetsune Rear gate, interior invasion Large mallet (*ōtsuchi*)	saké and kitchen manager	7 *koku*	37
Terasaka Kichiemon Nobuyuki Rear gate, interior invasion Spotlight	foot soldier	3 *ryō*	83

The rōnin were repeatedly warned to watch for fires.[37] Their sole aim was to slay Kira, not set the capital ablaze. The nearby Pure Land temple, the Ekōin, dedicated to those who perished in the Meireki Conflagration of 1657, was testimony to the horrors of carelessness. Moreover, there would be no wanton killing, looting, or destruction. Multiple copies of a document explaining the exact nature of the vendetta were drafted, with the names of each of the rōnin participants included. These documents would provide, in the event of capture or failure, an explanation of the attack and clear identification of all involved. Kira's neighbors were to be reassured that the break-in was not some act of random violence that might spread. Instead, the rōnin attack was a specific attack on Kira, well-orchestrated, and its rationale extensively documented.

[37] *Kōseki kenmonki*, p. 273.

4 LAYING SOULS TO REST

Summary accounts of the vendetta often suggest that the rōnin acted on samurai honor in taking revenge. Without discounting that aspect, this chapter highlights a different dimension. The rōnin declaration of intent and presentation of Kira's head at Asano's grave reveal that the rōnin attack had strong contemporary spiritual nuances. Simply put, the rōnin sought to lay to rest the spirit of their deceased lord by completing his unfinished deed, slaying Kira. Those dedicated to Asano's service were also concerned ethically about why he had attacked. They saw his attack and then theirs as countering the evil that Kira embodied. The ethical motive was first defined in *Akō Castle League* in terms of the decree of heaven. In the rōnin declaration of intent, the vendetta is explained as one meant to set the world below heaven in right ethical order by eliminating the perceived enemy within it, Kira. Thus, in addition to Asano's, the rōnin arguably sought to lay their own souls to rest, providing for the greater spiritual good at both the personal and the cosmic levels.

The Attack

The multipronged invasion of Kira's mansion began around 4:00 AM on the fifteenth day of the twelfth month (January 30, 1703).[1] Earlier, it had been planned for the fifth, but was cancelled when word came in

[1] *Kōseki kenmonki*, p. 304.

that Kira would be attending a function at Yanagisawa's residence featuring Tsunayoshi as guest of honor. On the tenth, Ōishi confirmed reports that Kira was planning an end-of-the-year tea gathering for the fourteenth. Relatively certain that Kira would be home that evening, Ōishi set that date for mobilizing the league. As expected, Kira maintained a guard at his compound, still fearing the possibility of a vendetta. Consequently, the rōnin encountered some resistance following their penetration of the compound. However, with the attack coming in the middle of the night, Kira's retainers were off guard, while the rōnin, armed, armored, and psyched with rhetoric about their heaven-sanctioned, righteous mission and the need for disciplined, unto-death determination, were well-geared for the struggle.

The rōnin did more than track down Kira: they killed sixteen of his retainers and wounded twenty-three others in fierce fighting. By 5:00 AM, some rōnin, including Kayano Wasuke Tsunenari, had penetrated the inner recesses of the mansion, where they found Kira's bedroom. Kayano reportedly touched the bedding and noticed its warmth, and so concluded that the retired master of ceremonies must have recently fled his chamber. Kira was reportedly discovered when Hazama Jūjirō noticed sounds coming from a charcoal storehouse adjoining the kitchen. Hazama asked who was in the shed and probed it with his spear. Two armed guards jumped out and were promptly cut down. Next, an elderly man emerged wielding a short sword. Hazama stabbed him with his spear.[2] Other rōnin were called in to determine whether the elderly man was Kira. Although they could not determine from looking at his forehead, they did find a notable scar on the man's back, establishing, in their minds, that it was Kira. Hazama then decapitated him, wrapped the head in the victim's white robes, and whistled to signal that Kira's head had been taken. Per some accounts, while Hazama's spear inflicted the mortal wound, Takebayashi Takashige delivered the final blow, decapitating him. In addition to wrapping Kira's head, Hazama was reportedly allowed to carry the gruesome prize bundle, supposedly affixed to his spear, in the march across Edo to the Sengakuji.[3]

---

[2] Ibid., pp. 274, 276–277, lists the names, positions in service to the Kira household, the age, and location within the Kira compound where the individuals met their deaths or were wounded.

[3] The *Hakumyō waroku*, p. 122, offers a similar but brief account, based on Terasaka's records of the vendetta (*Terasaka shi kiroku*). Other accounts in the *Kōseki kenmonki* (vol. 4, pp. 275, 279, 283; vol. 5, pp. 305, 309, 317) claim that Takebayashi assisted in

The plan was to attack with surgical precision, with as little collateral damage as possible. Yet rather than a rapid search and decapitate, the invasion lasted more than two hours with the rōnin looking high and low for Kira, without quick success. Had neighboring samurai responded, the rōnin would likely have been trapped and their vendetta foiled. But apart from their extended fight with Kira's men, they had time to search and search again until right at the break of dawn, Kira was discovered and slain, with positive identification coming after he had been cut down. Collateral damage was substantial. According to one samurai who surveyed the scene the following day, every gate, door, and sliding panel had been smashed; ceilings, floors, folding screens, and storage chests were riddled with lance punctures. The mansion was left in chaotic upheaval, with furniture, dishes, and personal effects thrown about and broken everywhere. Blood was splattered throughout the wreckage. Kira's adopted son, Sahyōe, was "bloodied and severely wounded, but still alive." Walking the length of the mansion, the samurai reporter supposedly had to straddle the dead and wounded, sprawled in "obscene postures, ... beyond description." In the garden area, corpses were left as they had fallen. Later the morning of the attack, noted sword-wound surgeon Kurisaki Dōyū, who had earlier treated Kira following Asano's attack, reportedly arrived at the Kira compound along with seven disciples to treat the wounded. Kurisaki worked until 10:00 PM that evening, and his disciples remained until 5:00 AM the following day.[4]

The rōnin band – which sustained minor injuries, but not a single loss – apparently had not imagined that it would emerge from the attack with such complete success. Indeed, there seems to have been no definite plan as to what would follow now that Kira's head had been taken and the rōnin had not encountered heated battle with the shogunal authorities. Initially, the band went to the adjacent Pure Land temple, the Ekōin, to regroup, and apparently sought entry, reportedly considering committing seppuku there. But they were turned away by

the kill. Several secondary sources indicate that Hazama probed Kira out of the closet, but that Takebayashi delivered the death blow. In the same passage, Ōishi reportedly allowed Hazama to offer the first stick of incense at Asano's grave, and then he, Ōishi, offered the second (p. 279).

[4] Thomas Harper, "The Kurisaki School of Sword Wound Surgery," in Anna Beerens and Mark Teeuwen, eds., *Unchartered Waters: Intellectual Life in the Edo Period: Essays in Honor of W. J. Boot* (Leiden: Brill, 2012), pp. 236–238.

the cautious Ekōin, which had been given no warning as to the vendetta. The rōnin then decided on a bold move: marching across Edo to the Asano family temple, the Sengakuji, where Asano Naganori was interred. Perhaps it had always been considered as a remote possibility, but planning an entry at the Sengakuji probably seemed too presumptuous beforehand. Apparently, the rōnin thought that they would be dead or on the verge of death before daybreak. The day before the attack, formulating a best-case contingency plan for the day after perhaps would have smacked of hubris.

The rōnin took a safe, peripheral route, crossing the Sumida River at the Eitai Bridge (some accounts say the Shin-Ōhashi), proceeding through the Hatchōbori district, on to Tsukiji, and then southward to the Asano family temple, the Sengakuji, in the Takanawa section of Shiba.[5] The fifteenth was castle attendance day for daimyō residing in Edo. For that reason, the rōnin bypassed the main thoroughfares. Overall, they kept their distance from Edo Castle, apparently to avoid any chance confrontation with the authorities. The injured, including Hara Sōemon, who hurt his ankle, were carried by palanquin. The entire way, the rōnin feared an attack from either the shogunate or a contingent of Uesugi samurai acting on behalf of Kira, but none came.[6]

In Shock to the Sengakuji

Neither Ōishi nor the rōnin made prior arrangements with the Sengakuji for bringing the vendetta to a conclusion there. Their arrival surprised the temple and caused something of an uproar in the surrounding area. An account by a Sengakuji monk, Gekkai, entitled *Hakumyō's Memoir*, relates that after the attack, the rōnin proceeded one step at a time, as if shocked by their own success in taking Kira's

---

[5] *Kōseki kenmonki*, p. 279. The *Kōseki kenmonki* states that the rōnin crossed the Shin-Ōhashi, then went through Kobiki-chō, past the former Asano residence in Teppozu, and on to the Sengakuji. Later (p. 306), it states that they crossed at the Eitaibashi. The *Akō gishi jiten*, pp. 103–105, states that the rōnin first considered taking a boat down the Sumida to the Sengakuji, but none was for hire and so decided to walk the entire distance. It also states that the rōnin crossed the Sumida at the Eitaibashi. The *Hakumyō waroku*, p. 122, specifically denies that Kira's head was transported to the Sengakuji by boat, noting instead that it was brought to the Sengakuji wrapped in Kira's white robe and tied to a lance.

[6] Ibid., p. 279.

head and then marching across Edo unopposed. Ōishi Chikara, Ōishi Yoshio's son, reportedly suggested that the rōnin commit seppuku once they arrived at the Sengakuji, but his father differed, stating that they should not rush things. En route to the Sengakuji, Ōishi decided to report the vendetta, a task he entrusted to two rōnin, Yoshida Chūzaemon and Tominomori Suke'emon. They left the group at some point along the way and proceeded to the Atagoshita compound of the shogunal grand inspector, Sengoku Hisanao, to report their deed.[7]

Gekkai's account of the rōnin while at the Sengakuji provides invaluable and authentic details about the vendetta. The rōnin entered the main temple gate just before 9:00 AM, without prior notice or permission. Gekkai relates that that morning, the monks were in the Dharma Hall participating in a biannual Zen ceremony. Suddenly, a watchman appeared, announcing that "around fifty to sixty retainers of the late Asano Naganori, attired variously, had entered through the gates with lances, long swords, and other military weapons, and meant to proceed." The temple assistant promptly informed the chief priest about this.

Since the Sengakuji was the family temple of Asano Naganori, the rōnin were allowed in. To keep onlookers away, the main gate was closed and a watchman posted outside. The weapons that the rōnin carried – long swords, spears, bows, and lances – were reportedly still covered with blood, as were many of the rōnin. Gekkai observes that Ōishi and the rōnin had been so focused on slaying Kira that they gave little thought to the aftermath, and so proceeded tentatively. As the rōnin presented Kira's head, temple monks approached and began reciting sutras to provide the semblance of a Buddhist graveside ceremony. Gekkai suggests that the rōnin were clueless regarding what should be done next, and that without temple guidance, the grave presentation of Kira's head would have been a rather uncouth affair.[8]

Gekkai dismissed rumors that the rōnin had brought a "dirty, filthy severed head" and placed it before sacred, ritually clean icons meant to secure prayers for all below heaven.[9] According to Gekkai,

---

[7] *Hakumyō waroku*, pp. 106, 123. Henry D. Smith II, "The Trouble with Terasaka," pp. 41–42, earlier discussed Gekkai's *Hakumyō waroku* and its relevance to understanding the vendetta historically. *Kōseki kenmonki*, p. 279.

[8] Ibid., pp. 106, 123; *Kōseki kenmonki*, p. 284.

[9] Ibid., p. 525. Gekkai attributes this to Ogawa Tsunemitsu's *Chūsei gokanroku* (*Mirror of Loyalty and Sincerity*). A modern edition of the text is in *Akō gijin sansho*, vol. 3,

that was a rumor circulated by illiterates. Nevertheless, that Gekkai felt compelled to deny such pollution suggests that however the head was presented, on a Buddhist altar or at Asano's grave, the Sengakuji had been challenged if not radically defiled by the entry of the bloodied band carrying the decapitated head of a retired shogunal official. Ōishi had not exaggerated when he earlier described the Akō rōnin as *bukotsu*.

After the head was presented, Gekkai added that the rōnin were not sure what should be done with it. Curiously, they went to the temple kitchen, found a set of stacked boxes, took the largest as its final resting place, and left it there. Later, temple monks arranged to have the head returned to the Kira family. Note here that Gekkai never mentioned the rōnin having washed the head, even though *Things Seen and Heard* does relate that the rōnin cleaned the head with water from a graveyard bucket. Earlier, while at Kira's mansion, the rōnin had reportedly rinsed the filth off the head in the hopes of verifying that it was Kira's.[10] In an understatement, Gekkai, recording his memories decades later, noted that what had happened was nothing like the puppet play.[11]

The temple, noticing that the rōnin had no incense, provided some for offering before Asano's gravestone. Hazama reportedly lit the first stick and Takebayashi the second.[12] One of the earliest studies of the vendetta, *The Righteous Men of Akō Domain* by Confucian scholar Muro Kyūsō, claims that even as the rōnin offered incense, Ōishi sat down and drafted his "Ōishi's Prayer" (*Saimon*), addressed to the spirit of his deceased lord. There Ōishi admitted that in taking Kira's life, the rōnin had violated shogunal decrees. Nevertheless, he explained the attack by quoting the *Book of Rites*' passage regarding the inability of sons and retainers to live under the same heaven as the enemies of their fathers and lords.

Along with the head, Ōishi supposedly brought a dagger to Kira's grave. It was allegedly one of Asano's treasured possessions that

---

pp. 410–553. Gekkai takes issue with the *Chūsei gokanroku* several more times in *Hakumyō waroku*.

[10] *Kōseki kenmonki*, pp. 283–284. Later (p. 305), the *Kōseki kenmonki* relates that Hazama Jūjirō established Kira's identity by his shoulder scar. Once certain, he reportedly took his head.

[11] *Hakumyō waroku*, pp. 122–123. *Chūsei gokanroku, Akō gijin sansho*, vol. 3, pp. 472–473.

[12] The *Kōseki kenmonki*, p. 279, states, that before the head was presented, Hazama was to have the honor of offering the first stick of incense, and Ōishi would offer the second.

had been given to Ōishi after Asano had used it in his seppuku. Other accounts, also questionable, even claim that Ōishi had carried the dagger with him in the invasion so that he could use it to sever Kira's head, thus providing through the blade a kind of blood justice. With the presentation of the head, however, Ōishi was returning the blade, mission accomplished, to Asano. The prayer concluded with Ōishi inviting the spirit of the late Asano to take the dagger and strike Kira's head once more. After being read, the prayer was placed on Asano's grave, alongside Kira's head and the dagger. It was reportedly signed, "[Ōishi] Yoshio and the other retainers."

Following Muro's *The Righteous Men of Akō Domain*, numerous other accounts of the vendetta included "Ōishi's Prayer" in describing the rōnin's presentation of Kira's head. Another early study of the vendetta, Ogawa Tsunemitsu's *Mirror of Loyalty and Sincerity*, cited the text, but questioned its authenticity. Later, yet another Tokugawa-period study, Miyake Kanran's *Records of Resolute Samurai Revenge*, went further and declared the prayer apocryphal. Meiji historian Shigeno Yasutsugu, in his *True Accounts of the Righteous Samurai of Akō Domain*, mocked the notion that Ōishi, on the spur of the moment, could possibly have sat down in front of his master's grave, exhausted from the vendetta, and composed, on short order, a four-hundred-word prayer in Sino-Japanese. Shigeno claims that even a skilled writer would have been challenged to draft such a document so quickly.[13]

Since Shigeno, serious studies of the vendetta have rarely cited "Ōishi's Prayer" as anything more than an apocryphal embellishment. Nevertheless, in popular accounts and historical fiction, it has been repeated, often without question. The fabricated text perhaps reflected the need for a fuller, more spiritually infused articulation of what transpired than the relatively austere, somewhat inarticulate rōnin presentation of Kira's head, as recorded by Gekkai, allowed. Nevertheless, their act – presenting the head before Asano's grave – spoke volumes about their purpose and motivation. Theirs was a spiritual mission, meant to bring, with its success, peace to Asano's soul.

---

[13] Muro Kyūsō, *Akō gijin roku*, in *Kinsei buke shisō*, pp. 305–307. Ogawa Tsunemitsu, *Chūsei gokanroku*, p. 471. Shigeno Yasutsugu, *Akō gishi jitsuwa*, pp. 162–163. *Akō gishi jiten*, p. 559. Imao Tetsuya, *Kira no kubi: Chūshingura no imagineeshon* (Tokyo: Heibonsha, 1987), pp. 56–59.

Shortly after, the assistant head of the Sengakuji introduced Ōishi and some of the rōnin to the chief priest. Ōishi explained the obvious, that they had come to the Sengakuji because it was the Asano family temple in Edo. Earlier, after killing Kira, they had gone to the Ekōin to kill themselves, but apparently due to their strange appearance, the gates remained closed. While there was no question that the group would commit suicide, in the end they decided that they should await the verdict of the authorities. Thus, two of their group, Yoshida and Tominomori, had been sent to inform the grand inspector, Sengoku Hisanao, of their deed.

Realizing that a matter of this consequence would have to be reported, the chief priest, in deference to the magistrate of temples and shrines, stated that he needed to establish an exact count of the rōnin and so conducted a roll call. The result was forty-five, but after a recount, the total was forty-four. Temple authorities soon figured that the forty-fifth rōnin was Terasaka Kichiemon who, though part of the group, had disappeared. In addition to the forty-four present, two more, Yoshida and Tominomori, were at the grand inspector's residence. Without worrying why or when Terasaka, a foot soldier, had gone, the temple authorities sent their calculations to the magistrate.[14]

While Ōishi, his son, and the senior leaders of the rōnin met with the chief priest in the main hall, the other members rested in a temple dorm, warming themselves by a fire. Served rice gruel and tea, they ate heartily. They were invited to take baths, but fearing imminent attack, declined. Nevertheless, those in the dorms soon fell asleep. Takebayashi Tadashichi, however, remained very much awake and wrote a poem that Gekkai found interesting. It reads:

> Thirty years have come and gone as if in a dream.
> Discarding my life and choosing righteousness remains like a dream.
> My two parents are in ill health at their old home place.
> Choosing righteousness and abandoning my debt to them is also
> a dream, empty.

The Zen-Confucian themes most likely appealed to Gekkai, but he called attention to Takebayashi's reference to his "two parents," noting how it conflicted with a later tale claiming that Takebayashi's mother

---

[14] *Hakumyō waroku*, pp. 106–109, 120.

had committed suicide to prompt him to join the vendetta. Gekkai corrected similar such rumors throughout his text. On another count, he noted that stories had circulated about "a woman" having entered the temple with the "righteous samurai," but denied it, explaining instead that it was a "handsome young boy" (*bishōnen*).[15]

Confession and Verdict

One document, "The Declaration of Asano Takumi-no-kami's Retainers" (*Asano Takumi-no-kami kerai kōjō*), identifies the rōnin as signatories, one by one, and offers a brief explanation of why they attacked Kira's residence. It is generally recognized as one of the most authentic and therefore valuable documents for any study of the vendetta.[16] *Things Seen and Heard* describes it as a "'last testament' to be left behind by those who had resolved themselves to certain death." One copy, for example, was reportedly placed in a bamboo container in the entrance hall of Kira's residence for discovery by someone later, presumably investigating the carnage.[17]

Participants in the attack were also given copies, with every copy bearing the names of the forty-seven rōnin. When Ōishi decided, en route, to report the vendetta to the grand inspector, Sengoku Hisanao, he sent a copy with Yoshida Chūzaemon and Tominomori Suke'emon. The declaration reads:

> Last year in the third month, while hosting imperial emissaries, Asano Takumi-no-kami came to harbor a grudge against Kira Kōzuke-no-suke. Even though he was in the shogun's castle hosting ceremonies, he found it difficult to bear the grudge any longer and so struck and wounded Kira. He did this in disregard for the time and the place, making his action extremely out of harmony with ceremonial rules and regulations. He was made to commit seppuku, and his domain in Akō was confiscated by the shogun. We, his

---

[15] Ibid., pp. 120, 122–124.

[16] Shigeno, *Akō gishi jitsuwa*, pp. 118–122; Bitō, "The Akō Incident," p. 8; Miyazawa, *Akō rōshi*, pp. 175–176; *Akō gishi jiten*, pp. 85–86; Akō-shi, *Chūshingura*, vol. 1, pp. 174–180; Thomas J. Harper and Henry D. Smith II, "110 Manifesto," *Sengakuji Akō gishi kinenkan shūzōhin mokuroku/Memorial Hall of Akō Loyal Retainers, Sengakuji Temple Catalogue of the Collection* (Tokyo: Sengakuji, 2002), pp. 114–115.

[17] *Kōseki kenmonki*, vol. 4, pp. 280–281.

retainers, had to abide by this, surrendering the domain to the shogunate, and then being promptly cut off and scattered.

During the altercation, there were shogunal officials on the spot who stopped the attack on Kira. Therefore, Asano did not complete his plan and so harbored regrets to the bottom of his heart. Finding this difficult to bear, we, his retainers, became enraged at Kira, a man of exalted birth. While we hesitated to take action, we know that a person cannot live beneath the same heaven as the enemy of his lord or father. Thus, we found it impossible to remain silent.

Today we are resolved to make our way into Kira's residence and bring to a conclusion the intention of our deceased lord. After our deaths, we request that anyone investigating this incident please read this document.

The Retainers of Asano Takumi-no-kami Naganori.
Genroku 15, Twelfth month, ___ day.
Ōishi Kura-no-suke and others.[18]

The declaration offers a Confucian defense of the attack. The key allusion, "a person cannot live beneath the same heaven as the enemy of his lord or father," is to the *Book of Rites*. The latter states:

> Zixia asked Confucius, "How should a son act toward the man who has killed his father or mother?" Confucius said, "He should sleep on straw with his shield for a pillow; he should not take office; he must be determined not to live in the same world [literally, 'under the same heaven'] as the killer. If he encounters the killer in the market-place or at court, he should not have to go back for his weapon, but [should be ready instantly to] fight with him."[19]

This passage does not link "fathers" and "rulers," but the twelfth-century Song dynasty philosopher, Zhu Xi, in a memorial to his emperor, Xiaozong, did recast the *Book of Rites'* sanction of vengeance against the murderer of one's father to apply it to "the enemy of one's lord and master."[20]

---

[18] Ibid., pp. 280–281.

[19] James Legge, trans., *The Li Ki, or Collection of Treatises on the Rules of Propriety or Ceremonial Usages*, in F. Max Müller, *Sacred Books of China: The Texts of Confucianism*, vol. 27 (Oxford: Clarendon Press, 1885), p. 140.

[20] Zhu Xi, "Chui gong zou zha, er" (Second Memorial to the Throne), *Huian xiansheng Wengong wenji* (*Zhu Xi's Collected Works*), vol. 6, vol. 13, p. 3a.

Zhu Xi's main concern was explaining the universal sentiment of vengeance found equally in relations between lords and retainers, and fathers and sons. Nevertheless, Zhu's pairing of the *Book of Rites*' reference to "the enemy of one's father" with "the enemy of one's lord" justified, along Confucian lines, the rōnin's declaration of intent to slay Kira due to their inability to live in the same world as the enemy of their late lord. Given that the shogun, Tsunayoshi, regularly participated in lectures and discussions of Zhu Xi's Confucian thought, the allusion to Zhu Xi would not likely have been lost on him, nor on any number of other Tokugawa Confucians. Admittedly, the Confucian justification did not change the final verdict, nor, most likely, did the rōnin imagine that it would. Rather, they meant simply to reveal, it seems, that far from common murder, theirs was a philosophically informed act, arguably sanctioned by none other than the renowned Confucian scholar Zhu Xi, if not the shogunate. Philosophical justification or not, one fact must have been crystal clear to the authorities: the rōnin had not requested permission for their vendetta, and so on that count alone, it amounted to an egregious breach of shogunal law.

Equally if not more important, the declaration suggests that the rōnin viewed their actions in a spiritual dimension as carrying out and completing the last intentions of their now deceased master. With psychological and emotional insight, the declaration first notes the lingering regrets at the bottom of Asano Naganori's heart as he met death. Later, the declaration adds that the rōnin sought to complete the intention of their late lord. Implied, in a way consistent with Confucian understandings of spirituality, was that by doing so, the rōnin would pacify the spirit of Asano Naganori, which otherwise would fester, frustrated and angry in the afterlife over the unfulfilled deed, possibly wreaking havoc on things as a consequence. While concerns for society at large were hardly those of the rōnin, their declaration suggests that they saw their deeds as ones meant to lay their deceased master's soul to rest, even as they prepared, by doing so, to join him in death.

That evening, around 7:00 PM, the magistrate for temples and shrines called for the rōnin to proceed to the residence of the grand inspector, Sengoku, in Atagoshita, north of the Sengakuji. Before leaving, Ōishi and his son reportedly thanked the chief priest at the Sengakuji. The rōnin group did the same, bowing in gratitude for food, drink, shelter, and spiritual assistance at Asano's grave. Lanterns were provided for the evening procession, with three in front, two in the middle, and two more at the rear. Six rōnin who had suffered injuries rode in palanquins. Ōishi and his son also took palanquins, riding at the front of the procession. According to Gekkai, the other rōnin, as they departed, maintained their ranks correctly and marched forward. Reportedly, all the temple monks were out to send them off. As Gekkai noted, it was about the same time of day, approximately two months later, that the rōnin returned to the Sengakuji, in coffins and burial containers, following their seppuku on the fourth day of the second month, 1703.[21]

Kira's son, Sahyōe, had also sent a messenger to the shogunate reporting the murder of his father and the attack on their Honjo compound. Following protocol, the Sengakuji reported to the shogunal commissioner of temples and shrines that the rōnin were at the temple with Kira's head. After hearing Yoshida and Tominomori, the grand inspector, Sengoku, had them detained at his residence. He then went to discuss the incident with a shogunal elder, Inaba Masamichi. News thus reached Edo Castle from various corners of the shogun's capital. Sometime around 8:00 PM, the shogunal elders convened, but only concluded that for the time being, the rōnin would be divided up and placed in the custody of four daimyō who resided south of Edo Castle and in relative proximity to the Sengakuji.[22]

Temple monks contacted the Kira family to arrange for the return of his head. This occurred on the sixteenth. Two elder vassals of the Kira received Kira's head on behalf of the family and signed a receipt, which remains at the Sengakuji, documenting the transfer. Reportedly, Kurisaki Dōyū, the physician who earlier treated Kira's wounds following Asano's attack, sewed Kira's head back on his body before burial at the Banshōji, Kira's family temple. While Kira was reportedly interred at the Banshōji, there is no evidence corroborating the procedure attributed to Kurisaki. At that time, the Banshōji was located in Ichigoya, west of Edo Castle, but later, during the Taishō period, it was moved, along with Kira's grave, to the Nakano ward, west of central Tokyo. Kira later came to have, incidentally, yet another gravesite at the Kezōji in Nishio City, Aichi Prefecture.[23]

---

[21] *Hakumyō waroku*, p. 122. [22] *Kōseki kenmonki*, vol. 5, pp. 307–310, 320–322.

[23] A photograph of the receipt (ink on silk, 29.8 X 42.3 cm) for Kira's head, along with a translation, is in Harper and Smith, "17 Receipt for Kira's Head," *Sengakuji Akō gishi kinenkan shūzōhin mokuroku*, pp. 31, 120. The elder Kira vassals were Sōda Magobe and Saitō Kunai.

Accounts of the shogun's verdict frequently omit the punishment meted out to Kira's surviving retainers. One text, the "Opinion of the Supreme Judicial Council," however, addresses this first. This document, considered apocryphal, judged that Kira's adopted heir, Sahyōe, who was found alive next to Kira's bed, be sentenced to seppuku, and that Kira's retainers who did not defend him be sentenced to death as common criminals. The verdict also proposed confiscating the Uesugi domain, Yonezawa, because the Uesugi had not moved against the rōnin.[24] While the document is apparently a forgery, in the end Sahyōe was stripped of his fief and exiled to Shinano province, in the protective custody of the lord of Takashima Castle. Three years later, age twenty, he died of an illness. A *bakufu* inspector who learned of Sahyōe's punishment, announced the same day as the rōnin verdict, reportedly informed Ōishi of the same just before his seppuku.

Two days after the rōnin seppuku, the shogunate announced, with some leniency, that of the nineteen children of the rōnin, only males fifteen and older would be exiled to Izu Ōshima, a volcanic island approximately one hundred miles south of Edo. Thus, only four – the sons of Yoshida Chūzaemon, Mase Kyūdayū, Nakamura Kansuke, and Muramatsu Kihei – were exiled. Wives, daughters, and female relatives were not punished. Children under fifteen were permitted to remain with relatives. After reaching fifteen, sons were to be exiled to Izu Ōshima. However, in 1706, with memorial services for the recently deceased Keishōin, a pardon was granted for sons who became Buddhist monks. Ōishi's second son, incidentally, had joined the priesthood even before the vendetta. Although never punished, he passed away at nineteen. In 1709, following Tsunayoshi's death, the new shogun, Tokugawa Ienobu, in addition to abolishing Tsunayoshi's infamous edicts protecting animals, proclaimed a general pardon releasing all those exiled and imprisoned. Ōishi's third son thus avoided any punishment and, after attaining manhood, became a retainer of the Hiroshima Asano clan.

The shogunate's final decision, sentencing the forty-six rōnin to death by seppuku, was handed down in the second month of 1703. The verdict is often explained in terms of a text known as "Memorandum on Law" (*Giritsusho*), attributed to Ogyū Sorai,

---

[24] The "Hyōjōsho ichiza zonjiyorisho" is in *Akō gijin sansho*, vol. 3, pp. 148–149. Bitō, "The Akō Incident," pp. 165–166.

a Confucian scholar serving Yanagisawa Yoshiyasu. However, some Sorai scholars have questioned the authenticity of the text, at least insofar as it claims to be Sorai's thinking on the subject. That aside, the text is relevant to the issues and is a well-formulated analysis of the verdict, whether authored by Sorai or someone else. "Memorandum on Law" strikes a balance between the sense of "justice" and "righteousness" (*gi*) relevant to individual morality, and the "law" (*hō*), or the public instrument providing coercively for social and political order. While recognizing that revenge might be considered an act of personal justice, the text nevertheless insists that such thinking amounts to "private theorizing." If viewed from the perspective of the law, acts of public violence carried out without the permission of the shogunate were simply unacceptable. If permitted, they would undermine the legal foundations of the polity. For that reason, the rōnin, although allowed the samurai ritual of seppuku, should be sentenced to die.

Lacking the subtlety of "Memorandum on Law," the verdict, handed down by the shogunate and read to each rōnin group before their seppuku was as follows.

> Asano Naganori was assigned the official ceremonial duty of entertaining imperial messengers. However, with disregard for the occasion and the shogun's palace, he behaved outrageously and so was executed. Kira Yoshinaka did nothing wrong and so was left alone. Yet the forty-six, retainers of Asano, formed a conspiracy to take revenge on the enemy of their master. Armed, they invaded Kira's residence and killed him. From beginning to end, they showed no respect for the shogunate. Over and again, your behavior has been outrageous. Accordingly, you will commit seppuku.[25]

The Hosokawa Seventeen

Earlier, on the evening of the fifteenth day of the twelfth month, the rōnin were divided into four groups and assigned to the custody of

---

[25] "Hosokawa-ke oazuke shimatsu ki," Chūō gishikai, eds., *Akō gishi shiryō*, vol. 2 (Tokyo: Yūzankaku, 1931), p. 33. "Hisamatsu-ke Akō oazuke jin shimatsu ki," *Akō gishi shiryō*, vol. 2, pp. 58–106, p. 88. "Mizuno ke oazuke kiroku," *Akō gishi shiryō*, vol. 2, p. 118.

daimyō responsible for their confinement. Hosokawa Tsunatoshi, the powerful outer lord of Kumamoto Castle with a sizeable income of 540,000 *koku*, was assigned responsibility for the seventeen leaders of the vendetta listed here:

> Ōishi Kura-no-suke Yoshio
> Horibe Yahei Kanamaru
> Yada Goroemon Suketake
> Chikamatsu Kanroku Yukishige
> Hayami Tōzaemon Mitsutaka
> Mase Kyūdayū Masaaki
> Tominomori Suke'emon Masayori
> Hara Sōemon Mototoki
> Okuda Magodayū Shigemori
> Kataoka Gengoemon Takafusa
> Onodera Jūnai Hidekazu
> Ōishi Sezaemon Nobukiyo
> Akabane Genzō Shigekata
> Yoshida Chūzaemon Kanesuke
> Ushioda Matanojō Takanori
> Isogai Jūrōzaemon Masahisa
> Hazama Kihei Mitsunobu[26]

The Hosokawa reportedly sent a lantern-lit, guarded escort of eight hundred seventy-five retainers, with seventeen palanquins, one per rōnin, to transport the vendetta leaders to the Hosokawa sub-residence, conveniently located near the Sengakuji.[27]

Due to a change of plans by the shogunate, the guard proceeded first to the Sengakuji, only to learn en route that the rōnin were in custody at the residence of the grand inspector in Atagoshita, requiring them to reroute the grand escort northward. As a result, the guard arrived around 10:00 PM, and only returned to the Hosokawa compound well after midnight. Despite the hour, the Hosokawa daimyō was reportedly there to offer Ōishi and the others a brief but gracious

---

[26] Ibid., p. 14. Here, only the names are given. *Kōseki kenmonki*, p. 320, lists the names, domain positions, and family crests.

[27] Ibid., pp. 4–10, 14–15, 24–25, gives eight hundred seventy-five as the total count for retainers sent. The text breaks down the roles and numbers of retainers. In addition to samurai, lantern carriers, palanquin carriers, and spokesmen, Hosokawa sent a small contingent of physicians to tend to the injured. *Kōseki kenmonki*, vol. 5, p. 320.

welcome, praising their "loyalty and righteousness," and declaring that they had truly responded to the decree of heaven. After remaining weapons, including ten swords, had been confiscated, Hosokawa ordered a meal of vegetables, tea, saké, and pastries for the rōnin.

At the Hosokawa compound, the rōnin were provided fresh robes and other clothing. Their rooms had garden views. In one, nine rōnin were lodged, and in the adjoining room, the remaining eight. Baths were provided regularly. With the permission of shogunal councilors, "medicinal saké" and tobacco were also available, and drinking apparently was a daily activity for Ōishi and some of the rōnin. Exceptional meals were prepared, and reportedly food was always available. The Hosokawa daimyō was, by all accounts, pleased to have Ōishi and the other sixteen rōnin under his care. He even inquired into the possibility of a pardon for them.

Things Seen and Heard records that at the end of the first month, just days before the verdict was announced, Hosokawa sent Ōishi a farewell poem about plums in full bloom, along with a plum twig that he had broken off a tree. The sixth volume of *Things Seen and Heard*, where the poem appears, includes a mix of apocryphal and factual accounts. Even if a later fabrication, the poem and plum twig well symbolize the extraordinary level of hospitality the Hosokawa house provided the rōnin. Another indication took the form of an Edo ditty, "The Hosokawa and Mizuno streams are clean and pure, but the Matsudaira and Mōri are filthy," praising the first two houses for their kindness, while trashing the latter two for their cold-hearted custody of the rōnin. By all accounts, the Hosokawa treated the rōnin like honored guests, with exceptional consideration, rather than as criminals sentenced to death.[28]

On the twenty-second day of the first month of 1703, a Tokugawa official, Inaba Tango-no-kami, went to the Hosokawa residence to request compilation of genealogical records for each rōnin. These provided the authorities a record of who, precisely, their relatives were, their ages, where they lived, and so on. With this, the rōnin likely realized that their day was near. On the fourth day of the second month, shogunal representatives delivered the earlier quoted verdict. Yasuba Ippei Masayuki, one of Hosokawa's trusted retainers,

---

[28] Ibid., pp. 3, 32. Akō-shi, *Chūshingura*, p. 252. *Kōseki kenmonki*, pp. 311, 322. Hosokawa's poem is recorded in vol. 6, p. 326. Also, *Akō gishi jiten*, p. 425.

was chosen to serve as Ōishi's *kaishaku*. The others were assigned one *kaishaku* per man, selected from the lower ranks of the Hosokawa retainers. After the rituals were over, a shogunal magistrate instructed some attendants to clean the site where the seventeen had met their deaths. Per the memoir of Horiuchi Den'emon, a Hosokawa retainer who had daily contacts with the rōnin, his daimyō intervened, stating, "The seventeen brave samurai will be grand guardian deities (*yoki mamorigami*) for this residence. There is no need to clean up anything. Please leave everything as it is." Horiuchi added that Hosokawa appreciated the blessings that the seventeen seppuku had brought to the garden area. In the end, Hosokawa was persuaded that re-facing the tatami mats and sliding doors was in order. Even with some cleaning, the site became an immediate "famous place" in the area. When word circulated that the Hosokawa daimyō had not wanted it cleaned, he was praised even more.

Hosokawa favor was also evident in the burial provisions for the seventeen leaders. Following their seppuku, the remains of each were placed into a cask, then transported by individual palanquin, accompanied by horsemen, lantern bearers, guards, and watchmen, to the Sengakuji for burial. Hosokawa also provided, reportedly, the Sengakuji with ample funds, fifty *ryō* (eighteen grams per *ryō*) in gold, for the interment of the seventeen leaders.[29]

In the days leading up to the seppuku, Ōishi enjoyed continued rounds of saké with some of his fellow rōnin. Horiuchi Den'emon relates that Ōishi also reassured the others that the seppuku ceremony would be the way of maintaining honor specific to the samurai, and thus, presumably, something that all should greet with courage, pride, and appreciation. The Hosokawa rituals lasted from 4:00 PM until approximately 5:00 PM. While samurai honor was arguably respected, it was respected in short order.[30] For seventeen men to die in just over sixty minutes, the rituals must have proceeded at a pace of one seppuku every four minutes. Held in the front garden of the Hosokawa sub-

---

[29] Ibid., pp. 26–29, 32, 36–39, 46. These family records are included in *Kōseki kenmonki*, pp. 316, 328, 331. Akō-shi, *Chūshingura*, vol. 1, p. 258. Hosokawa's remark about the seventeen rōnin becoming grand guardian deities is drawn from "Horiuchi Den'emon oboegaki," in *Akō gijin sansho*, vol. 1, p. 383. Shigeno's *Akō gishi jitsuwa*, p. 1, recognizes this text as an authentic source. *Akō gishi jiten*, p. 491, calls it a valuable source.

[30] "Genroku gikyo no kōgai," *Akō gishi jiten*, p. 114.

residence, the ceremonies began with Ōishi, followed by the other sixteen.

White drapery defined two sides of the space enclosing three stacked tatami mats, on top of which a white cloth was spread. It was there that the rōnin committed seppuku. A third side was defined by a white folding screen. The rōnin proceeded, one by one, as called, without fanfare or incident. Overall, the order was determined by the status and stipend of the individual rōnin. A final cup of saké was provided, and some rōnin reportedly asked in jest why, given the special nature of the occasion, there was no tobacco and green tea. Reportedly, they were also provided ink and paper to record any final words for their relatives, as well as parting poems. After each rōnin sat erect on the tatami and bowed to the inspectors and his *kaishaku*, he disrobed to the waist and leaned forward to grasp the short sword placed on a small stand in front of him. Little more than leaning forward or grasping the sword was needed, at which point the *kaishaku* decapitated him. Although referred to as seppuku, the stomach was not typically pierced. Apparently, the *kaishaku* performed their roles without error.

Ōishi's *kaishaku*, Yasuba Ippei, commissioned a painting of Ōishi's seppuku depicting the moment that he, Ōishi, had grasped his short sword. In it, Yasuba is coiled, a split second before his raised blade swung. In the upper right are fifteen of the rōnin who were to follow. Already positioned between the white curtain and Ōishi is the next in line, Yoshida Chūzaemon, surrounded by three Hosokawa guards. To the left are shogunal inspectors witnessing the proceedings. The men in the lower right removed the corpses and readied them for transport to the Sengakuji. The painting presents the scene from an elevated frontal perspective, in the "Japanese picture style," with mostly stylized figures and calligraphy above identifying them.

The Matsudaira Ten

The second group, consisting of ten rōnin, including Ōishi Chikara, was assigned to Matsudaira Sadanao, daimyō of Matsuyama domain in Iyo province with a rice income of 150,000 *koku*. Matsudaira was ill on the day of their transfer and so one of the shogunate's elder councilors, Inaba Masamichi, sent a representative to receive the rōnin on Matsudaira's behalf. The ten were transported by ten guarded

Figure 4.1 Ōishi's seppuku. Courtesy of Waseda University, Department of Special Collections.

palanquins from the grand inspector's residence to the Matsudaira main residence, accompanied by an escort of two hundred eighty-six men, all provided by the Matsudaira. The guarded escort arrived at the residence well after midnight. That evening, Matsudaira declined to meet the group. There the rōnin were lodged in a row house including ten rooms, one for each rōnin. For the most part, they remained confined in their individual rooms. Sixteen days later, they were relocated to the daimyō's secondary residence in Shiba, where they were divided into two groups of five, each assigned to a separate row house, and again confined in separate rooms.

On the fourth day of the lunar New Year, the rōnin received new robes, presumably as a New Year's present, to wear the following day, the fifth, when Matsudaira Sadanao met briefly with the group. He explained that, unfortunately, he had been unable to come earlier, but wanted to express his admiration for them. He added that a banquet was in order, but regulations prohibited it. Similarly, saké was not to be allowed. Later that month, *bakufu* inspectors arrived to record their family lineages. On the fourth day of the second month, the verdict was read and shortly after, one by one, the rōnin proceeded to their seppuku, beginning with the young Ōishi Chikara. The Matsudaira retainer who supervised the confinement of the rōnin overall served as Chikara's *kaishaku*. Along with *bakufu* inspectors and witnesses, the Matsudaira daimyō attended. He provided that the remains of the rōnin be transported to the Sengakuji for burial. The Matsudaira also paid the expenses for their memorial services.

The rōnin assigned to the Matsudaira house were:

Ōishi Chikara Yoshikane
Okano Kinemon Kanehide
Ōtaka Gengo Tadao
Horibe Yasubei Taketsune
Fuwa Kazuemon Masatane
Kaiga Yazaemon Tomonobu
Sugaya Hannojō Masatoshi
Nakamura Kansuke Masatoki
Kimura Okaemon Sadayuki
Chiba Saburobei Mitsutada[31]

The Mōri Ten

Less is known about the Mōri and Mizuno houses. The ditty suggests that the Mōri were mean-spirited, while the Mizuno were more considerate, like the Hosokawa, in their hospitality for the rōnin. On the fifteenth, Mōri Tsunamoto, daimyō of Chōfu domain in Nagato with a modest income of 50,000 *koku*, was in Edo Castle participating in a ceremonial occasion when, around 11:00 AM, he was called by the grand inspector, Sengoku, and assigned responsibility for confining ten rōnin. Mōri sent two hundred twenty-nine retainers, including ten palanquins, to escort the ten to his main residence in Azabu. As with the Hosokawa, along the way the instructions were clarified with the pick-up location being Sengoku's residence in Atagoshita rather than the Sengakuji. The ten assigned to Mōri custody were, in the order of their seppuku:

Okajima Yasoemon Tsuneki
Yoshida Sawaemon Kanesada
Takebayashi Tadashichi Takashige

---

[31] "Hisamatsu-ke Akō oazuke jin shimatsu ki," pp. 58–106. Akō-shi, *Chūshingura*, vol. 1, p. 252. "Matsudaira Hisamatsu Oki-no-kami Sadanao," *Akō gishi jiten*, pp. 428–429.

Kurahashi Densuke Takeyuki
Muramatsu Kihei Hidenao
Sugino Jūheiji Tsugifusa
Katsuda Shinzaemon Taketaka
Maebara Isuke Munefusa
Hazama Shinroku Mitsukaze
Onodera Kōemon Hidetomi

Within days, Sugino Jūheiji developed an illness, Takebayashi Tadashichi's forehead and hand were bruised, Maebara Isuke developed a tumor, and Okajima Yasōemon had a pox requiring treatment.[32] Whether conditions at the Mōri residence or coincidence resulted in the rash of medical issues, the latter contributed to the perception that confinement there was foul.

New Year's presents were not recorded. By the twenty-seventh day of the first month, genealogies for each of the ten were complete. On the fourth day of the second month, the verdict was handed down. Five *kaishaku* were used in rotation, with each assuming responsibility for two rōnin. The ceremonies were held in the garden off the Red Chamber, with two tatami mats, covered with a white futon, arranged in front of the chamber. Corpses were wrapped in the futon and transported away. Additional tatami were brought next, with similar arrangements. The *kaishaku* concluded each seppuku by presenting the head to the witnesses, confirming death. The remains were placed in rough-hewn casks lined up in the rear curtained area.

The rōnin variously signaled to the *kaishaku*, reportedly either quietly asking for assistance, or requesting that they dirty their hands. One of the rōnin, Hazama Shinroku, rather than calling on his *kaishaku*, reportedly seized the short sword and plunged it into his stomach, opening a wound of approximately twenty centimeters (nearly eight inches) across his abdomen before being beheaded. This was witnessed, Mōri records note, by all the inspectors on the scene. The corpses were sent to the Sengakuji, each in a different palanquin carried by two foot soldiers. Once again, Hazama was an exception. His remains, per his request, were handed over to one of his relatives the following day for transport to the Tsukiji Honganji for burial according to Pure Land Buddhist rites. The remains of the rōnin transported to the Sengakuji, including their

---

[32] "Mōri Kai-no-kami Tsunamoto," *Akō gishi jiten*, p. 434.

clothing, futon, swords, armor, spears, and other personal effects, were reportedly given to the Sengakuji. The chief priest of the Sengakuji, Chō'on, had individual gravestones erected within a fenced-in cemetery, next to their deceased lord. One for Hazama was included even though his remains were ultimately buried elsewhere. A posthumous name was soon given to each rōnin, including Hazama.[33]

The Mizuno Nine

Mizuno Tadayuki, lord of Okazaki Castle in Mikawa province with a substantial income of 325,000 *koku*, had been involved in the Akō incident from the start. Following Asano's attack on Kira in 1701, Mizuno sent a contingent of samurai to Teppozu, where Asano had resided, to ensure that there would be no resistance to confiscation. Prior to that, Mizuno confirmed that the mansion where the imperial emissaries had lodged was cleared of Asano retainers. On the fifteenth day of the twelfth month, Mizuno, once again in the shogun's castle for a ceremonial occasion, was summoned by the elder councilors and instructed to escort ten rōnin to his residence for confinement. The transfer process was delayed by the change in instructions that rerouted the escorts from the Sengakuji to the grand inspector's residence in Atagoshita. Thus, the Mizuno escort, consisting of a modest one hundred and twenty men, only returned to the daimyō's main residence, located in Shiba, after midnight.

The nine rōnin were relocated, on the twentieth, to the secondary Mizuno residence in nearby Mita. The following day, less than a week after assuming charge of them, Mizuno personally met with the group. Thereafter, tea, food, clothing, baths, tobacco, and various dwelling arrangements were provided with evident concern for their well-being. On the third day of the lunar New Year, the group was reportedly served a version of a formal, full-course meal, along with new robes and outer sashes, as well as pairs of split-toed socks.[34]

---

[33] "Akō rōjin oazukari no ki," *Akō gijin sansho*, vol. 2, pp. 6–27. "Mōri Kai-no-kami Tsunamoto," *Akō gishi jiten*, pp. 434–435.

[34] "Mizuno ke oazuke kiroku," pp. 107–136. "Mizuno Kenbutsu Tadayuki," *Akō gishi jiten*, pp. 430–431.

Originally the plan was for Mizuno to confine ten men. At the grand inspector's residence, however, it was learned that one of those assigned to the group, Terasaka Kichiemon, had disappeared. Terasaka's name was on the rōnin declaration of intent, copies of which were left at the Kira mansion and given to the grand inspector and to various members of the group. Also, his name had somehow made the first roll call at the Sengakuji, though not the second. After that point, clearly there was a missing man. Apparently more concerned with securing the forty-six on hand, Terasaka, the forty-seventh rōnin, was not pursued. Though smaller and far less distinguished overall than the other groups, Mizuno's contingent included the rōnin who, despite youth and low standing, had first drawn Kira's blood when he, Hazama Jūjirō Mitsuoki, plunged his spear into the storage shed where Kira was hiding. Thus, the small group included, arguably, one hero of the vendetta.

The Mizuno group included:

Kanzaki Yogorō Noriyasu
Yatō Emoshichi Norikane
Yokokawa Kanpei Munetoshi
Hazama Jūjirō Mitsuoki
Mimura Jirozaemon Kanetsune
Muramatsu Sandayū Takanao
Mase Magokurō Masatoki
Kayano Wasuke Tsunenari
Okuda Sadaemon Yukitaka

Genealogies were recorded late in the first month of the lunar New Year, signaling the end. On the fourth day of the second month, seppuku ceremonies for the nine men ended their fifty-day period of captivity. After the verdict was read, one by one the men proceeded to a garden area surrounded by witnesses, inspectors, foot soldiers, and others assisting in the ceremonies, including the various *kaishaku*. Following their seppuku, the remains were transported to the Sengakuji in a procession of nine palanquins, each carrying a cask, led by a single official on horseback. A lantern bearer and two foot soldiers accompanied each palanquin. Funds for the burial were provided. The swords, clothing, and other personal effects of the rōnin were reportedly given to the Sengakuji as well.[35]

---

[35] Ibid., *Akō gishi shiryō*, vol. 2, pp. 107–136. "Mizuno Kenbutsu Tadayuki," *Akō gishi jiten*, pp. 430–431.

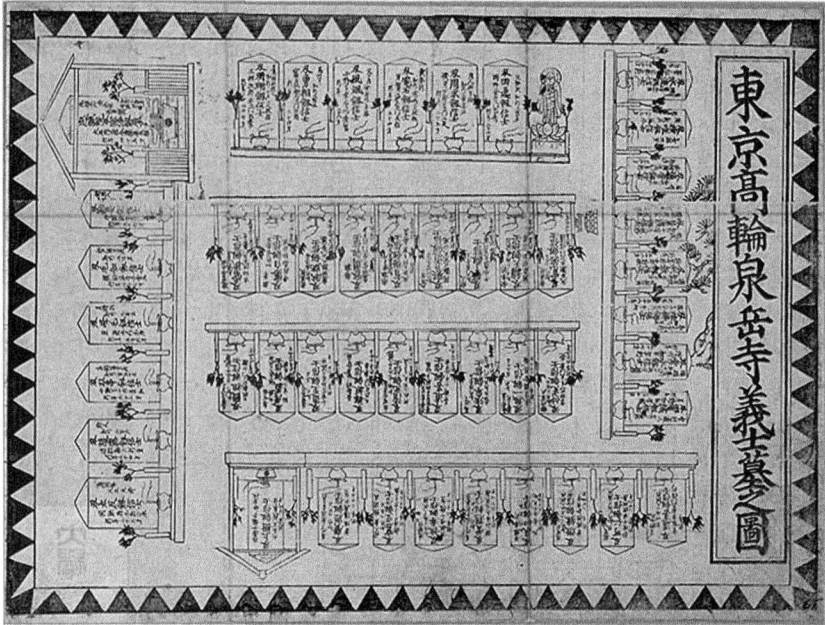

Figure 4.2 Chart of the Sengakuji cemetery. Courtesy of Waseda University, Department of Special Collections.

Final Rites

The chief priest at the Sengakuji, Shūzan Chō'on, who had earlier welcomed the rōnin following their beheading of Kira, had his assistants clear an area adjacent Asano's grave wherein the rōnin were buried individually.[36] Chō'on also offered the last rites and assigned posthumous names for the rōnin. In every case, these names included the word "blade" (*jin*), followed two characters later by a three-word compound *kenshinshi* (loyal samurai [of the] sword), beginning with "sword" (*ken*).[37] The words *jin* and *ken* allude to a Zen *kōan*, or enigmatic teaching, from the *Blue Cliff Record*, an esteemed text of the Sōtō Zen school. The *kōan*, entitled "Jōshū's Great Death," reads:

> Jōshū asked Tōsu, "How is it that one who has died the great death can return to life?"
>
> Tōsu replied, "I don't allow night-wanderers. You must come in the light of day."

[36] *Hakumyō waroku*, p. 122.
[37] Ibid., p. 122. "Genroku gikyo no kōgai," *Akō gishi jiten*, p. 115.

Jōshū (C: Zhaozhou) was a Tang dynasty Chan (Zen) Buddhist master known for his outrageous behavior, in word and purported deed. Tōsu was one of his comrades. Jōshū's question was meant to prompt realization of the Zen mind, yet Tōsu rebuffs him by saying, in effect, that he does not answer such beclouded questions, and will only consider Jōshū when the latter joins him in the light of day, i.e., with an enlightened mind.

Chō'on presumably understood the "great death" to be comparable to that of the rōnin, now returning to him as corpses at the Sengakuji. For Chō'on, those mind-blowing events must have amounted to a real life-and-death Zen *kōan*, the likes of which few priests and temples would ever encounter. Tōsu's response, "I don't allow night-wanderers," could easily be applied to the rōnin, who had wandered through the middle of the night, only to arrive at the Sengakuji with the light of day, as if performing a *kōan*, and bringing with them some form of enlightenment that Chō'on recognized. Then, once more, as corpses, they came at dusk, not as wanderers but for final repose at the Sengakuji following their seppuku. The chief priest did not mean to praise or condemn so much as to recognize how their vendetta resonated, uncannily, with the enigma of the *kōan*, meant to engender, at some level, the Buddha mind.

The "Instruction" that follows "Jōshū's Great Death" includes the words *jin* and *ken*, making the relevance of that *kōan* clearer. It states:

> Where right and wrong cross over, even the sage cannot know. Where rebellion and submission intersect, even the Buddha cannot distinguish. Acting as one who has cut off the world and divorced himself from ethics, he manifests the abilities of a great warrior who has broken loose from the crowd. He walks on top of icy peaks, and runs across sword blades, as though the head and horns of the *kirin*, or a lotus flower in a blazing fire. Seeing another who has transcended all barriers, he realizes immediately that person follows the same way. Who might be a good companion for him? To test, I cite this case. Look!

Chō'on's allusion to "Jōshū's Great Death" in the posthumous names assigned to the forty-six might be called the Sengakuji's Zen Buddhist reading of the rōnin and their vendetta. The rōnin had presumably trod the path where right and wrong, good and bad intersected. They had committed mass murder and then outrageously brought a grisly trophy,

Kira's head, as proof to the temple, without warning or permission, for direct presentation before the grave of their lord. As ordinary men, their deeds were utterly evil, but as samurai, they could not be called such. Even the shogunate had informed the four daimyō detaining the rōnin that they were not to be treated as "egregious criminals." Instead, their deeds arguably manifested the profound duty that they felt they owed their lord, nothing more.

The rōnin had also acted in a way that amounted to rebellion, even treason, against the shogunally decreed order. Tsunayoshi had declared their lord, not Kira, a criminal. In taking Kira as their enemy, the rōnin had positioned themselves against the political and legal order of the day, and Chō'on surely understood that too. But they also submitted to that order in reporting their deeds, making their act of rebellion a paradoxical one that, as the *kōan* suggests, even sages and Buddhas might not easily comprehend. The *kōan* also suggests that those who act in the space where right and wrong intersect, and where rebellion and subservience cross paths, reveal the ability of the great warrior standing out from the crowd. Such people, without equal and beyond compare, do the impossible, walking across icy peaks and running on top of swords, much as the rōnin had launched their invasion in the dead of a cold winter's night, and in battle with Kira's defenders, seemingly ran over the tops of swords to take vengeance. Such men, Chō'on suggests, were rarities, "as though the head and horns of the kirin ... and a lotus in fire," virtual impossibilities by any ordinary standards. Chō'on presumably saw in the rōnin those who had "transcended all barriers." Who would be a good match for them? Perhaps Jōshū and Tōsu. In any event, rather than as "loyal retainers and righteous samurai," as later Confucians would interpret the rōnin, Chō'on situates them in the realm of the incomprehensible, beyond even the discernment of the Buddha.

Many in Edo regretted the deaths of the rōnin, including some with bitter feelings toward the shogunate. Talk of the medieval loyalist Kusunoki Masashige, who died fighting for the imperial cause, was revived, along with worries about the angry, vengeful spirits of other loyalist warriors who met their ends tragically and then brought disaster and terror down on the world. Stories circulated shortly after the rōnin were buried that a typhoon, caused by their spirits, struck Edo. Other accounts claimed that during the middle of the night following their burial, violent winds, rain, thunder, lightning, and even hail storms came out of nowhere. Earthquakes were also attributed to their vengeful

Figure 4.3 Sengakuji gravestone of Ōishi Kura-no-suke. Photograph by the author.

spirits. Gekkai denies all of this, recalling how in the days after the rōnin seppuku, temple monks had worked in the cemetery, leveling the ground, clearing the area, removing bamboo, trees, and rocks, and making stone pagodas. Throughout that time, the weather was "most pleasant" and the monks had not needed an umbrella or a straw rain-coat. Gekkai admits that there were some evening showers, but denies that there was heavy rain.[38]

---

[38] *Hakumyō waroku*, pp. 125–126.

Important though the *seppuku* was, it soon vanished from the narrative, at least insofar as the latter was influenced by dramatic representations of the vendetta. While Chikamatsu Monzaemon's *Taiheiki on a Game Board* included it, the later dramatization, the great *Kanadehon Chūshingura*, with its romanticized reinvention of the vendetta, did not. Even before the rōnin were buried, reformulations of the incident in rumor, gossip, and street-level popular culture were taking shape, dealing with its ending variously. The vendetta thus reappeared in the form of successive cultural doppelgängers, double goers coexisting alongside the historical past and conjuring up the shocking deeds, but also representing them in ways that contested the ambiguities of the historical events and provided for, in some cases, a more palatable, even poignantly beautiful and spiritually significant reception for them. First, however, successive philosophical doubles were articulated, transforming the vendetta's brutish physicality into the rarified stuff of Confucian ethical discourse. While not as entertaining as the dramatic and artistic reincarnations, the philosophical debate defined the rōnin spiritually in ways important for their later reception in history.

5 CONFUCIAN VERSUS CONFUCIAN DEBATES

Historical accounts of the vendetta sometimes end with the rōnin seppuku, or leap to a brief survey of the incident as dramatized in puppet and kabuki theatre. Yet such narratives give short shrift to a crucial interpretive moment, the Confucian debates, wherein another verdict, the ethical and spiritual, was considered. This chapter explores the positions advanced praising, condemning, and both praising and condemning the rōnin. Overall, it suggests that the central issue was whether the rōnin merited recognition as *chūshin gishi*. While translatable as "loyal and righteous samurai," the notion also signified, in Confucian discourse, such retainers who died for a larger cause and so merited sacrificial reverence at a shrine dedicated to them. The debates were then, most profoundly, ones over the spiritual status of the rōnin. This chapter also discusses the political implications of such conclusions vis-à-vis the Tokugawa shogunate.

The Confucian Context

The first major reformulations of the vendetta were philosophical ones produced by a succession of Confucian scholars recording their ethical verdicts on what was the most sensational event of their day. By the early eighteenth century, Confucian learning was flourishing as the newly risen intellectual wave in Tokugawa cultural life. A host of scholars and teachers helped transform the philosophical horizons of the times, away from medieval Buddhist and nativist teachings and toward more progressive worldviews emphasizing the ultimacy of the self, the family, the polity, ethics, and the cosmos. With this transformation, semantically and ethically charged notions of righteousness, duty, justice, loyalty, courage, and humaneness came to occupy center stage of early modern sociopolitical discourse.

Evidence of this transformation appeared promptly as Confucian debates about the ethics of the vendetta spontaneously surfaced and then multiplied. Before long, commenting on the incident became a philosophical priority that nearly every major post-vendetta Confucian felt obliged to undertake. Even before the attack on Kira's mansion, some of the rōnin had already drafted a Confucian justification of the vendetta league and its goal of eliminating Kira, claiming that doing so was an expression of the decree of heaven (*tenmei*). Their text, *Akō Castle League*, praised the loyalty and righteousness of the rōnin band and denounced the disloyalty of those who had defected. The rōnin declaration of intent, also drafted before the attack, explained the group's determination to take Kira's life via an allusion to the Confucian *Book of Rites*, noting how a son could not live under the same heaven as the enemy of his deceased father. Thus, Confucian discourse informed the vendetta well before it had achieved success. It was an integral part of the rōnin mentality, evident in their conceptualizations of their imminent deeds. Moreover, Confucianism continued to inform discussions of the vendetta for the next two centuries, with the seminal positions articulated in the mid-Tokugawa affirmed or denied over and again.

Admittedly, Buddhists had contributed, as did the chief priest at the Sengakuji, in assigning posthumous names and providing for their burials. Also, the Sengakuji monk, Gekkai, in his *Memoir* of three decades later, recalled the rōnin at that Zen temple in the hours following their attack on Kira's mansion. Itinerant monks, noting the vendetta's draw, soon featured it in their sermons. Yet for Buddhists, the vendetta grew from misguided attachments to transitory, this-worldly things such as personal honor, loyalty to one's lord, domains, castles, ranks and titles, etc., rather than enlightened recognition of the non-substantial, ultimate emptiness of all things. As a result, Buddhists did not play as prominent roles in addressing the vendetta's mundane ethics and its sociopolitical weight as did more empirically minded Confucians determined, as they were, to investigate things and fathom their rational principles.

For Confucians, the vendetta became a hot-button issue about which it was difficult if not impossible to remain silent. Even though the incident recalled, in the minds of many Confucians, ancient, legendary loyalist-martyrs from the depths of Chinese history such as Bo Yi and Shu Qi, Japanese Confucians recognized in the dramatic events their contemporaries, now martyred, having made ultimately fateful, ethical decisions of perennial significance. The challenge for scholars was to assess the judgments and deeds of the rōnin vis-à-vis loyalty, righteousness, and the prerogatives of rulers. While there was no consensus on these issues, at least one question – whether the rōnin were "loyal and righteous samurai" (*chūshin gishi*) – came to inform virtually all Confucian statements about the vendetta.

The vendetta's impact on social and political discourse was considerable. Admiration for the rōnin was widespread early on, but the Edo man-in-the-street would not likely have concluded, one way or the other, that the rōnin had or had not exemplified the virtues of *chūshin gishi*. Conclusions eventually emerged, but only with ethical guidance generated by the ongoing discussions of Confucian scholars. As philosophy filtered down, popular conceptions incorporated ethical jargon, lauding the rōnin as "loyal retainers" (*chūshin*), "righteous samurai" (*gishi*), "righteous retainers" (*gishin*), or "righteous men" (*gijin*), or condemning them as the very antitheses. Yet in every case, popular discourse appealed to key Confucian concepts, elevating the vendetta to a decidedly ethical plane defined largely by the philosophical parameters earlier articulated by leading scholars. The vendetta thus transformed into a more decidedly Confucian incident, thoroughly permeated with Confucian values, metaphysics, and inescapable ethical judgments of praise or blame.

Along the way, the vendetta spawned successive philosophical doubles contesting, restating, and representing the events via essays and philosophical narratives addressing ethical questions, categories, and conclusions. Rather than just one cultural double appearing on the scene, multiple doppelgängers as philosophical dialectic affirming and denying rōnin righteousness surfaced time and again, overlaying knowledge and memories of the gruesome events, morphing them into something more theoretically and ethically abstract if not universal. With another step, the historical vendetta and its philosophical expressions assumed a decidedly different form, that of the spiritually substantial drama. Differences in genre and exposition aside, the Confucian genealogy of at least one such stage version was laid bare in its name, *Kanadehon Chūshingura.*

The notion *chūshin gishi* was pivotal throughout the Confucian debates. Although translatable via its components as "loyal and righteous samurai" or "loyal and dutiful samurai," such easy glosses hardly capture its larger spiritual significance. Ultimately, the notion meant far more than the sum of its parts. As a compound in religio-philosophical discourse spanning East Asia, it harbored spiritual nuances that vendetta discussions assumed as a crucial albeit typically unspoken subtext. Scholars understood *chūshin gishi* to denote persons who were not only loyal and righteous, but who had sacrificed their lives for some transcendent cause associated with a ruler or a realm. Those recognized as *chūshin gishi* were, according to key Confucians writings, fit to be enshrined and revered at spiritual venues specifically designated for such, via regulated sacrifice. They were, then, *kami*, or spiritually powerful deities.

The Hosokawa daimyō recognized as much in declaring that the rōnin who committed seppuku at his mansion would be its *mamorigami,* or protective deities. Confucian scholars, however, preferred classical authority rather than daimyō decree to legitimize such reverence. And the *Book of Rites*, part of the ancient Confucian canon, provided solid classical grounds for such. Yet Tokugawa discussions were more directly influenced by a late Song dynasty scholar, Chen Beixi (1159–1223), and his *Lexicography of Confucian Terms (Xingli ziyi, ca. 1226; J: Seiri jigi).* There, Beixi defined the religious contours of *zhongchen yishi* – as *chūshin gishi* is read in Chinese – in ways that became, in Tokugawa Japan, directly pertinent to the debates. Via commentaries on and colloquial explications of Beixi's *Lexicography*, Hayashi Razan and others introduced Beixi's ideas into the semantic arena of Tokugawa ideas, along the way transforming their nuances in accordance with the indigenous sociopolitical realities of the Tokugawa polity.

Reading the debates in terms of these nuances is important on three counts. First, a new religio-spiritual layer of significance emerges, one related to the status of the rōnin vis-à-vis sacrificial reverence and veneration. If recognized as *chūshin gishi*, the rōnin would merit shrines dedicated to them. Given the consequential nature of this for the spiritual horizon, the Confucian debates were hardly tedious anticipations of the popular dramatization, *Kanadehon Chūshingura.* Instead, they involved at their core an essentially religious question: were the rōnin worthy of spiritual remembrance?

Second, the shogunate's legal and political concerns appear in a new light. Recognizing the rōnin as *chūshin gishi* would raise sensitive and potentially embarrassing questions about the shogunate's judicial decisions. The shogunate had condemned the rōnin as criminals and punished them with death via seppuku. Allowing enshrinement would conceivably sanction spiritual venues for possible critiques of shogunal justice. Therefore, neither the shogunate nor obliging scholars concerned with the spiritual and legal foundations of Tokugawa authority were likely to acknowledge, graciously, that the rōnin were *chūshin gishi*. Affirming as much, however, did not necessarily imply political opposition. Rather, those recognizing the rōnin as *chūshin gishi* might simply mean to emphasize that the foundations of shogunal legitimacy should consist in personal bonds defined by loyalty, duty, and honor rather than legal relations. Yet even such a solicitous perspective might have seemed suspect to the shogunate that had, irrevocably, sentenced to death the rōnin and their lord.

Third, new insights about the nature of philosophical power struggles among contemporary Confucian schools emerge. In the debates, neither those lauding the rōnin as *chūshin gishi* nor those denying the same had any praise for Yamaga Sokō. Representatives of different Confucian schools blamed Yamaga's teachings for the vendetta, implying that they turned students into felons rather than *kami*. Consequently, one significant philosophical casualty of the debates was Yamaga's school, at least as an active force in Edo. Nevertheless, his teachings eventually resurfaced in outer hinterland domains such as Chōshū, where those advancing the Yamaga philosophy came to embrace and retool the spurious allegations of Yamaga's impact on the forty-seven rōnin for their own ideological purposes. In the Meiji period, with the political rise of former Chōshū samurai influenced by the retooled Yamaga teachings, the rōnin came to be revered in ways profoundly unprecedented in Tokugawa times, with an imperial rescript from the Meiji emperor read before their graves. With that act, the question of whether the rōnin merited spiritual remembrance seemed unequivocally answered.

Hayashi Razan and *Chūshin gishi*

Prior to the Tokugawa, Japanese history had produced no discussions of *chūshin gishi*. Its earliest appearance in Tokugawa discourse occurred when Hayashi Razan, in promoting Beixi's Confucian lexicon,

Figure 5.1 Hayashi Razan. Courtesy of Waseda University, Department of Special Collections.

explained the meaning of the Chinese term *zhongchen yishi*, read in Japanese as *chūshin gishi*. Beixi, a late Song dynasty disciple of Zhu Xi, addressed the notion several times while discussing legitimate forms of sacrificial worship. Hayashi's remarks were basically vernacular repetitions of Beixi, but they also added to what Beixi had simply adumbrated. For example, in discussing "ghosts and spirits," Beixi noted:

> In later ages, there were loyal subjects and righteous scholars (*zhongchen yishi/chūshin gishi*) who plunged into naked blades, sacrificing themselves to prevent calamities and dangers ... Zhang Xun and Xu Yuan died defending Suiyang; thus a double temple was founded to enshrine them. Su Zhongyong died in Yongzhou,

and so a temple was established for him there. The King of Manifest Spirit of Zhangzhou sacrificed his life to defend his people and therefore they built a temple so that they could offer sacrifices. These shrines for loyal subjects and righteous knight-scholars (*zhongchen yishi*) were, in each case, legitimate ones.[1]

Aware that Beixi's allusions to Zhang Xun, Xu Yuan, Su Zhongyong, and the King of Manifest Spirit would mean little to most readers, Hayashi annotated the *Ziyi* passage with material from Chinese dynastic histories detailing the heroic deeds of these *chūshin gishi*.

In identifying Zhang Xun and Xu Yuan, Hayashi drew biographical data from the *History of the Tang Dynasty*. One account related that Xu Yuan and Zhang Xun defended the city of Suiyang during the final year of the An Lushan (d. 757) rebellion. Although killed by rebels, Zhang and Xu were later enshrined as *zhongchen yishi* for their heroic defense of the dynasty. Hayashi also offered accounts from the *History of the Song Dynasty* relating that Su Zhongyong had been enshrined after he burned himself to death following his defeat by an invading force from areas south of China. Hayashi turned to the *History of the Tang Dynasty* and the *History of Fukien* for data on the King of Manifest Spirit, relating the real name of this Tang general, Chen Yuanguang, and his military and political exploits in establishing Chinese rule over what is today Fujian province.[2] Shrines honoring, then apotheosizing Chen Yuanguang followed.[3]

Hayashi's vernacular accounts thus made explicit what for Chinese Confucians was well known: that those who sacrificed themselves for the defense of their dynasty, culture, and people could be legitimately honored and worshiped at shrines established for that purpose. Hayashi's presentation of Beixi casts *zhongchen yishi* in terms of a proto-national realm: he explains that Beixi's mention of "those of great accomplishments" refers to "people who possess great, meritorious virtue and establish a political order encompassing the realm below heaven." Hayashi adds, "when those of great accomplishments are

---

[1] Chen Beixi, *Xingli ziyi*, 40b–41a. Wing-tsit Chan, trans., *Neo-Confucian Terms Explained* (New York: Columbia University Press, 1985), p. 156.

[2] Hayashi Razan, *Seiri jigi genkai*, vol. 8.

[3] Hugh Clark, "What Makes a Chinese God? Or, What Makes a God Chinese?" in Victor H. Mair and Liam Kelley, eds., *Imperial China and Its Southern Neighbors* (Singapore: Institute for Southeast Asian Studies, 2015), pp. 112–116.

revered and worshiped, so should *chūshin gishi*."[4] Hayashi's remarks were presumably meant to ensure that enshrined *chūshin gishi* would be compatible with the interests of the Tokugawa realm. Hayashi most likely had no inkling that a later band of vengeful rōnin would become Japan's most famous *chūshin gishi*.

Divided Minds

A high-ranking Confucian serving the shogunate, Hayashi Hōkō, wrote the first essay defending the rōnin even while simultaneously recognizing the importance of upholding the law. He had few choices regarding his judgment that the rōnin had broken shogunal law. His grandfather, Hayashi Razan, had served the first three shoguns as a scholar, advancing Confucian learning in the shogun's capital. As part of his work, Hayashi Razan founded the "Hall of the Early Sages," a Confucian temple-academy located just north of Edo Castle in the Shinobugaoka area (today, Ueno). In 1691, a decade before Asano's attack on Kira, Tsunayoshi had the Hall of the Early Sages moved to a new location in Yushima named Shōhei (after the birthplace of Confucius), and appointed Hayashi Hōkō to serve as its supervisor (*daigaku-no-kami*).

By then, the Hayashi were hereditary scholar-retainers, a status they would retain until the end of the Tokugawa. Hayashi Hōkō's grandfather, despite his commitment to Confucianism, had shaved his head and worn Buddhist robes as a condition for serving the shogunate, which early on expected its scholar-advisors to appear as Buddhists. Hayashi Hōkō had that requirement changed so that he and subsequent Confucian scholars would be received as Confucians. With his new standing as supervisor of the Confucian temple-academy and his professional status equivalent to that of a samurai, Hayashi Hōkō found personal cause to admire the rōnin, even as his service to the shogunate as a scholar-official prompted him to condemn the resort to violence first by Asano and later by the rōnin. Although Ogyū Sorai's thinking on the vendetta is often cited as the decisive influence on the shogunate's verdict, the text attributed to Ogyū in this context is dubious, making its significance in the judicial settlement questionable. Instead, Hayashi's

---

[4] Hayashi Razan, *Seiri jigi genkai*, vol. 8.

views, recorded shortly after the vendetta, appear to have been the most compelling ones.

Hayashi's essay "On Revenge" opens by recounting how forty-six men, including Ōishi Kura-no-suke, banded together, "uniting their minds and hearts as one," for the sake of their deceased lord. Hayashi does not name Asano, but instead simply refers to "a certain samurai retainer of the Kansai area." He relates that the rōnin took their revenge nearly a year later and were subsequently placed under arrest. After detailed investigations, the shogunate decided to have the men commit seppuku. Hayashi then considers a question from a hypothetical interlocutor: why must those who take revenge on the enemies of their lords or their fathers be sentenced to death? The questioner notes that the three bonds – between ruler and minister, father and son, and man and wife – are based on the highest principles of heaven and human ethics. The *Book of Rites* thus states, "One should not live under the same heaven with the enemy of one's father." The interlocutor claims that forbidding revenge against these enemies violates the ultimate principles of ethics as set forth by the early kings and as affirmed in the hearts and minds of "loyal retainers and filial sons" (*chūshin kōshi*).[5]

Hayashi responds by recalling that revenge is recognized in ancient Confucian classics such the *Book of Rites*, the *Rites of the Zhou*, and the *Spring and Autumn Annals*. He admits that Confucian discussions from the Tang, Song, and Ming dynasties also allow revenge against the enemy of one's lord. Hayashi adds that from the perspective of the hearts and minds of the rōnin, it was unbearable to continue sharing the same heaven, i.e., live in the same world, as the enemy of their lord. Moreover, he observes that enduring shame and humiliation is not the way of the samurai. Yet Hayashi also insists that the matter must be considered from the perspective of law (*hōritsu*), and that anyone who considers the law their enemy must be put to death. In fulfilling their lord's final intentions, i.e., in killing Kira, the rōnin inevitably made the law that prevails in the realm below heaven their enemy. Therefore, they were guilty of a capital crime. Because they

5 Hayashi Hōkō, *Fukushū ron*, in *Kinsei buke shisō*, NST vol. 27, ed. Ishii Shirō (Tokyo: Iwanami shoten, 1974), pp. 372, 374. A partial translation is in Wm. Theodore de Bary, Carol Gluck, and Arthur E. Tiedemann, eds., *Sources of Japanese Tradition, Volume Two: 1600–2000, Part One: 1600–1868* (New York: Columbia University Press, 2006), pp. 359–361. Also, Hiroaki Satō, *Legends of the Samurai* (Woodstock, NY: The Overlook Press, 1995), pp. 322–325.

rebelliously defied the authorities, they had to be sentenced to death for the sake of clarifying the legal standards of the realm.[6]

Hayashi adds, however, that while the two perspectives – those of the loyal samurai and the law – are not identical, neither are they necessarily contradictory. He explains:

> Above, there should be "humane rulers and worthy ministers" who hand down decrees clarifying the law. Below, there should be "loyal retainers and righteous samurai" (*chūshin gishi*) who express their fury in following through with their sense of purpose. If they submit themselves to the death penalty for the sake of upholding the law, why should their minds and hearts harbor any regrets.[7]

Hayashi thus suggests that rulers must do their duty in governing, while *chūshin gishi* must do theirs in fulfilling their sense of purpose and determination. That did not mean, however, that the rōnin were common criminals. Rather they were indeed *chūshin gishi* fulfilling their determination, and in the process, necessarily violated the law, for which they were put to death. Given their sense of purpose, this was nothing to regret. Rather, their fate reflected the ultimate nature of their purpose.

Having recognized the rōnin as *chūshin gishi*, Hayashi continues his discussion of the vendetta by relating:

> The ancients had a saying, "When the world is governed well for a long time, then people's minds and hearts become lax." Fortunately, we find ourselves in an age comparable to that [of the ancient sages] Yao and Shun, one in which people prosper and enjoy life. Indeed, there has never been a time of such abundance. Worldly samurai now immerse themselves in bounty and grow indolent in their minds and hearts ... The rōnin vendetta occurred at such a time, arousing and awakening the [samurai of the] age to confront their duty and bring it to bear on their minds and hearts. Accordingly, rulers will know they should be able to trust their retainers, and retainers will know that they should be loyal to their lords.[8]

---

[6] Satō, *Legends of the Samurai*, pp. 372–373, 374.   [7] Ibid., p. 373.   [8] Ibid., p. 373.

Hayashi thus recognizes the rōnin for awakening an indolent, self-indulgent age to the importance of duty, loyalty, and self-sacrifice. Their seppuku presumably displayed to the world, in Hayashi's view, their final and complete expression of selfless service.

Hayashi next cites several canonized Chinese retainers, including Yan Zhenqing, Wang Chu, Yu Rang, and Tian Heng who died serving their respective dynastic causes. In Tian Heng's case, his five hundred retainers, upon hearing of his suicide, reportedly committed mass suicide to join him in the afterlife. Much as Tian Heng was a heroic figure in his day, so were the rōnin "outstanding heroes of their generation." Hayashi's essay ends with a poem commemorating the rōnin. The final lines read:

> Pure sincerity penetrates the sun, so why regret death.
> Righteous energy overcomes mountains, while existence is trifling.
> The forty-six men all bowed to their swords.
> Heaven above, without partiality, assists the loyal and the strong.[9]

While Hayashi no doubt upholds the importance of the law, he praises the rōnin far more than might be expected from a shogunal scholar. In suggesting that the rōnin were *chūshin gishi*, he forged a new ethical identity for them, one casting them as moral exemplars of loyalty and righteous duty, virtues central to any conception of the way of the samurai.

Hayashi Hōkō knew Chen Beixi's text through the commentaries of his grandfather, Hayashi Razan, and in referring to the rōnin as *chūshin gishi* was suggesting, as an implicit subtext, that they could be legitimately worshiped as exemplars of loyalty and duty. As things turned out, the rōnin were promptly and spontaneously worshipped at the Sengakuji. Muro Kyūsō's writings on the vendetta note that once people learned there were gravestones for the rōnin, they visited the Sengakuji in large numbers, mourning before their graves, weeping and offering incense for months on end.[10] Popular reverence for the rōnin clearly did not wait on the Confucian debates for its sanction. That aside, in casting the rōnin as *chūshin gishi*, Hayashi Hōkō surely defined one of the most fundamental positions informing later Confucian

---

[9] Ibid., pp. 373, 375.
[10] Muro Kyūsō, *Akō gijin roku, Kinsei buke shisō*, NST vol. 27, p. 315.

writings on the vendetta. Whatever else might be said, scholars were subsequently obliged to declare whether they considered the rōnin worthy of status as *chūshin gishi*.

Praising the Righteous Men

The first detailed study unequivocally praising the rōnin as righteous samurai (*gishi*) was by Muro Kyūsō, a scholar-retainer serving Maeda Tsunanori, lord of Kanazawa domain. Muro's *Records of the Righteous Men of Akō Domain*, completed less than a year after the rōnin seppuku, provides an in-depth narrative, historical and philosophical, of the incident from Asano's attack on Kira, through the deaths of the rōnin in the spring of 1703, to their burial at the Sengakuji. The second half of *The Righteous Men* includes biographies of the rōnin, arranged according to the daimyō houses where they met their ends. Although Muro's work includes uncorroborated details, legends, and naïve fictions, it is sometimes referred to as the first quasi-historical examination of the vendetta. No doubt, however, when considered from the perspective of rigorous modern historical scholarship, Muro's early eighteenth-century study is lacking.[11] In addressing the problem of Terasaka, the rōnin who vanished, Muro explains that he was sent by Ōishi to inform Asano Daigaku of the vendetta's success. For that reason, Muro did not consider Terasaka a coward, but instead included him as one of the "righteous men." By Muro's count, then, there were forty-seven. Following Muro's text, the rōnin were widely – though not in every case – referred to as forty-seven in number.[12] While Muro's count of the rōnin has been influential, he offers no real evidence for his claim that Terasaka left the group honorably to report on the outcome of the attack.

In assessing the vendetta, Muro errs on the side of generosity: his title announces his view that the rōnin were "righteous men" (*gijin*) who did what they felt right duty compelled them to do, regardless of the consequences. Muro does not mention *chūshin gishi* as such, but so frequently broaches the notion via its constituent parts that his familiarity with the term and its nuances seems more than evident. For

---

[11] Shigeno, "Preface," *Akō gishi jitsuwa*, pp. vi–vii. Miyazawa, *Akō rōshi*, p. 5.
[12] Miyazawa, *Akō rōshi*, p. 172. Hayashi Hōkō referred to the "forty-six" rōnin.

example, he refers to the rōnin not as rōnin but glowingly as "righteous samurai" (*gishi*), "righteous men" (*gijin*), and as "loyal retainers" (*chūshin*), adding that they "illuminated the way of loyalty and righteousness (*chūgi no michi*) for posterity." Muro's correspondence with other scholars refers to Beixi's *Ziyi*, leaving little doubt that he knew that text and was familiar with Beixi's thoughts on *chūshin gishi*. Muro also alludes to major figures in Chinese loyalist literature such as Wen Tianxiang, suggesting that he understood the spiritual significance of *chūshin gishi*. Muro's signature praise for the rōnin as *gijin*, however, need not be interpreted as critical of the shogunate so much as a reflection of his belief that the authority of the shogunate grew from ethical foundations, specifically the kind of absolute loyalism evident in the vendetta.

Muro's preface to *The Righteous Men* introduces his philosophical sympathies. The opening lines relate how one autumn afternoon some of his students stopped by to visit. Together, they read portions of his text and wept, saddened that there were no rewards for "loyalty and goodness," and that no one seemed to understand the way of heaven. Nevertheless, Muro and his disciples remained confident that the ancient Confucian text, the *Mencius*, was correct in declaring that "ethical principles and righteousness please the minds and hearts of people everywhere" (6A/7). One student then asked whether Muro's view, affirming the rōnin as righteous, undermined public law by elevating personal opinions. After all, the shogunate had already passed judgment on the matter.

Replying on Muro's behalf, another student reportedly recalled how, in ancient China, Bo Yi and his brother Shu Qi had stood in front of King Wu's war chariots when they felt that Wu's military initiatives were wrong. Somewhat similarly, the rōnin opposed the leniency shown Kira by taking matters into their own hands and killing him, even though that meant giving up their lives in the process. Thus, in Muro's opinion, the Akō retainers had sacrificed themselves for what they believed was a righteous cause. Just as King Wu's advisor, Lü Shang, praised Bo Yi and Shu Qi even though they had tried to block King Wu's military expedition, so might Muro praise the Akō retainers as righteous men even though the shogunate had condemned them to death as criminals. Muro's high moral estimation of the men did not, then, mean that he meant to undermine the integrity of the law or the shogunate. Another student added that since Muro's discussions were restricted to his school, they did not impair the shogunate's verdict. With this, the students departed and Muro recorded the exchange in his preface.[13]

The comments of Muro and his students amount to a defense of "righteous opposition," and something akin to civil disobedience. Overall, Muro's adulatory narrative stands as the single most positive Confucian ethical assessment of the rōnin, one comparing them to the ancient legendary figures, Bo Yi and Shu Qi, who made repeated principled stands in opposition to unjust political systems, and ultimately starved themselves to death for the sake of righteousness. For their high-mindedness, they were later praised as worthies if not sages. In likening the rōnin to Bo Yi and Shu Qi, Muro grouped the rōnin with some of the most esteemed figures in the entire Confucian tradition.

Criticizing the Rōnin?

Studies of the vendetta typically highlight the writings of Ogyū Sorai, a scholar-advisor of Yanagisawa Yoshiyasu. Because Yanagisawa had a key role in sentencing Asano, Ogyū's influence on the verdict is thought to have been considerable. A work attributed to Ogyū, "Memorandum on Law," is typically cited in this context. However, in his study of the debates, Tahara Tsuguo questioned the authenticity of that text. Another piece by Ogyū, "Essay on the Forty-Seven Samurai," though infrequently mentioned, is arguably more authentic. Nevertheless, the two works, although profoundly different, are discussed in tandem, albeit with the caveat that "Memorandum on Law" is suspect, and might well have been written by a later disciple or someone imitating Sorai's style. Yet that two very different opinions on the vendetta would be attributed to Sorai indicates the extent to which the vendetta was indeed a philosophical site of ongoing controversy, disagreement, and debate. Either Sorai himself changed his mind about things, or others writing under his name decided to realign his high standing as a thinker to fit their agenda vis-à-vis the rōnin controversy.

Further complicating matters is that Yanagisawa Yoshiyasu's memoir relates that Ogyū only communicated his thoughts on the vendetta orally, and that he, Yanagisawa, then discussed the matter

---

[13] Muro, *Akō gijin roku*, pp. 272–273, 343.

Figure 5.2 Ogyū Sorai. Courtesy of Waseda University, Department of Special Collections.

the following day with the shogun. Yanagisawa thus does not assign much credit to Ogyū's views, and none to his writings, in the decision-making process.[14] Nevertheless, Ogyū's alleged writings are important insofar as they stand as another set of expressions of Confucian thinking on the vendetta. If the texts attributed to him are authentic, Ogyū was among the first, if not the first, to criticize the vendetta. Curiously, however, Ogyū's supposed critique of the vendetta never elicited the counterstatements that later critiques by Satō Naokata and Dazai

[14] Tahara Tsuguo, *Akō shijūroku shi ron: bakuhansei no seishin kōzō* (Tokyo: Yoshikawa kōbunkan, 1978), pp. 68–69. Also, Akō sōmubu shishi hensanshitsu, *Chūshingura* vol. 1 (Akō: Akōshi, 1989), pp. 330–331, suggests that the *Giritsusho* was most likely a later work written by a scholar. Instead, it discusses Ogyū's "Essay on the Forty-Seven Samurai" as the authentic expression of his views. The *Giritsusho* is not included in the *Kinsei buke shisō*, NST vol. 27. James McMullen's "Confucian Perspectives on the Akō Revenge," *Monumenta Nipponica*, pp. 299–300, briefly discusses Sorai's *Giritsusho*, but only mentions Ogyū's "Essay on the Forty-Seven Samurai" in a note, suggesting, contrary to Tahara, that it is questionable and the *Giritsusho* is more reliable.

Shundai certainly did. One can only conclude that if Ogyū indeed recorded his thoughts, he did not think it prudent to circulate them widely. Overall, the impact of the writings attributed to him on the vendetta and the larger debate seems to have been exaggerated.

Ogyū's "Essay on the Forty-Seven Samurai" opens with a recapitulation of the vendetta. He first notes that Asano, acting on a "personal grudge," drew his sword and attacked Kira in the shogun's castle. That evening, Asano was sentenced to death and his domain confiscated. However, Kira was not punished. Later, in the twelfth month of the following year, a band of forty-seven rōnin invaded Kira's residence and beheaded him. After being arrested and confined, they were put to death in the second month of 1703. Thereafter everyone praised them as "righteous samurai" (gishi) for having sacrificed their lives on behalf of their deceased master. Ogyū, however, objects unequivocally to such praise for the rōnin, asserting that their deaths were as senseless as the suicide of Tian Heng's five hundred retainers. Ogyū emphasizes that it was Asano who wanted to kill Kira. Kira, however, had no desire to kill Asano. Therefore, Ogyū reasons, Kira was not Asano's enemy, and so the rōnin had no reason to kill him.

Ogyū declares that Asano attacked Kira in a moment of anger, forgetting his responsibility to maintain his family line. Therefore, his actions were "not righteous" (fugi). At best, Asano's retainers simply carried out his "wicked intentions." How, Ogyū asks, can that be called righteous? Ogyū concludes that the whole matter was an egregious tragedy. In closing his essay, Ogyū mentions the case of Ichibei, a peasant who lived in Kazusa. After his village headman was exiled for having committed a crime, Ichibei assumed responsibility for the headman's family, all the while petitioning for the return of his master's estate. Finally, the petition was granted. Ogyū judges Ichibei's approach to righteous objection to misrule to have been vastly superior to that of the rōnin.[15]

"Memorandum on Law" presents a different analysis of the matter, one similar to Hayashi Hōkō's in its balance of praise and condemnation. It explains that righteousness is the way that brings honor to the self, while the law is the standard for all below heaven. In taking revenge on their lord's enemy, the forty-six samurai well understood the shame that comes to samurai who fail to act rightly. Thus, they followed

---

[15] Ogyū Sorai, "Shijūshichi shi no koto o ronzu," *Kinsei buke shisō*, pp. 400–401.

the way that brings honor, and in that respect their vendetta could be called righteous. However, such righteousness is ultimately a private matter. "Memorandum on Law" adds that Asano's disregard for the shogun's castle was, from the perspective of his public duty, inexcusable and something that the law simply could not permit. "Memorandum on Law" concludes by observing that if private interests injure public interests, then a legal system will not be able to stand.[16]

Implied in Ogyū's supposed analysis in "Memorandum on Law" is that while the rōnin might be recognized as having exhibited personal righteousness, they had to be punished as criminals according to public law. Compared to Ogyū's "Essay on the Forty-Seven Samurai," "Memorandum on Law" is far more lenient regarding the extent to which the rōnin might be considered righteous, but clearly favors upholding the law and one's public duties as superior to any private, personal obligations. Although his other writings advocated revering and even worshiping the ancient sages who had founded the sociopolitical order of China, Ogyū would not likely have agreed with the notion that the rōnin might be legitimately worshiped in shrines established for that purpose.

Denouncing the Vendetta

One of Yamazaki Ansai's disciples, Satō Naokata, authored the first major denunciation of the rōnin. Satō's "Notes on the Forty-Six Men," written around 1706, opens with a terse account of the vendetta focusing on the rōnin invasion of Kira's residence. Tellingly, Satō highlights the fact that during the attack the rōnin wore "helmets and armor, and carried bows, arrows, and spears." Satō adds that not only did the rōnin behead Kira, they also "wounded his son, and killed or wounded many of his men." Satō notes that the rōnin sent two members of their group to report the vendetta to the authorities. The vendetta band was later placed in the custody of four daimyō houses, and then on the fourth day of the second month, ordered to commit seppuku. Satō repeats the shogunate's verdict, which declared the vendetta completely disrespectful of the shogunal authorities, and most outrageous.

Mercifully, in Satō's mind, the shogunate allowed the rōnin to commit seppuku rather than be publicly decapitated. Despite the verdict,

---

[16] *Giritsusho, Akō gijin sansho*, vol. 3, p. 150.

Figure 5.3 Yamazaki Ansai. Courtesy of Waseda University, Department of Special Collections.

common people echoed one another in praising the forty-six men as "loyal retainers and righteous samurai" (*chūshin gishi*). Satō was willing to excuse the uneducated for not knowing better, but targets Hayashi Hōkō for extolling the rōnin as "loyal and righteous retainers" (*chūgi no shin*) and comparing them with ancient Chinese exemplars of loyalty and righteousness such as Tian Heng and his disciples. Satō cites, with contempt, Hayashi Hōkō's claim that "in taking revenge, the rōnin were pursuing righteousness." He finds it incredible that Hayashi could praise the men as righteous, and yet also affirm that the shogunate's verdict reflected ethical principles. Satō insists that one or the other was true, but not both.[17]

Satō claims that the rōnin made an egregious mistake in thinking that Kira was Asano's enemy, and in invoking the *Book of Rites*' passage as justification for their revenge. Kira was not Asano's enemy. This was clear because Kira never attacked Asano. Had he done so, he would have been his enemy. Asano was sentenced to death because he acted disrespectfully toward the authorities. Satō especially faults Asano for having attacked Kira during the ceremonies hosting imperial emissaries at the shogun's castle, calling such lack of consideration "reckless, unmanly, and cowardly." If an attack was inevitable, Asano should

[17] Satō Naokata, *Shijūroku nin no hikki, Kinsei buke shisō*, p. 378.

have done it elsewhere. Moreover, Satō mocks Asano's ineptness in striking Kira without being able to kill him. Such, Satō states, was "extremely laughable." Kira fares no better: he collapsed in shock, never even drawing his sword, thus becoming "the laughingstock of samurai throughout the realm." His shame was so profound, Satō suggests, that death would have been a better fate for him. But the bottom line for Satō remains that Kira was not Asano's enemy.[18]

Because they mistakenly viewed Kira as Asano's enemy, the rōnin, rather than regret their master's crime, conspired to commit an even greater one, arming themselves for an attack that would, in their minds, avenge their master's humiliation. Satō allows that if the rōnin had, after killing Kira and presenting his head at Asano's grave, killed themselves, they might have earned respect and sympathy. But instead they reported their deeds to the shogunate and awaited its verdict. In explaining their actions, the rōnin claimed to respect the authorities. Yet, Satō asks, was their behavior not simply a subterfuge by which they could win praise, escape punishment, and receive a stipend. Otherwise, there was no need to report their deed, much less wait for a verdict. They should have known that they were to commit seppuku, immediately. In Satō's opinion, the rōnin did not do so because they had not readied themselves sufficiently for death.[19]

Satō next blames the teachings of Yamaga Sokō for the vendetta. He recalls how the Asano had long revered Yamaga's teachings, and even claims that Ōishi, the leader of the rōnin vendetta, had studied them from early on. Although without explaining how, Satō asserts that the rōnin's conspiracy to murder Kira was consistent with Yamaga's teachings. He adds that their plot arose not from any sense of "loyalty and righteousness" (chūgi) to their deceased lord, nor from deeply rooted feelings of sadness about his death, but instead from their determination to escape from becoming rōnin forever. In Satō's view, the rōnin acted out of self-interest rather than self-sacrificing devotion to Asano.

Yet Satō shows no sympathy whatsoever toward Kira, explaining that people praised the rōnin as chūshin gishi because Kira was a greedy, arrogant, perverse, and deceitful man, one detested by all. Accordingly, when Asano's attack failed, people pitied Asano rather than Kira. Upon learning that the rōnin had killed Kira, they were

---

[18] Ibid., pp. 378–379.   [19] Ibid., p. 379.

overjoyed, praising them as *chūshin gishi*. Satō concludes by blaming the vendetta on Kira, whose wickedness had set in motion the events that caused an uproar throughout Edo and confused people regarding the true nature of *chūshin gishi*. Yet in Satō's view, no matter how much Kira was to blame, he, Satō, could hardly consent to the widespread misconception that the rōnin were loyal retainers and righteous samurai.[20] Those who thought otherwise, praising criminals as *chūshin gishi*, were, according to Satō, blindly following the claims of Hayashi Hōkō and Muro Kyūsō. The rōnin did not, Satō declares emphatically, exemplify "loyalty and righteousness" (*chūgi*).[21]

Satō, a follower of Yamazaki Ansai, thus initiated allegations that Yamaga's ideas were behind the vendetta. Although Dazai Shundai later attributed the same view to Ogyū, there is no evidence that Ogyū ever made such a charge. Yamazaki Ansai's school had been an enemy of Yamaga's teachings ever since Yamazaki's disciple, Hoshina Masayuki, purportedly had Yamaga exiled from Edo for publication of *Sagely Confucian Teachings*, a work harshly criticizing the Zhu Xi philosophy that Yamazaki held in highest regard. Satō revived the attack on Yamaga, now long dead, by blaming his teachings for the "outrageous" vendetta. There is no evidence, other than circumstantial, that Yamaga had any impact on Asano Naganori, Ōishi Yoshio, or the rōnin. Rōnin writings explaining their actions and intent make no mention of Yamaga or his teachings.

Between 1688 and his own passing in 1719, Satō served as the Confucian teacher for Sakai Tadataka, the long-standing lord of Maebashi domain. Given his proximity to the shogunate and service to one of its most loyal daimyō, Satō would hardly have endorsed the rōnin unequivocally as righteous. Unlike Hayashi Hōkō, Satō had no hereditary position providing him philosophical security. Perhaps like Yamaga Sokō, Satō dreamed of serving the Tokugawa more closely as a Confucian lecturer. Indeed, in criticizing the rōnin after the fact, Satō's views might be construed as an exercise in self-serving flattery of the judicial wisdom and legal authority of the shogunate, one meant to enhance his own chances for advancement. That aside, his views can surely be regarded as an attempt to accelerate the atrophy of the Yamaga school in Edo. The latter school, without attempting to rebut Satō's allegations, largely abandoned Edo in the 1740s.

[20] Ibid., pp. 379–380.   [21] Ibid., pp. 378–380.

Extolling the Vendetta

Like Satō Naokata, Asami Keisai was a disciple of Yamazaki Ansai. However, Asami and Satō differed on virtually every count, leaving them badly estranged in their final years. To a degree, their differences reflected their philosophical settings: Satō, although born in southwestern Japan, resided in Edo most of his professional life, teaching one of the shogun's close vassals. Asami stayed in Kyoto, the birthplace of Yamazaki Ansai's learning, remaining relatively independent of daimyō patronage. While Satō expressed disdain for vulgar samurai culture even as he served a daimyō in the shogun's capital, Asami, on the other hand, living in the imperial capital and so more isolated from the martial elite, was also more an admirer of the samurai world, reportedly wearing a sword and riding a horse. And it was from Kyoto that Asami set forth his high praise for the rōnin, and from Edo that Satō, backing the shogunate rather than popular opinion, denounced them for betraying righteousness and seeking professional advancement through a murderous vendetta.

Satō's condemnation of the rōnin as pathetically misguided men lacking any real grasp of loyalty and righteousness prompted Asami's adamant praise for them as *chūshin gishi*. In his "Essay on the Forty-Six Samurai," Asami declared that the loyalty of the rōnin to their lord could hardly be questioned. Sharing some ground with Satō, Asami has little respect for Kira, casting him as a selfish, uncaring bully who forced Asano to blunder his way into ceremonial humiliation, hounding him until he lost his temper, drew his sword, and attacked. Asami suggests that if the attack had been successful, Asano would have next committed suicide, bringing immediate closure to the whole matter. Unfortunately, Asano was stopped, and so completion was left to his rōnin.

In Asami's opinion, far from being an innocent in the attack, Kira had been the aggressor, bullying Asano to the point of outburst. The shogunate therefore erred, in Asami's view, in not adjudicating the matter according to the principle of "equal punishment for all involved in an altercation." Asami emphasizes that the rōnin showed neither animosity nor opposition to the shogunate. Rather, they simply attacked and killed the enemy of their deceased lord. Asami thus explains that rather than commit seppuku after the vendetta, the rōnin notified the authorities and then waited for a judgment. According to Asami, their behavior reflected their lord's lifelong loyal service to the shogunate. He adds that "even an ignorant person would have known that they could not expect to be pardoned." To imagine that they hoped for a pardon or a stipend was absurd. Asami thus affirms that the rōnin were loyal and righteous in their vendetta.[22]

Asami insists the rōnin did not mean to defy the shogunate itself. He admits that while the murder might appear, in retrospect, to have been an act of defiance, that was not the rōnin's intent. Instead, they thought of nothing other than acting on behalf of their lord and master. Asami suggests that the ancient Confucian philosopher, Mencius, thought similarly about the filial piety of the sage ruler Shun when he, Mencius, asserted that if Shun's blind father had committed a murder, Shun would have fled the empire carrying his father on his back. Doing so would not have amounted to an act of defiance against the authorities so much as an act of filial compassion for his father. Similarly, Asami implies, the rōnin thought only of completing their lord's task, i.e., killing Kira, without worrying over the implications vis-à-vis the authorities.[23]

Asami next considers the "despicable" assertion that the rōnin, having nothing left but life as masterless men, launched the vendetta in the hopes of gaining new employment and a rice stipend. Asami calls this a foul allegation. Instead, he emphasizes that from start to finish, the rōnin realized that the vendetta would mean sacrificing their lives for the sake of killing Kira. Yet nothing else mattered to them. To suggest otherwise amounted to extreme ignorance. Asami then addresses the suggestion that Asano should have waited until another time and place to attack Kira. He admits that when one neglects public responsibilities for the sake of private ends, one cannot hope to escape punishment. However, he adds that if a private act is not undertaken in defiance of the authorities, it makes no real difference when and where it might be staged. Over and again Asami asserts that neither Asano nor the rōnin had any grudge against, or intent to defy, the shogunal authorities, claiming instead that they were attentive to matters of ritual decorum and reasonable in every respect. Asami insists that the forty-six rōnin were of a high caliber, and fully merited recognition as *chūshin gishi*.[24]

---

[22] Asami Keisai, *Shijūrokushi ron, Kinsei buke shisō*, pp. 390–392.   [23] Ibid., p. 393.
[24] Ibid., pp. 394–395.

Asami deems "laughable" Satō's criticisms of the rōnin for revering the martial teachings of Yamaga Sokō and equipping themselves as a fighting force with armor, mail, swords, spears, bows and arrows, and other kinds of military ware. Although forming such a militia band violated shogunal law, Asami emphasizes that the rōnin had no alternatives if they were to succeed. Moreover, they went to great lengths not to disturb Kira's neighbors or kill women and children. Asami suggests that it is most important to focus on the overall intent of the deeds rather than be distracted by minor infractions. Regarding Yamaga's teachings on military strategy, Asami recalls that the deeds of heroic figures in history such as the imperial loyalist Kusunoki Masashige were informed by military strategizing, and that Kusunoki and others were still judged to be exemplars of loyalty and righteousness. Since Kusunoki lived long before Yamaga Sokō, Asami's suggestion is that relying on military strategy is sensible if one wants to succeed, and that no single teaching, such as Yamaga's, was inherently necessary to explain the vendetta.

In his lectures on Beixi's *Lexicography*, Asami also mentioned Kusunoki as a local exemplar of the *chūshin gishi* ethic.[25] Kusunoki was, incidentally, later, in the early Meiji period, enshrined at the Minatogawa Shrine. Well before that, in the late seventeenth century, Tokugawa Mitsukuni, lord of Mito domain, had a memorial stone erected near the Minato River, where Kusunoki died fighting for the imperial cause, calling attention to Kusunoki's loyalty and righteousness. Arguably, that memorial stone was a Confucian precursor, with its brief allusion to Kusunoki's "loyalty and righteousness," of the later Shinto shrine formally established by the Meiji government. In comparing the rōnin and Kusunoki, Asami hints at his understanding of the spiritual significance of the rōnin.

One of Yamazaki Ansai's disciples, Satō Naokata, thus took the debate as an opportunity to denigrate Yamaga's school by blaming it for the rōnin outrage, while another disciple, Asami Keisai, minimized if not mocked the significance of Yamaga's teachings in relation to the vendetta that it viewed as righteous and loyal. In this regard, the debate reflected rivalries among early eighteenth-century Confucian scholars, and especially the Yamazaki school's multifaceted, even internally divided opposition to what remained of the Yamaga teachings.

[25] Ibid., pp. 395–396. Nakamura Gihō, *Seiri jigi kōgi* (1783), 4:27a.

Moreover, the Confucian debates exemplified the extent to which the vendetta was becoming boldly contested public ground in Japanese cultural history. This dialectical development of the vendetta as a site of controversy and disagreement rather than consensus and homogeneity continued and indeed emerged as the most salient aspect of its unfolding over the three centuries that followed.

6   CONFUCIAN VERSUS CONFUCIAN, ROUND TWO

The vitality of the Confucian debates reflected a strong appetite for vendetta commentary at all levels. The arguments advanced were anything but monolithic. The most controversial claims in the so-called second round of the debates were those of Dazai Shundai, the harshest critic of the rōnin and their vendetta. Dazai's criticisms in turn became the targets of successive pro-rōnin writings. The second round thus added vigor to the debates, and an emerging consensus favoring the rōnin rather than their critics. This chapter emphasizes that in the debates, Yamaga Sokō's teachings were increasingly blamed for everything. While evidence establishing Yamaga's impact on the rōnin is lacking, allegations asserting that his ideas were behind the criminal incident hurt his already reduced teachings in Edo. Although a philosophical casualty of the debates, Yamaga's teachings survived in outer domains such as Chōshū, where their impact on the rōnin vendetta came to be viewed positively.

Denunciation Redux

Writing thirty years after the incident, Dazai Shundai, a student of Ogyū Sorai, kept the debate red hot by lambasting the rōnin as common criminals who staged a vendetta for the sake of fame and reputation.[1]

---

[1] Tahara Tsuguo, *Akō Shijūroku shi ron: Bakuhansei no seishin kōzō* (Tokyo: Yoshikawa kōbunkan, 1978), pp. 108–109.

In advancing this line of attack, Dazai shared common ground with Satō Naokata, the first harsh critic of the rōnin. However, Satō's early, more circumspect essay never elicited nearly the reaction that Dazai's did. By the time Dazai wrote, the vendetta had become a more central and public topic of discourse, Confucian and otherwise. During the decades following Dazai's essay, the debate over the rōnin transformed largely into a multilateral counterattack on Dazai's harsh condemnation of them.

Born into a lower samurai line in the castle town of Iida, west of Edo in Shinano province (now Nagano), Dazai moved to Edo in 1711, a decade after Asano's attack on Kira. In the shogun's capital, Dazai became a student of Ogyū Sorai's teachings. However, Dazai apparently did not have a close relationship with his teacher.[2] This might explain why he later stated, mistakenly, that Ogyū had not written an essay on the vendetta. As noted earlier, Ogyū, by most accounts, wrote at least one essay, and possibly two, even though neither was widely known, not even, apparently, by students such as Dazai. Nevertheless, Dazai claimed to have heard the gist of Ogyū's thinking, presumably in the context of a lecture or discussion. And what he heard was presumably critical. Like Ogyū had in his "Memorandum on Law," Dazai condemned the rōnin's attack on Kira, denying that it was an expression of righteous duty. However, Dazai was apparently as much influenced by Satō Naokata, a follower of Yamazaki Ansai's teachings, as he was by Ogyū. Significantly, both Satō and Dazai denounced the vendetta, and blamed the ideas of Yamaga Sokō for the military strategy evident in it. The combined, multi-school critiques of Satō and Dazai spelled short-term ruin for the Yamaga school, in Edo at least.

Dazai's "Essay on the Forty-Six Samurai of Akō Domain," written around 1732, opens with a summary of the incident, beginning with the New Year's ceremonies of 1701 when representatives of "the emperor of Yamashiro" were sent to the "eastern court," i.e., Edo. Dazai thus conveys disrespect for the emperor, whose power, he implied, extended no further than the imperial capital. Yet he extols the shogunal capital, Edo, as the supposed "eastern court." Dazai adds that few samurai had any real grasp of court rituals and so sought assistance by means of gifts to the master of ceremonies. Two young

[2] Tetsuo Najita, "Political Economism in the Thought of Dazai Shundai (1680–1747)," *Journal of Asian Studies*, vol. 31, no. 4 (August 1972), p. 823.

Figure 6.1 Dazai Shundai. Courtesy of Waseda University, Department of Special Collections.

daimyō, Asano and Daté, were hosting the imperial emissaries. Daté's retainers provided Kira gifts. In return, Kira praised Daté throughout the ceremonies, embarrassing and angering Asano. On the fourteenth day of the third month, while the emissaries were in Edo Castle, Asano suddenly attacked Kira, wounding him on the forehead before attendants could stop the attack. Dazai adds that the shogun was "greatly angered." Asano was placed in the custody of the Tamura daimyō and sentenced to death that evening. Akō Castle was confiscated and Asano's family line extinguished.

Kira soon resigned his position as master of court ceremonies, and was assigned a new residence on the outskirts of Edo. Then, more than a year later, the rōnin, led by Ōishi, invaded Kira's residence, tracked him down, and decapitated him. They next marched to the Sengakuji with Kira's head and presented it before the grave of their deceased lord, thus reporting their successful revenge. They also informed the shogunate of their deeds and awaited its sentence. The shogunal authorities had the men divided and confined among four daimyō until they were sentenced to die on the fourth day of the second month, 1703.[3] Dazai thus gives one of the most historically accurate recapitulations of the vendetta found in the Confucian debates.

Dazai adds that everyone, from scholars and high officials down to cart-pullers and horse groomers, praised the rōnin as "righteous samurai." Dazai recalls that as a young man, he agreed that the rōnin had embodied righteousness. He admits that he even mourned their passing. Later, however, he realized that they gambled in waiting for an opportune moment to attack because there was no guarantee that the elderly Kira would still be alive. If Kira had died earlier, the rōnin would have accomplished nothing. Dazai therefore reasoned that the rōnin's success was simply a matter of luck. Soon, he had doubts about the vendetta overall.[4]

Dazai claims that the rōnin had the sanction of the Confucian classics. The *Book of Rites* states that a son should not dwell under the same heaven, i.e., live in the same world, as the murderer of his father. Rather, he should make it his personal responsibility to slay the murderer. He acknowledges that the *Book of Rites* does not mention rulers and lords, but adds that the *Classic of Filial Piety* (*Xiaojing*) relates how "one's lord should be served and treated with the same respect as one's father." Therefore, the man who kills one's lord may be dealt with in the same manner as the man who kills one's father. Dazai states that this principle was understood throughout history, and was why Ōishi and the rōnin had been lauded as righteous samurai. But in Dazai's view, Kira was simply not to blame for Asano's death. Therefore, Kira should not have been considered Asano's enemy. Clearly, Dazai asserts, Ōishi and his men never realized where their animosity needed to be directed. Instead, they wrongly blamed Kira and so targeted him.[5]

Dazai admits that his views did not please people and so he kept them to himself for years. He claims that he discussed the matter with his teacher Ogyū, who concurred by stating, "The Akō samurai did not fathom righteousness." Per Dazai, Ogyū also remarked, "Their murder of Kira reflected their study of Yamaga Sokō's military strategies." Dazai then adds that Ieyasu established the law that if anyone

---

[3] Dazai Shundai, *Akō shijūrokushi ron*, *Kinsei buke shisō*, pp. 404–405.
[4] Ibid., p. 405.   [5] Ibid., p. 405.

committed murder in the shogun's castle, they would be put to death. Yet Asano only wounded Kira. Even though Asano's attack was not a capital crime, the shogunate treated it as one and sentenced him to death. In Dazai's view, the sentence admittedly far exceeded what was proper and just. Dazai therefore declared that what the rōnin should have resented was not Kira, but instead the shogunate's verdict.[6]

Paraphrasing the *Mencius*, Dazai goes on to state that when the shogunate treats the lord of a domain with respect, the retainers serving that lord will stand in awe of the shogunate. If the shogunate does not treat their lord with respect, however, the retainers will feel resentment against the shogunate. Incredibly enough, Dazai's suggestion, then, is that the rōnin should have viewed the shogunate's verdict as the enemy of their lord and resented it rather than Kira. Dazai adds that samurai of the eastern region around Edo deal with the murder of a father or lord by immediately springing into action, ready to die in a moment to manifest their righteous duty. Dazai then notes that not only did Ōishi and the rōnin resent what they should not have resented, they went contrary to the way of the eastern samurai in waiting so long to attack Kira. Consequently, Dazai suggests that, on at least two counts, the rōnin were simply pathetic.[7]

In Dazai's view, the rōnin should have expressed their opposition to the shogunate's verdict by standing their ground at Akō Castle rather than surrendering to the shogunate without a fight. Had Ōishi made such a stand, Dazai claims, more than forty-six would have fought for their lord's honor. Resistance would have meant defeat, but they would have remained with the castle until the end, then set it afire and died there, fighting together defending their master's honor. Instead, they made a cowardly display in yielding the castle. By doing so, they forfeited their best opportunity to do their righteous duty.

Another option would have involved going directly to Edo and attacking Kira without delay. Had they succeeded, they should have committed seppuku promptly. If they failed, they would have died in the process. Either way, death was their certain fate. With it, their righteous duty to their lord would have been fulfilled. Instead, Ōishi and the rōnin spent more than a year biding their time, waiting with the seasons for the right moment. They plotted, conspired, and engaged in intrigue for the sake of success. Their primary objective was not defending their lord's

[6] Ibid., p. 405.   [7] Ibid., pp. 406–407.

honor by dying on his behalf, but instead achieving a victory that would bring them "fame and profit." Dazai therefore declares the rōnin vendetta simply "despicable."[8]

Criticizing the rōnin on yet another count, Dazai declares that they should have committed seppuku immediately after presenting Kira's head at their master's grave. Why, Dazai asks, did they wait? His answer is that the rōnin thought that their success might earn them praise and honor as exceptional samurai. Possibly they might be spared death, and even gain stipends from daimyō who wanted such samurai in their service. On the other hand, if ordered to commit seppuku, they would do as the law required, somehow imagining that there would be no blame for having awaited the verdict of the shogunate. In the meantime, they apparently saw no reason to rush into death. With contempt, Dazai asks, "Are people like Ōishi who feign devotion to supreme righteous duty but are driven by a desire for profit worthy of being deemed righteous?" Dazai adds that if the shogunate had pardoned Ōishi and the rōnin, they would have taken a stipend and ended up living well rather than doing the honorable thing, committing seppuku.[9]

That aside, in Dazai's view, the most fundamental errors of the rōnin flowed from their "not recognizing the proper target for their resentment," i.e., the shogunate's verdict rather than Kira. More remotely, the problems "began with Master Yamaga Sokō serving the lord of Akō domain as an instructor in military strategy." Like Satō, Dazai notes that Ōishi had studied under Yamaga, and that he and the rōnin used Yamaga's teachings on military strategy in their conspiracy to murder Kira. But despite their success, they had not rightly identified the proper object of their resentment and so failed to fulfill the duty they owed their deceased master. Such, Dazai claimed, was the nature of Master Yamaga's teachings.[10] Like Satō Naokata, Dazai thus used his essay on the vendetta to incriminate Yamaga Sokō and his teachings.

Defending the Rōnin Anew

One of the first responses to Dazai's claims emerged from the Kaitokudō merchant academy, a Kansai center of Confucian learning dedicated to

---

[8] Ibid., p. 408. [9] Ibid. [10] Ibid.

educating townspeople. Much of Kaitokudō thought was influenced by Kyoto scholars Itō Jinsai and Itō Tōgai, whose ideas stood diametrically opposed to those of Ogyū Sorai and his disciples. Not surprisingly, one of the Kaitokudō's intellectual leaders, Goi Ranshū, was an outspoken critic of Ogyū's thought. In his essay on the vendetta, however, Goi targeted Dazai Shundai rather than Ogyū, point by point critiquing Dazai's claims that the rōnin were neither loyal nor righteous.

In his "Refutation of Dazai's Essay on the Forty-Six Akō Samurai," Goi argues that the rōnin were loyal and righteous. Goi opens his essay noting that since antiquity, vendettas launched by "loyal retainers and cautious samurai" (*chūshin sesshi*) had to simmer patiently, waiting for the right moment if they were to succeed. The priority was that they did succeed. The short-tempered approach was that of small-minded, poor planners. Goi thus rebuts Dazai's criticism that the rōnin were slow to act. Addressing Dazai's speculation that Kira might have died while the rōnin were plotting revenge, Goi explains that had Kira passed before the vendetta was done, the rōnin would have informed their deceased lord of as much at his grave. Then they would have committed seppuku, and done so without shame. As things turned out, in Goi's view, the rōnin acted admirably, as had deliberate and successful "loyal retainers and cautious samurai" from ages past.[11]

Emphasizing the vendetta's spiritual dimensions, Goi claims that the rōnin killed Kira to console the anger of their dead master, now in the underworld. Goi admits that Asano's attack required that he, Asano, be put to death. However, in Goi's view, that did not mean that the shogunate's verdict should, as Dazai claimed, be considered the enemy. Whether Kira was rightly viewed as Asano's enemy made no difference because in Goi's view, Ōishi and the rōnin were not carrying out a revenge attack on their lord's enemy. Instead, they were simply carrying out Asano's last intention, i.e., completing the intended action that their deceased master had been unable to bring to completion. Goi doubts that Asano harbored anger toward the authorities as he neared death, but declares with certainty that Asano's utmost regret was that he had not killed Kira. Thus, the rōnin beheaded Kira to complete Asano's last intention and thereby soothe his anger and frustrations in the afterlife. While denying that the vendetta was an act of revenge, Goi allows

---

[11] Goi Ranshū, *Baku Dazai Jun Akō Shijūrokushi ron*, *Kinsei Buke shisō*, p. 418.

that given Kira's role in prompting it all, the popular view of the rōnin attack as an act of revenge should not be considered mistaken.[12]

Goi does not pretend that the rōnin were saints. He admits, for example, that Ōishi led "an armed attack in the shogun's capital and therein killed a high-placed person as if he were an orphan swine, which was indeed a major crime." Goi thus recognizes that Ōishi and the rōnin were guilty of capital offenses, including armed conspiracy and the murder of a government official, for which the punishment should have been severe. Yet rather than publicly display their severed heads, the shogunate had four daimyō houses assume custody of them, and eventually "granted them the honor of committing seppuku and having a decent burial" next to their deceased lord at the Sengakuji. In Goi's view, the consideration afforded the rōnin reflected the shogunate's recognition of a degree of righteousness even in their murderous behavior. Goi adds that scholars who praised the rōnin's deeds had seen things similarly, acknowledging the substantial righteousness in them. Goi charges that Dazai did nothing more than plagiarize the aberrant ideas of an earlier critic, Satō Naokata, while claiming to be explaining the meaning of righteousness. Goi therefore declares Dazai's essay to be "extremely laughable."[13]

Goi strongly criticizes Dazai's suggestion that the rōnin should have viewed the shogunate and its verdicts as their enemy rather than Kira. After all, Asano did not bear a grudge against the shogunate, so why should his retainers have done so? Asano died because of his outrageous behavior in the shogun's castle, which in turn was prompted by Kira's "perverseness." Knowing Asano's grudge against Kira, Ōishi and the rōnin felt the same grudge even more. Why should they have begrudged anything else? Most especially, Goi mocks as "preposterous" the notion that the rōnin would have been so foolish as to resent the shogunate. Emphasizing the importance of the latter, Goi asks, "Is it possible for anyone not to appreciate what the shogunate provides for everyone?" If retainers were to conspire in opposition to the shogunate every time it treated their masters slightly, chaos would ensue. Affirming that respect for the shogunate is the foundation of respect for one's lord, Goi declares that Dazai's claims will surely incite people to evil.[14]

Goi further asserts that Dazai's claim that the shogunate's verdict should have been deemed the enemy amounted to "an extreme

---

[12] Ibid., pp. 418–419.   [13] Ibid., p. 419.   [14] Ibid., p. 420.

case of treason," an oxymoronic affirmation of "righteousness which is not righteousness." Rejecting Dazai's suggestion that there is a righteousness specific to samurai of a particular region, Goi declares more universally that righteousness is the same for the entire world below heaven. He adds that if the rōnin had died in Akō Castle fighting against shogunal forces, that would not have dissolved Asano's grudge, and instead, would have only added to the domain's crimes, bringing greater misfortune on the Asano family.

Defending Ōishi's leadership, Goi notes that warriors going into battle must be prepared for death. At the same time, no one wants to die senselessly. Accordingly, Ōishi and the rōnin had to plot, plan, and calculate for every contingency. Their only concern was making their deaths count. Therefore, Goi asks, how could they possibly have entertained self-centered thoughts of fame and profit? Goi concludes his critique of Dazai's essay by explaining Ōishi's decision to report the vendetta to the authorities. Rejecting Dazai's suggestion that the rōnin were hoping for a pardon and a stipend, Goi emphasizes that Ōishi's decision be understood as an expression of the *Mencius'* Confucian teaching (4B/23) that "when one may either die or not die, simply dying is at odds with being courageous." Yet Goi adds that even if the rōnin had been pardoned, they would have expressed their gratitude and then committed suicide. Such, in Goi's view, was Ōishi's approach to things.[15]

Itō Jinsai's ideas also influenced another Kaitokudō scholar, Nakai Riken, who, like Goi, sympathized with the rōnin. Incidentally, Itō Jinsai's eldest son and philosophical successor, Itō Tōgai (1670–1736), supposedly wrote a poem, "The Deeds of the Righteous Samurai," extolling the rōnin as *gishi*. An anecdote, substantially apocryphal, relates that Ōishi studied with Itō Jinsai, and that the latter praised Ōishi as a "capable individual." Anecdotes aside, Itō was most likely aware of the vendetta: it occurred two years before his death in 1705. Moreover, his son's diary, the *Tōgai nikki*, records "news" of Asano's attempted murder of Kira in 1701.[16]

Essays affirming that the rōnin were *chūshin gishi* increased during the remainder of the Tokugawa period, making that appraisal the more popular one, at least in terms of the number endorsing it.

---

[15] Ranshū, *Baku Dazai Jun Akō Shijūroku shi ron*, pp. 420–422.
[16] Sasaki (1983), pp. 340–341, 460.

Noteworthy among them was one by Miyake Shōsai, another of Yamazaki Ansai's leading disciples. Also, Miyake Kanran, who studied with Asami Keisai before serving the lord of Mito domain, Tokugawa Mitsukuni, praised the rōnin as "ardent, fierce samurai" (resshi), and argued that they exemplified a more aggressive, often violent form of samurai loyalty. The eclectically inclined Edo-based scholar Matsumiya Kanzan also defended the rōnin against charges that their vendetta had been motivated by a desire for wealth and fame. Matsumiya, however, was one of the relatively few Edo scholars to praise the rōnin enthusiastically. Apparently, his standing with the shogunate did not rise because of it. When implicated in a 1767 conspiracy supposedly aimed at overthrowing the shogunate, Matsumiya was banished from Edo.

Perhaps the most unique essay defending the rōnin was by Yokoi Yayū. Born in Nagoya and of samurai lineage, Yokoi was a *haikai* poet, a student of the tea ceremony, and a scholar of Confucianism, Chinese literature, and nativist studies. In 1762, he wrote an amusing essay on the vendetta, "A Rustic's Conversations." Like so many of his day, Yokoi objected to Dazai's harsh criticism of the rōnin. Unlike his predecessors, however, Yokoi cast his philosophical thoughts in the form of a tale featuring one Kusaku, a "urine collector." In doing so, he suggests that even such a person could understand how wrongheaded Dazai's claims were. Yokoi's tale echoes Goi's essay in other respects. First, the matter of timing is addressed. Kusaku allows that if the rōnin had waited five or more years, they might have been guilty of procrastination, but a mere year and a half was not cause for objection. Kusaku hints that the careful pace ensured success. Alternatively, had the rōnin rushed their vendetta, they, like their lord, would have failed.[17]

Kusaku emphasizes that the intent of the rōnin was to eliminate the mortification gnawing away at Asano's bones as he lay beneath the grass in the world below. Thus, his "loyal retainers" executed their vendetta with care to ensure its success and thus the peace of their late lord. In making this claim, Yokoi reiterated a perspective that Goi had advanced: that the rōnin did not harbor a grudge against Kira; they were simply carrying out Asano's thwarted intentions. To retire his grudge in the hereafter "below the stream," they presented Kira's head at his

---

[17] Yokoi Yayū, *Yafudan, Kinsei buke shisō*, pp. 426–432. An abridged translation is in Satō, *Legends of the Samurai*, pp. 336–338.

grave. On another count, Kusaku expressed disbelief at Dazai's claim that Ōishi and the rōnin acted out of a desire for fame and profit when they had obviously abandoned their families and knew the future would bring only death. Such, according to Yokoi, was the loyalty and righteousness of the Akō rōnin.[18]

Any number of other pro-rōnin essays could be examined. Suffice it to say, however, that over time sympathy accrued decidedly to the rōnin. Most likely, this sentiment was encouraged by popular dramatizations of the vendetta. Also important was the broadcast of the incident as an oral tale circulating in undocumented form well into the countryside. There, versions of the incident were most likely recounted freely with embellishment and fabrications. Common approbation was most likely prompted by the vendetta's affirmation of triumph against all odds, offering hope to all, at some level or another, regardless of their circumstances.

The Hidden Critique

Prior to the early twentieth century, *Hidden Leaves* (*Hagakure*) was virtually unknown outside of Saga domain on the island of Kyūshū, where its author, Yamamoto Tsunetomo, lived. Reportedly, after the death of his daimyō, Yamamoto wanted to commit seppuku to follow his master in death. However, he refrained from doing so because of shogunal law forbidding it. After becoming a Buddhist instead, he wrote *Hidden Leaves* to record an ethos that he believed had once prevailed among authentic samurai. Yet his text was not published in the Tokugawa period, and so went unmentioned in the various debates over the ethics and spirituality of the vendetta. While a romanticized and nostalgic account of the way of the warrior, Yamamoto's work is significant here due to its harsh criticism of the vendetta. In the twentieth century, *Hidden Leaves* emerged from obscurity to become, ironically enough, one of the most famous works of Tokugawa samurai literature, and its critique of the rōnin vendetta is one of the most frequently cited.

Overall, *Hidden Leaves* criticizes the option of remaining alive when one is faced with a situation demanding certain and inevitable death. It suggests that excuses offered for living are the contrived

[18] Ibid., pp. 426–432.

products of minds given to excessive calculation. Instead, *Hidden Leaves* endorses a readiness to engage in direct, unmediated action. Rejecting the sort of thorough planning that Ōishi relied on, *Hidden Leaves* claims that samurai warriors should throw themselves into battle without thought of the outcome, with a "crazed willingness to die."[19] It thus explains:

> [W]hen you must choose between life and death, choose death immediately. There is nothing else to do. Simply resolve your mind and do it ... If you fail to do so and survive, then you will be deemed a coward. This is a shameful situation to be in. If you fail and you die, people may say your death was meaningless or that you were crazy, but there will be no shame. Such is the power of the martial way. When every morning and every evening you die anew, constantly making yourself one with death, you obtain freedom in the martial way, and an ability to fulfill your calling throughout your life without falling into error.[20]

Unlike those who deem righteousness an ultimate value, *Hidden Leaves* suggests that there are values loftier. It states:

> There is a way that is higher than righteousness. It is difficult to find, but one who finds it possesses unsurpassed wisdom. From its vantage point, righteousness itself is something small and narrow ... *Bushidō* consists in nothing other than charging forward wildly, without hesitation, into death. A warrior with this state of mind is difficult to kill even if attacked by twenty or thirty people. There is no need to think of loyalty and filial piety. In *bushidō*, there is nothing but charging forward wildly into death.[21]

In discussing the rōnin vendetta, *Hidden Leaves* reiterates these themes.

> Concerning the night assault of Asano's rōnin, the fact that they did not commit seppuku at the Sengakuji was an error. Also, there was a long delay between the time their lord died and the time they

---

[19] *Hagakure*, pp. 251–252. "The Way of the Warrior II," in de Bary, Gluck, Tiedemann, eds., *Sources of Japanese Tradition: Volume 2: 1600–2000*, pp. 474–475. Translation adapted.

[20] *Hagakure*, p. 220. Translations adapted from *Sources*, p. 476.

[21] *Hagakure*, pp. 233, 251–252. De Bary, Gluck, and Tiedemann, eds., *Sources*, p. 478.

> struck down his enemy. If Kira had died of illness within that period, it would have been extremely regrettable ... The way to avoid shame is different. It resides simply in death. Even if it seems certain that you will lose, retaliate. Neither wisdom nor technique has a place in this. A real man does not think of victory or defeat. He plunges with abandon towards an irrational death.[22]

Yamamoto's analysis of the vendetta echoes Dazai's, especially in its emphasis on the need for immediate action. Yet unlike Dazai's essay, which became the target of repeated attacks, Yamamoto's criticisms of the vendetta did not elicit, in Tokugawa times, counter-responses. They did not simply because *Hidden Leaves* was a text largely unknown to the Tokugawa world. It was "discovered" in twentieth-century wartime Japan and soon rose to prominence as a classic expression of *bushidō* thought. In tandem with its modern rise, the vendetta came to be somewhat deemphasized. Instead of unmitigated praise for the vendetta, the latter was, in some circles, cast as a "lesser form of righteousness," echoing *Hidden Leaves*' earlier critique of righteousness as an ethical notion. In that regard, *Hidden Leaves*' thinking on *bushidō*, righteousness, and the vendetta were arguably more important in mid-twentieth-century wartime discourse than that of the Tokugawa period.

The Philosophical Victim

Yamaga Sokō died in 1685, sixteen years before Asano Naganori's attack and eighteen years before Kira's beheading. In the debates, however, Yamaga was early on implicated in the whole incident as if he and Ōishi were coconspirators. Essays by Satō and Dazai charged Yamaga's teachings with somehow informing the vendetta, although the charges were never accompanied by specifics regarding how, precisely, Yamaga's ideas had done so. Neither Asano nor the rōnin ever hinted that Yamaga or his ideas lay behind their deeds. Nor do credible documents such as *Things Seen and Heard* and *Akō Castle League* so much as mention Yamaga. Moreover, the rōnin declaration of intent to kill Kira does not once cite Yamaga's teachings as even remotely relevant.

---

[22] *Hagakure*, p. 237. William Scott Wilson, trans., *Hagakure: The Book of the Samurai* (Tokyo: Kōdansha, 2002), pp. 29–30. Translation adapted.

Evidence of any compelling sort establishing that Yamaga's ideas were relevant to the vendetta is clearly lacking.

If anything, allegations blaming Yamaga were based on circumstantial evidence: between 1652 and 1660, Yamaga served Asano Naganori's grandfather, Asano Naganao, as his instructor of martial philosophy. But serving Asano, a small, outer daimyō, was not apparently Yamaga's dream. Rather, he accepted Asano Naganao's generous offer of an annual stipend of 1,000 *koku* largely due to the shogunate's push to have Edo rōnin take up service to a lord as retained samurai rather than remain loose swords in the capital. In Yamaga's second year serving Asano, he helped oversee the layout of Akō Castle. For a seven-month period during the construction of the castle, Yamaga remained in Akō, but thereafter resided in Edo, providing instruction for his daimyō when the latter was in the shogun's capital.

During those years, Yamaga was exceptionally productive, authoring and editing a series of texts and compilations on martial philosophy. Yamaga's samurai thought typically reworked the Song Confucian ideas of Zhu Xi and his later followers by emphasizing their practicality as the exclusive learning of samurai. As such, Yamaga's martial thought, called *shidō*, or "the way of the samurai" (he rarely used the word *bushidō*), was one of the earliest and most systematic attempts at defining a civil ethic for samurai in an age of peace and urban prosperity. In short, Yamaga was not an advocate of revenge killings, and surely not ones directed at elderly ceremonial officials serving the shogunate.

In 1660, Yamaga declined further service to the Asano, even while courting other offers. He evidently hoped to rise as a purveyor of samurai philosophy. In 1663, he announced his supposedly newfound reliance on the teachings of ancient Confucianism as opposed to those of Zhu Xi. By 1665, he had formulated a new expression of Confucianism, called "sagely teachings" or "sagely learning," rubrics highlighted in the title of his soon to be infamous publication *Sagely Confucian Teachings*. That text sought to define, term by term, an authentic understanding of Confucian discourse, one returning, purportedly, to the original teachings of Confucius, even while rejecting, often pointedly, the quietist, metaphysical interpretations of Zhu Xi and his followers. Yamaga's doctrines might seem harmless enough today, and to the untutored, might even seem like Zhu Xi's.

However, Sokō coupled his return to ancient teachings with brash criticisms of Zhu and others, asserting that they were "guilty of the world's greatest crimes because they misled the world while pretending to explain the Confucian way." Yamaga's students imprudently added that their master's teachings might bring about changes in government. Such claims greatly offended the shogunal leadership, which included followers of Zhu Xi. In the tenth month of 1666, approximately one year after the publication of *Sagely Confucian Teachings*, Yamaga was summoned before the authorities, his book was declared "an outrageous writing," and he was sentenced to exile from Edo for an indefinite period. Due to his earlier association with Akō, he was assigned to the custody of the Asano daimyō there. Yamaga might have ended up exiled for life, but as things turned out, his banishment lasted just short of a decade.[23]

Yamaga's exile in Akō brought another stretch of philosophical ferment and productivity. His seminal work from that period, *The True Central Dynasty (Chūchō jijitsu)*, claimed that Japan's unbroken imperial line and its unwavering loyalty to its emperor distinguished it, rather than China, as the true "central imperial dynasty" (*chūchō*). Yamaga's new appreciation for Japan's imperial line likely reflected his relative proximity to Kyoto. Yet if *The True Central Dynasty* defined Yamaga's legacy in Akō, it is difficult to see how Asano's homicidal outburst during a high ceremonial occasion hosting representatives of the imperial throne might have flowed from Yamaga's thinking. Asano's disruption brought momentary chaos to Edo Castle, plus polluting bloodshed, and so displayed outrageous disrespect for the imperial emissaries if not utter disregard for the throne. Apart from *The True Central Dynasty* and several other writings, Yamaga's exile passed uneventfully, without attempted escapes, plans for revenge vendettas, or strategic teachings about attacks on shogunal officials. During the same period, the young Ōishi – eight when Yamaga's exile began and seventeen when he was pardoned – reportedly delivered vegetables to Yamaga's residence regularly. Such was the nature of their personal bond.

[23] Yamaga's account of his exile experience is in his *Haisho zanpitsu*. See Tahara Tsuguo and Morimoto Junichiro, eds., *Yamaga Sokō*, Nihon shisō taikei vol. 32 (Tokyo: Iwanami shoten,1979), pp. 317–338. For a translation, see Shuzo Uenaka, "Last Testament in Exile: Yamaga Sokō's *Haisho Zampitsu*," *Monumenta Nipponica*, vol. 32, no. 2 (Summer 1977), pp. 125–152.

Figure 6.2 Yamaga Sokō. Photograph by the author.

In 1672, Hoshina Masayuki, a relative of and trusted advisor to the shogun, passed away. Hoshina had been, by virtually all accounts, responsible for Yamaga's exile. Hoshina had also been a disciple of Yamazaki Ansai's Confucian teachings. Three years after Hoshina's death, corresponding to the Confucian period of mourning, Yamaga was pardoned and allowed to return to Edo. But in Edo, he remained under semi-house arrest. He was, then, hardly a free or restored man. The reported thousands who once took him as their teacher had scattered. Several outer daimyō, including Matsuura Shigenobu, lord of Hirado domain on Kyushu, and Tsugaru Nobumasa, lord of Hirosaki domain in northwestern Honshu, remained faithful followers, but overall Yamaga's post-exile broadcast was greatly reduced. He was not, for example, allowed to lecture to large gatherings of rōnin as he had prior to 1666. Also, his *Sagely Confucian Teachings* was never republished. Reportedly, the woodblocks had been destroyed.

Ambitious and obliging Tokugawa vassals distanced themselves from Yamaga and his tainted teachings. Yamaga's return to Edo also coincided with the final eight years of his life. By the time of his pardon, he was a physically reduced man, the vitality that once animated his early years and drove his productivity all but gone. His last major project, a metaphysical text exploring the foundations of change, *Exposition of the Origins of Change and Our Springs to Action* (*Gengen hakki*), remained incomplete at his passing. Despite the blows to his professional life that exile brought, Yamaga's diary reveals that until the end he continued to dream, literally, of receiving robes with the Tokugawa crest, symbolic of his desire to become a Tokugawa retainer. By the time he died, apparently from malaria, Yamaga's fame and notoriety seemed like things of the past.

The vendetta further doomed his teachings, in Edo at least. Despite numerous essays declaring the rōnin "righteous samurai," the shogunal verdict was that they were capital criminals. A show of sympathy or solidarity with them was not the politically correct stance for prudent, ambitious Edo samurai. Amid the Confucian discussions, Yamaga and his teachings were assigned, if anything, ideological blame for the murderous outrageousness displayed first by Asano Naganori and then by his rōnin. Yet there is no evidence that Yamaga or his thought had any direct bearing on the vendetta.[24] Nevertheless, scholars belonging to Ogyū Sorai's and Yamazaki Ansai's schools lost no time in denouncing Yamaga's writings, knowing that such denunciations were safe and would sound convincing, especially since the shogunate had earlier punished Yamaga as a troublemaker. With the vendetta debates, then, the posthumous vilification of Yamaga's teachings began. By 1744, following decades of atrophy, what remained of the Yamaga school in Edo closed.[25]

Yet even as Yamaga's thought ended up as a pariah form of learning among pro-shogunal forces in Edo, its purported association with the rōnin vendetta seemingly facilitated its emergence in distant outer domains such as Chōshū. There it apparently was a philosophy favored all the more because of its supposed associations with a vendetta that had targeted a shogunal official. The thinking seems to have been that if Yamaga's teachings could inspire such loyalty, righteousness, and martial resolution, they were more than worthy of promotion in the distant, less loyal domains. For those domains, Yamaga's exile by the shogunate apparently made his thought even more appealing, giving it the credibility that comes with punishment by a regime not universally admired. Spurious allegations meant to condemn Yamaga's teachings

[24] Hori Isao, *Yamaga Sokō* (Tokyo: Yoshikawa kōbunkan, 1967), pp. 267–278.
[25] Hori, *Yamaga Sokō*, p. 319.

soon became bragging points for far-flung advocates of the Yamaga philosophy. In time, the latter teachings, reimagined positively in relation to the vendetta, came to inspire considerable anti-Tokugawa samurai activism, including that of "resolute samurai" such as Yoshida Shōin.

The cardinal question addressed in the debates, however, was whether the rōnin had acted as *chūshin gishi*, i.e., "loyal and righteous samurai," or simply as rōnin who behaved in an indefensibly "unrighteous" manner. An important subtext of those discussions was whether the rōnin might be legitimately enshrined. In many respects, this question was irrelevant because the reality of reverence if not worship had begun shortly after their seppuku. Even before that, to provide for remembrance of Asano Naganori, whom none deemed a *chūshin gishi*, Ōishi had acted to ensure that the foundations for spiritual remembrance were in place following his lord's demise. Also, the Hosokawa daimyō had declared Ōishi and the other rōnin who committed seppuku while in his custody to be protective deities for his retainers.

Confucian sanction or not, others made offerings to the rōnin where and when they could. Theoretical sanction as *chūshin gishi* simply would have legitimized what was surely in the making, one way or another. Most Confucian discussions favored gracious ethical regard for the rōnin rather than harsh and inflexible denunciations. It should be emphasized, however, that the issue was not, in Tokugawa times, a matter of majority rule. Indeed, despite substantial consensus that the rōnin were *chūshin gishi*, powerful counterstatements emerged. Also, until the shogunate reversed its stance on the vendetta, the rōnin remained officially among those whose deeds had resulted in shogunally decreed death sentences. And ultimately, the philosophical debates brought no absolute closure: in the nineteenth and twentieth centuries, similar discussions continued with intellectuals of all sorts advancing various and profoundly conflicting ethical assessments of the rōnin and their lethal acts of loyalty.

Tokugawa scholars who argued that the rōnin were not *chūshin gishi* were not simply defending the legal wisdom of the shogunate. Rather, they were in effect denying that the rōnin were worthy of spiritual honor and recognition. Since worship of the rōnin might have provided the beginnings of a cult of martyrs around which opposition might rally, checking that possibility theoretically was perhaps a far greater service to the regime than simple support for its notions of justice. On the other hand, those extolling the loyalty and righteousness of the rōnin were not merely offering posthumous praise for their heroes. Rather, they were, in effect, legitimizing theoretically their enshrinement and arguably ensuring the practical safety of Edo and the realm from the feared spiritual consequences of doing otherwise. Given that the rōnin had defined themselves in opposition to shogunal law, this legitimization was, incidentally, a boon for those intent on rallying self-sacrificing challenges to the shogunate.

Yet it might have seemed premature, especially in the early eighteenth century, for admirers of the rōnin eagerly to advocate their apotheosis. A crucial first step, if the pattern followed in China was any indication, was the production of a substantial literature recording heroic loyalism and providing a scriptural basis for adoration. Some of this literature appeared with the accounts of the rōnin produced by Muro and other later writers. It was supplemented by subsequent essays defending their deeds. From the perspective of those intent on revering the rōnin with sacrificial worship, heresies appeared with the writings of Satō and Dazai. But even the latter served a necessary purpose in eliciting essays reaffirming impassioned approbation of the rōnin as *chūshin gishi*.

In many ways, the rōnin literature continued an earlier genre of loyalist writings that appeared in late Song China. However, unlike the latter, wherein the spiritual glory of loyalist martyrdom was dimmed by the eventual conquest of Song China, the successful and popular rōnin cause seemed irrepressible, even ascendant throughout the late eighteenth century and well into the nineteenth, increasingly associated with, by shogunal default, imperial loyalism. Apotheosis was not accomplished via the debate, but some of the grounds for the possibility of the liturgical and spiritual recognition of the rōnin were established through it.

Partly because later proponents of the Yamaga School embraced allegations that Yamaga's teachings had played a crucial role in the vendetta, the rōnin rose to prominence in the early Meiji period in tandem with those educated in the Yamaga teachings, especially as the latter assumed powerful positions in the new imperial regime. The most striking example in Japanese history of spiritual veneration for the rōnin occurred when the new emperor, en route to his new capital, sent an imperial rescript to be read before Ōishi's grave

Figure 6.3 Gravestone of Asano Naganori at the Kagakuji. Photograph by the author.

at the Sengakuji. The emperor's pronouncement effectively eclipsed the judgment handed down by the now-fallen shogunate, praising the rōnin as utmost exemplars of loyalty and righteousness. By this historic and unprecedented rescript, the Meiji emperor effectively sanctioned, via his deed, reverent veneration for the rōnin at the Sengakuji.

Paralleling the growing consensus that the rōnin were *chūshin gishi* meriting sacrificial worship, a new development occurred in 1739 at the Kagakuji, the Sōtō Zen temple that Asano Naganao had founded as his family's place of worship in Akō. With the blessings of the chief priest, the Mori daimyō, then lord of Akō domain, and the efforts of one of the Mori retainers, Kobayashi Sadama, a set of gravestones was carved and a second rōnin cemetery established, providing in Akō a place of veneration for the rōnin. Symbolizing the close relationship between Asano Naganori and his retainers, the Kagakuji cemetery was eventually arranged around a gravestone for Asano, flanked by one for Ōishi Yoshio on the right and one for Ōishi Chikara, Yoshio's son, on the left. Smaller tombstones for the other rōnin surrounded them. The cemetery opened on the occasion of the thirty-seventh memorial service for the rōnin held at the Kagakuji. Reportedly, the gravesites included a lock of hair from each of the rōnin. Another gravestone was added for Terasaka after his death in 1747, due to the efforts of an *ashigaru* in service to the Mori who admired his fellow *ashigaru*'s "loyalty and fidelity" (*chūshin*).[26] Thus, a new site of rōnin reverence, a Sengakuji doppelgänger of sorts, appeared in Akō.

[26] Taiunzan Kagakuji website. 2009–2016. kagakuji.jimdo.com/赤穂義士について. Accessed September 24, 2016.

7 HISTORY ON STAGE

The vendetta of history is often marginalized in favor of its dramatic reinvention, *Kanadehon Chūshingura*. This chapter seeks to contextualize the play and its dramatic content in relation to the unfolding of the vendetta in history, especially its spiritual dimensions. This chapter suggests that early on its appeal reflected popular fascination with the vendetta, but also a need to experience, and perhaps contribute to, spiritual closure with the incident. Additionally, this chapter notes that the popularity of *Chūshingura* prompted parodies that stood, arguably, as counterstatements irreverently contesting dimensions of the drama. Similarly, the substantial quantities of woodblock ephemera *Chūshingura* generated soon elicited repeated parodies in artistic representation. By the late Tokugawa, the vendetta was so widely known, albeit along lines confusing history and drama, that woodblock maps of Edo identified the modest Sengakuji, typically adding, in a significant spiritual vein, that it was there that one could find "the graves of the forty-seven samurai."

Vendetta Remembrance: Spiritual and Secular

In the early 1750s, the Sengakuji, the Kagakuji, and other temples held fiftieth-anniversary memorial services for Asano Naganori, and then, nearly two years later, similar services were staged for Ōishi and the rōnin. Simultaneously, kabuki actor Yamamoto Kyōshirō gained fame playing Ōboshi Yura-no-suke – Ōishi Kura-no-suke Yoshio's dramatic reincarnation – in *Kanadehon Chūshingura*, staged at the Morita-za,

Figure 7.1 "Scene from the Play *Chūshingura* at the Nakamura Theatre." Museum of Fine Arts, Boston. Photograph © Museum of Fine Arts, Boston, 2016.

one of the licensed theatres in Edo. This historical coincidence of the spiritual and the secular was not lost on contemporaries. The postface to "Horiuchi Den'emon's Memorandum" notes how Buddhist ceremonies and theatrical performances resonated, with key historical figures from the vendetta appearing under aliases in the kabuki play.[1]

The link between traditional Buddhist memorial services and innovative dramatizations of the historical tragedy points to a widespread, heartfelt epistemological and spiritual need for some means of knowing, understanding, and reverently responding, spiritually and experientially, to the events comprising the vendetta. Buddhist temples offered one option, that of memorial services, for family and close associates. But even Buddhist services often ended with the fiftieth, leaving those feeling spiritual loss in a vacuum of remembrance and reverence. Yet as Carl Lumbly notes, theatre can serve as a form of secular worship.[2] Through it, admiration, adoration, entertainment, and mystical union with the past as recreated in the staged

[1] "Horiuchi Den'emon oboegaki," *Akō gijin sansho*, vol. 1, p. 409.
[2] Michael Rosen, "Carl Lumbly: 'Theatre is secular worship,'" *SFGate* (August 27, 2015). www.sfgate.com/performance/article/Carl-Lumbly-Theater-is-secular-worship-6469120.php. Last accessed September 24, 2016.

present can bring those watching a sense of personal, empathetic, and even ontological investment in the drama. Simultaneously, theatre can resolve otherwise unsettled spiritual forces inherent in one's historical experience. Most importantly, for the masses of townspeople in Edo and Osaka, theatre offered an outlet for immersion in the past, facilitating achievement of mystic commonality with those lost, yet still remembered and revered.

Tokugawa vendetta drama was thus in the tradition of Nō drama, often staged at temples and shrines, entertaining, teaching, and even spiritually touching those attending. Akō vendetta drama, most famously *Kanadehon Chūshingura*, likewise provided a religiously nuanced occasion as well, one wherein patrons got more than saké and samurai entertainment. On stage, moments of spiritual clarity and release were achieved as tragic conflicts found refined and suitably beautiful expression and closure. Through drama, people experienced a facsimile of history, and with intuitive reactions, responded to its truth and reality, spiritually and emotionally.

Literary critic Maruya Saiichi has suggested that much as the historical vendetta sought to appease Asano's vengeful spirit (*onryō*), the kabuki play, *Chūshingura*, was "a kind of 'carnival' in the European manner, a springtime festival involving the ritual killing of the king of winter – in this case, Moronao [Kira's dramatic double]."[3] Modifying Maruya's controversial interpretation, this chapter suggests that dramatic reformulations of the vendetta might be viewed more indigenously as *matsuri*, or religious festival events, meant to entertain as well as facilitate spiritual resolution, or a kind of religious catharsis through which audiences reliving the events vicariously revere the rōnin and then, with their victory and passing, achieve closure and release, epistemic and spiritual. Whether all who attended *Chūshingura* imagined themselves as engaged in such spirituality is questionable, but it would seem naïve to think that early modern rōnin vendetta dramas communicated no spiritual dimension whatsoever.

Early Dramatic Reincarnations

In Edo, the vendetta quickly became the talk of the town. The events had impacted a broad range of the city's population including those living

---

[3] Maruya Saiichi, *Chūshingura to wa nani ka* (Tokyo: Kōdansha, 1984). For a critical summary of the controversy sparked by Maruya's book, see Henry D. Smith II, "*Chūshingura* in the 1980s" in Wetmore, *Revenge Drama*, pp. 203–205.

and working near Edo Castle, the Tamura compound, the Sengakuji, the Asano residences, Kira's old and new mansions, rōnin lodgings all over Edo, the route from Honjo to the Sengakuji, the chief inspector's residence in Atagoshita, plus the four daimyō compounds – leaving a trail of sights and sounds that bred sensational rumor, gossip, and fantasy as well as bits and pieces of reliable history. And then there was the far-flung broadcast from Edo to Akō and beyond, with a special transmission in Kyoto via on-the-scene imperial emissaries after their return to court. Yet rather than scraps of scattered, hinterland hearsay, the fascinated public wanted the whole story, or at least "a whole story," and wanted this even more because the shogunate seemed determined to provide silence, initially quashing efforts to do otherwise.

Playwrights quickly noted how the Akō vendetta recalled the Soga vendetta, one of the most famous historical and then dramatic tales ever. In no time, there were attempts at a romanticized reinvention, representing the incident by embellishing and refining the historically macabre with a more humane, ethically clear-cut, and emotionally and spiritually moving dramatic storyline. Once the nitty-gritty of the rag-tag vendetta was wrapped in romantic, dapper, gender-diverse, righteous drama, supplemented with colorful woodblock ephemera, the staged reincarnation resonated with audiences as no other drama of history had, not even the Soga. In the process, the staged vendetta became, unquestionably, more dramatic fiction than history, with bloody realities tamed by well-orchestrated and choreographed reinventions of the past. But whatever the distortions of history, at least the story was told, in a coherent and attractive manner, rather than suppressed without consideration for the populace's need to know and spiritually respond to the profoundly moving events comprising the vendetta. The innovations in the dramatic reformulation were not terribly problematic because, after all, most contemporaries had no clear grasp of the difference between history and historical drama. In the aftermath of the phenomenally popular *Chūshingura*, sorting the two out would take centuries of scholarly effort, and still is hardly complete.

Dramatic reformulations emerged as quickly as the philosophical debates. On the sixteenth day of the second month, just two weeks after the rōnin seppuku, the first kabuki dramatization was reportedly staged, *The Soga Brothers' Dawn Vendetta* (*Akebono Soga no yōchi*). By presenting the vendetta with the nomenclature of the medieval Soga vendetta, already the archetype of revenge attacks, the popularity of both was compounded.[4] The tale of the Soga brothers, Gorō and Jūrō, traced back to the twenty-eighth day of the fifth month of 1193, when they reportedly took revenge on their father's murderer. Jūrō was killed in the attack and Gorō was later executed. The shogun, Minamoto Yoritomo, reportedly admired the brothers' filial dedication, but punished Gorō because Gorō's victim was one of his, Yoritomo's, retainers.

The Soga story was first recorded in a medieval work on the history of the Kamakura shogunate, *Reflections of Eastern Japan* (*Azuma kagami*), compiled a century after the vendetta. The story was subsequently popularized in narrative fiction as *The Tale of the Soga Vendetta* (*Soga monogatari*). Several Nō plays and an entire genre of dances, puppet plays, and kabuki performances followed. In the early Tokugawa, the Soga tale remained exceptionally popular, with woodblock prints amply embellishing kabuki performances. However, the play that was staged in 1703 was more than simply another expression of the popular medieval tale. Within days of its opening, the shogunate reportedly shut it down, thus censoring its disturbing echoes of the Akō vendetta. Earlier, the shogunate had prohibited dramatizations of "recent events," hoping to check popularizations of anti-shogunal incidents, i.e., the vendetta.[5] From the regime's perspective, *The Soga Brothers' Dawn Vendetta* was simply a thinly veiled representation of the Akō vendetta, glorifying those who had taken lethal vengeance on allegedly evil government officials. Drama of that sort could not be permitted.

Veiled explorations of the vendetta continued to surface, with kabuki giving way to puppet theatre. One reason for the shift was economic: since plays ran the risk of being shut down, the least expensive option was deemed the most cost-effective. Puppet theatre was centered in Osaka, while kabuki, more of an Edo form, was subject to tighter shogunal control. Puppet theatre was also enjoying the talents of its greatest playwright, Chikamatsu Monzaemon, whose works defined much of its repertoire. In 1683, Chikamatsu attained fame with *The Heirs of the Soga*, one of eleven plays he wrote on the Soga tale.[6]

[4] D. E. Mills, "Kataki-uchi: The Practice of Blood Revenge in Pre-modern Japan," *Modern Asian Studies*, 10/4 (1976), pp. 530–531.
[5] Mills, "Kataki-uchi," pp. 530–531, 536, 541–542. Donald H. Shively, *"Tokugawa Plays on Forbidden Subjects,"* in *Chūshingura: Studies in Kabuki and the Puppet Theatre*, ed. James R. Brandon (Honolulu: University of Hawaii Press, 1982), p. 36.
[6] Mills, "Kataki-uchi," p. 541.

He later authored a one-act play on the Akō vendetta, *The Taiheiki on a Game Board (Goban Taiheki)*, dating from around 1706.[7] In it, he presented Kō-no-Moronao, a villain of the *Chronicle of Great Peace*, as a surrogate for Kira, and Enya Hangan, the victim of Kō's villainy, as the dramatic double of Asano Naganori. Chikamatsu's play included all forty-seven of the historical rōnin in "the thinnest of disguises," with Ōishi Kura-no-suke presented as Ōboshi Yura-no-suke, Ōishi Chikara as Ōboshi Rikiya, etc.[8] The play altered the vendetta at every turn, so that history was soon masked by dramatic fiction. Chikamatsu thereby facilitated the metamorphosis of a dramatic event in history into a drama of historical legend, one full of nuanced fabrication and unabashed embellishment, making the vendetta even more coherent, entertaining, and spiritually satisfying.

By identifying the villain as Kō-no-Moronao, Chikamatsu offered possible resolution to a vendetta puzzle: why had Asano (Enya) attacked Kira (Kō)? Chikamatsu presents Kō as a lecher,[9] lusting after Lady Ayame, the wife of Enya Hangan, captain of the imperial police. Kō plotted to have Enya charged with treason to remove him from the object of his, Kō's, desires. Enya's retainers learned this and secured his wife and children. Later, the retainers killed Enya's family and committed seppuku themselves. When Enya heard this, he also committed seppuku. But in the end, Ōboshi Yura-no-suke took revenge on Kō. Chikamatsu thus hinted that Kira, like Kō, had designs on Asano's (Enya's) wife, which presumably prompted Asano to attack him. Of course, there is no evidence establishing this, but the human interest appeal of a fateful, conflicted love triangle resolved by seppuku, assassination, then more seppuku apparently fascinated mid-eighteenth-century audiences.

Chikamatsu's play further embellished history by having Ōboshi's wife and mother commit suicide the day he departed for Kamakura. In addition to these fabricated suicides, the play is set in Kamakura, the first shogunal capital, rather than nearby Edo, the

---

[7] Jacqueline Mueller, "A Chronicle of Great Peace Played Out on a Chessboard: Chikamatsu Monzaemon's Goban Taiheki," *Harvard Journal of Asiatic Studies*, 46/1 (June 1986), pp. 221–267.

[8] For a listing, see Mueller, "Goban Taiheiki," pp. 225–226.

[9] Chikamatsu actually deals with these events in another play, written months prior to *Goban Taiheiki*, entitled *Kenkō hōshi monomiguruma*. Some consider it a prelude to *Goban Taiheiki*. See Mueller, "Goban Taiheiki," p. 223.

capital of the third shogunate, the Tokugawa. The women – as loyal wife and mother – took their lives to protest Ōboshi's apparent dissipation and to ensure that he thought only of fulfilling his duty to Enya rather than worry over them. Thus, Chikamatsu injected a substantial, melodramatic dimension of self-sacrificing female heroics into the drama. In history, women – even Tsunayoshi's mother and Ōishi's wife – played peripheral, behind-the-scenes roles. Ōishi did, significantly enough, divorce his wife, sending her back to her family's home along with their young children. And he reportedly visited Kyoto's Gion tea houses, and a mistress there whom he later left pregnant even as he proceeded to the vendetta. Rather than marginalize women, Chikamatsu made sure that they had more assertive and heroic, albeit tragic roles in *The Taiheiki on a Game Board*.[10]

Chikamatsu's play fabricated in its presentation of the rōnin committing suicide on the same day as the vendetta against Kō,[11] and doing so at the Kōmyōji, the dramatic surrogate of the Sengakuji. Historically, the rōnin went to the Sengakuji, reported their vendetta to the grand inspector, and then awaited the judgment of the shogunate. Their seppuku came two months later, at the daimyō mansions where they were detained. Later vendetta debates criticized the rōnin for waiting rather than immediately doing what had to be done, commit seppuku then and there at the Sengakuji. By portraying Ōboshi Yura-no-suke's band carrying out prompt seppuku at the Kōmyōji, Chikamatsu reimagined the vendetta along proactively heroic lines.

One might even argue that Chikamatsu anticipated the criticisms of Dazai and others. His script allowed the staged rōnin to avoid being charged with selfish, ulterior motives, including greedy desires for pardons and future stipends. Chikamatsu's play also anticipated later critics' calls for quicker action, even a wild rush into death, by simply omitting the rōnin confinement during the shogunate's prolonged deliberations over their vendetta. Via prompt seppuku, the vendetta emerged crisper, its closure, more unequivocal, and the rōnin, even more heroic. Despite the dramatic virtues of Chikamatsu's play, the shogunate shut it down, leaving this early attempt at staging history and spiritually remembering the rōnin another victim of shogunal efforts to terminate the vendetta.

---

[10] Mueller, "Goban Taiheiki," p. 227.   [11] Ibid., pp. 227–228.

A Buddhist Priest's Sermons

Ties between vendetta performances and spirituality appeared variously, especially in the hinterlands. In 1744, Motoori Norinaga, then fourteen, took notes on a series of sermons delivered by an itinerant Buddhist priest, Jitsudō, at a Pure Land temple, the Jukyōji, in his, Norinaga's, hometown, Matsusaka, Ise province. Jitsudō's topic was the "loyal samurai of Akō domain." Jitsudō apparently attracted listeners with the tale, and sermonized along the way. As a mature scholar, Motoori was a leading proponent of nativist learning, rejecting Confucian and Buddhist moralizing in favor of unadulterated native traditions. However, when he set down Jitsudō's tale, he was simply an educated country boy recording a fascinating samurai tale. The sermons of priests such as Jitsudō helped spread news of the vendetta deep into the countryside, one temple at a time, transforming history into an expedient means for delivering Pure Land Buddhist teachings.[12]

Jitsudō's sermons overlapped with "quasi-public" productions known as "true accounts" (*jitsuroku*). Although claiming to be authentic history, true accounts were typically mixtures of history and historical fiction that circulated widely via both published manuscripts and oral performances. As with Jitsudō's sermons, true accounts were true in the sense that they did not disguise historical realities with aliases or doubles. Nevertheless, they were not true in any strict sense, and often included fabrications meant to appeal to audiences. In Jitsudō's sermons, details from puppet plays, kabuki, and vernacular works, as well as rumors and gossip, all surface. One of his more important, identifiable sources was Katashima Shin'en's *Biographies of the Righteous Samurai of Akō Castle* (*Sekijō gishiden*, 1719), a collection of short stories about the rōnin. Although the shogunate banned its publication, it circulated through handwritten copies, and to a greater degree through oral performances. Together, Jitsudō's sermons and Katashima's *Biographies* contributed significantly to quasi-historical, increasingly fictionalized broadcasts of the vendetta.[13]

---

[12] Federico Marcon and Henry D. Smith II, "A Chūshingura Palimpsest: Young Motoori Norinaga Hears the Story of the Akō Rōnin from a Buddhist Priest," *Monumenta Nipponica*, 58/4 (Winter 2003), pp. 467–493.

[13] The term *jitsuroku* is used here largely as in Marcon and Smith, "A Chūshingura Palimpsest," p. 448, especially note 23.

Federico Marcon and Henry Smith have identified "nineteen 'fictional' episodes" in Jitsudō's sermons that furthered the apocryphal metamorphosis of the vendetta. One concerns Ōishi's mistress, Okaru. Reportedly, Ōishi left her pregnant when he moved to Edo for the vendetta. In a letter written to a Kyoto priest late in the eleventh month, just weeks before the attack, he asked that the priest help with the impending "Nijō birth" (Okaru apparently lived on Second Street, i.e., Nijō, in Kyoto). Karu, as she was called, gave birth to a son. Jitsudō's sermons, however, have Okaru cut her hair, give it to Ōishi, and then kill herself. This fabrication, perhaps meant to magnify the drama by tapping into a variation of the love-suicide theme, was not a mainstay of later retellings of the vendetta. Another fictitious episode presents Ōishi, during the attack, single-handedly fighting and killing "three notable warriors, experts with the spear and sword, [who] clambered up the pillars and attacked him from above."[14] Credible sources, however, have Ōishi remaining in a command position at the front gate, without engaging in heated combat.

In another flight of fiction, Jitsudō presents Ōishi as the heroic avenger who, when the group had lost hope, discovered Kira and informed him that the rōnin had come to take his head. Ōishi explained to Kira that the attack was meant to "uphold the way of lord and vassal," and so invited Kira to commit seppuku. When Kira blamed Asano for the attack and demanded that the rōnin leave, Ōishi signaled Takebayashi Tadashichi to behead him. The other rōnin then struck Kira's corpse with their swords, reducing it "to shreds." Contrary to Jitsudō's narrative, another Buddhist, Gekkai, reported that Kira had been discovered in a charcoal closet, and that it was Hazama Jūjirō who killed him and carried his head to the Sengakuji.[15] Gekkai does not mention Ōishi's role in either the discovery or the killing of Kira. Apparently, Ōishi's role was that of a strategic leader, commanding but above the fray, while the rōnin cut down everyone in Kira's compound who resisted and asked questions later. With Jitsudō, Ōishi is cast as the single most heroic figure with an active combat role far surpassing anything documented in credible sources.

[14] Marcon, "The Story of the Loyal Samurai of Akō," *Monumenta Nipponica*, p. 487.
[15] Marcon and Smith, "A Chūshingura Palimpsest," pp. 447, 453–454, 458–459. Gekkai, *Hakumyō waroku, Akō gijin sansho*, vol. 3, p. 122.

Another apocryphal detail in Jitsudō's sermons concerns the journey of Kira's head to the Sengakuji. The most reliable account of that event, *Hakumyō's Memoir*, written by the monk Gekkai, specifically mentions that the head was not transported by boat. Instead, it was carried by Hazama Jūjirō, the rōnin who killed Kira.[16] Jitsudō claims, however, that there were two heads: one real, transported by boat and accompanied by Yoshida Chūzaemon and Tominomori Suke'emon, and another, a decoy, carried by the other rōnin on land.[17] But Gekkai relates that Ōishi had sent Yoshida and Tominomori to report the vendetta to the shogunate's chief inspector, while the rest of the group marched to the Sengakuji.[18] Jitsudō later adds his new twist to the story, oblivious to the double duty his accounts assign Yoshida and Tominomori. Apparently by Jitsudō's day, the boat voyage of the head in tandem with the rōnin march of the decoy around the fringe of eastern Edo had become intriguing parts of freely evolving narratives transitioning from credible documents to dramatic historical fiction.[19]

Jitsudō claims that after killing Kira, the rōnin stopped at a saké shop. Later, they were detained at the residence of Matsudaira Mutsu no kami, where they were called "true samurai" and treated to more saké. A contingent of Matsudaira's men reportedly escorted them to the Sengakuji. After arriving, they proceeded directly to the grave of their lord, according to Jitsudō, where Ōishi placed Kira's head in front of Asano's grave, and offered alongside it the dagger that he, Ōishi, had received from Asano following the latter's death. Ōishi then declared, "Today we have brought Kira here. My lord, strike him as you please." Jitsudō reports that the retainers next offered incense and wept for joy.[20]

[16] Gekkai, *Hakumyō waroku*, *Akō gijin sansho*, vol. 2, p. 122.
[17] Marcon, "The Story of the Loyal Samurai of Akō," p. 489.
[18] Gekkai concurs on this. *Hakumyō waroku*, *Akō gishi sansho*, vol. 3, p. 119.
[19] Marcon and Smith note (p. 456) that Imao Tetsuya's *Kira no kubi: Chūshingura to imajineeshon* (Tokyo: Heibonsha, 1987) has shown that shortly after the vendetta, rumors multiplied regarding what had become of Kira's head. Some claimed that there had been three heads and others allowed only two. The real head, rumor generally agreed, was taken to the Sengakuji in advance by a small group of rōnin, ranging in number from two to six. The means of transport varied, with some rumors citing a land route while others included boat transport. The head or heads carried by the remainder of the rōnin was either a "dummy" or the head of one of Kira's retainers.
[20] Marcon, "The Story of the Loyal Samurai of Akō," pp. 489–490.

However, Gekkai had earlier recorded that the rōnin were unsure what to do after taking Kira's head. Gekkai even notes that they stopped at the Ekōin to commit seppuku, but were turned away. Gekkai records no other stops until the rōnin arrived at the Sengakuji, exhausted, famished, and unaccompanied by samurai escort. After presenting the head at Asano's grave, they placed it in a box in the temple kitchen and left it. Gekkai denies accounts by illiterates suggesting that the rōnin had placed the foul, polluted head before a group of sacred, ritually clean Buddhist statues, icons, and memorials.[21] In short, the credible monk's eyewitness account of the graveside ceremony helps to lay bare the fabrications spun in Jitsudō's sermons.

Jitsudō's claim that Ōishi presented Kira's head and asked the deceased Asano to "strike him as you please" alludes to the apocryphal "Ōishi's Prayer" included in Muro's *Righteous Men of Akō*.[22] Muro concludes his account of "Ōishi's Prayer" by noting that the dagger Asano had bequeathed to Ōishi was being returned, with the invitation to Asano's spirit to use it against Kira so as to console the anger and resentment that he, Asano, had felt since first attacking Kira. This account of "Ōishi's Prayer" was widely repeated in later retellings of the vendetta even though Miyake Kanran, a Confucian disciple of Asami Keisai, early on declared it apocryphal.[23] One account has the reading of "Ōishi's Prayer" followed by the rōnin each picking up the dagger and striking Kira's head three times, presumably as a way of achieving completion for the group.

Confucians and Buddhists believed that those who died violent deaths, especially when wronged, carried anger into the afterlife and often, as a result, asserted themselves in the human world by wreaking vengeance. To pacify angry spirits, regular prayers, offerings, and memorial services were staged. The presentation of Kira's head was no doubt done, "Ōishi's Prayer" or not, with that intent. Jitsudō's sermons were also meant, even through fabrication, to help lay Asano's soul to rest. Despite their many apocryphal layers, the sermons remain significant because they document the vendetta being communicated deep into the

[21] Gekkai, *Hakumyō waroku, Akō gijin sansho*, vol. 3, p. 123.
[22] Marcon, "The Story of the Loyal Samurai of Akō," p. 490. Muro Kyūsō, *Akō gijin roku*, NST vol. 27, pp. 603–604.
[23] "Saimon," *Akō gishi jiten*, p. 559. Kanran made this claim in his *Account of the Vendetta of the Fierce Samurai (Resshi hōshū roku)*. However, later works still presented the *Saimon* as a legitimate document.

hinterlands. Moreover, in addition to Buddhist teachings, Jitsudō surely saw his retellings as a way of memorializing the rōnin throughout the land, thus aiding in their pervasive spiritual pacification. In the culture of representation and remembrance associated with the vendetta, his sermons were hardly the last contribution to this project of rōnin spiritual reconciliation. Indeed, a considerable portion of what followed in Tokugawa cultural developments was, arguably, of that nature.

Staged Doppelgängers

Kanadehon Chūshingura is the greatest work in the history of Japanese theatre.[24] Since first being staged at the Takemoto puppet theatre in Osaka, it has been presented more times, in more forms, and in more countries than any other Japanese play. In its first fifty years, *Chūshingura* was performed more than one hundred times, as kabuki and puppet theatre, in Edo, Osaka, and Kyoto, in "production runs lasting days, weeks, and even months." Before the end of the Tokugawa, there were an estimated seventy puppet theatre and two hundred eighty kabuki performances.[25] In the Meiji, it was even more popular. In the twentieth century, it soared as a regular stage hit and as the subject of countless movies and multi-episode TV series, plus runs in comic books

[24] The number of translations worldwide reflect *Chūshingura*'s impact. The standard English translation is Donald Keene, *Chūshingura: The Treasury of Loyal Retainers* (New York: Columbia University Press, 1971). The first into a foreign language, *Zhong chen ku*, was by Chen Hongmeng, a Qing scholar who recast a Sino-Japanese (*kanbun*) version of the text into Chinese, published in 1794. The first English translation was Frederick Dickins' *Chiushingura, or, The Loyal League: A Japanese Romance* (London: Allen & Co., 1880). Jukichi Inouye improved on Dickins' work in *Chūshingura, or The Treasury of Loyal Retainers* (Tokyo: Nakanishi-ya, 1894). Albert Dousdebès translated Dickins' rendition into French as *Tchou-Chin-Goura, ou Une Vengeance Japonaise* (Paris: Paul Ollendorff, 1886). The standard French translation is included in a set of translations by René Sieffert and Michel Wassermann, *Le Mythe des quarante-sept rōnins: Kenkō-Hōshi monomi-guruma par Chikamatsu Monzaemon; Goban Taihei par Chikamatsu Monzaemon; Le Trésor des vassaux fidèles par Takeda Izumo; Fantômes à Yotsuya par Tsuruya Namboku* (Paris: Publications Orientalistes de France, 1981) *Chūshingura* was rendered into Italian by Mario Marega, trans., *Il Ciuscingura, La vendetta dei 47 rōnin* (Bari: Gius. Laterza & Figli, 1948).

[25] William D. Fleming, "Restaging the Forty-Seven Rōnin: Performance and Print in Late Eighteenth-Century Japan," *Eighteenth-Century Studies*, vol. 48, no. 4 (Summer 2015), pp. 395–397.

and animated films. Nothing in the history of Japanese drama has matched the extensive, perennial broadcast of *Chūshingura*.

Three playwrights – Takeda Izumo, Miyoshi Shōraku, and Namiki Sōsuke – are credited with dramatically beautifying and transforming the vendetta. They did this by weaving the revenge narrative into romantic subplots, enhancing samurai history with personal dimensions involving women and children. Also, in addition to warrior values, they incorporated a range of socioeconomic sensibilities, thus giving the drama a far broader, urban appeal than the historical event ever had. Yet there was also a political subtext, that of righteous resistance to corrupt rule, coupled with, on two occasions, the heroic yet tragic fate met by those making a purportedly righteous stand against perceived wrongs. Whatever one's assessment of the historical Asano Naganori, in *Chūshingura* his counterpart, Enya Hangan, makes an aggressive stand for honesty, transparency, and fairness in political and administrative relations. In doing so, he was prepared to die and did, without second, by his own hand, surrounded by loved ones and ultimately by his chief retainer, Ōboshi Yura-no-suke.

Later, his avengers, long-suffering, ethically minded rōnin, plotted to fulfill their lord's spiritual intentions by opposing the forces of greed, bribery, and abusive power via resort to a well-planned move against the evil minister who brought about their master's downfall. Ancient East Asian political thought provided well-known precedents for this response. Arguably the rōnin were attacking evil much as King Wu, in remote Chinese antiquity, had overthrown the debauched and evil Shang dynasty and its inhumane last ruler, Zhou Xin. Zhou Xin had, incidentally, egregiously wronged King Wu's father, King Wen. While Kira's supposed abuses were not as insufferable, presumably, as those attributed to the last Shang monarch, the principle behind the rōnin resistance remained the same: attacking evil on behalf of good is justifiable as an expression of heaven's will. Whatever the provocation might have been, the evil of Kō-no-Moronao (Kira's dramatic double) was deemed sufficient grounds for considering him an offensive, detestable expression of political power against which the only righteous course was violent resistance. In being prepared to meet their fate once their deed was done, the rōnin on stage established their moral superiority and evident dedication to the larger good rather than mere selfish interests.

It is noteworthy that *Chūshingura* does not depict the deaths of the rōnin: it concludes with them, victorious, proceeding to their master's grave where, presumably, they were to present the head and then commit seppuku. Omitted, but understood by all, are those final deeds. Thus, the play bypasses considerable bloodletting, leaving it more focused on the success of the vendetta than the sad fate of the rōnin. Moreover, *Chūshingura* invites its audiences to join the march and pledge to advance the spiritual intentions of Ōboshi and the rōnin in resistance to evil. The authors of *Chūshingura*, incidentally, removed the action from the realities of the Tokugawa world, and situated it prudently in a more historically remote period, the beginning of the Ashikaga (1338–1573), the medieval period's second shogunate. However, the shift only made the play more interesting, even arguably universal in historical time, especially once the pressures of censorship were gone and the temporal charade no longer necessary. Most importantly, the grand drama of revenge against evil was suffused with spirituality, romance, love, and passion, and a host of characters who, in addition to the rōnin, were drawn from all major divisions of early modern society. In *Chūshingura*, there was something of meaning and significance for virtually everyone.

Chūshingura reuses the surrogate identities that Chikamatsu introduced in *Taiheiki on a Game Board*, with Kira having his double in Kō-no-Moronao. Asano Naganori has his in Enya Hangan. Assisting Enya in hosting Ashikaga Takauji's brother at the Tsurugaoka Hachiman Shrine is Momoi Wakasa-no-suke, the counterpart of Daté Sakyō-no-suke. Tsunayoshi's double is Ashikaga Takauji, founding shogun of the Ashikaga bakufu. Conveniently, by situating this reinvention of the vendetta at the start of the Ashikaga, *Chūshingura* sets the drama allusively in both the Momoyama area of Kyoto (the Ashikaga base), distant from Edo (but close, incidentally, to Yamashina, where Ōishi once lived), and in Kamakura, close to Edo, yet without being in it. *Chūshingura* thus preserves in amended fashion the Kantō-Kansai dynamic, and thereby appeals to large urban populations in both centers of culture, wealth, and power. The result, *Chūshingura*, is erudite and amusing, poignant yet playful, and convincing enough, especially for puppet theatre and the kabuki stage, where realism never ruled drama anyway. By purging the incident of its offensive, polluting dimensions and yet maintaining hints of the high moral, political, and spiritual drama, *Chūshingura* provided a moving and entertaining facsimile of the historical events. This was especially true as the play became more mainstream. Shogunal efforts to prohibit such performances had been relaxed, incidentally, following Tsunayoshi's death in 1709.[26]

A summary of *Chūshingura* reveals its spiritual resonance with and yet remaking of history. Act I is set at the beginning of the Ashikaga period, in 1338, with the founding shogun, Ashikaga Takauji, about to enshrine the helmet of his recently slain foe, Nitta Yoshisada, at the newly established Tsurugaoka Hachiman Shrine in Kamakura, dedicated to the god of war. The governor of Kamakura, Kō-no-Moronao (Kira), is coordinating the rituals. He has tapped two daimyō, Momoi Wakasa-no-suke (Daté Sakyō-no-suke), younger brother of the lord of Harima, and Enya Hangan (Asano Naganori), lord of Hōki Castle, to serve as ceremonial assistants. *Chūshingura* thus preserves the ritual background of the vendetta even as it makes it more spiritual and more thoroughly samurai in nature, with the helmet enshrinement rather than New Year's greetings from imperial emissaries as the occasion. The opening scene features Nitta, symbolized by his helmet, as a *chūshin gishi* of sorts, now being enshrined. *Chūshingura* hints that the rōnin – or properly speaking, the *chūshin*, or "loyal retainers," referred to in the title of the play – will merit similar enshrinement due to their anticipated self-sacrifices in the drama.

Enya's beautiful wife, Kaoyo, is brought in to confirm the identity of Nitta's helmet. After she has accomplished her task, Kō, lusting for her, approaches to slip a missive into her sleeve. Invoking his powerful, divine ally, Kō praises Ashikaga Tadayoshi, the shogun's brother, as "the deity who brought about their union." But Kaoyo rebuffs Kō's advances, dropping the letter. Frustrated, Kō pledges to pursue her until she consents, boasting that he "controls the rise and fall of all below heaven." He adds that the life of Kaoyo's husband will depend on her response to his, Kō's, overtures. Momoi then enters and witnesses the moment. Embarrassed, Kō bullies Momoi, threatening him with destruction. Momoi grasps his sword, but then remembers

---

[26] Donald H. Shively, "Tokugawa Plays on Forbidden Topics," in James R. Brandon, *Chūshingura: Studies in Kabuki and the Puppet Theater* (Honolulu: University of Hawaii Press, 1982), pp. 34–44. Tsunayoshi's passing in 1709 resulted in more license for veiled dramatic presentations of the vendetta. Shively notes that "By the time *Chūshingura* was performed, there was little concern about censorship since the writers followed the conventions, now well established, of how names and identities should be camouflaged."

Figure 7.2 Utagawa Hiroshige, "Act One, from the series *The Storehouse of Loyal Retainers (Chūshingura).*" Harvard Art Museums/Arthur M. Sackler Museum. Imaging Department © President and Fellows of Harvard College.

that he is in the presence of deities. Ashikaga Tadayoshi enters next, defusing tensions. Kō's lechery, coupled with threats directed at Momoi, reveal his evil and suggest that something similar prompted Asano's attack on Kira. The historical mystery haunting the Akō vendetta – why Asano attacked Kira – is inverted in *Chūshingura*: with Kō depicted as licentious and abusive, the mystery is why Asano did not attack sooner.

In Act II, Momoi tells his retainer, Kakogawa Honzō (Kajikawa Yosōbei's double), that he plans to kill Kō during the enshrinement ceremonies. Momoi knows that this will mean the end of his family line and the reduction of his retainers to rōnin, but affirms that in using his sword, he revers the deity of the samurai (*yumiya no kami*). He also explains that killing Kō will be for "the sake of the entire realm below heaven." After his master leaves, Kakogawa calls for a horse and rides off, intending to avert the impending disaster. In Act III, Kakogawa provides Kō with largesse in the hopes of kindness for his master, Momoi. Later, when Momoi arrives, Kō indeed praises him, apologizing profusely for his earlier harsh remarks. Momoi, ignorant of the bribe, is befuddled by the about-face and so, pleading illness, departs. When Enya arrives shortly after and is late, Kō turns bitter and lambastes him for his neglect of duty and righteousness. Enya endures Kō's anger and then naïvely delivers a poem – the contents of which he is unaware – from his wife. Kō reads it, only to learn that Kaoyo is again rejecting his passion. Livid, Kō taunts Enya obsessively, mocking him until Enya can no longer restrain himself. Finally, he draws his sword, strikes Kō on the forehead, and then strikes again. Kakogawa stops the attack, but the altercation has already created upheaval. Enya is confined and then transported to his residence, inside a bound prisoner's palanquin.

Enya's attack on Kō is thus made somewhat comprehensible: *Chūshingura* suggests it was the result of Kō's frustrated lust for Enya's wife, compounded by the absence of enticements from Enya for Kō that might otherwise have soothed the latter's rebuffed libido. History, however, has yielded no definitive answers about the nature of Asano's grudge, if there was one, or what, exactly, prompted his attack on Kira. In this respect, *Chūshingura* is more psychologically satisfying, leaving viewers with a sense of emotional and rational understanding, of sorts, regarding the attack. In short order, it introduces beauty, passion, anger, lechery, abuse, bribery, crime, and violence in a controlled but tense dynamic that makes sense, at least on stage, of one of the perennial mysteries of history. The opening acts of the drama moreover highlight a set of spiritual and ceremonial nuances integral to the beginning of its tale, and in the process, point to ones that were intrinsic to the contemporary Confucian discussions of the historical vendetta.

Act IV is set at Enya's residence in Kamakura where his family and retainers reflect on his fate. Hara Goemon (Hara Sōemon Mototoki) tries to be optimistic, but Ōno Kudayū (Ōno Kurobe Tomofusa) is critical of Enya's circumstances, reminding everyone that Enya attacked a high shogunal official and caused an uproar in the palace. A light sentence would be exile, a harsh one, seppuku. Ōno blames Hara for not having bribed Kō. Kaoyo next confesses that she bears responsibility for her husband's fate. She recalls Kō's passion, which she rejected in the letter Enya delivered. Kaoyo claims that Kō, angered at her, tormented Enya until he snapped. No sooner has Kaoyo confessed this than messengers arrive with the verdict: because of the disturbance Enya created due to a personal grudge, his domain would be confiscated and he, Enya, required to commit seppuku. Enya responds that his only regret is that Kakogawa stopped him from slaying Kō. Likening himself to Kusunoki Masashige, whose brother affirmed at the

Battle of Minatogawa that if reborn, he would fight for the imperial cause over and again, Enya declares that he will be reborn over and again until vengeance is achieved.

Just before Enya's seppuku, some of his retainers ask to see their lord one final time. Enya refuses to allow it without Ōboshi (Ōishi), his senior retainer, present. After calling out for Ōboshi, Enya stabs his left side and pulls the blade across. Suddenly, Ōboshi rushes in and bows to his dying lord. The other retainers follow suit. Enya pulls the dirk across his belly as he tells Ōboshi, "This dirk I leave with you, Yura-no-suke, for you to dissolve my grudge toward Kō." He then cuts his throat, drops the dirk, and collapses in death. Enya's last words penetrate Ōboshi's heart and soul, prompting him to resolve, bloodied dirk in hand, to take revenge on Kō, thus proving himself a "loyal samurai with a righteous mind" (chūshin gishin).

Reverently, Ōboshi has Enya's remains transported to the Kōmyōji, the Enya family temple. No sooner has Enya's body been taken away, however, than Ōno Kudayū and Sadakurō scheme to steal what remains of Enya's gold reserves. After the two thieving retainers leave, Ōboshi informs the others – some of whom want to take immediate action – of Enya's desire that they exact revenge on Kō. The act ends with Ōboshi proposing to use Enya's dirk, on which his soul (kon) – through his blood – now resides, to sever Kō's head and thereby complete his master's profound intent. Thus, almost miraculously, Ōboshi bursts onto the stage of Chūshingura, just in time to soothe his fated master's passing and then lead the bereft retainers in their determination to dissolve Enya's lingering anger by means of vengeance on Kō.

Clearly, Chūshingura fabricates the communication between Enya and Ōboshi, transforming Asano's pathetic and tragic end into an incredibly poignant one. Asano Naganori was fated to die alone, with neither family nor retainers anywhere nearby. Sparing Enya that sad fate, Chūshingura has Ōboshi receive his bloodied dirk, hear his final words, and then announce his plans for revenge over his deceased lord's remains. By doing so, no sooner is Enya gone than Ōboshi has launched the plan to save his, Enya's, soul from an eternity of anger and frustration in the underworld. In history, Ōishi was hundreds of miles away from Asano's seppuku and received only an enigmatic note from his lord regarding what should happen next. Moreover, the rōnin spent months discussing and debating their options before a clear resolution to take revenge emerged. *Chūshingura* eliminates the rōnin ambiguities and equivocations and instead portrays them immediately and unequivocally embracing the ultimate objective of deadly vengeance on Kō for the sake of bringing peace to the now agitated soul of their deceased master.

Act V features Hayano Kanpei, a retainer of Enya who forgot duty while sharing an intimate moment with his beloved, Okaru. In Hayano's absence, Enya attacked Kō, and so was sentenced to seppuku. Hayano was also absent when his master committed suicide. Had he been attentive to duty, Hayano might have kept Enya from attacking Kō, or, if not, he might have kept Kakogawa from stopping Enya's further attack on Kō. Shamed by his disloyalty, he retreats to the woods of Yamazaki and hunts for daily sustenance. Hayano is the *Chūshingura* takeoff on Kayano Sanpei. Along with Hayami Tōemon, Kayano traveled from Edo to Akō to inform Ōishi and the rōnin that Asano had committed seppuku. Although Kayano joined the vendetta conspiracy, his family arranged for him to serve another daimyō. Torn between conflicting obligations, Kayano committed seppuku on the fourteenth day of the third month of 1702.

In *Chūshingura*, Kayano's tragic fate is recast through Hayano, whose love for Okaru compromises his duty to serve Enya. While hunting in the Yamazaki woods, Hayano encounters one of Enya's retainers, Senzaki Yagorō (Kanzaki Yogorō). He tells Senzaki of his hope to become part of the vendetta, despite his earlier neglect of duty. Senzaki feigns ignorance of any vendetta, claiming instead that he and Ōboshi are raising funds for a memorial service for Enya. Thinking that "the memorial" is a metaphor for the vendetta, Hayano says that he will persuade his father-in-law, Yoichibei, to sell some property so that he, Hayano, can contribute. Senzaki promises to tell Ōboshi, and ask if Hayano might join the vendetta.

Shortly after, Ōno Sadakurō, Ōno Kudayū's son, appears in the woods nearby, stalking an old man. Moments before Ōno Sadakurō kills him, the old man explains that he has just sold his daughter to a tea house in Kyoto to raise funds for his son-in-law so that he might restore his honor as a samurai. Despite the old man's pleas, Ōno strikes him down without mercy, mockingly reciting the name of Amida Buddha and the *Lotus Sutra*, wishing the old man well in heaven. Suddenly, a wild boar runs by. From a distance, Hayano sees the boar and shoots. Yet when he searches for his kill, he finds a man, dead. Spotting a purse filled with fifty *ryō* in gold, he deems it a gift from heaven and quickly runs off, hoping that with the gold he can join the vendetta league.

In Act VI, Hayano returns home only to find the Kyoto proprietor, Ichimonjiya, who had purchased Okaru from Yoichibei, insisting that she go to Kyoto to begin her five-year service. Okaru's mother tells Hayano that her husband, Yoichibei, sold Okaru to Ichimonjiya's tea house to raise money for him. Okaru's mother knows her daughter must go, but first wants to wait for her husband to return. Hayano begins to realize that the man he shot in the woods must have been Okaru's father, but rather than confess, he sends Okaru off to her new life in Kyoto's pleasure quarters. Soon, Yoichibei's body arrives, brought by three hunters. Noting that Hayano is not surprised that Yoichibei is dead, Okaru's mother concludes that he, her son-in-law, had killed her husband, his father-in-law, and then robbed him. As she curses him repeatedly, Hayano feels "the punishment of heaven" upon him.

Two members of the vendetta league, Hara Gōemon and Senzaki Yagorō, arrive to inform Hayano that Ōboshi had decided that Enya's spirit would not be pleased with a gift wrongly gained. Declaring the gold unrighteous and immoral, Senzaki adds that Hayano does not understand the way of the samurai. Hayano's mother-in-law curses him even more, calling for his immediate punishment. Senzaki and Hara curse Hayano vehemently, accusing him of horrendous crimes. Unbearably shamed, Hayano plunges his sword into his stomach, confessing that he must have shot his father-in-law, Yoichibei, by mistake.

However, Senzaki then checks the old man's corpse and reports that Yoichibei was killed with a sword, not a bullet. Hara next recalls finding another dead body nearby, that of the evil Ōno Sadakurō, killed by a gunshot. Hara concludes that Hayano must have killed Ōno, and that the money Hayano took from Ōno had earlier been stolen from Yoichibei. It was Ōno, then, who had robbed and killed Yoichibei. Realizing that Hayano had not murdered her husband, Hayano's mother-in-law begs for forgiveness. As it dawns on Hara that Hayano had, in fact, exacted revenge on the murderer of his father-in-law, Hara takes out a copy of the "spirit oath" signed by forty-five rōnin and adds Hayano's name, making the total forty-six. Even as he lay dying, Hayano sealed the oath with his blood. Giving the purse of gold to Hara and Senzaki, Okaru's mother asks them to treat it with care because Hayano's spirit will dwell in it. With his parting words,

Hayano declares that he will not die, but instead continue to linger on earth to join, spiritually, the revenge attack on Kō.

Act VII features Okaru and Ōboshi. While residing in Yamashina, Ōishi reportedly had a mistress with a name similar to Okaru's. In assigning a major role to an attractive but fateful young lady, *Chūshingura* adds another female presence to the staged vendetta, thus enhancing history with greater gender diversity in its dramatic remake. Okaru's role is complemented by Ōboshi's, ranging from a drunken profligate, to a shrewd conspirator, and finally to an omniscient avenger. The act opens with the evil Ōno Kudayū and his retainer Bannai entering the tea house to spy on Ōboshi. Three rōnin also appear, hoping to save Ōboshi from chronic debauchery. Badly inebriated from a three-day binge, Ōboshi passes out, prompting the rōnin to depart in disgust. However, Ōboshi merely feigns drunkenness to deceive Kō's spies into thinking that he is drowned in saké and in no shape for revenge. One day before the anniversary of Enya's seppuku, Ōno Kudayū tests Ōboshi's degeneracy by offering him some fish, taboo for those in mourning. Ōboshi devours the fish, and even calls for chicken dishes and female entertainers to boot, adding to the façade of irreverent dissolution. When the entertainers arrive, Ōboshi playfully chases them around, oblivious of his rusted sword left behind.

Once alone, Ōboshi quits his charade and quite soberly reads a confidential missive from Kaoyo about the vendetta. From a veranda above, Okaru uses a mirror secretly to glean the contents of the communiqué. Ōno Kudayū, hiding below, gazes upward so that he too can read the dispatch as it unfurls downward. Aware of Okaru's eavesdropping, Ōboshi decides she must die to ensure that the vendetta remains a secret. Her brother, Teraoka Heiemon, soon realizes that Ōboshi knows that Okaru has read the letter. Understanding that Ōboshi must kill Okaru, Teraoka proposes to kill her instead so that, by doing so, he, a lowly foot soldier, might prove his loyalty to the cause and so join the vendetta. Okaru spares her brother, declaring that she will kill herself. Overhearing this, Ōboshi, impressed with their loyalty, decides to let Okaru live and Teraoka join the league. Ōboshi asks Okaru to offer prayers, once the vendetta is complete, for the repose of Teraoka's soul.[27]

---

[27] Donald Keene, trans., *Chūshingura* (New York: Columbia University Press, 1971), p. 122.

The act concludes with Ōboshi, fully aware that Ōno Kudayū lay spying underneath the veranda, guiding the blade Okaru held and plunging it through the floor, stabbing Ōno. Ōboshi curses Ōno, "a foot-soldier of the King of Hell," for betraying his former lord and becoming one of Kō-no-Moronao's spies. Ōboshi cuts Ōno repeatedly, and then has him hauled away from the Ichiriki tea house. Simply put, this act is one of the most complete flights of dramatic imagination in *Chūshingura*, having precious little grounding in history. It is also one of the most popular. Its popularity presumably has been due to the prominently courageous and engaged role assumed by Okaru. Though Ōboshi guides her hand, she assists like a female samurai in the attack on Ōno, helping to slay the villain who is second only to Kō in the drama.

Act VIII, the shortest, relates the journey of Kakogawa Honzō's wife and daughter, Tonase and Konami, from Kamakura to Yamashina, to meet Konami's fiancé, Ōboshi Rikiya, and his family. Konami fears that Rikiya has decided to shun her because her father, Kakogawa, prevented Enya from killing Kō. In Act IX, Tonase and Konami are greeted by Ōboshi's wife, who pretends that Ōboshi is absent. She politely notes that Konami should marry someone else now that Rikiya's father has become a poor rōnin. More directly, Mrs. Ōboshi declares that while Enya had acted with honesty in his attack on Kō, Kakogawa had proven himself "a corrupt samurai" in providing Kō with a bribe in return for his flattering treatment of Kakogawa's lord, Momoi.

When pressed, Mrs. Ōboshi flatly declares that Rikiya and Konami are divorced. Devastated, Tonase plans to slay her daughter and then kill herself. Just before Tonase can strike Konami, Mrs. Ōboshi intervenes, expressing admiration for their samurai spirit and offering her blessings for the marriage if they will give her, as a wedding gift, Kakogawa's head. Kakogawa next appears and is soon in an altercation with Mrs. Ōboshi. Rikiya then rushes out and plunges a spear into Kakogawa. Before Rikiya can finish the kill, his father appears to explain that Kakogawa had planned everything, including his death at the hands of Rikiya. This was his punishment for what he, Kakogawa, realized was the most egregious error of his life, stopping Enya from killing Kō.

Kakogawa further realized, according to Ōboshi, that if Rikiya killed him, Rikiya's anger would be released, enabling him to wed Konami. Thus, Kakogawa gladly planned to die for his daughter's happiness. Ōboshi then revealed his plan to avenge Enya's death, but, in doing so, to die as well. Since Rikiya was to participate in the vendetta, his death would leave Konami widowed. Thus, he must indeed divorce Konami, but only to spare her that fate. As he lay dying, Kakogawa unveils his wedding gift to Rikiya, a diagram of Kō's residence. Ōboshi rejoices, knowing that the diagram will ensure the vendetta's success. As father and son discuss their next moves, Kakogawa dies. As with the previous act, Acts VIII and IX are largely dramatic creations, featuring women in prominent, decisive roles, but lacking substantial counterparts in history. Nevertheless, the important roles assumed by women reveal the extent to which the dramatic reinvention of the vendetta served as a popular and thus effective means of pioneering new gender roles and identities for them.

Act X depicts Ōboshi and the rōnin procuring weaponry from an Osaka merchant, Amakawaya Gihei. Knowing that Amakawaya has done business with Enya, Ōboshi trusts him in ordering lances, spears, gauntlets, leggings, coats of mail, mallets, and other equipment needed for the attack. To maintain secrecy and to protect his family, Amakawaya sends his wife, Osono, to her father's home. However, Osono's father, Ryōchiku, not privy to the circumstances, doubts Amakawaya's marital fidelity and so demands divorce papers that will enable him to profit by arranging a new marriage for his daughter. Ryōchiku, incidentally, had formerly served the evil Ōno Kudayū, the ex-retainer of Enya who had become one of Kō's spies.

Late one evening, local authorities search Amakawaya's residence and threaten to kill him and his young son unless he divulges the contents of a suspicious container. The authorities claim to have proof that Amakawaya was supplying arms for the vendetta. Amakawaya steadfastly refuses, daring the authorities to slice him to pieces. When they try to open the box, Amakawaya stands on it, claiming that it contains lewd materials ordered by a prominent daimyō's wife. The authorities next threaten to kill Amakawaya's son. Amakawaya replies that he is prepared to go to hell if need be, but will tell them nothing. He then seizes his son and begins to strangle him himself to show that he cannot be intimidated.

Suddenly, Ōboshi springs out of the suspicious container, revealing that the search has been a rōnin test of Amakawaya's loyalty. Next, Osono returns and begs Amakawaya to accept her back, but Amakawaya hesitates, thinking that she might have truly wanted to

Figure 7.3 "Warriors Ōishi Sezaemon Nobukiyo and Terasaka Kichiemon Nobuyuki from the series *Kenroku Yamato Kagami* (*Chūshingura*)." Harvard Art Museums/Arthur M. Sackler Museum. Imaging Department © President and Fellows of Harvard College.

marry another. As Osono flees, a masked man grabs her, cuts her hair off, and steals the divorce papers that Amakawaya had earlier written for her father. As the rōnin depart, Ōboshi gives Amakawaya two presents: one, Osono's hair cut by one of the rōnin to make her look like a nun, and two, the divorce papers Amakawaya has written for the sake of maintaining secrecy. Now, without the divorce papers, and with

Figure 7.4 Katsushika Hokusai. "Act Eleven, from the series *The Storehouse of Loyal Retainers (Chūshingura).*" Harvard Art Museums/Arthur M. Sackler Museum. Imaging Department © President and Fellows of Harvard College.

Osono looking like a nun, her father cannot marry her off. Ōboshi explains that in one hundred days, the vendetta will be done and Osono's hair grown back. He promises Amakawaya that the rōnin will honor his loyal service by using the words *ama* (heaven) and *kawa* (river) as passwords during the attack.

As mentioned previously, *Things Seen and Heard* does relate that the rōnin used the words *yama* and *kawa* as passwords during the attack. However, apart from that, Act X lacks any foundation in the historical vendetta. Nevertheless, by featuring Amakawaya the merchant, it broadened *Chūshingura*'s appeal among townspeople generally. Also, it gave Ōboshi another opportunity to assume the role of the avenger of those, such as Amakawaya's father-in-law, who take advantage of honest and loyal men. Some accounts claim that Amakawaya was modeled after Amanoya Rihei, supposedly an Osaka merchant, but there is no real evidence for this. In captivity, the rōnin never mentioned an arms dealer, much less his identity. Most likely, the rōnin scrounged together the equipage needed, piece by piece over time, to avoid attention. Procurements would have been made in Edo, not Osaka. Physical remains from the attack suggest that the rōnin were outfitted ad hoc, rather than as a corps of smartly outfitted samurai armed with freshly bought weaponry. Claims that they were, as a group, dressed uniformly in firemen's outfits are apocryphal.

Act XI, the final one, depicts Ōboshi and the rōnin traveling by sea to their target site, Kō's residence. The men are dressed uniformly, with their names and one of the forty-seven characters of the *kana* syllabary on their jacket lapels. Inside the residence, Kō, exhausted from the evening's party, has passed out, along with the others. The prolonged fight that ensues leaves few of the assailants injured, although Kō's wounded and dead are numerous. Yet still Kō escapes detection. Then, Yazama Jūtarō (Hazama Jūjirō) discovers him hiding in a shed. The rōnin assemble around him, triumphant. Ōboshi reminds them that Kō was "one of those who governed all below heaven," so that "even in killing him, etiquette and ceremony must be observed." Respectfully, Ōboshi then says to Kō, "Although we are only retainers, we have broken into your residence and caused a disturbance because we wanted to avenge our lord's death. We beg you to pardon our want of manners. You will now bravely give us your head." Uncooperative, Kō throws Ōboshi off guard and rushes toward him with drawn sword. Ōboshi breaks Kō's charge, secures him, and delivers the death blow with the dirk "their lord left behind." The rōnin then rejoice over the deed done.

Ōboshi next takes from his robe Enya's "spirit tablet" and places it on a table in a nearby alcove. He washes Kō-no-Moronao's head and presents it before the tablet, offering incense saved in his helmet for this moment. Ōboshi bows repeatedly before the tablet and says:

> I have the honor to report this to the sacred spirit of our late lord, Renshōin kenri daikoji [Enya's posthumous name]. With the dagger that my lord used to commit suicide and then gave to me, with the request to give repose to your spirit, I have cut off Kō's head and now offer it before your spirit tablet. Please, from your resting place in the shade of the blades of grass [i.e., the underworld], my lord, accept it.[28]

The final act then relates that Ōboshi invites the rōnin to offer incense, one by one, beginning with Yazama Jūtarō, who had pulled Kō out from hiding in a woodshed. The second rōnin allowed to make an offering,

[28] Inouye, *Chūshingura*, p. 265. Translation adapted.

now posthumously, is Hayano Kanpei, who killed himself in Act
V. Ōboshi had kept Hayano's purse with him, and now has it placed
by the censer, along with a stick of incense. Just then, the men hear
horses approaching. Momoi enters to warn them that Kō's younger
brother, Moroyasu, is approaching with an armed force. Ōboshi
declares that it is time to withdraw to the Kōmyōji – the Sengakuji
double – to commit suicide in front of their lord's grave. After a final
scene in which Ōboshi Rikiya slays three attackers, the avengers proceed
triumphant toward the Kōmyōji.

Chūshingura's presentation of Kō's demise is one of the most
historically grounded and yet historically fictitious events in the play.
There was indeed an invasion, and many were killed. Kira was in the
end slain. But unlike Chūshingura, Ōishi was not present to engage in
a final dialogue with the fated master of ceremonies, nor did he take
his head. With Chūshingura, Ōishi in the form of Ōboshi emerges as
the heroic figure, especially in delivering the coup de grâce and then
reverently presiding over an on-the-spot presentation of the head
before Kō's spirit tablet. Far from an ad hoc rite, Ōboshi was well
prepared for it with incense in his helmet. Gekkai's Memoir account
of the presentation of the head was, as he himself noted, profoundly
different than that staged. At the Sengakuji, the rōnin seemed
exhausted from the battle and the march, and all but clueless regarding what would come next. Without assistance from the monks there,
the presentation would have been a crude affair indeed. Astoundingly
enough, opposition forces never appeared on the horizon, tracking
down the avengers.

One can only wonder whether the rōnin would have been
allowed quietly to exit Edo unpursued, their crimes hushed up and
cleaned up, had they not made such a fuss about turning themselves
over to the authorities. In doing so, however, they ensured that their
bloody deeds would necessarily be known to history. Chūshingura
does not dramatize Ōboshi's decision to have the rōnin report their
deeds to the shogunate. Instead, they march triumphant, presumably
to assume responsibility for their fate without awaiting any judgment
from on high.

By the mid-nineteenth century, there had been approximately
three hundred fifty kabuki and puppet theatre productions of
Chūshingura. If private and non-licensed performances, amateur thea-
tricals, Buddhist sermons, and commoner retellings are factored in, the

total would multiply many-fold[29] The play's popularity reflected its masterful representation of the vendetta, aesthetically sanitized and more inclusive socially than the gruesome historical realities from which it sprang. Its popularity also reflected the need, on the part of those who came to learn of the vendetta, for a means of remembering the rōnin. Performances served as opportunities to offer oneself visually, through the audience's gaze, to the vendetta experience, enabling both spiritual unity with it, as well as completion and solace. Most surely, attendance was not simply a matter of entertainment, but instead, as with Nō and other traditional forms of dramatic performance, harbored a spiritual dimension intimate to the experience.

At still another level, attendance was arguably a means of registering approbation for the ethics of the staged vendetta, especially the notion that greed, evil, and abuse from on high might be heroically opposed and defeated, in one way or another, as appropriate given one's status and station. The play also affirmed, as did admirers in the audience, aggressive and even heroic displays of ultimate individual autonomy, regardless of contemporary confines that might have otherwise senselessly limited the same. Most certainly, the unprecedented appeal of *Chūshingura* derived from the many seminal and seemingly timeless layers of significance – ethical, spiritual, political, and existential – aesthetically and philosophically integral to it, as well as from the socio-gender enhancements with which the dramatic double supplemented history.

Woodblock Reincarnations

Vendetta-related woodblocks appeared in tandem with vendetta dramas, but most profusely with the greatest of them, *Chūshingura*.[30] In its first four decades, the drama was staged forty-one times in major theatres in Kyoto (ten), Osaka (ten), and Edo (twenty-one),[31] with related woodblock prints numbering in the thousands, and perhaps in

---

[29] William D. Fleming, "Restaging the Forty-Seven Rōnin: Performance and Print in Late Eighteenth-Century Japan," *Eighteenth-Century Studies*, vol. 48, no. 4 (2015), pp. 413.

[30] Chelsea Foxwell, "The Double Identity of Chūshingura: Theatre and History in Nineteenth-Century Prints," *Impressions*, no. 26 (2004), pp. 25–26.

[31] Henry D. Smith II, "Part I: Theatre Texts and Color Woodblock Prints, 1–8," *Chūshingura On Stage and in Print*. May 5, 2017. www.columbia.edu/~hds2/chush ingura/exhibition/.

the tens of thousands. Yet as Henry D. Smith II observes, the most impressive legacies of *Chūshingura* were the "color woodblock prints ... made primarily to advertise upcoming performances." These included works by artists such as Katsukawa Shunshō and Ippitsusai Bunchō depicting famous performers in major roles.

In the 1770s, Katsukawa pioneered another development, the eleven-woodblock series with one illustration for each act in *Chūshingura*.[32] Soon, members of the Katsukawa and Utagawa schools were producing series after series of this kind. In some cases, as with the final act, extra illustrations were added. On average, one hundred prints per illustration were made, but in some cases, hundreds of copies per illustration. Thus, one eleven-illustration series could easily result in more than a thousand copies printed. In its first forty-one performances, *Chūshingura* conceivably generated more than forty-one thousand print copies, and possibly several times that number. Estimates for the total number of unique *Chūshingura* woodblock illustrations ever cut and printed in the Tokugawa range from two thousand to as many as five thousand.[33] Assuming again runs of one hundred copies per woodblock illustration cut, the total output might have ranged from two hundred to a staggering five hundred thousand copies. Some illustrations were diptychs and others, triptychs that, if counted separately, would again multiply the total number of prints made. Such was the exceptional popularity of *Chūshingura* in the latter half of the Tokugawa period.

From the 1840s forward, *Chūshingura* and woodblock prints went through another era of explosive growth coinciding with celebrations of the drama's centennial. Increasingly, however, woodblocks focused, in a quasi-historical manner, not on scenes from *Chūshingura*, but rather on those grounded in history, at least as imagined by artists such as Utagawa Kuniyoshi. Known for his warrior prints, Utagawa produced works such as the triptych, "Having Achieved Their Goal, the Loyal Retainers Retreat to Sengokuji [*sic*]," depicting the rōnin, still identified by their *Chūshingura* names, near the conclusion of their march, at the gate of the Sengakuji. The play, *Chūshingura*, however, ends with the rōnin taking Kō's head, and

---

[32] Foxwell, "The Double Identity," pp. 26–27.
[33] Smith, "Part I: Theatre Texts and Color Woodblock Prints, 10–21," www.columbia.edu/~hds2/chushingura/exhibition/.

Figure 7.5 Ōboshi Yura-no-suke. Courtesy of Metropolitan Museum of Art.

then preparing for their march to the Kōmyōji, not the Sengakuji. Utagawa's print nominally disguises the name Sengakuji as Sengokuji, but in adding the scene at the temple gate, takes woodblock illustrations of the vendetta beyond the dramatic confines of *Chūshingura* and back somewhat closer to the stage of history.[34]

Utagawa also pioneered individual portraits of the forty-seven in series such as "Lives of the Sincere, Loyal, and Righteous Samurai"

---

[34] Smith, "Part I: Theatre Texts and Color Woodblock Prints, 22." May 5, 2017. www.columbia.edu/~hds2/chushingura/exhibition/.

(1847–1848). There, he devoted one print to each "righteous samurai," changing their names only slightly. Major figures such as Ōishi Kura-no -suke were presented as Ōboshi Yura-no-suke, consistent with *Chūshingura* nomenclature, while minor figures were given different names. Along with action portraits of each *gishi*, Utagawa included snippets from historical records, popular legends, and oral narratives recounted by storytellers. In a series published in 1864, Utagawa Kunisada used the real names of the rōnin, but depicted them in the style of kabuki actors.[35] Andō Hiroshige contributed several series entitled *Chūshingura*, depicting key scenes from kabuki and the historical vendetta. Woodblock artists thus compounded conflations of history, oral traditions, and stage drama under the *Chūshingura* rubric, further blurring lines between history and legend. Yet vendetta consumers were not necessarily after hard-core history. Their prodigious consumption of woodblock prints shows their moral support for the rōnin and represents an implicit, aesthetically nuanced critique of shogunal justice. Woodblock consumption also provided rōnin enthusiasts with relics of a performance experience and rōnin memorabilia that might be revered within private spaces as tokens of their affirmed presence. It is doubtful, however, that many such prints were to be found in Edo Castle.

Vendetta Parodies

Parody, a form of cultural critique, is often bred by popularity. The appeal of *Chūshingura* and the rōnin as righteous samurai was soon countered by more than forty parodies in just one genre, that of illustrated works of fiction. Although based on visuals from kabuki performances, this genre used illustrations in jovial, occasionally sardonic ways. Just as *Chūshingura* was supposedly a "miracle cure" for distressed theatres, its subject matter was also a godsend for writers, offering economic incentive even for lampooning the vendetta. One little-known but significant parody appeared in 1796 in the form of *A Treasury of Chinamen: A Copybook of Exotica*, authored by Morishima Chūryō and illustrated by Kitao Shigemasa. This parody well understood the popularity of *Chūshingura*, noting in its preface

---

[35] Ibid., 22–25. May 5, 2017. www.columbia.edu/~hds2/chushingura/exhibition/.

that the play was like rice, "year after year, it's boiled and grilled up for picture-books and color prints in a hasty effort to put something on the table, and still nobody ever turns it down." With iconoclastic humor, *A Treasury of Chinamen* introduces things exotic and foreign, Western and Chinese into its yarn, mimicking the eleven acts of *Chūshingura* along the way. Rather than bold philosophical essays of the sort Satō Naokata and Dazai Shundai authored, *A Treasury of Chinamen* presents witty satire as critique, casting its rōnin-surrogates literally as the laughing stock of illustrated humor. It was not alone: another author-illustrator, Santō Kyōden, published three parodies of *Chūshingura* including his *Whipped-Up Meal of Chūshingura* (1796), time and again making a mockery of the rōnin and samurai conceits about loyalty and righteousness.[36]

In Act I of *A Treasury of Chinamen*, the shogun, Ashikaga Takauji, is presented as a connoisseur of exotica who is arranging his new collection, previously owned by his late enemy, Nitta Yoshisada, for an exhibition of recently acquired treasures. Helping the shogun are his brother, Ashikaga Tadayoshi, Kō-no-Moronao, and Enya Hangan. Because her family runs an import business, Kaoyo, Enya's beautiful wife, helps identify the artifacts. The text's first illustration presents Kō, Enya, and Kaoyo gathered around a large Chinese-style table inspecting Chinese lanterns, pottery, and vases. Kaoyo holds a coral sculpture affixed to a pedestal. Kō desires her, and soon he makes his move. Seeing Kaoyo compromised, Momoi intercedes. After Kō has humiliated him in return, Momoi returns home to smoke tobacco in a Chinese long pipe, explaining to his retainer, Kakogawa Honzō, that he plans to kill Kō the next day.

Kakogawa, wearing a pair of curled-toed, Chinese shoes, cuts a branch from a pine tree as a show of his resolution, but shortly after gallops off barefoot to bribe Kō and thus gain good treatment for his master. Yet when Enya appears, Kō abuses him mercilessly. As punishment for striking Kō, Enya must commit *shippoku*, i.e., devouring a Chinese banquet until he has eaten himself to death.

---

[36] Fleming, "Restaging the Forty-Seven Rōnin," pp. 391–415. Waseda University has posted a digital copy of a 1796 edition of *Karadehon Tōjingura*. www.wul.waseda.ac .jp/kotenseki/html/he13/he13_01961_0151/index.html. Illustrations discussed herein are from it. For a modern edition, see Ishigami Satoshi, ed., *Morishima Chūryō shū*, in Takada Mamoru and Hara Michio, eds., *Sōsho Edo bunko*, ed. vol. 32 (Tokyo: Kokusho kankōkai, 1994), pp. 285–316.

Figure 7.6 "A Treasury of Chinamen (*Karadehon Chūshingura*)." Courtesy of Waseda University, Department of Special Collections.

As Enya's rōnin leave their late master's castle, they look back one last time, using European telescopes, only to see and hear the Ashikaga forces occupying the castle blaring back at them with "speaking trumpets," or megaphones.

Hayano Kanpei is subsequently depicted in the Yamazaki woods holding an arquebus. Later, thinking that he has shot and killed his father-in-law, Hayano commits seppuku, with an assistant holding a Western anatomy chart, comparing the diagram of the human abdomen to Hayano, trying to figure out what is going on. In depicting Ōishi at the Ichiriki tea house, *A Treasury of Chinamen* shows Okaru, from a veranda above, spying the contents of Ōishi's letter through a mirror, with Ōishi's son, Rikiya, sailing off on a Chinese-style sailboat, presumably down the Kamo River. Chinese-style railing lines the veranda, and a Chinese table occupies the center of Ōboshi's pleasure quarters. Below Ōboshi is Ōno Kudayū, wearing glasses so that he too can read the letter. Mocking the multiple consumption of the missive, *A Treasury of Chinamen* adds a foreign sheep nibbling the tail end of it.

Act X features the merchant Amakawaya from whom Ōboshi plans to secure military equipment for the attack. In *A Treasury of Chinamen*, Amakawaya's store is an import shop specializing in exotica. When the rōnin test Amakawaya's loyalty, they demand an *erekiteru*, or a static electricity generator, for an unnamed daimyō. In the final, fatal confrontation with Kō, he is surrounded by large Chinese treasure tablets, apparently his most prized possessions, while Ōboshi and some rōnin wearing Chinese-style helmets bear down on him with large, curved-blade Chinese spears and swords.

A *Treasury of Chinamen* thus lampoons the vendetta by exoticizing it with things foreign. The text hardly reveres the rōnin, their spiritual fate, or the ethics of their deeds, but rather deconstructs the vendetta with parody, even while exploring another variety of worship, that of foreign things. At another level, *A Treasury of Chinamen* might be construed as satirizing shogunal efforts to limit access to foreign things by injecting them at every turn. At the very least, the text can be read as an illustrated critique of the notion that the Tokugawa realm was, in any real way, a closed country. Even the forty-seven rōnin, it suggests, enjoyed exotica.

Woodblock printmakers worked in tandem with kabuki, gaining inspiration from stage scenery for their visually stunning copy.[37] Utagawa Kuniyoshi returned to *Chūshingura* nearly two dozen times with prints promoting kabuki productions. Some of his works also parodied the same. His *Ghosts and Goblins of Chūshingura*, published around 1836, consists of a series of prints depicting, act by act, the *dramatis personae* sporting grotesque, ghoulish, but ultimately comic monster faces.[38] The suggestion – that the rōnin might be viewed as monsters – was, of course, hardly complimentary. Later, in *Pillow Book of Revenge: A Treasury of Loyal Retainers* (1857), he parodied the vendetta again, depicting scene after scene including oversized penises and vaginas, climaxing with the brutal gang rape of Kō's residence, including five different forced acts, plus two victimized, loin-clothed retainers of Kō fleeing, enlarged members in tow, and apparently, lucky to still have them. In the last print, Kuniyoshi portrays the rōnin marching across the Sumida River carrying spears from the tops of which large

[37] For a detailed study of *Chūshingura* and related woodblock prints, see David Bell, *Chūshingura and the Floating World: The Representation of Kanadehon Chūshingura in Ukiyo-e Prints* (Richmond, Surrey: Japan Library/Curzon Press, 2001).

[38] The Princeton University Art Museum has a digitized copy of *Bakemono Chūshingura* posted at artmuseum.princeton.edu/collections/objects/110647. Accessed May 5, 2017.

Figure 7.7 "The Monster's Chūshingura (*Bakemono Chūshingura*)." Courtesy of the Princeton Art Museum/Art Resource, NY.

severed penises dangle, most likely indicating Kira's men who had gone down fighting. At the front is Kira's severed manhood, clearly oversized, being marched across Edo for presentation at Asano's grave.[39] Depicting the vendetta squad as a gang of rapists and sexual mutilators was as disturbingly offensive, and surely unflattering, as it was perversely comic.

Another of Utagawa Kuniyoshi's series, *A Toad's Treasury of Laughs* (ca. 1847–1848), depicts *Chūshingura* with frogs dressed in costume, performing all roles. Although not handsome, frogs are associated with fecundity and good fortune, and so provide a positive nuance to an otherwise slimy representation of the rōnin. Yet another,

[39] Yasunori Kojima, "Laughter Connects the Sacred (*sei*) and the Sexual (*sei*): The Blossoming of Parody in Edo Culture," in James E. Ketelaar, Yasunori Kojima, and Peter Nosco, eds., *Values, Identity, and Equality in Eighteen and Nineteenth Century Japan* (Leiden: E. J. Brill, 2015), p. 209. Ritsumeikan University's Art Research Center has posted a digitized copy of this text at www.dh-jac.net/db1/ books/results-thum.php?f1=arcBK03-0138&f12=1&-sortField1=f8&-max =30&enter=portal#. Accessed May 5, 2017.

Utagawa Kuniyoshi's *Satire of Samurai Loyalty*, portrays the rōnin enjoying their invasion of Kō's residence, and in one print, frightening one another with a Kō-no-Moronao scarecrow, and in another, building an enormous snow head looking like Kō.[40] Still another, *Eight Successful Plays Performed by Frolicking Bats*, published between 1844 and 1846, parodies *Chūshingura* and other kabuki plays with anthropomorphized bats depicted in key scenes as the main characters. As with frogs, bats, though not attractive, are considered auspicious, and so need not be interpreted in an entirely unfavorable light. Another woodblock artist, Kitagawa Utamaro, parodied the vendetta play in his series, *Chūshingura as Celebrated Temptresses* (ca. 1794–1795), substituting stunning female beauty for samurai prowess. In every case, these parodies were counterstatements that challenged, ethically and aesthetically, *Chūshingura* and the historical vendetta behind it.

Mapping the Graveyard

Parodies aside, a sightseeing guide published between 1834 and 1836, *Famous Places of Edo, Illustrated*, reveals that the vendetta had attained recognition and some respectability by the final decades of Tokugawa rule. Therein, the Sengakuji makes the tourist map of the shogun's capital. The Zen temple is presented from an aerial perspective, with surrounding areas cast as stylized woods and empty space rather than the urban bustle of the Takanawa-Shiba area evident in other prints in the same guide. The Sengakuji's large, hipped roof building (right page) is the main hall, to the right of which is the priest's residence, and the temple kitchen. Left of the main hall across from the kitchen is the meditation hall. A double row of pines flanked by dorms defines the lower-central half of the temple. At the end of the pines is the central gate.

An inscription on the left page, upper left corner informs readers that this is the final resting place of the righteous samurai of the Asano family. Below is a cluster of gravestones labeled the "graves of the forty-seven samurai." The grave of their daimyō, Asano Naganori, however,

---

[40] Basil William Robinson, *Kuniyoshi* (London: H. M. Stationery Office, 1961), p. 85. www.kuniyoshiproject.com/Miscellaneous%20comic%20series,%20Part%20I.htm. May 5, 2017.

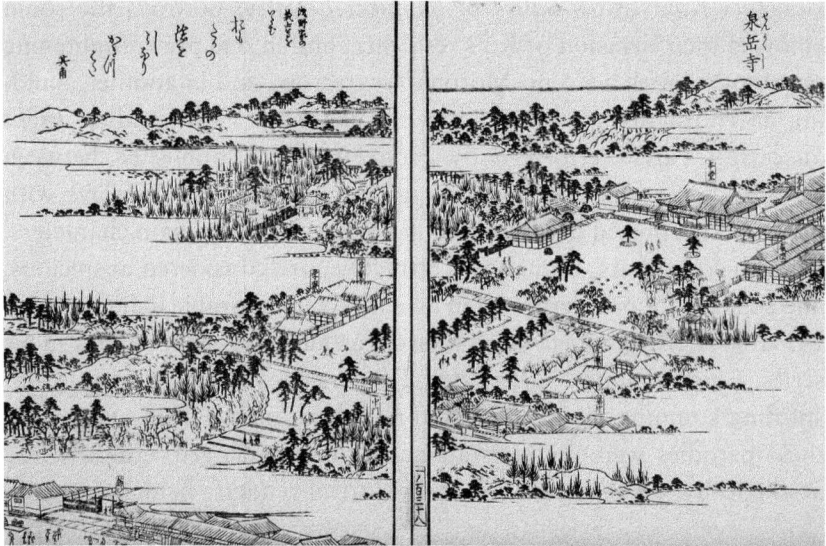

Figure 7.8 *Edo no meisho.* Courtesy of Waseda University, Department of Special Collections.

is not labeled. The text preceding the illustration refers to the temple as Banshōzan Sengakuji, including its "mountain [temple] name," Banshōzan, meaning "Temple of Ten Thousand Pines." The mountain name alludes to the first syllable of the Tokugawa family's earlier name, Matsudaira, or "field of pines," indicating the Sengakuji's mission of supporting the Matsudaira (Tokugawa) shoguns for ten thousand years.

The text adds that the temple is one of the three most important Sōtō Zen temples in Edo. It was founded in 1612, by decree of Tokugawa Ieyasu, the first shogun, just outside the Sakura Gate of Edo Castle, and placed under the leadership of the Sōtō priest, Monnan Sōkan. Although the text does not mention this, Ieyasu reportedly had the Sengakuji founded in spiritual remembrance of Imagawa Yoshimoto, a warlord under whom he served as a young samurai. In 1641, the original compound was destroyed by fire, resulting in its relocation in Takanawa, in Edo's southeastern coastal route. The main object of worship is a statue of the historical Buddha, flanked by two bodhisattvas, Monju, personifying wisdom, and Fugen, personifying practice.

Famous Places of Edo suggests that the Sengakuji's standing as a distinguished Sōtō Zen temple pales by comparison with its historic ties to the forty-seven "righteous samurai." Reflecting increasing sho-gunal laxity in prohibiting publications or performances about the vendetta, *Famous Places of Edo* maps the graves' location and labels those buried there unambiguously as righteous samurai. Well over half of the written entry discusses the temple's ties with the Asano family, Asano Naganori's attack on Kira, and then the vendetta. Mention is also made of the "remaining possessions and artifacts" of the "righteous samurai" ending up at the Sengakuji. In relating the vendetta, *Famous Places of Edo* observes that with Asano Naganori's death, Ōishi realized that he was "unable to remain under the same heaven as the enemy of his lord," and so organized a "blood league" with those of "like inten-tions," and then bided his time, waiting for the right moment. On the fourteenth day of the twelfth month, 1703, after beheading Kira, Ōishi reverently presented the head before his deceased lord's grave. Afterward, they waited the judgment of the authorities. The following year, on the fourth day of the second month, they com-mitted seppuku.[41]

Famous Places of Edo leaves the story at that. Although brief, this relatively accurate summary reflected both the late Tokugawa loosening of restrictions on information about the vendetta, as well as the persistent fascination with it as history, and with the Sengakuji as the final resting place of "the forty-seven samurai."[42]

---

[41] Saitō Gesshin and Hasegawa Settan, *Edo meisho zue*, vol. 3 (Tōto [Edo]: Suharayaihachi, 1834), pp. 48b–50b.

[42] Also see Kageyama Muneyasu et al., eds. "Shiba Takanawa atari ezu," *Edo kiriezu*. (Edo: Owariya Seishichi, 1849–1862). *Kokuritsu kokkai kokushokan dejitaru kor-ekushon*. Accessed May 5, 2017. info:ndljp/pid/1286255. This map labels the Sengakuji and notes that "the graves of the forty-seven men who were righteous samurai are here" (*gishi shijūshichi nin haka ari*).

8 DOMESTIC, FOREIGN, AND ANTI-FOREIGN REFLECTIONS

This chapter explores the vendetta's legacy in late Tokugawa historical and philosophical literature, as well as that produced by foreign writers during the same period. The Tokugawa shogunate itself established the vendetta's importance as history in its official historical chronicles by detailing the events time and again. Two Western officials serving in Japan, the chief Dutch trade representative, Isaac Titsingh, and a British consul, Rutherford Alcock, furthered the broadcast of vendetta lore internationally, albeit in distorted, Orientalist ways. This chapter concludes by examining the vendetta in Yoshida Shōin's late Tokugawa philosophy of anti-foreign, anti-shogunal activism. With Yoshida, the rōnin became role models for resolute samurai intent on driving out the foreign enemies and revering the emperor. With the downfall of the Tokugawa regime, the fortunes of the Akō rōnin rose to new, utterly unprecedented heights.

The New Age in Vendetta History

By the late Tokugawa period, the vendetta was transitioning to a new age. Widely discussed, performed, and visualized on stage and in woodblock prints, it had long since left the days of shogunal efforts to censor it. While the Tokugawa regime continued to stand by its verdict, it recognized, with regular and often lengthy entries in its historical chronicle, the vendetta as one of the most noteworthy and indeed sensational events of the times. Surprisingly, Tokugawa historical accounts even acknowledged salient currents of popular discourse, bringing the rōnin crimes closer to the orthodox fold of shogunal history. Popular guides to Edo's famous places had already graphically situated the Sengakuji and its rōnin cemetery within the oft-visited landscape of the shogun's capital. With shogunal historical writings, the rōnin were recognized as some of the regime's most cunningly defiant rebels. The vendetta also achieved significant broadcast globally, appearing in two Western works introducing Japanese history and culture to primarily European readers. In the process, the story was badly told, but nevertheless ethically assessed, from a Dutch and then British perspective, reflecting the mores and sensibilities of foreigners looking in, and misunderstanding much that was seen and heard.

Most significantly for the internal dynamic of native political history, the vendetta came to be incorporated into the discourse of anti-shogunal anti-foreignism, inspiring those intent upon taking direct action against perceived evil rulers, this time out of loyalism not to a daimyō lord but instead, to the imperial line. This final development was the most significant for later vendetta history since it contributed to a highly significant event at the intersection of the end of the Tokugawa and the beginning of the Meiji periods: an imperial rescript read before their Sengakuji graves, from the newly ascendant Meiji emperor, recognizing with high praise Ōishi and the rōnin vendetta.

The Tokugawa Chroniclers

The *Veritable Records of the Tokugawa House* (1809–1849) chronicles the Tokugawa shogunate from the founding of the regime until the early nineteenth century, i.e., the reigns of the first ten shoguns. While generally a reliable source, it advances the shogunate's view of the past. As such, it should be factored into any historical study of the Tokugawa period, but with careful skepticism regarding interpretive biases. Hayashi Jussai, director of the shogunate's Confucian academy, the Shōheikō, coordinated the massive project involving nearly two dozen historians. One of the shogunate's historians, Narushima Motonao, edited the *Veritable Records*. Narushima also compiled the *Veritable Records of the Tōshōgū*, a chronicle of the shrine devoted to Ieyasu. While the *Veritable Records of the Tokugawa House* gives an official, government-sponsored account of events, due to its late compilation –

completed in 1849 – it was oblivious neither to the cultural atmosphere of the times nor to changing perspectives on the vendetta. As a result, it presents surprising details, reflecting not simply facts, but rumors, nascent legends, popular opinion, and interpretive perspectives apparently drawn from *Chūshingura* and many other sources. Overall, its record of the vendetta is diverse, presumably reflecting the looser standards of the late Tokugawa vis-à-vis the Akō incident than had prevailed during the century and a half prior.

The *Veritable Records* discusses the vendetta sporadically, but nevertheless in considerable detail. Not surprisingly, it contextualizes it in relation to the arrival of imperial emissaries on the eleventh day of the third month, 1701. Valuably, it provides substantial detail, such as a listing of the Nō plays held on the thirteenth. Supplementing its account of the New Year's rituals is another, drawn from Kajikawa Yosobei's diary, relating his eyewitness record of Asano's attack on Kira. The *Veritable Records* does not, incidentally, draw on Okado Denpachirō's memoir. Instead, it advances something akin to an official narrative, one affirming that Asano's attack was meant to redress a "grudge" held against Kira. Kira, however, was deemed "innocent." The *Veritable Records* quickly adds that Asano was placed in the custody of the Tamura house. That evening, he was made to commit seppuku for his "evil behavior, disregarding the time and place." But the *Veritable Records* also adds accounts that "circulated widely," including mention that Kira was a man with years of experience in the practice of court ceremonies. For this, the ruling elite sought him out, in need of his guidance. In return, he eagerly accepted and even expected gifts. Because Asano offered no inducements, Kira shamed him at every opportunity. It was this, reportedly, that Asano resented.[1]

In its entry for 1703, the *Veritable Records* relates that forty-six of Asano's men, led by Ōishi Kura-no-suke, broke into Kira's Honjo residence during the night and beheaded him, wounding his son, killing sixteen of his retainers, and leaving another twenty victims lacerated. They then proceeded to the family temple of their lord, the Sengakuji, and presented Kira's head before their lord's gravestone. Two rōnin, Yoshida Chūzaemon and Tominomori Suke'emon, reported the vendetta to the *bakufu* inspector, Sengoku Hisanao, explaining that their

---

[1] Kuroita Katsumi, ed., *Tokugawa jikki*, in Kokushi taikei, vol. 43 (Tokyo: Yoshikawa kōbunkan, 2003), vol. 6, pp. 432–433.

deeds were meant to bring completion to their late lord's grudge against Kira by fulfilling his intent to kill him. Having done that, they were turning themselves over to the authorities. The *Veritable Records* then relates that the other rōnin were summoned from the Sengakuji to the inspector's residence and subsequently assigned to the custody of four daimyō: the Hosokawa, Matsudaira, Mōri, and Mizuno.

The *Veritable Records*' accounts of discussions that "circulated widely" partly reflect the elevation of Ōishi as the heroic figure of the vendetta in "true accounts," dramatizations, and art. Thus, the popular accounts claimed, according to the *Veritable Records*, that after learning of the incident, Asano's chief retainer, Ōishi Kura-no-suke, described as "a man of deep feelings," assembled the three hundred retainers at the castle and informed them of Asano's death. He added that there should be no hatred toward the authorities, only hatred of the fact that their lord's determination to slay Kira remained unfulfilled. Because Kira lived, their master's grudge would need to be completed. Alluding to the ancient Confucian *Book of Rites*, Ōishi supposedly declared that he could not live under the same heaven as Kira, his lord's enemy. Some favored following their lord in death then and there, inside the castle, yet as the discussions continued, more than half of the three hundred retainers had a change of heart. After more discussion, only sixty signed a blood pledge to take action. Ōishi became even more dedicated and deeply perceptive, divorcing his wife, cutting off relations with his family, and moving to Yamashina. There, Ōishi caroused with prostitutes and immersed himself in saké and lewd activities, creating the impression that he had no intention of taking revenge. Hearing about this, Kira began to relax. Yet as time passed, more rōnin dropped out so that by the fall of 1702, only forty-six remained dedicated. Gradually they gathered in Edo, taking up life as merchants and artisans near Kira's residence. Kira, in the meantime, had retired and devoted himself to practicing the tea ceremony.[2]

Upon hearing that Kira planned to host a tea party during several days of intermittent snow (and here is one of the few mentions of snow, otherwise so frequently depicted in woodblocks of the rōnin attack), they decided the time was right. In the middle of the night, the rōnin band broke into Kira's residence and murdered their deceased lord's enemy. With their collective sense of purpose supposedly unified

---

[2] *Tokugawa jikki*, vol. 6, pp. 492–494.

by a common devotion to righteous duty, "the forty-six men were truly able to do the impossible, surely an incomparable feat."[3] Here, the *Veritable Records'* willingness to report the success of the vendetta with such enthusiasm is surprising. By the end of the Tokugawa, even Tokugawa official historians had apparently become admirers of the rōnin and their vendetta. Then again, these reports were said to be those that "circulated widely," i.e., rumor and popular thinking about the vendetta, and not necessarily the opinion of the shogunal chroniclers.

In relating the end of the rōnin, the *Veritable Records* states that Asano's forty-six retainers had violated the rules of the realm by form-ing an armed conspiracy in utter disregard for the law. Therefore, they would have to die. Accordingly, they were divided up into four groups and placed in the custody of four daimyō houses with inspectors assigned to supervise their confinement. Their children were sent into distant exile. The same applied to Kira's son, Sahyōe. The *Veritable Records* then lists the forty-six men by name, according to the daimyō house to which they were assigned. Although not referred to as "loyal and righteous" (*chūgi*) from the start, soon discussion of them (alluding to the Confucian debates) seemed to never end. When it was learned that the rōnin might be punished as commoners because of their conspiracy, sentiment shifted in their favor and note was taken of their loyalty and how they had acted on behalf of their deceased lord. Yet even the imperial abbot of the Ueno Kan'eiji and Nikko Tōshōgū, when asked by Tsunayoshi whether mercy might be shown the rōnin, declined to respond in their favor. Taking the abbot's silence as an endorsement of death for the rōnin, Tsunayoshi's regime handed down its verdict. Shogunal reasoning was apparently that even if the rōnin were par-doned, they, as loyal men, would never be able to bring themselves to serve another lord. Rather than allow the rōnin to starve themselves to death in the mountains and forests (alluding to the principled suicide of the ancient Chinese righteous martyrs, Bo Yi and Shu Qi), it was deemed best, the *Veritable Records* relates, for the authorities to establish "the way of the samurai" by asking for their lives. In that way, their deter-mination to fulfill their master's intentions would not have been in vain. Official punishment, then, would rightly resolve the matter.[4]

The *Veritable Records* thus concludes its discussions, seeing in the shogunate's verdict a righteous and judicious resolution, one that

[3] Ibid. [4] Ibid., pp. 499–500.

came to be accepted by all. In the process, it casts Tsunayoshi as the loyal and righteous ruler, justly concluding the incident with fairness, mercy, and consideration for all. Noteworthy is the mention of the shogunal consultation with the imperial abbot, suggesting the kind but righteous heart of the shogun, made stronger in justice by the abbot's silence. Or, considered differently, in noting the abbot's silence, the *Veritable Records* meant to hint that in the end, it was the abbot, not Tsunayoshi, who sealed the fate of the rōnin. In the process, the shogunate's history arguably would have been attempting to wash Tsunayoshi's hands of the fateful blood of the rōnin. If so, then this detail was another indication of changing attitudes within the shogunate regarding the rōnin vendetta. Perhaps, very late in the Tokugawa, the shogunate was beginning to rethink its role in the verdict, and thus, rethink the verdict itself.

The Dutch Trade Official

In different ways, Western accounts added to the controversies, advancing global understandings and misunderstandings of the vendetta and Japan. The first discussion appeared in Isaac Titsingh's *Illustrations of Japan: Consisting of Private Memoirs and Anecdotes of the Reigning Dynasty of the Djogouns, or Sovereigns of Japan*, published in English in 1822. As an official in the Dutch East India Company, Titsingh was based in Dejima, an artificial island established in Nagasaki Bay as the shogunally supervised residential and commercial space for trade with Japan. In the eighteenth century, trade was not a privilege widely held. Distrust of Westerners and their religion prompted the shogunate to restrict commercial and other access largely to the Dutch. Titsingh's position thus gave him an exceptional window on Japan, at least as he could experience it from Dejima, and on two occasions while in Edo, in audiences with Tokugawa officials. Titsingh passed away in 1812, before his writings were published. Two French scholars edited what came to be published as the French edition of 1820,[5] entitled *Mémoires et anecdotes sur la dynastie régnante des djogouns, Souverains du*

---

[5] Timon Screech, ed., "Introduction," *Secret Memoirs of the Shoguns: Isaac Titsingh and Japan, 1779–1822* (London: Routledge, 2006), pp. 2–3, 63–74.

Japon. The English text cited here is a translation of the 1820 volume, published in London in 1822.

Illustrations of Japan includes skewed accounts, curiously Romanized words, and illustrations that seemingly confuse Titsingh's later time in Beijing's Forbidden City with his visit to Edo Castle.[6] The frontispiece, for example, presents "the residence of the Djogoun at Yedo" as a vertically stacked succession of rectangular palatial enclosures, with each progressively larger, culminating in the final, grand compound facing south. Symmetry defines the illustration at every level. While not as grand as the Forbidden City, the illustration looks nothing like Edo Castle. Titsingh's contributions to the beginnings of Asian studies, and especially Japanese studies (and arguably Orientalism as well), came to be monumental. The glaring errors in his work were no doubt due to his not having had a final hand in their editing prior to publication. Nevertheless, the errors were accepted as truth, misleading many along the way.

The boom in *Chūshingura* performances, parodies, and woodblocks bypassed Titsingh. His one-page account, presented in the context of his discussion of the fifth shogun, Tsunayoshi, was grounded in something akin to the historical facts rather than the *Chūshingura* narrative. It reads:

> On the 14th of the 3d month of the 14th year Gen-rok (1701), Assan-no-takoumi-no-kami-Naganori, prince of Akō, who had been several times treated contemptuously by Kira-kotsouki-no-ski, having received a fresh affront from him in the palace of the Djogoun, drew his sword with the intention of revenging the insult. Some persons, on hearing the noise, ran up and separated them, and Kotsuoki was but slightly wounded. It is an unpardonable crime to draw a sabre in the palace; the prince was therefore ordered to rip himself up, and his descendants were banished for ever. His adversary who, out of respect for the palace, had abstained from drawing his sabre, was pardoned.
>
> This injustice exasperated the servants of the prince so much the more since it was Kotsouki, who, by his repeated insults, had caused the destruction of their master. Forty-seven of them, having agreed to revenge his death, forced their way, in the night of the 14th of the

---

[6] I. Titsingh, "Frontispiece," *Illustrations of Japan: Consisting of Private Memoirs and Anecdotes of the Reigning Dynasty of the Djogouns, or Sovereigns of Japan* (London: R. Ackermann, 1822).

12th month of the following year, into the palace of Kotsouki; and, after a combat which lasted till day-light, they penetrated to his apartment and dispatched him. The Djogoun, on the first intelligence of this desperate attack, sent troops to the assistance of the unfortunate Kotsouki, but they arrived too late to save him. The assailants, not one of whom lost his life in the scuffle, were all taken and condemned to rip up their bellies, which they did with the greatest firmness, satisfied with having revenged their master. They were all interred in the temple of Singakousi, near the prince. The soldiers, in token of respect for their fidelity, still visit their graves, and pray before them. Kotsouki's son, who had been withheld by cowardice from hastening to the assistance of his father, though he was then in the palace, was deprived of his post and banished, with all his kindred, to the island of Awasi.[7]

For better or worse, Titsingh's account influenced nearly every subsequent Western rendition of the vendetta, at least until the early twenty-first century. Titsingh mentions neither the bribery thesis, tracing back to Muro Kyūsō's *The Righteous Men*, nor the *Chūshingura* addition that Kira's (Kō-no-Moronao's) bullying of Asano (Enya) resulted from Kira's frustrated advances toward Asano's wife. Rather, Titsingh simply notes that Asano "had been several times treated contemptuously" by Kira. Then, on the fourteenth day, he "received a fresh affront from him in the palace," so that he "drew his sabre with the intention of revenging the insult." In Titsingh's view, Kira, apparently for no stated reason, verbally abused Asano to the point that the latter tried to strike him down. Titsingh returns to this in explaining the outrage of Asano's retainers who thought that Kira was to blame for their deceased master's attack because of his "repeated insults."[8]

Titsingh offers no hint that Asano simply lost his senses and attacked Kira in a moment of madness. Titsingh's book is subtitled *A Description of the Feasts and Ceremonies Observed throughout the Year at Their Court*, making it peculiar that the ceremonial context of Asano's attack – receiving imperial emissaries for New Year's greetings – is omitted. Instead, Titsingh simply places Asano within the inner confines of the shogun's castle, as though that were an ordinary event for the young daimyō. Titsingh offers no account of Kira's status or of his relationship to Asano. The attack is presented simply as the response

---

[7] Titsingh, *Illustrations of Japan*, pp. 22–23.   [8] Ibid., pp. 23.

of one man, treated with contempt to the breaking point, against another. Any number of subsequent Western vendetta narratives offered similarly terse accounts, bracketing out the ceremonial occasion that made the attack an egregious and outrageous breach of ritual circumstance and civility.

Titsingh claims that it was "an unpardonable crime to draw a sabre in the palace." This legalistic explanation, however, is not consistent with primary sources describing the incident. Instead, the chief inspector, Shōda Yasutoshi (1650–1705), speaking at the Tamura residence where Asano committed seppuku, delivered the shogunal verdict as follows: "This person [Asano], due to a grudge that he harbored, irrationally, cut down Kira, showing no respect even for the [shogun's] palace. Despite the time and circumstances, his actions were repeatedly unyielding to the most extreme point. Accordingly, he must commit seppuku."[9] What the shogunate found offensive was that Asano had, for no clear reason other than some unspecified grudge, attacked, with murderous intent, the shogunate's senior master of court ceremonies, in Edo Castle, just as the final day of the most important ceremony of the year was about to begin. In the process, blood was spilled and the ritual venue polluted. By any count, such behavior was outrageous. Most likely, even if he had not drawn his sword but instead simply struck Kira and spilled blood, Asano would have been punished similarly for the violent disruption. This is not to deny that drawing one's sword in the shogun's castle was offensive. However, the shogunate explained its verdict not in terms of a drawn sword, but rather as the consequence of Asano's outrageous disregard for the ceremonial time and place. Nevertheless, any number of later Western accounts echoed Titsingh on this count, mentioning the unsheathed sabre as, in itself, a capital offense.

Titsingh claims that the shogunate "sent troops to the assistance of the unfortunate Kotsouki, but they arrived too late to save him." As things turned out, the rōnin reported their deed to the shogunate while en route to the Sengakuji, but were never pursued by shogunal forces. After reaching the Sengakuji and being offered baths, they declined for fear that forces pursuing them might arrive, but none did. Amazingly, the rōnin encountered no official police or security

---

[9] "Tamura Ukyōdaibu dono ni Asano Takumi-no-kami oazuke ikken," *Akō gijin sansho*, vol. 2, pp. 4–5.

resistance, other than that by Kira's guards, during or after their attack. Outside forces supportive of the Kira house did not arrive. The suggestion that such troops were on the horizon is in *Chūshingura*, making this detail in Titsingh's account the only one even remotely alluding to that drama.

Despite these issues and many others, Titsingh's account remains significant insofar as it provided the first description of the vendetta for the Western world. Later Western writings on Japanese history and culture included similar accounts, and like Titsingh's, typically omitted mention that Asano attacked Kira at the start of a high ceremonial occasion. In the absence of that ritual context, Asano's supposed breach of shogunal law, drawing his sword within the shogun's palace, came to be emphasized. Western accounts have also mistakenly suggested, as did Titsingh, that seppuku in the Genroku period required samurai to "rip up their bellies," when in fact, they simply signaled to their second to behead them mercifully. Either way, the punishment was strange and unusual for Westerners, but Titsingh and later Western raconteurs, in describing seppuku, portrayed the Genroku period in ways that horrifically sensationalized its exoticism, rendering it far less refined than the more ritualized and arguably humane version of seppuku then practiced warranted.

The British Consul

Two years after the Opium War (1839–1842), Sir Rutherford Alcock, a surgeon by training, was appointed British consul in Fuzhou, and then later, consul in Shanghai. In 1858, as the Ansei Treaties opened trade relations with Japan, Alcock was named the first British consul-general there. As things turned out, he established the first British legation in Japan at a Zen temple, the Tōzenji, in the Takanawa area, not far from the Sengakuji. The Tōzenji, incidentally, was the family temple of the Tamura lords, who had, in 1701, supervised Asano Naganori's seppuku. The Hosokawa residence where seventeen rōnin leaders, including Ōishi, had committed seppuku, was also nearby. Not surprisingly, Alcock's book, *The Capital of the Tycoon*, published in 1863, discusses the Akō vendetta and its relevance to contemporary history in some detail. Unlike Titsingh, Alcock resided in Japan as the highest diplomatic minister of the world's most powerful nation. In Edo, he lived and worked proximate to several emotionally charged vendetta sites, during the most xenophobic

Figure 8.1 "Sir John Rutherford Alcock." © National Portrait Gallery, London.

period of early modern Japanese history. To ensure its security, the British compound reportedly had a "Japanese guard of one hundred and fifty men." Alcock recorded that he kept "two cases of revolvers placed on my dressing-table," and slept "with revolvers under my pillow."[10]

Nevertheless, in 1861, the British legation was attacked by rōnin carrying a signed pledge declaring their inability to endure foreigners defiling the "sacred empire," and affirming their mortal determination to "cause the foreigner to retire, and partly tranquilize both the minds of the Mikado and the Government (Tycoon)." By Alcock's count, twenty-three of the rōnin were killed or wounded during the failed night attack. Reflecting on it, Alcock wrote, "There is probably not in all the annals of our diplomacy an example of such a bloodthirsty and deliberate plot to massacre a whole Legation, and certainly none so boldly and recklessly carried to partial execution."[11]

[10] Sir Rutherford Alcock, K.C.B., *The Capital of the Tycoon: A Narrative of Three Year's Residence in Japan*, vol. 2 (New York: Harper and Brothers, 1863), pp. 146–158.
[11] Ibid.

Alcock's account of the Akō vendetta is paired with his account of the assassination of Ii Naosuke (1815–1860), the shogun's regent, killed "in broad daylight, on his way to the palace, ... in the midst of a large retinue of his retainers!" Alcock noted that such violence reminded him of "feudal times of Europe, when the streets and thoroughfares of every capital were scenes of daily bloodshed and murder." Alcock next addressed "the popular idea of heroism and poetic justice as exemplified in a hundred legends and traditions, which form the staple of their theatrical pieces, their picture-books, and their popular tales."[12] Conflating history, "true accounts," art, oral traditions, and *Chūshingura*, Alcock related:

> One of the most celebrated of these is a story of a small Daimio, who, having a feud in past times with one of the Tycoon's Council of State, determined to avenge himself by slaying his enemy when he met him in the palace. He made the attempt and failed, inflicting only a slight wound, some of the attendants having seized him from behind as he was aiming his blow. Foiled in his object, he returned to his house; and having collected his officers and retainers about him, and made his preparations for disemboweling himself, he deliberately performed the operation in their presence, and then, handing the short sword covered with his blood to his secretary, he laid his dying injunction upon him, as his liege lord, with that very weapon to take the life of his enemy. The latter, being freed from his antagonist, seized upon the house and property of the deceased Daimio, and turned out all his faithful servitors.[13]

Seemingly unaware of Titsingh's account, published in 1822, forty-one years before his own, Alcock refers to the story of the rōnin not as history, but instead as "a popular legend ... recited" to him. Personal names, perhaps too foreign, are simply omitted. Instead, Alcock refers to the Tycoon (Tsunayoshi), a "Daimio" (Asano), and "one of the Tycoon's Council of State" (Kira). No attempt at explaining the "feud" is made. The circumstances of the attack, crucial factors in the shogunate's verdict, are not given.

Alcock notes that the attack took place in the palace (Edo Castle), but suggests that the occasion was a random one that occurred when "the Daimio" happened to meet his enemy there. Alcock draws on

---

[12] Ibid.   [13] Alcock, *The Capital of the Tycoon*, vol. 1, pp. 312–313.

Act IV of *Chūshingura*, or accounts echoing it, in stating that the seppuku took place in the house of "the Daimio," and in describing the dying instructions "the Daimio" left to his "Secretary" (Ōishi). Finally, the suggestion that "the enemy" of "the Daimio" confiscated his domain is mistaken. It was Tsunayoshi who took advantage of the opportunity to seize the domain, not Kira. Alcock continues his rendition by explaining:

> These, to the number of forty-seven, become *Lonins*, under the command of the secretary, all bound together by an oath to accomplish the destruction of their master's enemy. Accordingly, choosing their time, they stormed his castle during the night when they knew he was inside, and entered into a terrible conflict with all his retainers, to the number of some three hundred; and such was their valor and heroism that they finally vanquished them, and immediately proceeded to search for their chief victim. He was concealed in a secret recess between two rooms, with one of his friends; but they had obtained information of the existence of such a hiding-place, and one of them thrust a spear through the partition. The blade wounded the Daimio, but not in a vital part; and as it was drawn out he took care to wipe it with his sleeve, so that on examining it and seeing no mark of blood, they came to the conclusion that no one was there, and that he had escaped their vengeance. Nothing then remained but an act of self-immolation; and, stripping off their armor and dress, they were just in the act of performing the Hara-kiru, when a stifled cough reached their ears from the very hiding-place they had pierced in a vain search. Satisfied now that their enemy was still in their grasp, they sprung to their feet, tore down the walls, and dragged him and his friend out, when the secretary, with the very sword received from his dying chief, struck off both their heads. Their vengeance thus satisfied, and not a living being remaining to be slain, they then performed the disemboweling with the greatest heroism and complacency. They were all buried in one cemetery in Yeddo, which was pointed out to me, and they live to this day in the hearts of all brave and loyal men in Japan as types of true heroism![14]

Alcock's account is quite the work of historical fiction. He describes Kira's residence, admittedly a sprawling compound, in overstated

---

[14] Ibid., p. 313.

terms, as a "castle," and then inflates the number of Kira's men, citing three hundred. The discovery of Kira, referred to as a daimyō, is an elaborate fabrication, with Kira wiping blood from the blade that pierced him to fool the rōnin into thinking he was not there. The double beheading that followed was one too many, and fictitiously credited to Ōishi. Given the proximity of the British legation to the Sengakuji, it is surprising that Alcock only mentions "one cemetery in Yeddo" rather than cite its name. Perhaps with little exaggeration, Alcock noted that "they [the rōnin] live to this day in the hearts of all brave and loyal men in Japan as types of true heroism." By prefacing his vendetta narrative with descriptions of the assassination of Ii Naosuke and the later attack on the British legation, Alcock also suggested that one legacy of the rōnin vendetta was the use of lethal terror and violence in the political arena.

Critiquing the ethics of the vendetta, Alcock expressed concerns about the influence of the rōnin on the "character, as well as the habits of thought and action of a nation." In Alcock's view, the Japanese were embracing criminal lore, beginning with Asano's attempted murder of Kira, and concluding with the vendetta's bloody triumph. He thus warned:

> What its exact influence may be we can not determine, perhaps; but that it is deep and all-pervading, affecting their general estimate of all deeds of like character, whether it be the slaying of a Regent or the massacre of a Foreign Legation, is very certain, and presents a state of things well worthy of serious consideration.[15]

Alcock's anxieties about the "deep and all-pervading" respect for the rōnin, as well as his condescending, at times arrogant interpretive perspectives, were arguably alternative expressions of Britain's larger imperialist domination of East Asia and the world. It must be added, however, that Alcock had Japanese precursors in the form of Ogyū, Satō, and Dazai, and that his critical appraisals of the rōnin were later echoed by Fukuzawa Yukichi and other modern commentators. Still, Alcock was British, and so his views must be interpreted through that foreign lens and all that it implies about their interpretive nuances.

---

[15] Ibid., pp. 313–314.

Figure 8.2 Kodomo shibai. Courtesy of Waseda University, Department of Special Collections.

Regardless of how misguided and perhaps arrogantly Orientalist, Alcock's account became the first widely read English retelling of the vendetta. It should be added that in 1864, after successive Japanese attacks on foreigners, Alcock, then British minister to Japan, abandoned negotiations and endorsed the bombing of Shimonoseki and Kagoshima, as well as a punitive expedition against Chōshū.[16] Knowing well the rōnin legend, Alcock, in advocating violent retaliation, was apparently swayed equally by its values. Whether he realized their pernicious impact on his own decisions is questionable.

The Resolute Samurai

Alcock's assessment of the vendetta's relevance for late Tokugawa political culture might seem farfetched. However, corroboration appears in Yoshida Shōin. Yoshida's life was dominated by Yamaga

---

[16] Michael Austin, *Negotiating with Imperialism: The Unequal Treaties and the Culture of Japanese Diplomacy* (Cambridge, MA: Harvard University Press, 2004), pp. 108–117.

Sokō's teachings and their convoluted historical and philosophical legacy. The Yoshida family, hereditary teachers of Yamaga's thought in Chōshū domain, first gained certification in those teachings in 1714, a decade after the vendetta. At that time, close vassals of the Tokugawa were rallying behind the shogunate and its verdict regarding the rōnin, much as they had earlier following Yamaga's exile to Akō domain. During the vendetta debates, Yamaga's teachings, blamed repeatedly for the rōnin violence and lawlessness, became even more a pariah form of learning in Edo, at least from the perspective of those supporting Tokugawa authority and judicial wisdom. However, in distant Chōshū domain, Yamaga's ideas came to be valued precisely because of their alleged links to the vendetta.

As outer lords, the Mōri daimyō of Chōshū were not the most enthusiastic supporters of the Tokugawa shogunate. Prior to their defeat by Tokugawa forces at the Battle of Sekigahara in 1600, the Mōri had ruled the second wealthiest domain in the realm, with holdings totaling 1,250,000 *koku*. But after Sekigahara, the ascendant Tokugawa decided to quarter their power, reducing the Mōri to 298,480 *koku* and the territory it comprised to two provinces, Nagato and Suō, "less than a fourth of their previous domains."[17] Over time, resentments engendered by these reductions in wealth and power fed a fascination for, and even vengeful dedication to, Yamaga's teachings. After all, those teachings were, via their alleged connection to the Akō vendetta, linked to examples of heroic direct action supposedly based on heavenly mandated opposition to arrogance, greed, and abusive rule. That Yamaga's teachings were blamed for the rōnin vendetta directed against a supposedly evil shogunal official, then, was arguably a point of pride for their Chōshū advocates and patrons.

Yoshida was born in 1830 to a low-ranking samurai-peasant family in the village of Matsumoto, outside the castle town of Hagi. In 1834, he was adopted by his uncle, Yoshida Daisuke. The following year, 1835, with his uncle's passing, he became head of the Yoshida line and hereditary teacher of Yamaga Sokō's martial philosophy in Chōshū. Another uncle, Tamaki Bunnoshin, assumed responsibility for educating Yoshida in Confucian and martial philosophical studies, which Yoshida apparently mastered quickly. Incredibly, in 1840, at ten, he began

---

[17] Albert Craig, *Chōshū and the Meiji Restoration* (Cambridge, MA: Harvard University Press, 1961), pp. 21, 11–25.

Figure 8.3 Yoshida Shōin. Courtesy of the National Diet Library, Portraits of Modern Japanese Historical Figures.

lecturing his daimyō at the domain school, the Meirinkan, on Yamaga's *Complete Writings on Martial Teachings*, a compilation that Yoshida would lecture on for the remainder of his life. With his daimyō's support, Yoshida traveled, in 1850, to Kyūshū, spending significant time in Hirado, another center of Yamaga's "way of the samurai" teachings. There, Yoshida studied under Yamaga Bansuke, a distant relative of Yamaga Sokō.[18]

Yoshida read voraciously, reportedly more than one hundred books, including ones on the Opium War and Western munitions. Yoshida also read works such as *New Theses* by a leading advocate of political reform, Aizawa Seishisai. In 1851, Yoshida accompanied his daimyō to Edo and enrolled in Yamaga Sosui's newly opened school. Although convinced of the importance of Western military studies, Yoshida believed that Confucian thinking would provide a necessary

[18] Yoshida Shōin, *Saiyū nikki,* in *Yoshida Shōin*, Nihon shisō taikei vol. 54, eds. Yoshida Tsunekichi, Fujita Shōzō, and Nishida Taichirō (Tokyo: Iwanami shoten, 1978), pp. 403–406, 413–418, 423, 425–426, 430–433, 441.

foundation for reform. During this period, he remained an official instructor of Yamaga's Confucian teachings, lecturing his daimyō twice monthly at the Mōri residence in Edo.

Yoshida revealed how strongly the exploits of the Akō rōnin figured in his thinking when he, along with two other students of the Yamaga teachings, embarked, without their daimyō's permission, on travel to northeastern Japan. The date of their departure was the fourteenth day of the twelfth month, 1852. Yoshida recorded in his diary how the three had pledged to leave Edo on the same date that the rōnin had launched their vendetta. The group's destination was Tsugaru domain, the stronghold of Yamaga teachings in northeastern Honshū. During their pilgrimage, they often discussed the rōnin vendetta and *Chūshingura*.[19] After returning to Edo in the spring of 1853, Yoshida reported his deed to his daimyō, much as the rōnin had reported their vendetta to the shogunal authorities. As punishment, Yoshida was returned to Chōshū where he was reduced to rōnin status. Nevertheless, his daimyō gave him permission to travel for ten years, enabling Yoshida to return to Edo to resume study under Yamaga Sosui.

In 1854, Yoshida attempted to stow away on Commodore Matthew Perry's flagship, the USS *Powhatan*, but was returned to Japanese soil by Perry's men. Not satisfied with an uneventful conclusion to his breach of shogunal law, Yoshida reported his deed to the authorities. Although execution was recommended, the shogunate had him imprisoned. Writing from Denma-chō prison, Yoshida reasoned, "When Akō was offended, the forty-seven righteous samurai sacrificed themselves to take revenge on their lord's enemy ... The Akō samurai, in serving their lord, defied the law. For the sake of my country, I too had to defy the law."[20] Yoshida's *Prison Memoirs*, finished while he was incarcerated in Chōshū, reveal that he modeled his life in confinement after what he knew of the rōnin by, among other things, allowing himself nothing more than an austere diet. His *Prison Memoirs* claim that his suffering for a righteous cause would benefit the nation just as the righteous samurai of Akō had benefited Japan, and as the righteous martyrdoms of Bo Yi and Shu Qi had benefited ancient China. Yoshida then added that the Akō rōnin, Bo Yi, and Shu Qi were all "sages" who

---

[19] Yoshida, *Tōhoku yū nikki*, in *Yoshida Shōin*, NST vol. 54, pp. 447, 505, 507, 522.
[20] Quoted from David M. Earl, *Emperor and Nation: Political Thinkers of the Tokugawa Period* (Seattle: University of Washington, 1964), pp. 125–126.

deserved respect as "the teachers of hundreds of generations."[21] Thus Yoshida revealed that his martyr's course was partly modeled after that of the Akō rōnin, Japanese exemplars of a sagely way arguably traceable to ancient Chinese Confucian martyrs.

After being released from Noyama prison in 1856, Yoshida was permitted to give lectures at his uncle's private academy, the Shōka Sonjuku, in Chōshū. His pupils included an impressive list of local samurai who later became leaders of Meiji Japan, including Itō Hirobumi and Yamagata Aritomo, both future prime ministers. Yoshida frequently lectured on Yamaga's *Complete Writings on Martial Teachings*, and praised Yamaga's impact on the Akō rōnin. In Yoshida's view, the alleged connection between Yamaga and the rōnin, far from a negative, only enhanced the value of the Yamaga teachings. As Yoshida emerged as a powerful advocate of the "revere the emperor, expel the foreign barbarian" line, his praise for Yamaga's impact on the rōnin vendetta was linked to imperial loyalism and anti-foreignism. Thus, he stated:

> We samurai ... must strive to repay the grace and bounty provided for us through this imperial land by striving always to fulfill the way of the samurai ... If samurai wish to comprehend their way, they must accept the precepts of our samurai teacher, Yamaga Sokō. Throughout history, myriad books have been written, so why are Master Yamaga's so worthy of belief? When you have studied what Master Yamaga recorded in the *Complete Writings on Martial Teachings*, you will fathom this completely. But allow me to explain just one point ... When one thoroughly examines the Akō vendetta, one realizes what Ōishi Kura-no-suke, the leader of the Akō samurai, learned from Master Yamaga.[22]

Yoshida hints, without specifics, that somehow the heroics of the rōnin exemplified how Yamaga's "way of the samurai" teachings could inculcate in "resolute samurai" (*shishi*) an admirable willingness to act on behalf of the imperial nation, even in ways that might transcend mere shogunal decrees. Yoshida's understanding of "resolute samurai" reflected his admiration for the rōnin and his readiness, as a Yamaga

---

[21] Yoshida, *Kaikoroku*, NST, vol. 54, pp. 549.
[22] Tahara Tsuguo, "Yamaga Sokō to bushidō," *Yamaga Sokō*, Nihon no meicho, vol. 12 (Tokyo: Chuō kōron sha, 1971), p. 16.

instructor, to incorporate his master's most famous (alleged) disciples, the rōnin, into his vision of what future disciples of the Yamaga teachings might embody. Earlier, in his diary accounts of his travels to Tsugaru, Yoshida mentioned the need for "samurai having resolute purpose," describing the latter as impassioned activists ready to sacrifice themselves for their cause, much as the Akō rōnin had for their lord.[23]

Rather than interpreting Yamaga's thought in terms of historical stages, Yoshida merged Yamaga's later thinking about the supremacy of imperial Japan, expressed in his exile-period work, *The True Central Dynasty*, with Yamaga's earlier, Edo-based "way of the samurai" thinking, synthesizing the two and thus allowing loyal samurai to think in terms of directing ultimate loyalty to the imperial line and its divine realm. In this context, Yoshida asserted that the gist of Yamaga's *Elementary Learning for Samurai* consisted in its accounts of "the distinctive national essence of Japan."[24] Yoshida's interpretations of Yamaga's thought, characterized by his elevation of the Akō rōnin as exemplary activists, was one of the stronger, more resilient threads in his intellectual development. Indeed, in his final years, Yoshida arguably sought to match the loyalism-unto-death ethic of the rōnin, only in his case, as directed toward the emperor and the divine imperial homeland. After hearing that Ii Naosuke, the dominant political figure in the shogunate, planned to conclude treaties with several Western nations despite imperial opposition, Yoshida decided the shogunate had to be stopped. In his eyes, the shogunate had become the enemy of the emperor and the imperial land.

In late 1858, he and seventeen Chōshū samurai apparently made a blood pledge to assassinate Manabe Akikatsu, a senior counselor whom the shogunate planned to send to Kyoto to quash anti-Tokugawa sentiment there. Similarly, a band of Mito samurai plotted to assassinate Ii Naosuke, and indeed they succeeded. However, in 1859, the shogunate uncovered the conspiracy that Yoshida figured in and subsequently beheaded him. In his final testament, Yoshida supposedly vowed, "even if I return seven times from the dead, I shall never forget to drive away the foreigner," paraphrasing the famous remark by Kusunoki Masashige's brother, Masasue, as the two samurai faced certain death on the battlefield fighting for Emperor Go-Daigo's cause.

[23] Shōin, *Tōhoku yū nikki*.
[24] Hori, *Yamaga Sokō*, pp. 143–144. Also, Tahara, "Yamaga Sokō to bushidō," *Yamaga Sokō*, pp. 13–18.

Yoshida's vow implicitly added his fate to that of Kusunoki as another expression of ultimate, imperial loyalism.

Yoshida was buried by his former pupils, including Itō Hirobumi and Kido Kōin. Another of his former students, Yamagata Aritomo, remarked that Yoshida's death was "an ineradicable tragedy, causing great sadness to all loyalists and ineffable sorrow to me."[25] Yoshida's disciples soon made sure, however, that his interpretations of Yamaga Sokō's philosophy gained a kind of legitimization via imperial decree. By Tokugawa legal standards, the rōnin remained outlaws, rightly punished by death. Their widespread following, theatrically and otherwise, had not changed their status as criminals, guilty of a murderous conspiracy that rampaged the residence of a former shogunal official. Yoshida identified with, and even glorified, the rōnin because he too was an outlaw of sorts, one intent on aggressively challenging if not overthrowing the regime, which in his view was compromising the integrity of the sacred imperial land. Much the same could have been said about the legal standing of Yoshida's former disciples turned revolutionaries, including Itō Hirobumi, Yamagata Aritomo, and Kido Kōin.

The Emperor's Rescript

As the Chōshū revolutionaries found themselves on the cusp of political power in a new regime, they engineered the rehabilitation of their late teacher, and arguably themselves, by having some of their idols, the Akō rōnin, imperially designated as exemplars of samurai loyalty. In the process, they also legitimized Yamaga's way of the samurai since it was the teaching widely thought to have been behind the rōnin vendetta. In an incredible twist that marked the opening of the Meiji period, Yoshida's praise for the rōnin as teachers of samurai virtue for "one hundred generations" was paraphrased by none other than the young Meiji emperor. On the fifth day of the eleventh month of the first year of the Meiji period (1868), as his procession approached Edo, soon to be renamed Tokyo, the emperor sent an emissary to the Sengakuji to relay, on his behalf, an imperial rescript (*chokugo*) before the graves of Ōishi and the other rōnin. It read:

[25] Roger F. Hackett, *Yamagata Aritomo in the Rise of Modern Japan, 1838–1922* (Cambridge, MA: Harvard University Press, 1971), p. 17.

You, Yoshio, and the others resolutely grasped the righteous duty informing relations between lords and retainers. You took revenge on your lord's enemies, and then died according to the laws. Thereby you inspired the sentiments of one hundred generations. We convey our profound approbation.[26]

In addition to the rescript, the imperial messenger delivered an offering to the temple. At a certain level, the presentation of the rescript curiously recalled the rōnin presentation of Kira's head before Asano's grave one hundred and sixty-five years earlier. In other respects, the emperor's message was another expression of reverence and respect, reiterating innumerable previous occasions when local people and pilgrims made the trek to the Sengakuji to offer incense before the rōnin graves, or, in a different register of reverence, attended a performance of *Chūshingura*. In still other respects, the imperial rescript foreshadowed the century to come in which the celebration of the rōnin, although not without critique, would reach unprecedented and yet ultimately tragic heights.

Quite possibly, the significance of the Meiji emperor's message was not something he, sixteen at the time, fully understood. Almost certainly the decision to send a rescript was made by the leaders of the Chōshū entourage managing the emperor in his journey to what would become his new capital. Along the way, they made sure that their martyred teacher, Yoshida Shōin, found a modicum of vindication via imperial recognition of the rōnin that he, Yoshida, so admired. Kido Kōin coordinated the transfer of the imperial capital to Edo and worked closely with the Meiji emperor as he and those around him consolidated the power of the new regime. Also close to the emperor during the same time was Asano Nagakoto, daimyō of Hiroshima domain and head of the main branch of the Asano family. He would have favored such a move since recognizing Ōishi with praise by implication cast the Akō branch of the Asano line in a new light. Additionally, the emperor's message could be viewed most generally as a metaphorical statement of support and approval for resolute samurai bent on revering the imperial line and expelling the barbarian, who, like the rōnin earlier, acted boldly and defiantly out of a sense of loyalty to the political figure they identified as their lord.

[26] Kunaichō, *Meiji tennō ki* (Tokyo: Yoshikawa kōbunkan, 1968), vol. 1, p. 888.

Figure 8.4 "Portrait of the Meiji Emperor." Courtesy of the Metropolitan Museum of Art.

In significant ways, the Meiji emperor's praise for the rōnin signaled the beginning of yet another boom in vendetta culture, one that pervaded the Meiji period and the twentieth century, through 1945. For the next century, the Meiji emperor's rescript would be cited over and again by those intent on revering the rōnin. The same year, the chief priest of the Kagakuji began a campaign for the establishment of an Ōishi shrine (Ōishi *jinja*) in Akō, on the grounds of Akō Castle. Similarly, momentum for establishing an Ōishi shrine in Yamashina began to emerge. Early the following year, two leaders in the Meiji regime, Sanjō Sanetomo and Iwakura Tomomi, initiated plans for a lay shrine for the "righteous samurai" near the Sengakuji. With assistance from the Hiroshima branch of the Asano family and descendants of the Ōishi family, the effort resulted in a hall displaying wooden statues, celebrated with a Shinto-style "completion ceremony." This initiative, along with an earlier, 1848 contribution of wooden statues of the rōnin, marked a union of forces from on high, along with those from society at large, toward revering the rōnin and their vendetta.[27]

In 1873, as part of a new code of laws, the Meiji state declared private revenge vendettas illegal, affirming instead the primacy of state laws and official justice. While the prohibition might be viewed as another example of Meiji Japan copying Western models without fully endorsing them, it also complicated perceptions of the rōnin and their vendetta. In the end, however, rather than a contradiction in policy, the move to outlaw private revenge arguably did little more than affirm that the imperial state would assume the role Ōishi had played earlier, deciding who, when, why, and how the efforts of righteous and loyal samurai would be deployed. Private revenge was outlawed, but the new regime expected from its subjects nothing less than the loyalty and devotion of the rōnin, in response to its directives and for its ends. In effect, imperials subjects were to manifest the virtues of the forty-seven rōnin, but now in relation to their new sovereign, the Meiji emperor.

---

[27] "Genroku gikyo ni kankei aru jinja, bukkaku, iseki," *Akō gishi jiten*, p. 735. Miyazawa, *Kindai Nihon to Chūshingura gensō*, pp. 30–31.

9 MODERN REVIVALS

The Meiji emperor's 1868 rescript praising Ōishi and the rōnin before their graves at the Sengakuji signaled the beginning of a new age for the vendetta, one wherein it flourished as never before. Kabuki performances and woodblock print production continued on a grand scale in Tokyo, Osaka, and Kyoto. Modern Japan's emerging networks of communication facilitated deep penetration of vendetta culture into the hinterlands. Ideologies of all sorts enlisted the rōnin in support of their causes, no matter how farfetched the connection. Western writings on the vendetta also attained new heights. Yet the vendetta remained in Meiji times the subject of ongoing controversies and disagreements reflecting divisions within Japanese society, and internationally as well, regarding its political ethics, or lack thereof. Nevertheless, it must be admitted that by the end of the Meiji, the rōnin and their supposed teacher, Yamaga Sokō, had been elevated to unprecedented heights as role models for the nation and its future generations.

Early Meiji Intellectuals

Sounding the first contrarian view was Fukuzawa Yukichi, one of Meiji Japan's most influential intellectuals. A long-standing advocate of Western learning, Fukuzawa provoked the ire of Meiji conservatives in *An Encouragement of Learning* when, in pamphlets six and seven (1874), he addressed people's relationship to public law. In the sixth pamphlet, he rejected the notion that individuals should take matters into their own hands. Doing so amounted to "private, vigilante justice," which he condemned. Fukuzawa's ideas drew strongly from a work by an American thinker, Francis Wayland's *Elements of Moral Science*. However, in denouncing private justice, Fukuzawa clarified his points with indigenous examples, noting that Asano's forty-seven retainers had murdered Kira as an act of revenge because, in their view, Kira had caused their lord's death. Fukuzawa agreed that Kira should have been punished, but denied that the rōnin, in exacting their own justice, acted righteously. Why, he asked, did they not make a principled appeal to the authorities? Fukuzawa acknowledged that in doing so the retainers might have been put to death, but argued that if they had proceeded, one by one, courageously protesting and dying, the shogunate would have been eventually swayed by the display of ultimate loyalty to their master and respect for the laws.[1]

In the seventh pamphlet, Fukuzawa considered three responses to abusive rule. The first, simple submission, he rejected as immoral, emphasizing that people have a duty to follow the just way of heaven, which does not condone compliance with misrule. The second, violent opposition, he denounced as a detestable form of vigilantism, something only praised by uncivilized peoples. The third, nonviolent protest coupled with a readiness to become a martyr, he endorsed as the principled way to make a stand on behalf of what is right. Fukuzawa then introduced a fictitious samurai, Gonsuke, to clarify his point. Once given a gold coin by his master, Gonsuke carelessly lost it. Humiliated, he tied his loincloth to a tree and hanged himself. Fukuzawa claimed that Gonsuke's suicide was neither more nor less shameful than the deaths of "loyal and righteous samurai" (*chūshin gishi*) who fought bravely against their enemies. Facetiously, Fukuzawa asked why was there no memorial stone commemorating Gonsuke? Along utilitarian lines, he concluded that the only legitimate way to distinguish a meaningful death from Gonsuke's is by determining whether it benefits society and advances the cause of civilization.

Fukuzawa noted that only one figure in Japanese history had sacrificed himself while petitioning the government in advocating human rights and just rule: Sakura Sōgorō. Fukuzawa confessed that

---

[1] Fukuzawa Yukichi, *Gakumon no susume* (1874 woodblock) pamphlet six, 4a–6a. David Dilworth, trans., *Fukuzawa Yukichi: An Encouragement of Learning* (New York: Columbia University Press, 2012), pp. 45–48.

the story of Sakura's life, although popularized in fiction and legend, had not been studied by historians.[2] Thus, he remained silent about Sakura's deeds. Traditional accounts relate, however, that Sakura was a village headman in Sakura domain, Shimosa province, during the early Tokugawa period. The local daimyō, Hotta Masanobu, taxed the peasantry of that domain excessively, prompting Sakura's petitions. When Hotta ignored Sakura's appeals, Sakura went to the shogunate with a direct appeal that, because it bypassed the established bureaucracy, was punished by death. Sakura's petition for tax relief was supposedly granted, but he was crucified, reportedly, along with his wife, after they were forced to witness the decapitation of their children. Despite his tragic end, Sakura was later venerated by the peasants of the village, who established a shrine honoring him. Implied in Fukuzawa's mention of Sakura is that he, Sakura Sōgorō, modeled a more praiseworthy and civilized strategy for political opposition than had those who, like the rōnin, took matters into their own hands, exacting murderous, vigilante justice.

Fukuzawa's criticism of the rōnin, and more generally the notion of *chūshin gishi*, elicited considerable controversy, including attacks on Fukuzawa, many of them personal and threatening. In response, he authored "A Defense of *An Encouragement of Learning*," published in November 1874, in a newspaper, *News of the Government and People* (*Chōya shinbun*), under an assumed name, Gokurō Senban. There, Fukuzawa explained that *An Encouragement of Learning* criticized *chūshin gishi*, but only because they had not died for the sake of civilization. Exacerbating things, Fukuzawa added that *chūshin gishi* of old had died "a stubborn dog's death." Yet he quickly retreated, noting that people of the past lived in their own peculiar historical circumstances, while moderns had contemporary standards. Fukuzawa responded to charges that *An Encouragement of Learning* implicitly equated the tragicomic Gonsuke with imperial loyalist-martyr Kusunoki Masashige by reminding his readers that Kusunoki's name appeared nowhere in *Gakumon*. That aside, Fukuzawa insisted that Kusunoki distinguished himself through his living example as an imperial loyalist, not because of his suicide.[3]

---

[2] Ibid., pp. 5b–10b. Dilworth, trans., *Fukuzawa*, pp. 54–58.
[3] Fukuzawa Yukichi, "Fukuzawa Yukichi zenshū shogen," *Fukuzawa Yukichi zenshū* (Tokyo: Iwanami shoten, 1958), pp. 75–95.

During the controversy, Fukuzawa began writing *Theories of Civilization* (*Bunmeiron no gairyaku*). There, without broaching the rōnin directly, he discussed *chūshin gishi* in a more conciliatory but still critical way, suggesting that old values such as loyalty between a lord and subject might well serve the ends of civilization, and did not necessarily have to be condemned. In the end, their value was a function of their benefit to society in its advance toward civilization. In making this allowance, Fukuzawa implicitly pioneered a line of thought wherein the rōnin might be reinterpreted to serve the ends of civilization, or – going well beyond Fukuzawa – whatever modern causes might require traditional exemplars of ultimate devotion and service. In leaving room for the latter and all the ambiguities of modernity, Fukuzawa most likely never anticipated that those enlisting the rōnin would, in some cases, seek to advance the causes of liberalism, yet in other cases, twentieth-century militarism and fascism, via appeal to their vendetta.

Following Fukuzawa's contextualization of modern political issues vis-à-vis the vendetta, Ueki Emori, a radical advocate of the early Meiji Freedom and People's Rights Movement, took another tack, aggressively defending the rōnin. In his 1879 essay, "On the Forty-Seven Samurai of Akō Domain," Ueki argued that the laws of the state should be respected, provided they are the creation of a people enacting them freely of their own accord. However, Ueki denied that the laws of an autocratic regime had to be obeyed. In his view, the Tokugawa verdict regarding Asano and Kira was neither fair nor just. Therefore, the rōnin naturally viewed the government with disgust and took Kira as their lord's enemy. Recognizing the rōnin as traditional exemplars of the legitimacy of popular opposition to unjust rule, Ueki suggested that it was wrong to condemn them for their vendetta.[4]

Meiji Christians also found room for accommodating the rōnin. In an English-language essay, "Moral Traits of the 'Yamato-Damashii,'" published in the *Methodist Review* in 1886, the young Uchimura Kanzō cited three key traits of Japanese ethics: filial piety, loyalty and sincerity to superiors, and compassion for subordinates. The exemplars of these traits included the Soga brothers, the loyal and righteous rōnin, and Sakura Sōgorō. Uchimura added that loyalty and sincerity to superiors was "the crown" trait since Japanese sometimes turn against their parents in service to their lords, but not against their

[4] Miyazawa, *Kindai Nihon to Chūshingura*, pp. 44–46.

lords in serving their parents. If Jesus, rather than a secular ruler, were recognized as their lord, then Japanese would follow and serve him with utter sincerity in mind and intent. In this context, Uchimura briefly reviewed the vendetta wherein Asano was a wrongly punished victim, and the rōnin stood as devotees to sacred, righteous duty. Along the way Uchimura hinted that righteous duty, remolded by Christianity, would result in Japanese Christians ready to devote themselves wholeheartedly to their religion even to the point of martyrdom.[5] Uchimura's essay thus expanded themes suggested in Fukuzawa's writings, even while linking them specifically to the cause of Christianity in Meiji Japan.

Further reflecting the vendetta's conflicted reception in the Meiji period, the 1881 edition of government-approved textbooks on Japanese history and language discussed the rōnin, but the textbooks on ethics did not. Earlier history texts from the 1870s mentioned the vendetta, but only in a few lines. With the 1881 edition, seventeen hundred words were devoted to it, largely following accounts in Muro Kyūsō's *The Righteous Men of Akō Domain*. In the 1885 language textbook, published a decade before the Sino-Japanese War, Muro's accounts were accompanied by mention of the Hosokawa daimyō's observation that "the loyal spirits" (*chūkon*) of the seventeen rōnin who committed seppuku at his Takanawa compound would serve as eternal guardian deities for his clan.[6] Thus, young Meiji students were reminded of one spiritual reading of the rōnin, at least as affirmed in language textbooks via reference to Hosokawa's statement. Even so, the silence in ethics textbooks arguably served as a counterstatement to the positive entries on the rōnin vendetta found in other government-approved texts. At the same time, kabuki performances of *Chūshingura*, still the vendetta's most popular dramatic double, had become, by the 1880s, a staple of Meiji stage culture, representing the fictionalized vendetta to large audiences in Tokyo, Osaka, and Kyoto annually. Regardless of government-approved textbooks, popular consumption patterns in the private sector's entertainment districts ensured that vendetta memories, commemorations, and even attendance as acts of secular worship, did not become a thing of the past, not even in modern Japan.

---

[5] J. K. Uchimura, "Moral Traits of the 'Yamato-Damashii' (Spirit of Japan)," *Methodist Review*, vol. 68, Fifth Series, vol. 2 (January 1886), pp. 56–72. Miyazawa, *Kindai Nihon to Chūshingura*, pp. 42–44.

[6] Miyazawa, *Kindai Nihon to Chūshingura*, p. 49.

The British Secretary's Tale

The Meiji tendency toward approbation for the rōnin was beautifully echoed in Western accounts. Following stints in St. Petersburg and Shanghai, Algernon Bertram Mitford was appointed second secretary to the British legation in Japan in 1868. In addition to his official duties, he authored a two-volume work, *Tales of Old Japan* (1871), which included as its first chapter "The Forty-Seven Rônins." The book's frontispiece is a woodblock illustration entitled "The Rônins Invite Kôtsuké no suké to Perform Hara-Kiri," highlighting the prominence of the vendetta tale therein. Mitford's stay in Japan coincided with the beginning of the Meiji period and its relative openness to new patterns of social, political, and economic relations, making his experiences far happier than Alcock's had been in xenophobic Japan just a decade prior.

In his account, Mitford, like Alcock, indulged in Western conceits, arrogantly claiming to explain, along essentialistic lines, the minds and hearts of the Japanese. Perhaps looking for an interesting story rather than credible documents, he drew on vendetta history, *Chūshingura*, popular storytelling, and "true accounts" (*jitsuroku*) circulating, thus crafting a well-written mixture of fact, fiction, and pure fancy. Mitford was no historian, and so it would be unfair to judge his retelling as history. As a raconteur of historical fiction, he excelled as few other Westerners had or would.

Mitford opens his account with admiration for the natural beauty of the Sengakuji, a scenic bayside temple that also happened to be "renowned throughout the length and breadth of the land for its cemetery, which contains the graves of the Forty-Seven Rônins, famous in Japanese history, [and] heroes of Japanese drama." Inside is a "chapel ... in which are enshrined the images of the forty-seven men, and of the master whom they loved so well." Mitford also describes a small well with an inscription stating, "This is the well in which the head was washed; you must not wash your hands or your feet here." In his text, a woodblock illustration follows.[7] With that, Mitford made famous, at least for English readers, the notion that the rōnin had washed Kira's head before presenting it at their master's grave. Credible sources, however, say nothing about a well washing, although the Tokugawa source, *Things Seen and Heard*, mentions a graveside washing using water from a

[7] A. B. Mitford, *Tales of Old Japan* (London: Macmillan and Co., 1871), pp. 3–8.

bucket. It is not entirely clear, however, that the rōnin even unwrapped the head before presenting it.

Mitford differs significantly from Titsingh and Alcock by first contextualizing Asano's attack on Kira, and thus the beginnings of the vendetta, vis-à-vis the New Year's ceremony in Edo Castle. Like many previous accounts, he cast Kira as "a man greedy for money." Also, Mitford somewhat accurately described the verdict: Asano "committed an outrage in attacking another man within the precincts of the palace," but, as Westerners since Titsingh typically have, he interpreted the infraction as a legal violation rather than an outrageous disregard for the ceremony. Unlike Titsingh and Alcock, Mitford celebrates Ōishi Kura-no-suke, referring to him by name, and recalling his shrewd leadership. He adds that the rōnin followed a strategy of subterfuge, disguising themselves as carpenters, craftsmen, merchants, etc., and in the case of Ōishi (following *Chūshingura*), as a debauched wastrel mired in the pleasure quarters of Kyoto.

Mitford added a memorable fabrication not from *Chūshingura*: the story of the Satsuma samurai who, finding Ōishi passed out in a street, cursed him as a "faithless beast! ... Unworthy the name of Samurai!" and then trod on his face and spat on him. A woodblock illustration of the same followed. Mitford next described the rōnin's attack on Kira's residence, including mention of their announcement that they were neither robbers nor ruffians, but instead men intent on taking revenge on their lord's enemy. Mitford also named several of Kira's men, including "Kobayashi Héhachi, Waku Handaiyu, Shimidzu Ikkaku," thus respectfully adding identities rather than the collective, anonymous references of Titsingh and Alcock.[8]

Mitford also presented a fabricated account of Kira's final moments, relating that after Kira had been ferreted out and his identity verified, Ōishi knelt before the emeritus master of ceremonies and explained, courteously and reverently:

> My lord, we are the retainers of Asano Takumi-no-kami. Last year your lordship and our master quarreled in the palace, and our master was sentenced to hara kiri, and his family was ruined. We have come to-night to avenge him, as is the duty of faithful and loyal men. I pray your lordship to acknowledge the justice of our

[8] Ibid., pp. 6–24.

purpose. And now, my lord, we beseech you to perform hara kiri. I myself shall have the honor to act as your second, and when, with all humility, I shall have received your lordship's head, it is my intention to lay it as an offering upon the grave of Asano Takumi-no-kami.

When Kira refused to cooperate, Ōishi turned brutal, taking the dagger Asano had used to commit seppuku and promptly decapitated Kira with it.[9]

Mitford's version of Kira's end drew on popular retellings of the vendetta, especially those glorifying the role of Ōishi as the thoughtful, brave, and well-spoken hero of the vendetta. By inserting Ōishi's voice and actions apocryphally into his account of the decapitation of Kira, Mitford's narrative recalled an earlier tale, also apocryphal and included in his account, of Ōishi authoring the *Saimon* at Asano's grave just before the presentation of Kira's head. In both cases, where the vendetta lacked, according to credible documents, clear leadership and focus, crucial roles were invented and assigned to Ōishi so that he, the designated hero, could provide it with wise and decisive direction. In the process, Ōishi emerged, in Western accounts of the vendetta, as the brave, sagacious, and humane force leading the bloody vendetta to its noble success.

Somehow finding solid historical ground, Mitford next related that the rōnin, in approaching the Sengakuji at dawn, "presented a terrible appearance" with their "clothes and arms all blood-stained." Nevertheless, he claimed, with grand exaggeration, that "everyone praised them, wondering at their valor and faithfulness." At the Sengakuji, the rōnin were, according to Mitford, received at the front gate by the abbot of the temple who then led them to their deceased master's gravestone. After washing Kira's head in a nearby well, they "laid it as an offering before the tomb." They then engaged the priests to recite sutras while they offered incense. Ōishi reportedly gave the Sengakuji abbot all his money, requesting that the temple bury them decently after their seppuku and pray for the repose of their souls. Impressed with their "faithful courage," the abbot promised, "with tears in his eyes," to fulfill their wishes. Thereafter, their "minds at rest," the rōnin "waited patiently until they should receive the orders of the Government."[10]

---

[9] Ibid.   [10] Ibid., pp. 24–30.

With sketchy fidelity to the historical record, Mitford had the rōnin "at last ... summoned to the Supreme Court," where they were sentenced to seppuku for their outrageous and murderous deeds. Thereafter, they were divided into four groups and sent to the compounds of four daimyō, in whose presence they eventually performed seppuku. Their remains were then carried to the Sengakuji and buried near their deceased master. Soon, Mitford added, "people flocked to pray at the graves of these faithful men." Graphically making the site real, Mitford included a woodblock illustration of the rōnin gravestones at the Sengakuji. Among those who paid homage was the Satsuma samurai who earlier spat on Ōishi's face while the latter lay drunk on a road in Kyoto. The Satsuma man asked for forgiveness, pleading ignorance of Ōishi's true intent. After prostrating, he reportedly committed seppuku before Ōishi's grave. The chief priest, pitying him, had him buried alongside the forty-seven, thus bringing the total number of tombs to forty-eight. With that apocryphal detail, Mitford ended his narrative of "the story of the forty-seven Rônins."[11]

Reflecting on the vendetta tale, Mitford acknowledged that it amounted to "a terrible picture of fierce heroism," but added that he thought it was one "impossible not to admire." Mitford next stereotyped Japanese thinking about the vendetta by observing:

> [I]n the Japanese mind, this feeling of admiration is unmixed, and hence it is that the forty-seven Rônins receive almost divine honours. Pious hands still deck their graves with green boughs and burn incense upon them; the clothes and arms which they wore are preserved carefully in a fire-proof store-house attached to the temple, and exhibited yearly to admiring crowds, who behold them probably with little less veneration than is accorded to the relics of Aix-la-Chapelle or Trèves; and once in sixty years the monks of Sengakuji reap quite a harvest for the good of the temple by holding a commemorative fair or festival, to which the people flock during nearly two months.

Mitford added that the Sengakuji treated him to a private showing of vendetta relics, which he described as "a curious medley of old rags and scraps of metal and wood!" The historical provenance of what Mitford

[11] Ibid.

saw is, of course, questionable,[12] but reliable accounts produced by the four daimyō houses do relate that the personal effects of the rōnin were sent to the Sengakuji, along with their corpses. What became of them, however, is unknown. Mitford also mentioned seeing a floorplan of Kira's compound (now considered a fabrication), which, he related, clearly following legendary accounts, "one of the Rônins obtained by marrying the daughter of the builder who designed it."[13]

Mitford concludes his account by introducing three documents: (1) the receipt establishing that Kira's family received Kira's head from the Sengakuji, (2) a copy of the declaration explaining the vendetta, and (3) an invocation that Ōishi supposedly presented at Asano's grave. The receipt for Kira's head is considered authentic. The second document, known as the "Declaration of the Retainers of Takumi-no-kami," is also authentic. Mitford deserves credit for bringing these to the attention of those curious about the vendetta. However, as discussed earlier, the last document, *Ōishi's Prayer*, is apocryphal. Continuing his reflections, Mitford noted that Confucianism was integral to the incident. Here he cites his contemporary, Confucian scholar James Legge, who had earlier recognized Confucius' thinking affirming "the duty of blood-revenge in the strongest and most unrestricted terms."[14] On these counts, apart from *Ōishi's Prayer*, Mitford deserves credit for pioneering a document-based, scholarly approach to vendetta understandings.

Mitford ends by adding an experience of his own. He noted that in September 1868, "a certain man" prayed before the grave of Ōishi Chikara and then committed suicide. Reportedly, the man had earlier petitioned to become a retainer of Chōshū domain, but was rebuffed. He therefore decided to take his own life and knew no better place than before the graves of the loyal retainers at the Sengakuji. Mitford related that this happened just two hundred yards from his residence in Takanawa, and that he personally saw the blood splattered ground

---

[12] Thomas J. Harper and Henry D. Smith, translators, *Memorial Hall of Akō Loyal Retainers, Sengakuji Temple Catalogue of the Collection* (Tokyo: Sengakuji, 2002), pp. 117–118, notes that armor, helmets, face guards, chain mail, fire hats, arm guards, a whistle, a drum, and a spotlight, among other artifacts, are "said to have been used in the attack." Mitford might have seen some of these items, which may indeed have belonged to the rōnin, though that is by no means certain.

[13] Mitford, *Tales of Old Japan*, pp. 30–34.   [14] Ibid.

within two hours of the suicide. Apparently, his point was that even one hundred and sixty-five years after the rōnin were buried, their final resting place remained a center of reverence and literal self-sacrifice, one wherein the living and yet macabre legacy of the vendetta might still be experienced.[15]

Mitford's account marked a new stage in Western understandings of the vendetta. Previously, brief summaries sufficed, but Mitford included more than thirty pages, with more historical detail and fiction, than either Titsingh or Alcock. Significantly, by recognizing key historical figures by their names, Mitford humanized the story considerably. With English translations of three documents supposedly related to the vendetta, his account at least appeared more historical in methodology, even though one of the three was a fake. Most importantly, in authoring a highly readable narrative accompanied by illustrations, Mitford crafted an appealing English-language version of the vendetta story, one that continues to attract those looking for a good read.

Early on, Robert Louis Stevenson noted that the "Forty-Seven Rônins" was "the gem of Mr. Mitford's collection," while later Western works such as Frederick V. Dickins' *Chiushingura, or The Loyal League*, and M. Gausseron's *Les Fidèles Rônins*, were "imaginative" take offs. For decades, Mitford's tale was even used in English-language textbooks for advanced Japanese junior high school students. Thus, his rendition contributed to the broadcast of the vendetta in a quasi-historical way within the new Japan, and internationally as well. Finally, Mitford's mixed feelings about the tale, from horror to admiration, marked a shift away from the ominous and stern critique that Alcock offered in the late Tokugawa. Mitford's more positive estimation reflected the extent to which he and much of the world had come to admire early Meiji Japan's ability to transform itself into a modern, civilized state. Given the nation's accomplishments, and its move away from murderous attacks on foreign legations, Mitford's thinking was presumably that its cultural heroes, including the rōnin, must not have been as pernicious as Alcock had earlier feared.

[15] Ibid.

A Vendetta Novel

An abiding priority for the Meiji regime was undoing the unequal treaties imposed during the 1850s by five Western powers: the United States, Britain, France, the Netherlands, and Russia. To achieve that, Japan felt compelled to prove to the West, especially the United States and Britain, that it merited recognition as a modern, civilized nation. Through a new government-sponsored study abroad program, Saitō Shūichirō traveled to Boston for a Western-style education, and to promote, as an individual, recognition of the Japanese as a civilized people. Japan's larger mission vis-à-vis the unequal treaties is quite evident in Saitō's later work, *The Loyal Ronins* (1880).

In introducing his text, Saitō noted that Japan made a "brilliant display" at the International Exhibition at Philadelphia in 1876 with its exhibit of Japanese art that "commanded the wonder, and admiration of the world." Saitō added that literature was another means of establishing "the degree of civilization and refinement attained by a nation." Confidently, he affirmed that the Japanese had "a literature of no mean order." To establish that, he recruited Edward Greey, an Englishman fluent in Japanese, for the project culminating in *The Loyal Ronins*, an English translation of Tamenaga Shunsui's late Tokugawa novel, *Iroha bunko* (*The ABC Library*), a *Chūshingura* spin-off. Saitō predicted that the West would appreciate "the wit and pathos" of Tamenaga, one of Japan's most "celebrated writers," the reputed "Charles Dickens of Japan." Yet Saitō was aware of the controversial, even repugnant nature of the tale. Although he claimed to be "the last person to defend lawless acts," Saitō, like Mitford, added that he could not "avoid feeling a certain admiration" for the rōnin tale, and added further, along nationalistic lines, that it contained "the germ of patriotism."[16]

Saitō and Greey took extraordinary liberties with Tamenaga's text. They rearranged its one hundred and eight miscellaneous chapters sequentially into forty chapters that followed the structure and progression of *Chūshingura*. Also, while the length of *The Loyal Ronins* exceeds anything previously published in English, running two hundred seventy-five pages, *Iroha bunko* is even longer, running seven hundred

---

[16] Shiuichiro Saito and Edward Greey, translators, *The Loyal Ronins: An Historical Romance, Translated from the Japanese* of Tamenaga Shunsui (New York: G. P. Putnam's and Sons, 1880), pp. iii–vi.

seventy-eight pages in one of its many modern editions. Even while abridging *Iroha bunko* in their translation, Saitō and Greey added supplementary information clarifying allusions for foreign readers. The most striking dissimilarity, however, concerns the names of the characters. *Iroha bunko* followed *Chūshingura* nomenclature with Enya Hangan (Asano), Kō-no-Moronao (Kira), and Ōboshi Yura-no-suke (Ōishi) as the main characters. *The Loyal Ronins*, however, reversed the guise, substituting the real name, Ōishi Kura-no-suke, for the dramatic alias, Ōboshi Yura-no-suke, etc. Yet even while basing their work on the real names and thus presumably creating the semblance of a concern for historical fidelity, Saitō and Greey decided to "translate" most personal and place names into English. While Kira Kōzuke-no-suke remained "Kira," Asano became "Lord Morning-field of Akō"; Ōishi became "Sir Big-rock"; the Sengakuji, the "Spring-hill Temple"; the Ryōgoku Bridge, the "Two-provinces Bridge"; the Hosokawa daimyō, "Lord Narrow-river"; Matsudaira, "Pine-plain"; Mizuno, "Water-field"; Terasaka, "Temple-cliff," etc. Mitford had referred to those involved in the vendetta by their Japanese names. Whether Saitō's call or Greey's, the decision to translate the names of history in a literalistic manner into descriptive phrases seems, compared to Mitford's approach, gratuitous and ill advised as a strategy of literary presentation.

The Loyal Ronins* thus contributed to the further fictionalization of history, establishing an even larger legend, and publicizing it internationally under yet another set of identities. At the same time, Saitō and Greey were men of their era. Tamenaga's *Iroha bunko* includes many details unprecedented in *Chūshingura*, but completely omitted from *The Loyal Ronins*. For example, chapter 13 of *Iroha bunko* explains the starting point of the vendetta, Enya's grudge, which, according to *Iroha bunko*, grew from the conflicting desires of Enya and Kō-no-Moronao for the same young man, Hibiya Ukon. Tamenaga prefaces his remarks by noting that among samurai and townspeople of the time, many preferred male love (*nanshoku*) and were passionate over young boys, even to the extent of pledging themselves to them in life and death. In such contexts, love suicides were not uncommon. Tamenaga cites Ihara Saikaku's *Great Mirror of Male Love* as proof. Enya Hangan, according to Tamenaga, had such a love for Hibiya Ukon, a handsome young boy. Kō-no-Moronao, also, developed an intense passion for Hibiya and wanted to take him from Enya. Enya

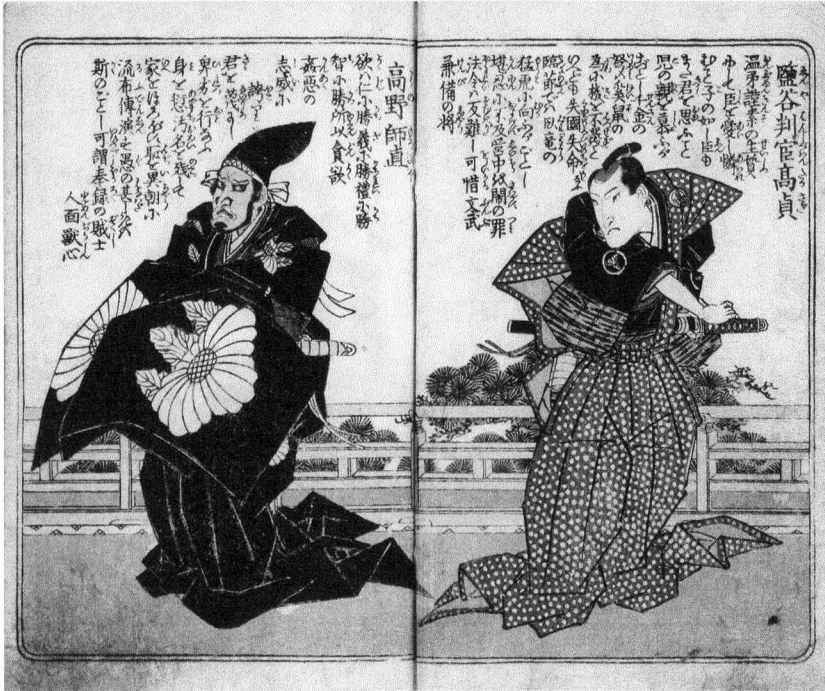

Figure 9.1 *Iroha bunko*. Enya Hangan and Kō-no-Moronao. Courtesy of Waseda University, Department of Special Collections.

refused. This infuriated Kō-no-Moronao, and eventually led to Enya's grudge, and then his tragic fate. Tamenaga concludes the chapter by quoting a proverb suggesting that a mind enraged with desire can becloud even a sagely and courageous general.[17] Saitō and Greey's translation, a Victorian recapitulation of Tamenaga's text, does not mention this salacious detail.

When Tsuda Umeko, a pioneer of women's education in Japan, met Theodore Roosevelt, the latter reportedly asked if she was familiar with *The Loyal Ronins*. Roosevelt allegedly added that the book had helped him understand Japan and the reason for Japan's victories in the Sino-Japanese War (1894–1895) and Russo-Japanese War (1904–1905). Miyazawa Seiichi has noted, skeptically, that if Roosevelt had indeed been so influenced by *The Loyal Ronins* that he decided to help broker the peace treaty concluding the Russo-Japanese War, it was a

[17] Tamenaga Shunsui, *Iroha bunko: seishi jitsuden* (Tokyo: Yūhōdō shoten, 1911), volume 7, section 13, pp. 95–96.

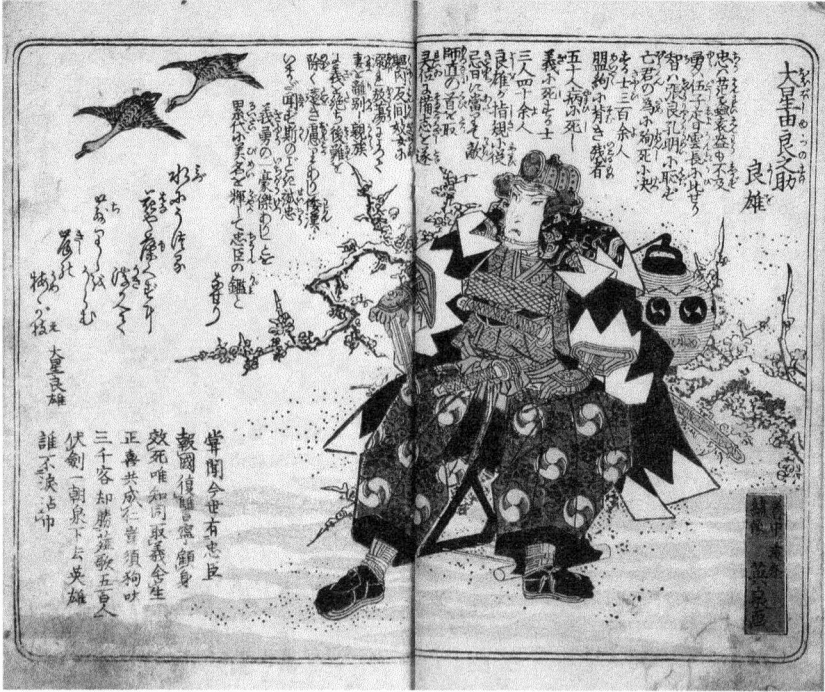

Figure 9.2 *Iroha bunko*. Ōboshi. Courtesy of Waseda University, Department of Special Collections.

rare example of a work of Japanese literature impacting international politics. Geopolitical considerations of the regional interests of Czarist Russia, Qing dynasty China, Britain, and Germany were surely far more important factors. Yet the fact that President Roosevelt even mentioned the text – if in fact he did – in a conversation with a young Japanese studying abroad is testimony to its wide circulation in the West, and its broadcast of what, with every retelling of the story in historical fiction, were becoming increasingly complex, multifaceted apocrypha, some removed from anything resembling reliable historical knowledge.

The Ōishi Shrine

The 1836 edition of *Iroha bunko* includes woodblock illustrations by various artists. The first portrays Enya Hangan about to attack Kō-no-Moronao. The second features the hero of the drama, Ōboshi Yura-no-suke (Ōishi Kura-no-suke Yoshio), armed and in an action pose before a plum tree laden with snow. In the 1911 edition, the latter illustration – a two-page spread of Ōboshi, now billed as the iconic figure of the vendetta – is the first presented.[18] In 1868, the Meiji emperor's rescript addressed to Ōishi left no doubt about Ōishi's standing, nor did it equivocate regarding ways in which Ōishi and the rōnin might be honored and revered. The Sengakuji was, as the first and primary grave site of Asano, Ōishi, and the rōnin, the de facto center of reverence. By the mid-eighteenth century, the Kagakuji, the Asano family temple in Akō, had emerged as another Buddhist site for remembrance of Asano and the rōnin. In a way, Ōishi had pioneered all of this by recognizing the need for spiritual sites devoted to his lord, Asano Naganori. To facilitate the same, Ōishi provided gifts to Akō temples, as well as temples on Mt. Kōya and in Kyoto, to ensure that Asano's spirit would be honored respectfully.

In the early Meiji, the abbot of the Kagakuji helped launch a movement to establish yet another place for remembrance of the vendetta, the Ōishi Shrine, in Akō. In doing so, he surely realized that the Meiji imperial government's religious agenda meant to privilege Shinto shrines, even to the point of persecuting Buddhist temples. Rather than simply maintain the Buddhist monopoly on sites for rōnin veneration, the Kagakuji abbot apparently decided that it would be helpful for his temple to assist, graciously and proactively, in sponsoring a separate site, a Shinto shrine devoted to nativistic veneration of Ōishi. Thus, in 1883, the abbot cosponsored a request to the Hyogo prefectural offices for permission to establish a shrine for Ōishi. The request recalled that the Meiji emperor had recognized Ōishi and the rōnin with an imperial rescript delivered before their graves at the Sengakuji, and added that a Shinto shrine for their worship would significantly contribute to the strength of the nation.

The proposed shrine was a response to the growing reverence for the rōnin at the popular level, and the imperial rescript honoring Ōishi and the rōnin, arguably signaling sanction for such worship from on high. Moreover, the Ōishi Shrine was to serve as more than a place for worshiping the rōnin: it would enhance, spiritually, the imperial nation's drive for wealth and power. Concerns had presumably surfaced, at the Kagakuji and elsewhere, that the forces of liberalism and

---

[18] Tamenaga Shunshui, *Iroha bunko* (Tōto: Sanrindō, 1836), pp. 3b–4a, 4b–5a. 1911 Yūhōdō edition, vol. 1, sec. 1, pp. 4–5.

people's rights might seek to enlist Ōishi and the rōnin for their own purposes, especially in the absence of an official place of worship guarding their memory, dignity, and spiritual integrity. A Shinto shrine for Ōishi and his rōnin league therefore seemed imperative.

Nevertheless, it was only in 1900 that permission to establish the Ōishi Shrine was granted. Rather than the Kagakuji initiative, priority was first given to the Sengakuji, which, with support from the Meiji government's Home Ministry, began work in 1885 on refurbishing its front gate, which had fallen into disrepair after the loss of Tokugawa support following the Meiji Restoration. Among others, the minister of communications in the first Itō cabinet, Enomoto Takeaki, helped raise funds for the Sengakuji cause. Also, a new site showcasing the personal effects of Ōishi and the rōnin was soon completed there, and in 1889, attracted more than one hundred thousand people.[19] Competing with the Sengakuji, based in what was now the imperial capital, Tokyo, would be a tall order, even when the competition was a shrine to be devoted to Ōishi Kura-no-suke. While the latter was to be established on the terrain where Ōishi and rōnin had lived, that was Akō, which remained a lengthy trek even with modern advances in rail transportation.

In 1910, construction of the Ōishi Shrine in Akō began. Two years later, coinciding with the passing of the emperor and the end of the Meiji period, the Ōishi Shrine was dedicated as a Shinto place of remembrance devoted spiritually to commemorating and revering Ōishi and the rōnin. The enshrined included Ōishi Kura-no-suke, the other rōnin, and Kayano Sanpei, who committed suicide before the vendetta. Along with these "chief deities," the Ōishi Shrine provided for the memory of the three Asano lords of Akō domain, Naganao, Nagatomo, and Naganori, as well as the Mori daimyō who ruled Akō after the Asano. The shrine's Treasure Hall featured items that supposedly belonged to Ōishi and the rōnin. A restored version of Ōishi's home and garden, later designated a national historic relic, was built on the shrine grounds subsequently, as were seven collateral sites of worship. These seven included one dedicated to Yamaga Sokō; a Tenmangu shrine, dedicated to the *kami* of education; a Hatta shrine, dedicated to the Akō salt fields; an Inari shrine, dedicated to agricultural prosperity; an Ebisu shrine, dedicated to maritime prosperity; an Awashima shrine focused on women's health; and a Chūkon shrine, dedicated to those who died fighting for imperial Japan. In 1928,

---

[19] Miyazawa, *Kindai Nihon to Chūshingura*, pp. 51–53.

the Ōishi Shrine was upgraded from unranked to prefectural status. With the Ōishi Shrine, the rōnin were recognized not only as spiritual icons, but as *kami,* or divine spiritual presences in the Shinto landscape of early twentieth-century Japan. Moreover, the shrine served as an important site encouraging loyal and self-sacrificing devotion to the emperor and the imperial nation.

The Kagakuji, the Asano family temple in Akō, had long served as a Buddhist site of reverence for the rōnin. That Sōtō Zen temple, like its counterpart in Tokyo, similarly featured various personal effects, letters, calligraphy, swords, bows, and samurai equipment, as well as a small cemetery in which the gravestones of the rōnin surrounded the central monuments for Asano Naganori, his senior retainer, Ōishi Yoshio, on the right, and Ōishi Chikara, on the left. The Kagakuji Treasure Hall came to have as its central images a mortuary tablet of Asano Naganori and a thousand-armed bodhisattva, Kannon, the guardian deity of the Ōishi family. Flanking these to the right were, eventually, twenty-three wooden statues of the rōnin who attacked the front gate of Kira's mansion (plus one of Kayano Sanpei), and to the left, twenty-four statues of those who attacked the rear gate.

Just as the Kagakuji was the Akō counterpart of the Sengakuji in Tokyo, so did the Ōishi Shrine in Akō come to have a counterpart in Yamashina. The famous minstrel performer, Yoshida Naramaru, an admirer of the rōnin, was one of the driving forces behind the founding of the new Ōishi Shrine, located outside of Kyoto, in the Yamashina area where Ōishi had lived the year before the vendetta. After successful fundraising, permission to establish the shrine was granted in 1933. The main hall was completed in 1935. Two years later, the Ōishi Shrine in Yamashina was recognized as a prefectural shrine. Unlike the Akō Ōishi Shrine, the Yamashina shrine was meant to enshrine Ōishi exclusively, and to commemorate his life in that area, from the seventh month of 1701, until the ninth month of 1702. Compared to the Sengakuji, the Kagakuji, and Ōishi Shrine in Akō, the Yamashina Ōishi Shrine, the last of the main four, came to house fewer personal artifacts. Nevertheless, it did have the unique claim of preserving and remembering as sacred the Yamashina space where Ōishi spent much of the final year prior to the vendetta. The establishment of the two Ōishi shrines amplified the Meiji emperor's 1868 rescript, and contributed to the further elevation of Ōishi in the Meiji period and beyond as the vendetta's single most heroic and spiritually significant figure.

A Historian's Monograph

Modern historical studies of the vendetta date from Shigeno Yasutsugu's *A True Account of the Righteous Samurai of Akō Domain*, published in 1889. The same year, Shigeno, along with Ludwig Riess, a disciple of Leopold von Ranke, founded the Japanese Historical Association. As a professor of history at Tokyo Imperial University, Shigeno led in the establishment of the objective, scientific study of history generally advocated by Rankean positivists. While the pursuit of objectivity is now considered, by some, naïve, its ideals provided Shigeno a path beyond the traditional Confucian vision of history as a didactic narrative of goodness rewarded and evil punished. Shigeno's approach often entailed iconoclastic conclusions about subjects of inquiry once considered sacrosanct. His dedication to positivistic historiography prompted him to declare, for example, that Kojima Takanori, a fourteenth-century imperial loyalist described in the *Records of the Great Peace*, was a fabrication of that text's author, Kojima Hōshi, who wanted his family name glorified. Despite Shigeno's claims, Kojima Takanori was enshrined in the late nineteenth century at a subsidiary of the Yoshino Shrine where Emperor Go-Daigo was revered. Because he seemed bent on debunking legend-infused pseudo-history, Shigeno came to be called "professor iconoclast." Personal threats coupled with official proclamations from on high, such as the 1889 Constitution and its description of the imperial line as divine, unbroken, and inviolable, came to temper Shigeno's scientific ardor.

In *A True Account*, Shigeno's positivism seems circumscribed. Admittedly, Shigeno opens his work with a valuable classification of dozens of vendetta documents and texts as: (1) reliable and authentic, (2) mixtures of truth and fabrication, (3) apocryphal, (4) unexamined, (5) dramatic renditions, (6) correspondence, and (7) miscellaneous. This taxonomy of kind and credibility typifies Shigeno's critical, scientific methodology. Shigeno next juxtaposes the popular conception of the rōnin vendetta, based largely on *Chūshingura*, with the historical record set forth by reliable texts such as *Kajikawa's Diary* and *Things Seen and Heard*, thus revealing how the vendetta as credibly documented history differed from dramatic retellings. Nevertheless, Shigeno was not an entirely objective historian. The frontispiece of his book features a calligraphic reproduction of the Meiji emperor's rescript delivered before the graves of Ōishi and the rōnin at the Sengakuji. Also, the

Figure 9.3 Shigeno Yasutsugu. Courtesy of the National Diet Library, Portraits of Modern Japanese Historical Figures.

book's full title, *A True Account of the Righteous Samurai of Akō Domain*, endorses the popular estimation of the rōnin as *gishi*, or righteous samurai.[20] Shigeno's intent was presumably not to debunk the *gishi* so much as elevate them via the methods of empirical history, or at least the façade of such. Thus, in discussing the invasion of Kira's residence, Shigeno addressed the problem of Terasaka. Henry D. Smith notes, however, that Shigeno's naïve conclusion, that Terasaka was sent to report the success of the vendetta, is more a leap of faith than one established by credible documents.[21]

The limits of Shigeno's empiricism also appear in his appraisal of the rōnin's ties to Yamaga Sokō. Shigeno recalled that while Akō was small in terms of its area, it produced great men, including the *gishi*. Shigeno added that great men are not born overnight: Asano Naganori's grandfather, Asano Naganao, was an enlightened lord who first built

[20] Shigeno, *Akō gishi jitsuwa*, frontispiece (unnumbered), pp. 1–10.
[21] Henry D. Smith, "The Trouble with Terasaka," p. 31.

Akō Castle. He also invited Yamaga Sokō, a scholar of military learn-ing, to Akō as his guest instructor. Shigeno described Yamaga as a rare, heroic figure. Later, however, Yamaga resigned his position and returned to Edo. Subsequently, after offending shogunal officials with publication of his *Sagely Confucian Teachings*, Yamaga was banished from Edo and exiled to Akō domain indefinitely. While in exile, Yamaga was frequented by Ōishi Yoshio and his great uncle, Ōishi Yoshishige. According to Shigeno, they both studied with him then. Shigeno cites Yamaga's *Autobiography in Exile* (*Haisho zanpitsu*) as relating that during Yamaga's exile, Asano Naganao continued to treat Yamaga as his teacher. Other retainers presumably had contacts with Yamaga as well. Thus, Shigeno claimed, "samurai of the entire domain came to receive his influence."[22] It must be added that despite Shigeno's claims, nothing in Ōishi's writings or in rōnin records indicates that their vendetta drew upon Yamaga Sokō's teachings. Nevertheless, Shigeno, as a respected Tōdai historian, gave this fabrication new credibility in modern Japan.

Shigeno adds that *Chūshingura*'s allusions to the words of Sunzi (544–496 B.C.E.) and Wu Qi (440–381 B.C.E.), two ancient Chinese military philosophers, are references to the military learning that pre-vailed in Akō via Yamaga. The legacy of Asano Naganao's enlightened rule and Yamaga's transformative teachings appeared in the adminis-tration of the domain, and the fact that it produced "loyal retainers and righteous samurai." Shigeno concludes his volume noting how the impact of Yamaga and the later *gishi* eventually spread far and wide, encompassing the entire nation. In this context, Shigeno recalls the remarks of Hosokawa Tsunetoshi, lord of Kumamoto domain, that the rōnin would be guardian deities of his domain. Shigeno adds that in neighboring Satsuma, the fourteenth day of the twelfth month of every year is remembered, and writings such as *Records of the Righteous Men* and *Biographies of the Righteous Retainers* are widely read. Similar customs developed in other domains as well. Thus, two centuries later, with the Meiji Restoration, the impact of the samurai way became more evident, and the indirect influence of Yamaga and the *gishi* more fragrant. The more the vendetta was discussed and debated, Shigeno claimed, the more fragrant the influence of Yamaga and the righteous samurai had become.[23]

---

[22] Shigeno, *Akō gishi jitsuwa*, pp. 250–259.   [23] Ibid.

Shigeno's evidence for Yamaga's impact on the vendetta consists of Yamaga's *Autobiography in Exile*. There Yamaga relates that
while he was in exile, Ōishi Yoshishige, the chief retainer of the Asano
family, delivered vegetables to him twice daily, morning and evening.
However, Uenaka Shōzō, who has translated Yamaga's *Autobiography
in Exile* into English, has criticized the claim that Yamaga influenced the
vendetta as "chronologically untenable." Uenaka notes that, first, Ōishi
was "only two years old when Yamaga resigned his instructorship
under Lord Asano, and, secondly, there is no evidence that Yamaga
engaged in teaching while in exile." Uenaka also relates that Yamaga's
biographer, Hori Isao, maintained that Yamaga "never influenced the
rōnin directly or indirectly" primarily because the revenge occurred
seventeen years after Yamaga's death.[24]

Equally if not more significant is that neither Ōishi nor the other
rōnin ever claimed that they had been inspired by or were following the
teachings of Yamaga. Moreover, there is little in Yamaga's teachings
that might be construed as legitimizing revenge vendettas, especially
vendettas without official sanction. Thus, Shigeno's readiness to affirm
Yamaga's influence on the rōnin prompts questions about his "empirical" approach to the study of the vendetta. Nevertheless, Shigeno
deserves considerable credit for emphasizing in principle, if not always
in practice, the use of authentic, credible sources in crafting a historical
narrative. Despite its clear weaknesses on matters such as Yamaga's
influence, Shigeno's study must be recognized for having elevated docu-
mented-based critical historical scholarship on the vendetta to new
heights.

Late Meiji Intellectuals

Popular historian Yamaji Aizan mixed mockery and praise for the rōnin
in his own conflicted writings on the vendetta. In an 1891 essay, he
called the rōnin "bumpkin samurai," led by Ōishi, "the general of an
army of hungry ghosts." Overall, Yamaji mocked the common view
that the rōnin deserved being called loyal and righteous as akin to the
senseless yelping of dogs following the bark of one. Two years later,

---

[24] Shuzo Uenaka, "Last Testament in Exile: Yamaga Sokō's Haisho zampitsu,"
Monumenta Nipponica, 32/2 (1977), pp. 128–130.

however, Yamaji recalibrated his harsh appraisal, recognizing the rōnin as historically significant. In an essay published in *Friend of the People* (*Kokumin no tomo*), Yamaji credited the bumpkin samurai of Akō, the so-called righteous samurai of Akō domain, with having tried to revive *bushidō* in a world of effeminate warriors. In noting the endless number of people who went to pay homage at their graves, Yamaji referred to the rōnin in quasi-spiritual terms as "prophets." But in the end, samurai culture crumbled, leaving Ōishi as the last exemplar of the old ways of martial life. Their spirit lived on only in the education of youth in distant Satsuma domain where every year, on December 14, young people took turns reading *Tales of the Righteous Samurai*.[25] More than likely, as with Fukuzawa earlier, Yamaji had encountered flak when speaking so disrespectfully of the rōnin and thus decided to tone down his appraisals.

Discourse on the vendetta intensified during and after the Sino-Japanese War of 1894–1895. Following that war over hegemony in Korea, Japan's victory was spoiled by the Triple Intervention in which Czarist Russia, Germany, and France forced Japan to renounce concessions gained from Qing dynasty China. National humiliation at the hands of Western powers thus once again befell Japan, compromising its impressive victory and standing as the dominant power in northeast Asia. Journalist-historian Tokutomi Sohō soon fanned the flames of national revenge by calling on Japan to endure hardships to reverse the humiliation. After the Japanese victory in the Russo-Japanese War (1904–1905) was short-changed by the West with the Treaty of Portsmouth and its denial of an indemnity for Japan, Tokutomi identified the European powers and the United States as Japan's prime enemies, grouping them together as the "white people" oppressing Imperial Japan and quashing its aspirations.[26]

In that context, a biographical study entitled *Ōishi Yoshio*, attributed to Ameya Issaian but apparently written by Tokutomi, praised Ōishi and the rōnin not simply as righteous samurai but as courageous, heroic figures who endured hardships to complete the wrath of their lord and realize social justice in their age. The implied lesson was that modern Japanese might well model themselves on the

[25] Yamaji Aizan, "Ōishi Kura-no-suke," *Kokumin no tomo*, no. 197–199, pp. 145–147, 191–192, 236–238. Miyazawa, *Kindai Nihon to Chūshingura*, pp. 60–61.
[26] Miyazawa, *Kindai Nihon to Chūshingura*, pp. 60–61.

rōnin, enduring hardships to prevail over the West and thus undo Imperial Japan's national humiliation. Yet as before, there were other, contrary voices. Along profoundly different lines, Kitamura Tōkoku, a Christian pacifist and founder of the Japan Peace Association, criticized the rōnin by calling revenge a primitive tendency that sometimes manifested itself as war. Kitamura added that laws might forbid revenge vendettas, but such laws simply substituted the power of society for that of the individual in vengeance. In the end, he claimed, only religion, i.e., Christianity, had the power to stop both revenge and war.[27]

Late Meiji educated opinion on the vendetta was by no means unanimous. Politician-academician Katō Hiroyuki, echoing ideas attributed to Ogyū Sorai, argued that the rōnin acted on emotion rather than reason, and so were neither righteous samurai nor fit to be compared to the imperial loyalist martyr, Kusunoki Masashige. Allowing emotion to prevail would make it impossible to provide peace and security for the realm. Instead, Katō emphasized that reason and the law must be respected. Literary and cultural critic Tsubouchi Shōyō also criticized the rōnin and their vendetta, claiming that rather than devotion to duty and their lord, the rōnin acted for the sake of their reputations. Tsubouchi thus echoed charges earlier advanced by Satō Naokata and Dazai Shundai. However, one foreign interpreter, Lafcadio Hearn, impressed by Mitford's account of the vendetta, praised the Japanese practice of revenge as issuing from a "religion of self-sacrifice" that transcended morality in its readiness to face death without thought of oneself. Hearn added that the feudal values the rōnin exemplified, "loyalty and righteousness," had been redirected toward the emperor and imperial nation following the Meiji Restoration, and thus served as the spiritual ethic behind contemporary patriotism and Japan's modern development.[28]

By the late Meiji, Japanese public opinion was developing on a range of issues, national and international. Many agreed with Tokutomi that the Western powers were suppressing Japan by compromising its hard-won victories over China and Russia. A reaction soon set in against Western ways of thinking such as individualism, capitalism, liberalism, democracy, socialism, and communism. Instead,

---

[27] Ibid., pp. 61–66.
[28] Ibid., pp. 76–77. Lafcadio Hearn, "The Religion of Loyalty," *Japan: An Attempt at Interpretation* (New York: Macmillan, 1905), pp. 320–329.

reassertions of Japanese nationalism and a heightened emphasis on military values in service to the imperial order appeared ascendant. Within that environment, distinctly Japanese expressions of vendetta culture flourished. Minstrel performances, popular at the time, drew repeatedly on rōnin lore, broadcasting it to large audiences well before radio, film, and TV supplanted them as forms of mass entertainment. One popular performer, Tōchūken Kumoemon, flourished with emotionally charged vendetta tales delivered to packed houses in Osaka, Kyoto, and Tokyo. Some of his performances were recorded and sold exceptionally well as phonographic recordings, thus spreading vendetta lore at the mass entertainment level.[29]

Another new technology, "moving pictures," soon helped broadcast the boom in vendetta culture. In 1907, just a decade after film was introduced, one of Japan's first cinematic works was made by recording a live kabuki performance of the fifth act of *Chūshingura*. Subsequently, Makino Shōzō, the founding father of Japanese cinema, made nine different films on the vendetta, with his first in 1910 and his last, *A True Account of Chūshingura*, in 1928, the year before his death. Mass broadcast of rōnin tales – via minstrels (*naniwabushi*), phonographs, radio, and cinema – made the vendetta and its fictional lore integral components in the emerging popular ideology of nationalism, patriotism, and loyal self-sacrifice for the imperial cause.[30] After all, with the Meiji emperor's 1868 rescript, the rōnin had become his vassals, in service to his cause. Identification with them thus became, in modern Meiji Japan, identification with one's imperial destiny.

Between 1904 and 1905, journalist Tsukahara Jūshien authored a series of fictional pieces for the *Tokyo Daily News*, later republished as the first modern novel about the vendetta, *Ōishi Yoshio*. Tsukahara extolled Ōishi not so much as a *chūshin gishi*, nor as an exemplar of *bushidō*, but instead simply as a "great hero" distinguished by his strategic intelligence and wisdom. Tsukahara's work created a new image for Ōishi, one all the more meaningful for a nation emerging victorious from regional wars with two much larger, seemingly more

---

[29] Hyōdō Hiromi and Henry D. Smith II, "Singing Tales of the Gishi: *Naniwabushi* and the Forty-Seven Rōnin in Late Meiji Japan," *Monumenta Nipponica*, 61/4 (Winter 2006), pp. 459, 460–508.
[30] Ibid.

powerful nations, China and Russia.[31] Along nativistic lines, literary scholar Haga Yaichi, in *Ten Essays on the Nature of the Japanese People* (1907), suggested that the spirit of *bushidō* evident in the vendetta was a samurai expression of the "true heart" first manifested in ancient times as loyalty to the emperor, and then in modern times as the fundamental essence of the nation. In his 1912 publication, *The Japanese*, Haga gave the vendetta a global dimension by suggesting that the spirit of self-sacrifice evident in it was comparable to that exhibited by Joan of Arc in French history and culture.[32]

The Meiji General and Tōdai Philosopher

Yamaga Sokō's rise to historical prominence in the Meiji reflected the ascendance of the vendetta during the same era. On December 29, 1907, the Imperial Household Agency, prompted by General Nogi Maresuke, elevated Yamaga to senior level, fourth imperial court rank. Nogi personally read the announcement before Yamaga's grave at the Sōsanji, a Sōtō Zen temple in Tokyo. Earlier, in 1885, ceremonies commemorating the two hundredth anniversary of Yamaga's death had been held at the Sōsanji. In 1906, after the Russo-Japanese War, another service honoring Yamaga was held there. Subsequently, ceremonies were held at the Sōsanji annually. Nogi's respect for Yamaga was an outgrowth of the writings of Shigeno and, more importantly, those of Tokyo Imperial University professor of philosophy Inoue Tetsujirō.

Inoue's voluminous writings on Tokugawa Confucian philosophy lauded Yamaga more than any other, and gave scholarly prestige and credibility to alleged ties between Yamaga and the vendetta. In his *Philosophy of the Japanese School of Ancient Learning*, published in 1902, Inoue reiterated many of Shigeno's earlier claims: that Ōishi, eight when Yamaga was exiled and seventeen when he was pardoned, was taught by Yamaga. Like Shigeno, Inoue added that Yamaga's impact spread to virtually all Akō rōnin. He declared that Yamaga's years of

---

[31] Tsukahara Jūshien, *Ōishi Yoshitaka* (Tokyo: Ryūbunkan, 1906). Miyazawa, *Kindai Nihon to Chūshingura*, pp. 84–86.

[32] Haga Yaichi, *Kokuminsei jūron* (Tokyo: Fuzanbō, 1907). *Nihonjin* (Tokyo: Bunkaidō shoten, 1912).

Figure 9.4 Inoue Tetsujirō. Courtesy of the National Diet Library, Portraits of Modern Japanese Historical Figures.

teaching Akō samurai while an Asano retainer between 1652 and 1660, and while in exile in Akō between 1666 and 1675, forged in the domain, mentally and physically, a discipline that later enabled its samurai to execute their vendetta. Inoue also explained Yamaga's alleged influence on the vendetta in relation to Yamaga's *True Reality of the Central Kingdom*, which claimed that Japan was the true "central dynasty" because of its unbroken imperial line, made possible by the utter loyalty of the Japanese people to their emperor. On the other hand, China, which prided itself on being the "central dynasty," had a history of chronic dynastic overthrow, revealing its people to be less than loyal to their dynasty. Inoue added that Yamaga's teachings – especially those exemplified by the rōnin and emphasizing devotion to the throne – were interrelated for modern Japanese as essential aspects of their spirit and national morality.[33]

Reacting against Nitobe Inazō's claim, made in *Bushidō: The Soul of Japan* (1899), that *bushidō* was an "unwritten tradition," Inoue asserted that Yamaga Sokō was the "constitutional theorist" of *bushidō*, and that his writings provided a substantial literature on the subject. In Inoue's view, the rōnin were exemplars of *bushidō* as the latter had been pioneered philosophically by Yamaga. Discussions of *bushidō* prior to 1945, and well after, typically cited the rōnin as exemplars. Even Nitobe had recognized as much, albeit without citing Yamaga as the theorist of *bushidō* and teacher of the rōnin. Inoue, however, defined an orthodox lineage for Yamaga's samurai teachings as first evident in the Akō vendetta, then in Yoshida Shōin's self-sacrificing loyalism, and then, following the suicide of General Nogi and his wife in 1912, in them as well. It should be added that the day before his suicide, Nogi had presented the crown prince, the future Taishō emperor, with a modern edition of Yamaga's *The True Central Dynasty*, publication of which he had personally underwritten. In commenting on Nogi's suicide, Inoue acknowledged that the deaths of Nogi and his wife were shocking, but added that they were beautiful expressions of the utter loyalty and service distinguishing Yamaga's teachings and Japanese ethics. With Inoue, then, the rōnin came to be linked even more closely with Yamaga Sokō, Yoshida Shōin, and, innovatively, General Nogi, as well as *bushidō*, the imperial throne, and discourse on Japan's national essence. In effect, Inoue's writings helped to make the rōnin and their vendetta a central axis in the emerging discourse of imperialism, militarism, and ultranationalism.[34]

Inoue's views on Yamaga Sokō and the forty-seven rōnin became the standard narrative for nearly every twentieth-century publication on Japanese cultural and intellectual history. However, the alleged connections between Yamaga and the rōnin were circumstantial at best. Inoue, for example, never explains why Yamaga's teachings were never mentioned by Ōishi or any of the Akō rōnin either before or in the wake of their vendetta. Connections between Yamaga and the vendetta were first

---

[33] John Allen Tucker, "Tokugawa Intellectual History and Prewar Ideology: The Case of Inoue Tetsujirō, Yamaga Sokō, and the Forty-Seven Rōnin," *Sino-Japanese Studies*, 14 (April 2002), pp. 38–71.

[34] Ibid.

broached not by the rōnin nor by their defenders, but instead by critics who knew that Yamaga had earlier violated shogunal sensibilities and been punished for the same. In first linking Yamaga and the vendetta, Satō Naokata and Dazai Shundai blamed Yamaga for blatant violations of righteousness, suggesting in short that criminal philosophers bred criminal samurai. It was only with Yoshida Shōin that these critical allegations became bragging points as Yoshida moved in the direction of anti-*bakufu* activism that was inevitably criminal as well. While the supposed lineage between Yamaga and the vendetta came to be, in Meiji Japan, regularly affirmed by Shigeno, Inoue, and a host of others, there is no evidence, other than circumstantial, establishing the same.

Nevertheless, in 1925, the Yamaga Sokō Society in Akō had a bronze memorial statue established on the grounds of Ōishi Yoshio's grand uncle's residence near Akō Castle, commemorating Yamaga's days in exile there. That period was commemorated because it was then that Ōishi Yoshio supposedly received teachings from Yamaga, and then that Yamaga wrote his *The True Central Dynasty*, extolling Japan's loyalty to its imperial line.[35] The next year, an inscription recognizing Yamaga's birth in Aizu-Wakamatsu was dedicated. In 1934, the two hundred fiftieth anniversary of Sokō's death was commemorated at the Sōsanji. In Tokyo's Hibiya district a festival supposedly attended by four thousand people was held in his remembrance. Taishō (1912–1926) and early Shōwa (1926–1989) scholars repeated the myths about Sokō and the rōnin, making them salient aspects of *bushidō* lore circulating in the 1920s and 1930s. Tokyo University professor of literature Nakayama Kyūshirō, in his *Yamaga Sokō* published in 1937, even boasted that Yamaga and his school of military philosophy had influenced every age. By endorsing the Yamaga line of transmission that Inoue had defined, Nakayama and others were, like Inoue, suggesting that the Yamaga teachings were very alive and relevant for modern Japan. Implied was that future exemplars would be praised as well.

The Ultranationalist Intellectual and His Critics

The Remarkable Achievement of the Genroku Period (1909), by the journalist-politician-historian Fukumoto Nichinan, glorified the

---

[35] "Yamaga Sokō takyo seki," *Akō gishi jiten*, p. 742.

vendetta and associated ideological myths and legends even further.[36] According to Henry D. Smith II, Fukumoto's text was "the pivotal work in the modernization" of the vendetta narrative wherein the latter came to serve as "a piece of propaganda on behalf of martial values and selfless sacrifice to the state." Fukumoto's voluminous writings, while informed by a treasure of credible sources, often border on fiction rather than reliable history. A member of the right-wing ultranationalist organization, "Black Ocean Society," Fukumoto coupled admiration for the vendetta with advocacy of military expansion into the Philippines and on the continent. His retelling of "the remarkable achievement," as he called the vendetta, began in 1908 as a serial in the Gen'yōsha publication, the *Kyūshū Daily News*, just three years after the Japanese victory in the Russo-Japanese War. As a journalist, Fukumoto continued Shigeno's approach, distinguishing dramatic fabrications and popular fiction from credibly documented history. However, even after his efforts on behalf of reliable history, the distilled result for Fukumoto remained, along distinctly sensational lines, "the glorious work of righteous samurai."

Fukumoto's writings were enhanced by publication of Nabeta Shōzan's *Documents Related to the Righteous Men of Akō*, a multivolume compilation of sources, some of which were authentic and primary, between 1910 and 1911. A few years later, Fukumoto brought out a revised edition of his work, *True Records of the Magnificent Achievement of the Genroku Period*. To commemorate the vendetta throughout the imperial nation, Fukumoto helped found the Central Office of the Righteous Samurai Society, thus contributing to the "nationalization of the story of the righteous samurai." Fukumoto's efforts, in sum, sought to establish, according to Miyazawa Seiichi, "the logic of the vendetta" as the original, unitary principle of the nation and the people, one exclusive of things foreign and indicative of the uniqueness and superiority of Japan vis-à-vis the world. Interpreting the vendetta along populist lines, Fukumoto emphasized that "the glorious achievement" was not made exclusively by high-level samurai, but also by middle- and lower-level retainers. Although Ōishi was the

---

[36] Fukumoto Nichinan, *Genroku kaikyo roku* (Tokyo: Keiseisha, 1910). Fukumoto, *Genroku kaikyo shinsō roku* (Tokyo: Tōadōshobō, 1914). Henry D. Smith II, "*Chūshingura* in the 1980s," in Kevin J. Wetmore Jr., ed. *Revenge Drama in European Renaissance and Japanese Theatre* (New York: Palgrave Macmillan, 2008), pp. 195–196.

chief retainer of Asano Naganori, he lived simply and treated others with respect, modesty, and humility, prompting Fukumoto to call him "a rare embodiment of the commoner philosophy of life."[37] Implied was that modern commoners might strive to be, like Ōishi and the rōnin, *chūshin gishi*, advancing the imperial nation toward wealth and power via their readiness to sacrifice themselves loyally for the cause.

The ideological agendas of Inoue and Fukumoto dominated, but were not unchallenged. In his *Alternative Account of the Magnificent Achievement of the Genroku Period* (1910), Mitamura Engyo turned the vendetta on its head, presenting it from the perspective of Kira and his retainers.[38] Though overlooked in historical fiction and drama, Kira's men were, after all, Japanese, and displayed praiseworthy qualities such as selfless loyalty, even to a despicable master. In addition to providing information about them, Mitamura added that the Japanese "way of the retainer" required that a retainer be a retainer, even when the master does not behave as a master. In this regard, he noted, Japan differed from China. Emphasizing this point, Mitamura repeated the apocryphal tale that the ancient Confucian text, the *Mencius*, which recognized that retainers might overthrow their lords, had been lost at sea, one time after the next, as it attempted to make its way into Japan. Mitamura added that while the written word for "loyalty" used by China and Japan were the same, the two differed in meaning: in China, loyalty hinged on rational principle and so was variable, while in Japan, it had distinctly emotional nuances and did not admit alteration or compromise. Regretting that Asano's retainers were deemed "loyal and righteous" while Kira's were considered "wicked," Mitamura recognized them nevertheless as ones who "died loyally" (*chūshi*).[39]

Japan and the Japanese: A Special Issue

In 1910, a special issue of the journal *Japan and the Japanese* featured an extensive series of all-star essays praising the vendetta. General Nogi

---

[37] Fukumoto Nichinan, *Genroku kaikyo shinsō roku* (Tokyo: Tōadō shobō, 1914). Miyazawa, *Kindai Nihon to Chūshingura*, pp. 90–93.

[38] Mitamura Engyo, *Genroku kaikyo betsuroku* (Tokyo: Keiseisha, 1910).

[39] Miyazawa, *Kindai Nihon to Chūshingura*, pp. 90–93.

Figure 9.5 Sengakuji 1902. Courtesy of the National Diet Library, the Meiji and Taisho Eras in Photographs.

authored the opening piece, "Growing Up with the *Gishi*," recalling how he had heard stories about the rōnin from birth, having been born in the Mōri residence where earlier, in 1703, ten rōnin had been confined and eventually committed seppuku. His daimyō's family temple was the Sengakuji, and his father served as grave keeper there twice a month. Nogi often accompanied him and thus heard more vendetta tales there. Nogi's family later returned to Chōshū, where he was placed in the care of Yoshida Shōin's uncle, Tamaki Bunnoshin, from whom he studied military thought, especially that of Yamaga Sokō, and learned of his purported impact on the rōnin. Nogi's essay thus gave the rōnin and their vendetta a living testimonial, linking them to modernity and selfless service to the imperial state. Following the Meiji emperor's death in 1912, well after contributing to the *Japan and the Japanese* issue, Nogi committed suicide together with his wife. The Nogi suicides shocked the nation, but were soon compared, by Inoue Tetsujirō and others, to the rōnin seppuku, and Nogi was grouped with Kusunoki

Masashige and Ōishi Kura-no-suke as one of "the three great loyalists" in Japanese history.[40]

In his essay for *Japan and the Japanese*, future prime minister and the founder of Waseda University, Ōkuma Shigenobu, suggested that the rōnin had embodied values cherished by the Japanese people, including loyalty, righteousness, and bravery. Moreover, *Chūshingura* had, for more than a century and a half, presented those ideals on stage, in times of peace and hardship, thus guaranteeing the education of society and the transformation of the nation.[41] Future prime minister Inukai Tsuyoshi included a relatively moderate essay praising the "devotional spirit" of the forty-seven. More enthusiastically, Tōdai professor Hoshino Hisashi praised Ōishi as one of the great men of Japanese history, noting how he had first and foremost worked for the restoration of the Asano house, but when that failed, joined forces with the radical vendetta faction. The same issue of *Japan and the Japanese* included brief essays by Admiral Tōgō Heihachirō, Inoue Tetsujirō, Katō Hiroyuki, and Fukumoto Nichinan, plus dozens of other luminaries of the day praising the rōnin in succession, establishing that the late Meiji was the era of the righteous samurai, now celebrated unabashedly as self-sacrificing loyalist exemplars who might inspire the imperial land.[42]

[40] *Nihon oyobi Nihonjin*, 524 (Tokyo: Seikyōsha, 1910). Miyazawa, *Kindai Nihon to Chūshingura*, pp. 93–95.

[41] Miyazawa, *Kindai Nihon to Chūshingura*, p. 95.

[42] *Nihon oyobi Nihonjin*, 524 (1910). Miyazawa, *Kindai Nihon to Chūshingura*, pp. 95–99.

10 THE VENDETTA THROUGH 1945

This chapter explores the vendetta's versatility in twentieth-century Japan through 1945, tracing its many reverberations in literary works, historical studies, imperialist culture, fascism, and war. Overall, this chapter owes much to the scholarship of Miyazawa Seiichi and his studies of *Chūshingura* in modern Japanese history. Even during the Taishō period (1912–1926), often described as a time of liberalism and democratic developments, the vendetta was appropriated, nationally and internationally, in ways that resonated with Japan's participation in World War I. Later, when Japan felt mistreated by the Western powers, the revenge impulse was whipped up via easy references to the vendetta. Liberal and left-wing interpretations contested right-wing glorifications of the vendetta, but in the end amounted to little more than a minority report. During the 1930s, political and military incidents echoed the vendetta's modus operandi repeatedly, even as some warned against its glorification in tandem with fascism. Through 1945, works of popular culture time and again advanced reworkings of the vendetta along militaristic lines.

The Vendetta and World War I

The Taishō period (1912–1926) was a time of relative liberalism and democracy in modern cultural history. Compelling evidence of its liberal quality appeared in 1925 with legislation providing for universal manhood suffrage. Political parties, as well as left-wing ideologies, achieved a presence and some power within the political landscape. Reflecting the openness of the age, the vendetta served various ends, but not necessarily liberal or democratic ones. As in earlier history, the Akō vendetta was, in Taishō times, more a narrative site of controversy, conflicting interpretations, and culturally contested ground than unity and consensus. Thus, one year after Japan declared war on Germany, entering World War I as a British ally, nativist scholar Haga Yaichi discussed the vendetta in his *War and Japanese Character*. Haga noted that throughout history, war had elicited displays of Japan's fighting spirit, as well as its readiness to engage in self-sacrifice. Contrary to Westerners who saw the deaths of the rōnin as tragic, Haga noted how Japanese viewed their seppuku as acts that preserved righteousness and honor. Rather than see *Chūshingura* simply in terms of revenge, Haga interpreted the drama as one elevating the spirit of self-sacrifice, and for that reason, the foundation of *bushidō* as well. In that regard, Haga mobilized the rōnin of drama and history for the allied cause, readying Imperial Japan for inevitable sacrifices in World War I.[1]

Among the allies, the vendetta was used similarly, albeit in historically mangled form. In 1915, *Chūshingura* was appropriated internationally in *The Faithful*, a reworking of the rōnin drama by English poet John Masefield. Masefield's play modified the tale by casting Kira and Asano as rival warlords, with Kira offending Asano by invading Asano's holdings. Written at a time when the German offensive remained unchecked, Masefield's drama meant to encourage the fighting spirit in British and Allied troops. Asano and the Akō rōnin became surrogates for the Allies, including Japan, while Kira represented the Kaiser's German forces. Somewhat successful in England and America, the play was later translated, in 1921, as *Loyalty and Righteousness* (*Chūgi*), by Japanese dramatist Osanai Kaoru and staged in Tokyo. Osanai chose not to correct the modifications that Masefield introduced, preferring instead to let the play serve as a telling reflection of one Westerner's reinterpretation of Japanese history and its famous drama. Osanai and others were perhaps proud that an ally, an Englishman no less, drew from their native dramatic tradition to encourage values essential to the survival of liberal nation-states.[2]

---

[1] Haga Yaichi, *Sensō to kokuminsei* (Tokyo: Fuzanbō, 1915). Miyazawa, *Kindai Nihon to Chūshingura*, pp. 116–117.

[2] Miyazawa, *Kindai Nihon to Chūshingura*, pp. 129–130. John Masefield, *The Faithful: A Tragedy in Three Acts* (London: W. Heinemann, 1915).

It was also in 1915 that Fukumoto Nichinan helped found the Righteous Samurai Society as a branch of the nationalistic Vast Way Society. The following year, seeking to coordinate branches nationwide, the Central Office of the Righteous Samurai Society was established in Tokyo, promoting awareness and understanding of the rōnin legacy, especially during times of national hardship. Historian Mikami Sanji was a participant, and subsequently Watanabe Yosuke of the Bureau of Historical Records at Tokyo Imperial University led the society. In 1918, it published a beautiful volume, *Righteous Samurai Illustrated*, with contributions by sixty artists accompanied by remarks from scores of politicians, military officers, and scholars. For the 1921 edition, former prime minister Ōkuma Shigenobu addressed the vendetta in a preface praising the rōnin as "models for ten thousand generations," thus echoing the Meiji emperor's rescript of 1868. Along somewhat liberal lines, Okuma added that the rōnin had "opposed the oppression of the strong and sought to assist the weak and downtrodden," and had done so with a "consciousness of human rights." Supplementary volumes featured calligraphy by Ōishi Yoshio and Yamaga Sokō, as well as selections from Fukumoto's writings.[3] The same year, Ōishi and the vendetta reappeared in government-approved history textbooks, no doubt another legacy of the Righteous Samurai Society's efforts.

Literary Explorations

Author Akutagawa Ryūnosuke, in his short story "One Day in the Life of Ōishi Kura-no-suke," published in 1917, added to the diversity of Taishō interpretations of the vendetta by exploring its psychological ambiguities. Overall, Akutagawa describes Ōishi's mind as given to contrary, even contradictory feelings about the attack. The story opens with Ōishi reading an ancient Chinese military history, *Records of the Three Kingdoms*, while privately musing about the vendetta. However, when another rōnin mentions the vendetta's popularity, Ōishi turns cold and disappointed. He confesses his shame that so many high-level retainers had quit the league. Yet rather than lambaste them as others had, Ōishi allows that their decisions were natural, even honest. Akutagawa does not deny that Ōishi was a righteous samurai,

---

[3] Fukumoto Nichinan, *Gishi taikan* (Tokyo: Gishikai shuppanbu, 1921).

but instead emphasizes the prism-like nature of his mind, capturing through his psychological equivocations his heartfelt responses to the realities that he had encountered. Akutagawa's depiction of Ōishi thus contributed to the literature of individualism in vogue in the Taishō period, as well as to the growing body of historical fiction and legends based on the vendetta.[4]

Novelist Osaragi Jirō, in *The Masterless Samurai of Akō* (*Akō rōshi*), furthered Taishō trends toward rethinking the vendetta by leaving off moralistic praise for the rōnin as righteous samurai. Osaragi's novel began as a serial installment in the *Tokyo Daily News*, running from May 1927 through November 1928, but was later published as a book. In it, Osaragi did not characterize the Akō band as *gishi* "righteous samurai," or as rōnin "masterless men." Instead, he preferred a relatively new rubric, *rōshi*, or "masterless samurai."[5] This term was somewhat oxymoronic because samurai were, by definition, supposed to serve a lord. When that service ended, they became rōnin, literally "floating men." Osaragi's idea was apparently that the Akō men were still samurai in that they served the ideal of justice for their late lord, and so, accordingly, had a master – their integrity – making them samurai. Instead of simply vilifying Kira individually as a greedy bully, Osaragi depicted Tsunayoshi's entire regime as one given to arrogance, corruption, and misguided policies. Osaragi noted, for example, how Tsunayoshi issued laws protecting dogs, and had them enforced with the death penalty. Tsunayoshi's regime, as Osaragi described it, was both perversely bureaucratic and ever greedy for bribes. Although Asano was a decent daimyō who revered *bushidō* and was compassionate toward his retainers, Tsunayoshi's administrative cohort treated him like a bumpkin lord.[6]

Osaragi cast Asano's attack as one of passion, but also as an attack that was against more than just one man: it was against something larger and deeper. Through Asano's mind, two currents supposedly ran: one related to preserving the customs of the *bushi*, and the other to something new that was smothering samurai traditions. Ultimately, Asano dwelt in the old, which his grandfather Naganao

[4] Akutagawa Ryūnosuke, "Aru hi no Ōishi Kura-no-suke," *Chūō kōron* (32/9), pp. 79–92. Miyazawa, *Kindai Nihon to Chūshingura*, pp. 120–123.
[5] Smith, "The Capacity of *Chūshingura*," p. 32.
[6] Osaragi Jirō, *Akō rōshi* (Tokyo: Kōdansha, 1986), pp. 22, 37, 84–85.

had transmitted. Osaragi depicted Ōishi and the *rōshi* as consciously opposing the laws of land and plotting violence, leaving no doubt about their crime. Nevertheless, he also portrayed them thinking on a grand scale, envisioning their self-sacrifice as contributing to a reinvigorated *bushidō*, one that was not simply for Akō domain, but rather for the sake of the entire realm below heaven. Osaragi suggested that deep inside Ōishi's mind was the realization that the vendetta "rebelled against the authorities of all below heaven" and stood as a "protest" for the sake of completing their lord's grudge.[7]

Intellectually, however, Osaragi cast the Akō band overall as one devoted to past traditions that they were intent on preserving. When ideas are discussed, Osaragi differs from the views of Shigeno and Inoue by describing Ōishi not as a student of Yamaga Sokō, but instead of Zhu Xi's Confucian learning. Bringing Ōishi more closely into the nativist fold, Osaragi also posits that Ōishi developed a later interest in the ideas of Kada no Azumamaro, affirming that Japan had, in antiquity, embodied "the great way of the kami." Yet these intellectual topics are discussed only briefly, without suggesting that Ōishi and the rōnin were of a deeply philosophical bent.[8]

Osaragi's characterization of the vendetta as a protest for the sake of all below heaven, according to Henry Smith, "perfectly suited" the vendetta revival in popular culture – movies and television especially – in Japan's postwar democratic era. In 1963, for example, Osaragi's novel served as the basis for the second NHK year-long historical drama series.[9] At another, more immediate level, Osaragi's work arguably influenced political activism in the 1920s and 1930s. First, in the Taishō period, the activistic interpretations that Osaragi advanced presumably inspired a range of politically engaged players taking up liberal and other causes. Yet later, in the 1930s, those behind the right-wing assassinations and militaristically driven coup d'état attempts of that decade similarly claimed to be rebelling against corrupt government for the sake of all, imagining that by martial terror they might usher in a return to an ideal moment from the imperial past. The multifaceted implications of

---

[7] Ibid., pp. 84–85, 464.   [8] Ibid., pp. 84–85, 464.

[9] Smith, "The Capacity of *Chūshingura*," pp. 32–33. Also, Smith, "The Media and Politics of Japanese Popular History," pp. 87–88; and Smith, "*Chūshingura* in the 1980s," pp. 198–200.

Osaragi's writings were, no doubt, what made them both fascinating and, in the eyes of some, problematic.

Histories, Native and Foreign

Other Taishō thinkers addressed the vendetta's historical significance. In 1917, Yamaji Aizan, upon his passing, left an unpublished manuscript, *A History of the Japanese People*.[10] There Yamaji argued that historical progress depended on resistance and opposition, citing rebel leaders such as Yui Shōsetsu and Saigō Takamori, as well as loyalist Kusunoki Masashige, and, of course, the Akō rōnin, as driving forces of historical change. More than mere exemplars of loyalty and righteous duty, these men stood their ground and died for their beliefs, meriting praise for furthering "the spirit of resistance." This spirit, Yamaji claimed, was an expression of "the spirit of Japan" (*Yamato damashii*). In setting forth this view, Yamaji's historical writings anticipated some of Osaragi's literary interpretations of the *rōshi* as activists rebelling against social and political wrongs of the day.

From a more nativistic perspective, Waseda University historian of Japanese culture Tsuda Sōkichi questioned ethical readings of the vendetta, claiming instead that it issued purely from the emotions. Accordingly, the Confucian debates were senseless and inappropriate, disconnected from the realities of the time, which had nothing to do with "righteousness." In Tsuda's view, the rōnin had internalized the emotional wrath of their master, and sought to provide that wrath with closure through vengeance on Kira. Similarly, Tsuda criticized modern efforts to read the vendetta in terms of *bushidō*, which he saw as a modern expression of spiritual support for the imperial state. According to Tsuda, interpreting the vendetta as *bushidō* perpetuated the wrongheaded Confucian debates via anachronistic misunderstandings of ancient samurai thought under the guise of what was, in modern times, called *bushidō*.[11] Thus, rather than endorse the view of the rōnin as activists serving the cause of human rights, Tsuda interpreted them in a more historically and spiritually specific way, as men devoted

[10] Yamaji Aizan, *Kirisutokyō hyōron/Nihon jinmin shi* (Tokyo: Iwanami shoten, 1966).
[11] Tsuda Sōkichi, *Bungaku ni arawaretaru waga kokumin shisō no kenkyū*, vol. 5 (Tokyo: Rakuyōdō, 1921). Miyazawa, *Kindai Nihon to Chūshingura*, pp. 124–125.

to assuaging the posthumous anger and frustrations of their late lord by carrying out his unfinished deed.

Yet another perspective emerged from the writings of James Murdoch, the foremost Western historian of Japan active in the Taishō period. In the final volume of his trilogy, *A History of Japan* (1915), Murdoch included a twenty-page chapter entitled "The Forty-Seven Ronins." There, he described the vendetta as "one of the greatest feats of derring-do that has ever been accomplished within the four seas of the Empire." Emphasizing the international reach of the story, Murdoch added:

> There is no tale better known in Japan than the story of the Revenge of Akō, or the Loyal League, while the story of the Forty-Seven Rōnin, as it is usually known among Europeans, is the only episode in the Tokugawa annals with which foreigners are almost universally acquainted. The incident has become so famous that it has been deemed advisable to devote a short chapter to its consideration.[12]

Murdoch acknowledged receiving guidance from Tokyo Imperial University historian Shigeno Yasutsugu, noted author of *A True Account of the Righteous Samurai of Akō Domain*. As a result, Murdoch's interpretations are generally informed by credible documents, even though he does not cite them. Significantly, in describing the retreat from Kira's residence to the Sengakuji, Murdoch noted the indecision of the rōnin, as well as their ad hoc plan to commit suicide at the Ekōin. After being rebuffed at that temple, Murdoch related, "they paused and bethought themselves that it would be well to await the sentence of the Shogun, as the world would then better understand their motives." In describing the rōnin at the Sengakuji, Murdoch apparently followed information from the account by Gekkai, the monk whose memoir is one of the most valuable texts for documenting what happened immediately after the attack. In concluding his survey of the vendetta, Murdoch praised Shigeno's work as a historian, especially for having illuminated the "moral and intellectual stature" of Ōishi by showing "that his conduct throughout was marked with singular

[12] James Murdoch, *A History of Japan, Vol. III: The Tokugawa Epoch,* 1652–1868 (London: Kegan Paul, Trench, Trubner, 1926), pp. 218–219.

moderation and foresight, and, when it came to the point, determination and audacity."[13]

Murdoch added that "this episode was so startling and thrilling that it appealed to the imagination with greater force than any other single incident ... in the history of the empire. From Satsuma to Tsugaru it focused the national attention – for the time men spoke of nothing else, thought of nothing else." Eventually, this fascination produced "*Chūshingura*, the most popular play ever put upon the boards in Japan." Yet rather than praise, Murdoch concluded by quoting the following ominous remarks that Alcock had earlier offered.

> I could not help reflecting on what must be the influence of such a popular literature and history upon the character as well as the habits and thoughts of a nation. When children listen to such fragments of their history or popular tales, and, as they grow up, hear their elders praise the valour and heroism of such servitors, and see them go at stated periods to pay honour to their graves centuries after the deed – and such is the fact, it is quite obvious that general talk and unhesitating approval of what with us, perhaps, would be considered great crimes, may have very subtle and curious bearings on the general character and moral training of the people. What its exact influence may be we cannot determine, perhaps, but that it is deep and all-pervading, affecting their general estimate of all deeds of like character, whether it be the slaying of a Regent, or the massacre of a Foreign Legation, is very certain, and presents a state of things well worthy of serious consideration.[14]

British assessments thus ranged from Mitford's laudatory, early Meiji recounting, to Masefield's ideological drama of the early Taishō, and then Murdoch's more historically reliable survey that, in invoking Alcock's late Tokugawa appraisal, returned to the ominous and critical.

Murdoch's concerns would have multiplied had he seen the history textbook for primary instruction approved by the Ministry of Education and published in 1921. Rather than emphasizing liberal, democratic developments, the history text strengthened nationalistic tendencies in education and arguably prepared the way for future militaristic developments. It credits, for example, the vendetta with "renewing the minds of men" and "invigorating the righteous

[13] Ibid., pp. 219–230.   [14] Ibid., pp. 230–235.

mentalities of samurai." It also praises the seppuku of Ōishi and his son as an excellent display of wisdom and courage, thus encouraging among young Japanese similar devotion in serving their superiors. After World War I, the government, apparently wary of activist, democratic trends, sought to check them by having more conservative, nationalistic thought, including *bushidō*, written into the history text. Thus, the latter presented the vendetta as an important historical event offering spiritual support to the modern imperial state system and guidance regarding people's duties to it, i.e., the very matter about which Murdoch and before him, Alcock, had serious concerns.[15]

Influential journalist-historian Tokutomi Sohō recorded his thinking about the vendetta yet again in *The Genroku Age*. This work, first published in 1925, was the eighteenth volume of his monumental *History of Early Modern Japan*. Tokutomi was not an academic historian, but rather a journalist who published his reflections serially as newspaper articles, and then as books. Overall, Tokutomi cast the rōnin realistically, as flawed individuals rather than ethical paragons. He suggested, for example, that Terasaka – the supposed forty-seventh rōnin – simply ran, abandoning the group the night of the vendetta. Tokutomi explained Kira's expectation of a bribe as part of the culture of that time, not something unusual or corrupt. In Tokutomi's view, the Genroku was "the age of the bribe." That Asano did not understand that was simply absurd. Kira thus treated him like an idiot, and Asano complied, behaving badly without ceremonial reserve. Tokutomi thus viewed the clash between Asano, an obstinate, self-centered lord, and Kira, a self-righteous "grand-goblin," as well deserved on both counts.

Regarding Asano's attack, Tokutomi related a conversation he had with Inoue Tetsujirō. Tokutomi mentioned how Kajikawa described Asano attacking from behind. In response, Inoue recalled his discussion of the issue with General Nogi. Nogi stated that he thought Asano had attacked from the front because attacking from behind was not the samurai way. Regardless, if Asano delivered two blows and only cut Kira's ceremonial hat, it was a poor attack. When Inoue asked Nogi what he should have done, Nogi replied, "He should have simply approached from the front and plunged his sword into his

[15] Miyazawa, *Kindai Nihon to Chūshingura*, pp. 132–133. Also, Karasawa Tomitarō, *Kyōkasho no rekishi: Kyōkasho to Nihonjin no keisei* (Tokyo: Sōbunsha, 1956), and Kawahara Kunimatsu, *Rekishi kyōjuhō seiei* (Tokyo: Kōgakudō, 1928).

[Kira's] abdomen." Tokutomi added that Nogi's words, as reported by Inoue, were worthy of consideration.[16] Clearly, Nogi's insights did not cast Asano in the best light, and even implied that apart from being inept, Asano's attack was cowardly. Thus, even those who most admired the rōnin, like Nogi, found aspects of the Akō incident not beyond critique. In repeating the exchange, Tokutomi was apparently of like mind.

Tokutomi characterized Ōishi realistically as a man of his times. Thus, he explained Ōishi's visits to the pleasure quarters as simply reflecting Genroku hedonism. Tokutomi emphasized that those who thought that Ōishi feigned debauchery to disguise his true intentions were being too defensive. To cast Ōishi as a flawless individual, like Confucius, robbed him of his predilections as a human being, and thus killed the true Ōishi. At another level, Tokutomi contextualized the vendetta in relation to Song Confucian ethics, noting how that discourse pervaded the age and was reflected in the vendetta and the language used to discuss it. Yet he also described the tactics and strategies used by the rōnin as akin to those of warfare, with the invasion amounting to "a small-scale war." Ultimately, Tokutomi praised Ōishi for having maintained his duty toward his master, evident in his patient and long-suffering efforts to restore the Asano house. Tokutomi esteemed Ōishi on this count, even while offering only muted praise for him and the rōnin as "righteous samurai."[17] That aside, Tokutomi's realistic interpretations recognized the many ambiguities and imperfections of the vendetta instead of glossing over them with omnibus praise or attempting to transform them into inspirational examples for modern Japan.

A *Gishi* Picture Album

In 1921, the Sengakuji published a small picture book, *Sengakuji Gishi Album*, as a commemorative item for those visiting the temple and paying their respects at the rōnin cemetery.[18] The images included

---

[16] Tokutomi Sohō, *Kinsei Nihon kokumin shi*, vol. 18, *Genroku jidai, chū kan, Gishi hen* (Tokyo: Minyūsha, 1925), pp. 1–14, 54–58.

[17] Tokutomi, *Genroku jidai*, pp. 25–26, 126–130. Miyazawa, *Kindai Nihon to Chūshingura*, pp. 134–138.

[18] *Takanawa Sengakuji sanpai kinen gishi yonjūshichi shi gachō* (Tokyo: Tenshōdō shokyoku, 1921).

hardly compare aesthetically with the woodblocks of the late Tokugawa and Meiji periods, but nevertheless are indicative of the early twentieth-century nuances that came to be attached to the vendetta, especially by those recruiting the rōnin for martial causes. The album opens with an illustration of Asano, short sword in hand and ready to strike Kira a third time, but being restrained by Kajikawa. The picture does identify the place as the shogun's castle, but says nothing about the New Year's ceremony that was about to conclude. The image is one of violence frustrated, but real and righteous in passion, and likely to find its channel eventually.

The second illustration presents Asano about to commit seppuku in a garden area of the Tamura daimyō's mansion near the Sengakuji. The garden site is makeshift, with a curtain tied loosely around a tree. The caption fabricates yet another apocryphal detail, claiming that Asano has just written a note to Ōishi expressing his regrets, and asking Hara Goemon, who is sitting next to him, to deliver it to Ōishi. While Asano did write a brief, enigmatic missive that was delivered to Ōishi, Hara was not at Asano's seppuku, nor did Asano offer any final instructions to him. Rather than a mentally troubled man, the illustration depicts Asano as a resolute communicator relaying the intent of his mission vis-à-vis Kira.

Figure 10.1 *Gishi gachō*. Asano attacks Kira. Author's copy.

Figure 10.2 *Gishi gachō*. Asano's seppuku. Author's copy.

Figure 10.3 *Gishi gachō*. The rōnin at Asano's grave. Author's copy.

Figure 10.4 *Gishi gachō*. The rōnin. Author's copy.

One of the final illustrations included depicts the rōnin band at the Sengakuji presenting Kira's head, unwrapped and freshly washed (per a previous illustration of that), before Asano's grave. With the head, the group communicates intently, with gazes locked on Asano's grave, that his will has been done. The album does not depict the rōnin seppuku, but instead shifts to the grand inspector receiving rōnin reports about their deeds. Paralleling that, the album then depicts Terasaka, described as one of the *gishi*, energetically reporting the rōnin deeds to Asano's relatives, and then to Ōishi's. The album concludes first with a group picture of the rōnin, armed and in full, apocryphal uniform, as though ready to launch another attack on whatever enemy might compromise their lord's purpose. The final illustration is of the rōnin cemetery at the Sengakuji.

Late Tokugawa and Meiji woodblocks did not typically focus on Asano's attack, his seppuku, or the presentation of Kira's head at the Sengakuji. These violent and bloody scenes were avoided in favor of the more clever twists and turns in the dramatic narrative. Or, when warriors were depicted, they posed, perhaps fiercely, as if on the kabuki stage. In the *Gishi Album*, however, these ghastly moments are depicted in no uncertain terms, for all who might take the small volume home and admire its illustrations to see. The net effect, most likely, was to normal-ize righteous anger attacks and glorify revenge vendettas with the sug-gestion that those bringing such tasks to completion would be remembered and revered by posterity. That Murdoch would echo Alcock's concerns in such an environment is not surprising.

Capitalist and Marxist Views

Economically minded theorists offered diverging perspectives on the vendetta, both praising and condemning it. Considered as an intellec-tual, the Meiji entrepreneur Shibusawa Eiichi is best known for equating Confucius' teachings and entrepreneurship in his classic work, *The Analects and the Abacus*. Shibusawa also commented widely on Japanese history and culture, and in that vein offered a positive, even openly sympathetic view of the vendetta. Shibusawa noted that some-times human feelings and the law are not always at one. Those, such as Ogyū Sorai, who more esteemed the law, might applaud the spirit evident in the brilliant achievement of the "righteous samurai," but would most likely refuse to praise their deeds. However, those – and Shibusawa admits he belongs to this group – who more value human feelings find Muro Kyūsō's praise for the rōnin appropriate. Shibusawa suggested that people are generally of this second mind. He did not deny that the rōnin violated the law, but insisted that their display of human feelings was splendid. In that respect, he called them "model samurai."

In another essay, "The Beauty of Akō's Righteous Deeds," Shibusawa concurred with others in stating that the vendetta "was a good resource for teaching *bushidō*." Without question or critique, Shibusawa readily echoed affirmations of Yamaga Sokō's impact on the vendetta. In his essay, "Concerning the Revenge of the Righteous Samurai of Akō Domain," he stated that Yamaga's time in exile in Akō exerted an "extremely positive transformation" on Ōishi as well as on the spirit of the Akō samurai generally. Shibusawa even stated that the spirit of rōnin was an expression of the Yamaga school of martial arts. He added, "Ōishi received the teachings of Yamaga Sokō, especially those emphasizing the unity of knowledge and action, and led others by means of the power of those teachings." Considered in that regard, Ōishi's greatness consisted in his superior leadership skills and espe-cially his ability to transform the rōnin into a unified group that acted with "one mind and one body."[19] Shibusawa's thoughts thus echoed themes from the writings of Shigeno Yasutsugu and Inoue Tetsujirō, especially regarding Yamaga Sokō's impact on the vendetta. Even if derivative, Shibusawa's views held sway among bankers, financiers, and businessmen, nationally and internationally, in part because he was, after all, the wealthiest, most successful, and well-known entrepreneur of Meiji-Taishō Japan.

One contrarian line emerged from a Taishō thinker interpreting the vendetta positively, but in the service of socialism. Labor leader Asō Hisashi, in his essay "*Chūshingura* and the Japanese Character," noted that the spirit of revenge is "the main theme of *Chūshingura*." Similarly, he encouraged in the labor movement not only opposition to the "capitalist class," but application of the mind of revenge in the struggle. In thus appropriating the spirit of the vendetta, Asō was arguably making the foreign teaching of socialism more natural and nativistic in local expression.[20]

However, by 1929, slightly beyond the Taishō period, left-wing historian Hani Gorō had developed a Marxist critique in his article "Ōishi Yoshio's Circumstances." There, Hani claimed that the vendetta began with the shogunate's policy of eliminating "members of the feudal elite" (i.e., daimyō vassals), such as Asano Naganori. As a result, Asano's rōnin were hard hit: they could not find employment, join forces with the "proletariat," or challenge the *bakufu*. Desperate, they partnered with the emerging urban class, the *chōnin*, and targeted one individual, Kira Yoshinaka. Hani denied that the move against Kira was an expression of political opposition against the *bakufu* or an attempt at social reform. Instead, he saw it as a "last-ditch empty show" issuing from a collapsing feudal elite. Yet conceptually, within the confines of the decaying feudal society, the vendetta appeared as a glorious deed. The rōnin were therefore extolled as *chūshin gishi*, and their vendetta was transformed into the drama *Chūshingura*.[21]

---

[19] *Shibusawa Eiichi zenshū*, vol. 6, pp. 150–151, 153–154; vol. 2, pp. 253–255.

[20] Miyazawa, *Kindai Nihon to Chūshingura*, pp. 126–127.

[21] Ibid., pp. 162–164. Hani Gorō, "Ōishi Yoshitaka no baai," *Shinkō kagaku no hata no moto ni* (March 1929). Smith, "*Chūshingura* in the 1980s," p. 198, adds that radical Marxist historian Tamura Eitarō (1893–1969) furthered the economic reading of the vendetta, tracing back in embryo to Satō Naokata, claiming that the rōnin were simply looking for another job and never meant, necessarily, to sacrifice their lives.

Critically, Hani added that if Japan continued to maintain the petty bourgeoisie mentality perpetuating the collapsing class of feudal elites, then accounts of the "glorious deeds" of the Akō rōnin would continue to capture the minds of people. However, Hani predicted that if people could put an end to the false images of human existence, rightly discern the inhuman, existential realities inherent in the vendetta's tendencies toward self-denial, and diligently work to overcome them, then it would be possible to situate the "tragicomic incident" known as the glorious deed of the Genroku period, within the history of human liberation. Hani's opposition to the continued revival of the vendetta stemmed not only from his critique of "feudal society," but also from his fear that reactionaries would use the vendetta to advance the ends of militarism. For that reason, he advocated liberation of the masses from its "spell."[22]

Although the Taishō period ended in 1926, tendencies toward liberalism continued until the early 1930s when successive incidents shifted the political balance toward military expansion abroad and fascist domination at home. Taishō trends remained evident in the writings of liberal journalist Hasegawa Nyozekan. In his 1931 essay, "A Materialist's Historical Perspective on the Righteous Samurai of Akō Domain," Hasegawa offered an imaginative critique of the vendetta via a dialogue between one of Asano's senior retainers, Ōno Kurobei, who absconded from the league early on, and foot soldier Terasaka Kichiemon, who mysteriously disappeared following the attack on Kira. Ōno Kurobei, serving as Hasegawa's voice, explains the irrational nature of the vendetta to Terasaka, claiming, for example, that relations between samurai lords and their retainers were nothing more than those of "feudal slavery" that had evolved into relations of fictitious kinship. While the lord/retainer bonds were meant to be reciprocal, daimyō had used them to exact absolute obedience from their retainers, just as sons were expected to show their fathers. From that deception, the "noble deed" was born. However, Ōno claimed, what was praised as a noble deed was in fact the antithesis, an ignoble one, making it necessary for townspeople to create the drama *Chūshingura*, transforming and beautifying it. Ōno ended his discourse by taking up the contradiction between the Meiji emperor's rescript and the 1873 prohibition of revenge vendettas, noting – with sarcasm – that it could

[22] Miyazawa, *Kindai Nihon to Chūshingura*, pp. 162–164.

be understood in terms of the leap from "feudal politics" to bourgeois political circumstances.[23]

Earlier, an essay that sounded like Hasegawa, "Political Reactionaries and Artistic About-Faces," criticized contemporary praise for the vendetta as a noble deed by suggesting that such praise was based on the pursuit of "illusions from the past," and amounted to nothing more than an expression of "feudal romanticism."[24] Despite such views, by the time Hasegawa's 1931 essay was published, the Manchuria Incident, marking the beginning of Japan's Fifteen-Year War (1931–1945), had already erupted. The following year, Hasegawa moved from critiques of misguided praise for the vendetta to an analysis of the rise of chauvinistic, illiberal ultranationalism and what he called "Japanese fascism."[25] While definitions vary, the common threads relevant to fascism include opposition to liberal parliamentary political systems; elevation of the nation, national lore, and national identity; and rabid opposition to communism, socialism, and left-wing politics generally. In Japan's case, fascism was also typically tied to the rise of military authoritarianism, achieved internally with propaganda and terror attacks on individuals and organizations identified as enemies of the unity of emperor and imperial nation.

Fascism and War

Tokyo University political scientist Maruyama Masao has distinguished Japanese fascism from European varieties due to the rōnin element in the former. He explains:

> The true outlaw type did play an important part in Japanese fascism. But as the name rōnin suggests, one of their characteristics was precisely that they did not attain any influential position; instead this eerie gentry operated behind the scenes, scurrying in and out of the offices of the men in power, and receiving an unfixed income in return for such services as they could render. This type of

[23] Ibid., pp. 164–165. Hasegawa Nyozekan, "Yuibutsu shikan Akō gishi," *Chūō kōron* (May 1931).

[24] Ibid., pp. 164–165.

[25] Andrew E. Barshay, *State and Intellectual in Imperial Japan: The Public Man in Crisis* (Berkeley: University of California Press, 1988), pp. 191–202.

outlaw differed entirely from his Nazi counterpart ... The men who held supreme power in Japan were in fact mere robots manipulated by their subordinates, who in turn were being manipulated by officers serving overseas and by the right-wing rōnin and ruffians associated with the military. In fact the nominal leaders were always panting along in a desperate effort to keep up with the *faits accomplis* created by anonymous, extralegal forces.[26]

The ascent of Japanese fascism and militarism in the 1930s was, in Maruyama's view, initiated "from below" by vigilante bands, civilian and military, attacking government offices and political institutions, and in some cases assassinating statesmen identified as enemies of the imperial nation. Over and again, these attacks recalled the modus operandi of the rōnin vendetta, if not always its level of success.[27]

Recently, vendetta historian Miyazawa Seiichi has noted resonance between the Akō Incident and the advent of fascism in the May 15 Incident (1932) wherein a band of young imperial navy officers, army cadets, and members of the "League of Blood" attempted a coup d'état. The officers assassinated the prime minister, Inukai Tsuyoshi, at his official residence in Tokyo. Simultaneously, a group of cadets and their "League of Blood" allies attacked the residence of Makino Nobuaki, Lord Keeper of the Privy Seal. The headquarters of Inukai's political party, the Constitutional Government Party, was also attacked. With the May 15 Incident, civilian rule was egregiously threatened. Indeed, the incident was a defining moment in an era known as "government by assassination."[28]

Inukai's offense consisted in supporting the London Naval Treaty of 1930, which limited Japanese naval expansion, and in opposing the ambitions of the Imperial Army in its push into Manchuria. Miyazawa notes that the naval prosecutor, in requesting punishment for the officer-assassins, paraphrased words attributed to Ogyū Sorai in his early eighteenth-century argument that if the Akō rōnin were pardoned, there would be no end to lawlessness.[29] Seeing the relevance of that argument vis-à-vis contemporary deeds that clearly echoed the earlier vendetta, the prosecutor aptly paraphrased what he took to be Ogyū's judgment. Thus, the vendetta had its reverberations in both the May 15

---

[26] Maruyama Masao, *Thought and Behavior in Modern Japanese Politics*, Ivan Morris, ed. (New York: Oxford University Press, 1963), pp. 91–92.

[27] Ibid.   [28] Miyazawa, *Kindai Nihon to Chūshingura gensō*, pp. 167–175.   [29] Ibid.

crimes and the prosecutor's case for strict punishment of the modern-day rōnin insurgents.

Other scholars have detected resonance between the vendetta and the February 26 Incident of 1936,[30] yet another attempted coup d'état wherein army officers assassinated two former prime ministers, Saitō Makoto and Takahashi Korekiyo. These two were targeted because they had sought to weaken the military. An attempt was also made on the life of then prime minister Okada Keisuke at his official residence in Tokyo. While Okada escaped, the assassins killed his brother-in-law, mistaking him for Okada.[31] Several other attacks and attempted assassinations were launched. Once it was apparent that the coup had failed, the officers and their cohort either committed suicide or surrendered to the authorities.

Unlike the rōnin, all of whom were sentenced to seppuku, the February 26 rebels, comprising more than fourteen hundred men, were treated leniently, with only one hundred and twenty-four brought to trial, and then only half of those being convicted and punished. Whether the popularity of the vendetta in the Meiji and Taishō periods translated into relative leniency for the insurgents is open to question. Nevertheless, following the February 26 Incident, military rule intensified and civilian government was a thing of the past. Liberals, political parties, and organs of constitutional government were marginalized and often vilified as Western evils that had to be purged or dominated by the military for the sake of national and imperial glory.

Earlier in this emerging milieu of government by assassination, the journal *Historical Discussions* published a special issue on the "Righteous Samurai of Akō" addressing the verdict handed down for the rōnin. The essays echoed popular discussions of the verdict for the May 15 rebels, which was exceedingly light, considering that Prime Minister Inukai had been assassinated. One of the leading journalist-intellectuals of the period, Miyake Setsurei, likened the vendetta to a modern-day gang assassination of a minister of imperial court ceremonies. Like Dazai Shundai, Miyake hardly saw the rōnin as righteous or honorable. However, Miyake added that the *bakufu* erred in sentencing all the rōnin to death. Instead, it should have executed Ōishi and a

[30] Richard Storry, *The Double Patriots: A Study of Japanese Nationalism* (Boston, MA: Houghton-Mifflin, 1956). Cameron Hurst, "Death, Honor, and Loyalty: The Bushidō Ideal," *Philosophy East and West* 40/4 (October 1990), p. 525.

[31] Miyazawa, *Kindai Nihon to Chūshingura gensō*, pp. 167–175.

handful of the leaders, and exiled or imprisoned the rest.[32] Thus, even as vendetta-like acts of political terror defined the 1930s, some intellectuals like Miyake who otherwise criticized the rōnin also criticized the harsh verdict – death by seppuku for all – handed down for them, seemingly echoing the leniency shown the May 15 insurgents, and perhaps influencing the subsequent leniency that would be shown the February 26 rebels.

Internationally, praise for the vendetta came from unusual quarters: Georges Bagulesco, Romanian wartime ambassador to Japan, published a series of short stories, written in the mid-1930s under the title *Yamato damashii*, lauding the rōnin and their heroic expression of the Japanese spirit in opposition to injustice. Bagulesco emphasized that Ōishi not only opposed the *bakufu*'s verdict for Asano, he and the rōnin made a stand against injustice that anyone in the world would approve. Whether Bagulesco's book facilitated Japan's later participation in the Axis alliance with Germany, Rumania, and Italy is questionable. Nevertheless, it is noteworthy that the vendetta had admirers among European writers who later supported fascism.[33]

Other foreign voices denounced the rōnin-like modus operandi evident during the 1930s. Former president of Throop College of Technology (later, California Institute of Technology) and founder of the Japan Evangelical Lutheran Church, James A. B. Scherer, in his *Japan Defies the World* (1938), called attention to what he saw as the beginnings of a fascist dictatorship. In a chapter entitled "Suicide on the Stage and Off," Scherer distinguished *Chūshingura* from the historical vendetta, adding that the revenge drama was more popular in Japan than *Hamlet* and *Macbeth* were in England. Regarding the spiritual appeal of the historical vendetta, Scherer noted that there was a regular flow of "pilgrims" at the Sengakuji graves, whose "white votive offerings always cover the mortuary shrine." He condemned, however, the pernicious impact of both forms of the vendetta, historical and dramatic, recalling Alcock's questions posed eighty years prior regarding the effects that their values would have on the Japanese. Scherer added that in his day, the tale was even more cherished, and blamed it in part for the prevalence of political assassinations, which were "almost always condoned."[34]

[32] Ibid., pp. 169–171.   [33] Ibid., pp. 175–177, 195–196.
[34] James A. B. Scherer, *Japan Defies the World* (Indianapolis, IN: The Bobbs-Merrill Press, 1938), pp. 97, 107–116.

In his concluding chapter, "Climax, 1937," Scherer declared that "fascism [had] been steadily strengthening itself since the February 26 incident" by "keeping alive the story and example of such swashbucklers as the Forty-Seven Rōnin so as to foster [others] as a disciplinary aid for General Araki's or General Minami's army." Pointedly, Scherer criticized the "pernicious influence" of *Chūshingura*, which "spreads the suicide habit until it becomes a national stigma, and condones political assassinations such as the Forty-Seven Rōnin themselves committed." Thus, Scherer saw the vendetta of history and drama as an egregious force undermining the ethics of the nation rather than serving as the basis of the same.[35]

Vendetta drama embraced the heightened militarism prevalent during Japan's 1937 invasion of China. With the fall of Nanjing, the capital of Chiang Kai-shek's Nationalist regime, the Tokyo Kabuki Theatre followed its featured show, *The Tale of Kanzaki's Grass Hut*, "a chauvinistic rewrite" of *Chūshingura*, with an impromptu celebration featuring the two hundred-member cast joining the audience in waving flags and shouting *banzai*.[36] In 1939, the Central Office of the Righteous Samurai Association published a pocket-size volume, *Lessons from the Noble Genroku Vendetta*, for distribution to Japanese troops in China. The book emphasized how the "spirit of the righteous samurai" could overcome any threats Japan faced. After the attack on Pearl Harbor, the Central Office staged an event in Hibiya's Public Auditorium, on December 14, commemorating the two hundred fortieth anniversary of Asano's attack on Kira. The main speaker, the president of the Imperial Subjects Association, Matsui Shigeru, likened Japan's attack to Asano's attack on Kira, prompted by long humiliation at the hands of an arrogant and abusive power. Regardless of the challenges ahead, Matsui forecast a glorious, righteous victory akin to that of the vendetta. When Imperial Japan's military situation worsened and the threat of national destruction became a reality, the vendetta continued to play a major role in last-ditch inspirational calls for "national revenge" against the "evil demons," Great Britain and the United States.

---

[35] Ibid., pp. 255–257.

[36] James R. Brandon, *Kabuki's Forgotten War, 1931–1945* (Honolulu: University of Hawaii Press, 2009), pp. 80–82.

Intensification of warfare challenged the bonds between militarists and vendetta admirers. Despite the Meiji emperor's rescript of 1868, the rōnin, strictly speaking, had not been, in Tokugawa times at least, imperial loyalists. Historically, their vendetta issued from samurai devotion to a samurai lord who disrupted, with murderous intent, shogunal ceremonies hosting imperial emissaries. The vendetta's clear target was a shogunal official whose specialization was in imperial court ceremonies. Perhaps fearing other such misguided displays of loyalty, military propagandists downplayed the vendetta as an expression of "a lesser form of righteous duty," especially as compared to the Japanese people's "great duty" of loyalty and righteous devotion to the imperial throne.[37]

Government-approved primary school history textbooks soon reduced the space devoted to the vendetta to a section on Ōishi and Confucian thinker Arai Hakuseki. Eliminated were discussions of the rōnin attack on Kira. Instead, the entry described Ōishi's study of military learning and Chinese philosophy from Yamaga Sokō and Itō Jinsai, respectively. Yet as things worsened, distinctions between lesser and major duties gave way to a last-ditch revival of vendetta lore for the sake of victory. In 1943, coinciding with the death of Admiral Yamamoto Isoroku, the leader of the attack on Pearl Harbor, *Chūshingura* was being performed at all three major kabuki theatres in Tokyo. In 1944, publication of *Stories about the Lives of the Righteous Samurai*, a collection of song-tales for minstrels, helped revive vendetta lore in wartime culture. Adolescent publications such as *National Youth* contributed as well, stressing the revenge imperative against the enemies of humanity, the United States and Britain.[38]

Not all efforts to appropriate the vendetta turned out well. Early on government propaganda officials, realizing the vendetta's appeal, commissioned film director Mizoguchi Kenji to produce a cinema version of *Genroku Chūshingura* in the hopes of coopting popular culture for the war cause. However, Mizoguchi's 1941 film, based on Mayama Seika's contemporary kabuki play by the same name, ended up being a sluggish and lengthy flop. Nevertheless, one ideologically nuanced scene is worth noting. In it, Ōishi worries whether the emperor considered Asano's attack an act of *lèse majesté*. However, Ōishi is informed by a retainer that the emperor pitied Asano because he had failed to kill Kira.

---

[37] Miyazawa, *Kindai Nihon to Chūshingura gensō*, pp. 202–222.   [38] Ibid.

Reportedly, many nobles felt similarly, prompting Ōishi, shocked by the supportive news, to weep while bowing toward Kyoto. This news meant, in Ōishi's mind, that Asano had been "saved" from the worst charge, offending the throne. It also meant that Ōishi and the rōnin, in plotting their attack, were saved insofar as they would be proceeding with implicit imperial sanction.

Some have explained Mayama's inclusion of this fabrication as historically "plausible" due to Ōishi's tutelage under Yamaga Sokō, "who regarded the imperial line as of great importance to Japan." Yet any impact that Yamaga might have had on the rōnin was not documented in their extensive writings. Nor does Mayama suggest this connection with Yamaga explicitly. The scene depicting Ōishi's anxieties about imperial sanction was, instead, one Mayama added, lacking any credible Tokugawa precedent.[39] Rather, it revealed the extent to which Yoshida Shōin, Shigeno Yasutsugu, and Inoue Tetsujirō had effectively coopted the critical allegations about Yamaga and the rōnin, and transformed them into bragging rights, thereby refashioning the general perception of the rōnin as agents of imperial loyalism unto death.

Until his passing in 1944, Inoue Tetsujirō continued to discuss Yamaga, the rōnin, General Nogi, and national morality. His *Commentary on Instructions for Warfare*, published in 1941, featured a bold frontispiece with calligraphy by another general, then minister of war, General Tōjō Hideki, stating, "Extend the Imperial Way throughout the World." In it, Inoue examines the history of *bushidō*, again noting Yamaga's impact on the rōnin and their unparalleled role in making society aware of the power of *bushidō*.[40] In 1942, Inoue published *Fundamentals of Bushidō*, further evidencing, at least as a civilian scholar, his authoritative role in defining an ethic for imperial Japan at war. In his last two years, Inoue oversaw compilation of the thirteen-volume *Complete Works of Bushidō*. In these, Inoue's distinctive interpretations of Yamaga, the rōnin, Japan's national essence, and *bushidō* echoed time and again.[41]

[39] Donald Keene, "Variations on a Theme: *Chūshingura*," in James Brandon, ed., *Chūshingura: Studies in Kabuki and the Puppet Theatre* (Honolulu: University of Hawaii Press, 1982), pp. 15–16.

[40] Inoue Tetsujirō, *Senjinkun hongi* (Tokyo: Kōbundō shoten, 1941), pp. 18, 24–28. Inoue's preface explains that he authored the "Introduction" and "Conclusion" to the work. Nakayama Kyūshirō (1874–1961) authored the main text.

[41] Inoue Tetsujirō, *Bushidō no honshitsu* (Tokyo: Hakkōsha, 1942). Inoue Tetsujirō, general editor, *Bushidō zensho* (Tokyo: Jidaisha, 1942–1943). Also, John A. Tucker, "Tokugawa Intellectual History and Prewar Ideology: The Case of Inoue Tetsujirō,

One popular volume affirming Inoue's views was a work of juvenile fiction, *Ōishi Yoshio*, published in 1936. By 1943, it had been through eight printings. Its author, Takagi Giken, readily took the novelist's liberties with even the most basic facts. Takagi stated, for example, that Ōishi was among those Akō samurai serving Yamaga as bodyguards, escorting him to Akō. During Yamaga's passage from Edo to Akō, the various routes departing from Edo were, according to Takagi, carefully watched by thousands of Yamaga's disciples, enraged that their master was being banished. Supposedly these followers were armed, even with rifles, ready to attack anyone who threatened Yamaga with physical harm. Launching into another flight of fantasy, Takagi claimed that Yamaga incurred the wrath of the *bakufu* by explaining, in a book on military strategy, the best way to attack Chiyoda Castle.[42] Takagi also reminded his readers, credibly in this case, that General Nogi had studied Yamaga's writings on samurai ethics and military strategy. In concluding his account, Takagi fabricated the circumstances surrounding the Meiji emperor's entrance to Tokyo in 1868, when he sent an imperial message to the gravesite of Ōishi and the other Akō rōnin, remembering their heroic deed and praising them for it.[43]

A more historically grounded work, apparently meant for high school students, appeared in 1943 with Hirao Kojō's *Yamaga Sokō and Ōishi Yoshio*. Well illustrated and simply written, the book opens with pictures of the commemorative bronze bust of Yamaga in Akō, a wooden statue of Ōishi preserved at the Kagakuji, the text of the Meiji emperor's rescript sent to Ōishi's grave, a hand scroll depicting Akō Castle, a folding screen of the Akō gishi, an illustration of Ōishi's residence, a woodblock of Ōishi's suicide at the Hosokawa mansion, and the Shinto gate at the Ōishi Shrine in Akō. Not surprisingly, Hirao affirms that the rōnin vendetta, from beginning to end, was based on the teachings of Yamaga Sokō as the latter were most directly communicated to Ōishi.[44] Additionally, Hirao emphasized three spiritual legacies of Yamaga's thought for modern Japan: first, belief in national autonomy; second, faith in the eternal development of the Japanese race; and

---

Yamaga Sokō, and the Forty-Seven Rōnin," in Joshua A. Fogel, ed., *Crossing the Yellow Sea: Sino-Japanese Cultural Contacts, 1600–1950* (Norwalk, CT: EastBridge, 2007), pp. 249–287.

[42] Takagi Giken, *Ōishi Yoshio* (Tokyo: Dai Nippon yūbenkai, 1943), pp. 45–55.

[43] Ibid., pp. 409–410.

[44] Hirao Kojō, *Yamaga Sokō to Ōishi Yoshio* (Tokyo: Echigoya shobō, 1943), p. 9.

third, faith in the fusion of divinity and humanity within Japan. Hirao added that these culminated in the "movement to transform the eight directions into a single imperial universe."[45] In Hirao's view, Yamaga was clearly one of the most prescient and quintessential thinkers of modern Japan. Looked at differently, Hirao's summary of Yamaga's teachings cast them as key expressions of the nationalist discourse that had become standard fare for young and old in wartime Japan.

Popular culture advanced similar conventional wisdom about Yamaga and the rōnin. The picture book *Cherry Blossoms of Japan* (*Yamatozakura*, 1935) includes sixty depictions of samurai exploits in history, beginning with the battle between the deity Susanoō and an eight-headed serpent. This mythic event is sacred within imperial lore because it was by cutting the serpent open that Susanoō got a miraculous sword, which subsequently became one of the three treasures of the imperial throne. The second illustration features Emperor Jinmu standing before an all-penetrating blaze emanating from the rising sun, thus presiding over the military ascent of Yamato imperial rule. The fifty-eighth illustration, depicting the rōnin, includes a caption stating, "The Righteous Samurai of Akō Domain Whose Honor Will Instruct One Thousand Generations," alluding to the Meiji emperor's rescript. The caption adds that Ōishi led the attack via tactics taught by Yamaga Sokō. This illustration is followed by one depicting the assassination of Ii Naosuke (1815–1860) by a band of rōnin. The final illustration portrays anti-Tokugawa forces from Chōshū, presumably inspired by Yoshida Shōin's (and thus Yamaga's) teachings, prevailing over pro-*bakufu* troops.[46] By concluding its survey of Japanese history with these three scenes, *Cherry Blossoms of Japan* implied that Yamaga's teachings decisively shaped warrior strength and spirit culminating in the Meiji restoration of imperial rule. In doing so, it further implied that Yamaga's legacy in *bushidō* would provide modern Japan with similar success in pro-imperial warfare.

Though few, there were dissenting voices: historical novelist Kaionji Chōgorō, in his *Ōishi Yoshio* published in 1944, argued that it was anachronistic to interpret the vendetta in terms of modern notions of imperial loyalty. In early modern times, *bushidō* was the ethic of loyalty and righteous duty between retainers and their lords. That was

---

[45] Ibid., pp. 124–126.

[46] Kokushi meiga kankōkai, eds., *Yamatozakura* (Tokyo: Shōbunsha, 1935), pp. 58–59.

the context of the vendetta. To suggest that the rōnin thought twice about the imperial throne was, in Kaionji's view, farfetched. Kaionji thus judged the scene in Mayama's *Genroku Chūshingura* where Ōishi weeps upon learning that the emperor had expressed sympathy for Asano to be historically out of place. While acknowledging that *bushidō* had contributed to Japanese morality, Kaionji's view was that its value did not depend on pretending that it was, in early modern times, what the modern age might wish it to be.[47] Nevertheless, with the ideological frenzy of fascist discourse during the wartime years, little attention was paid to Kaionji's historically sensitive thinking about the vendetta and its misappropriation by militarist propaganda.

---

[47] Kaionji Chōgorō, *Ōishi Yoshio* (Tokyo: Chōbunkaku, 1944). Miyazawa, *Kinsei Nihon to Chūshingura no gensō*, pp. 198, 200–225.

11   DOMESTICATING THE VENDETTA

This chapter shows that despite prior associations with wartime propaganda, the vendetta came to be embraced by postwar Japan in new ways. Most typically, it served as mass entertainment made possible by new technologies emerging from Japan's middle-class consumer society and its economically driven relationship with the world. With televised broadcasts, the vendetta entered every home, becoming a thoroughly domesticated form of nostalgic entertainment. Internationally, an American scholar, Donald Keene, translated *Chūshingura* into English, providing a more definitive basis for global study of the drama and the history behind it. In 1960, Grand Kabuki performances of *Chūshingura* were staged in New York City, extending Japan's embrace of the vendetta drama as entertainment internationally. Ultimately, the same technologies of popular culture that saturated Japan with vendetta broadcasts also produced cultural rivals advancing life-affirming ethics, often in gender-diverse ways, fascinating young Japanese with alternative cultural visions and idols. As a result, the vendetta's appeal has subsided, but hardly vanished in the consumer-dominated, high-tech world of early twenty-first-century popular culture.

American Censorship

On September 22, 1945, three weeks after the formal surrender of Japan, the Supreme Command of the Allied Powers (SCAP) led by

U.S. General Douglas MacArthur issued a decree forbidding movies and works of drama encouraging feudal loyalties and acts of revenge. This decree was part of SCAP's efforts, during the postwar-Occupation period, at eliminating Japanese militarism and promoting instead a demilitarized, democratic polity. Thus, as Japan's premier drama about samurai loyalties and revenge vendettas, *Kanadehon Chūshingura*, approached its two-hundredth year, it was declared taboo. Needless to say, MacArthur's decree recalled for some historically minded observers the earlier attempt by shogun Tokugawa Tsunayoshi to ban stage versions of "recent events," i.e., the Akō vendetta. In neither case were the prohibitions effective as long-term solutions.

Even while suppressed domestically, the vendetta attained new heights internationally. In 1946, Ruth Benedict's study, *The Chrysanthemum and the Sword*, originally commissioned by the U.S. Office of War Information as research on the psychology of the Japanese, was published. Conflating history, drama, and legend into a work she called *The Tale of the Forty-Seven Rōnin*, Benedict identified the latter as "the true national epic of Japan." She added:

> It is not a tale that rates high in the world's literature but the hold it has on the Japanese is incomparable. Every Japanese boy knows not only the main story but the subordinate plots of the tale. Its stories are constantly told and printed and they are retold in a popular modern movie series. The graves of the forty-seven have been for generations a favorite pilgrimage where thousands went to pay tribute.[1]

Benedict offered a detailed yet apocryphally ridden rendition of the vendetta. Issues of historical fidelity aside, Benedict's account was consequential. According to historian Miyazawa Seiichi, Benedict's text prompted SCAP – and presumably others as well – to distrust the Japanese even when they, the Japanese, were submissive and law-abiding. The fear was that postwar Japanese, like Ōishi and the rōnin, were hiding their true feelings and waiting for an opportune moment to unleash their secret revenge agenda.[2]

[1] Ruth Benedict, *The Chrysanthemum and the Sword* (New York: Houghton Mifflin Harcourt, 1946), pp. 198–199.
[2] Miyazawa, *Kindai Nihon to Chūshingura*, pp. 227–228.

Perhaps so. At the same time, the vendetta was marshalled to facilitate Japan's postwar transition to peace and stability. General Shimomura Sadamu, who oversaw the demobilization of imperial troops, worked with the abbot of the Kagakuji to appropriate the vendetta, subtly but meaningfully, in public efforts to convince the Japanese to come to terms with surrender. Together the general and the abbot called for compliance with the Occupation forces, citing Ōishi's counsel to the rōnin to surrender Akō Castle in the hopes that the Asano line would be restored.[3] At issue for postwar Japan was the survival of the imperial line and, in some form, Japan's "national essence." To the extent that the Shōwa emperor remained on the throne, unharmed, Japanese cooperation with the Occupation was successful, far more so than had been the surrender of Akō Castle for the sake of continuing the Asano line. Perhaps because the emperor was allowed to remain on the throne as a national symbol, whatever tendencies toward revenge might have been harbored were neutralized. Regardless of lingering fears over secret revenge agendas, the Occupation authorities found overall Japanese compliance a welcome response to their efforts to remake the polity. Even if in a small way, the vendetta thus contributed to a successful and sensible transition to peace.

By late 1947, Faubion Bowers, an aide-de-camp to MacArthur and admirer of Japanese drama, had persuaded SCAP to lift the ban on *Chūshingura*. Along the way, the kabuki world had come to realize that for its survival, it would need to focus on the drama's more aesthetic dimensions, as well as those related to passion and desire rather than themes related to revenge, assassination, and militarism.[4] After all, SCAP and McArthur were overseeing the constitutional reinvention of Japan as a nation dedicated to the cause of international peace through renunciation of war. Although imposed, these pacifistic dimensions of postwar Japanese social and political culture were quickly embraced by the war-weary nation emerging from cruel and utter defeat. In such a traumatized environment, there hardly would have been a need for forbidding *Chūshingura* in the first place. Nor did the kabuki world need to be ordered subsequently to rethink the drama to render it appropriate to the new times and circumstances emerging in postwar Japan. Resilience and adaptability had always been part of the vendetta modus operandi, in earlier history and drama, and they continued to be so in the postwar years.

[3] Ibid., pp. 228–229.   [4] Ibid., pp. 227–229.

On the Silver Screen

With the end of the Occupation in 1952 and the beginnings of national economic recovery well under way, postwar Japan witnessed a revival of vendetta-related culture in the form of a succession of films, beginning with Tōei Studios' *Akō Castle*. Yet what was revived was not the vendetta of wartime propaganda. Instead, the seminal incident was recalibrated for the new era dawning. When production began even before the Occupation ended, Tōei explained to SCAP authorities that Ōishi and the rōnin were being portrayed as "democratic forces seeking to destroy the feudal order by opposing the *bakufu*." Also, Tōei chose a title that avoided the word *Chūshingura*, realizing that the latter might raise red flags. Thus, the vendetta as popular culture experienced its own reverse course, turning away from the themes of wartime propaganda and finding within its earlier developments politically acceptable interpretive nuances that would serve it well in the future.

From 1952 forward, vendetta films appeared annually. In 1956, Tōei released another, Matsuda Sadatsugu's *The Masterless Samurai of Akō Domain*, reviving themes from Osaragi Jirō's novel. As with Osaragi's work, the film presented the rōnin acting in opposition to Tsunayoshi's corrupt and abusive regime. Indicative of the new sensibilities of postwar Japan, the rōnin came to be commonly referred to as "masterless samurai" (*rōshi*) rather than as "righteous samurai" (*gishi*). Other studios followed suit, employing their most talented directors and featuring their most famous stars in one major production after the next. In 1958, Daiei Films released Watanabe Kunio's *Chūshingura*, with an all-star cast including Hasegawa Kazuo and a host of others. These later films marked the golden age of forty-seven rōnin cinema with entertaining themes from kabuki and the minstrel repertoire supplanting problematic ideological motifs of the 1930s and 1940s. However, following Tōhō Films' 1962 production, *Chūshingura*, directed by Inagaki Hiroshi, vendetta films declined somewhat as the newest form of mass entertainment, television, emerged as a nimbler medium for presenting the vendetta *ad infinitum* and *ad nauseum*, broadcasting the forty-seven rōnin invasion into the living rooms of homes throughout the archipelago on a regular, often weekly basis.[5]

---

[5] Ibid., pp. 229–231. Donald Keene, "Classic Spectacular from Japan," *New York Times* (May 22, 1960), pp. 317, 321, 325, 327.

Chūshingura in the United States

In 1960, *Kanadehon Chūshingura* attained a new level of international celebrity with a "Grand Kabuki" production in New York City
at the City Center. The performances featured actor Onoe Shōroku
masterfully playing two different roles, the villain, Kō-no-Moronao,
and the hero, Ōboshi Yura-no-suke. The *Chūshingura* scene presented, in abbreviated form, was the seppuku of Enya Hangan, following his attack on Kō. The *New York Times* covered the theatrical
novelty with consistently positive reporting and reviews. In doing so,
it signaled how far the two countries, and indeed the vendetta and its
cultural spin-offs, had come in the fifteen years since the end of World
War II.

One of the most informed pieces about the Grand Kabuki
performances was by young Columbia University associate professor
of Japanese Donald Keene. With evident enthusiasm, Keene recalled the
appeal of kabuki for American visitors in the past, adding that the
dramatic excitement had also "fascinated Japanese audiences for over
350 years." Well into his exposition, Keene defused any sense of horror
that might have arisen in reaction to the sometimes macabre
Chūshingura plot by noting that much "as Greek tragedies with their
terrible strains of murder and incest stirred Athenians living in the
sunshine of Periclean civilization, so the violence of Kabuki moved
Japanese who were normally sedate and occupied chiefly with trade."
Keene added, preemptively, that in Tokugawa Japan, "Men studying
severed heads and children sacrificing themselves were hardly more
common than they are today in the United States."[6] Given the full
court media coverage of the Grand Kabuki presentations, Japanese
culture – with *Chūshingura* billed as its most famous theatrical expression – became quite the dramatic sensation in New York City as of
1960.

Just over a decade later, Keene added to American understandings of Japanese theatre and *Chūshingura* with his translation

---

[6] Donald Keene, "Classic Spectacular from Japan," *New York Times Magazine*
(May 22, 1960), pp. 50–60. Brooks Atkinson, "Theatre: More Kabuki,
'Chūshingura' Heads City Center Bill," *New York Times* (June 10, 1960), p. 37.
Brooks Atkinson, "Visit by Kabuki: City Center Is Host to Troupe of Japanese,"
New York Times (June 12, 1960), sect. 2, p. 1.

of the classic puppet and kabuki drama as *Chūshingura: The Treasury of Loyal Retainers*. Published by Columbia University Press, Keene's work furthered efforts that he and William Theodore de Bary pioneered in introducing the classic texts of East Asian civilizations to Western audiences. Keene's translation was thus meant primarily for undergraduates and general readers interested in grasping the work, despite having little understanding of the Japanese language, modern or classical. By far surpassing earlier translations of the drama, Keene's rendition became an instant hit, a classic in its own right, remaining in print without new editions for nearly fifty years. Reviewers praised Keene for producing an excellent, accurate, and readable translation – definitive by one count – of the difficult classic.[7]

Keene's contribution to *Chūshingura* studies in the United States was pivotal. Since his translation, other works, including James R. Brandon's anthology, *Chūshingura: Studies in Kabuki and the Puppet Theatre*, have added significantly to the field. Not surprisingly, Brandon's work includes another of Keene's classic contributions, "Variations on a Theme: *Chūshingura*," as well as essays by several other respected American scholars.[8] Before Brandon's book, San Francisco-based psychedelic rock group Jefferson Airplane offered its own homage to Keene's promotion of the play by including an acid rock electronic instrumental on its 1968 album, *Crown of Creation*, entitled "*Chūshingura*." Most recently, another Columbia University scholar, Henry D. Smith II, has assumed a leading role in Western scholarship on the vendetta, authoring and orchestrating a succession of excellent, scholarly publications on the historical incident, the drama *Chūshingura*, and their seemingly endless interactions over the past three centuries. Without Keene's and Smith's multifaceted work, this study would not have been possible.

---

[7] Donald Keene, *Chūshingura: The Treasury of Loyal Retainers* (New York: Columbia University Press, 1971). Marian Ury, "Review: *Chūshingura* (*The Treasury of Loyal Retainers*) by Takeda Izumo, Miyoshi Shoraku, Namiki Senryu, Donald Keene." *Journal of the American Oriental Society*, vol. 93, no. 3 (July–Sept. 1973), p. 411. Frank T. Motofuji, "*Chūshingura* by Donald Keene," *Journal of Asian Studies*, vol. 31, no. 3 (May 1972), pp. 677–678.

[8] James R. Brandon, *Chūshingura: Studies in Kabuki and the Puppet Theatre* (Honolulu: University of Hawaii Press, 1985).

The Rōnin on TV

The 1964 Tokyo Olympics, the first ever staged in a non-Western nation, provided Japan with a unique opportunity to showcase its phenomenal transformation from postwar defeat to one of the world's most vibrant economic powers. The same year, in a mixture of tradition and modernity, NHK broadcast as its grand, yearlong drama, *The Masterless Samurai of Akō Domain* (*Akō rōshi*), featuring an all-star cast. The televised version coincided, at another level, with the rise of a consumer-driven society enjoying world-class broadcast technology. Not surprisingly, the NHK vendetta series achieved unprecedented ratings throughout its fifty-two-week run. Themes of political resistance from Osaragi's novel were toned down, incidentally, to suit Japan's emerging fashion culture. A new age – that of domestic TV – in vendetta culture had clearly begun, setting in motion a boom the likes of which minstrel shows, kabuki, and cinema combined could only approximate.

From the mid-1960s, the vendetta was broadcast repeatedly in the homes, bars, and coffee shops of Japan's newly affluent, technologically sophisticated society. Before long, however, the vendetta ended up domesticated, tamed by family members wielding their power as entertainment consumers with the click of a remote. New technologies in communications and entertainment, including video players, cable TV, and the Internet, so saturated homes that the vendetta, seeming more and more old-fashioned with the years, ended up stripped of its very uniqueness. Reduced from the grand stage of dramatized history to small electronic boxes, it had become both more available and yet a lesser entity, literally belittled by new technologies and innovative forms of popular culture. Critics of the postwar vendetta boom also emerged. Waseda University historian Matsushima Eiichi, in his 1964 publication, *Chūshingura: Its Establishment and Evolution*, regretted the revival of a drama that had earlier enhanced the rise of militarism, and continued still to glorify the values of self-sacrifice. Another critic, Marxist historian Tamura Eitarō, also expressed his fear that a revival of militarism might be facilitated, at least in part, by broadcasts of the rōnin.[9]

---

[9] Matsushima Eiichi, *Chūshingura: Sono seiritsu to tenkai* (Tokyo: Iwanami, 1964). Tamura Eitarō, *Akō rōshi: Sono rekishiteki haikei to ningensei* (Tokyo: Yūzankaku, 1964).

Critics aside, the popular response to the vendetta, already past its two hundred and fiftieth year and now mass-marketed on TV, remained strong for decades. In 1971, NET (Nihon Educational Television, now TV Asahi) broadcast its yearlong, fifty-two-episode, primetime *Chūshingura Epic* (*Dai Chūshingura*), featuring Mifune Toshirō and a large cast of stars. In 1975, NHK responded to the continued demand for grand televised productions with yet another yearlong drama, *Chronicle of the Genroku's Great Peace* (*Genroku Taiheiki*), based on Nanjō Norio's novel. NHK returned to the vendetta a third time in 1982, with another yearlong drama, *The Mountain Pass* (*Tōge no gunzō*), based on Sakaiya Taichi's novel exploring the collapse of the salt industry in Akō and the economic consequences for the vendetta. Then in 1999, NHK staged its fourth yearlong presentation, *Genroku's Full Blossom* (*Genroku ryōran*), which concluded with the beginning of the new millennium, just one year before the three hundredth anniversary – according to the Western calendar – of Asano's 1701 attack on Kira in Edo Castle. For NHK alone, the four year-long series entailed the production of more than two hundred individual episodes, televised nationwide and so watched, per episode, by tens of millions. The total tabulation of viewings – though not by unique viewers – easily ran into the billions.

Vendetta Studies in the 1970s and 1980s

In tandem with the TV boom, intellectuals contributed insightful essays seeking to explore new dimensions of the vendetta. Film critic Satō Tadao presented a spiritual reading. Satō noted that while the rōnin died violently and therefore could have become angry ghosts (*onryō*) cursing the *bakufu*, they avoided that fate because they were allowed to commit seppuku and thus attain spiritual union with their deceased lord in the afterlife. By extension, the play *Chūshingura*, along with worship of the rōnin at the Sengakuji, arguably became a means of revering and pacifying their spirits. Literary scholar and cultural critic Katō Shūichi emphasized how the rōnin vendetta, more than conveying individualism, was most fascinating as a display of the collective, group-based power of the rōnin in loyalty to their lord. Tsurumi Shunsuke and Yasuda Takeshi stressed the finality of death in service to loyalty and righteousness as central to the vendetta's appeal. Tahara Tsuguo's

Essays on the Forty-Six Samurai, published in 1978, focused historically on the Confucian discussions regarding whether the vendetta was the work of righteous samurai. Tahara found in the complex debates two layers of samurai intellectual and spiritual discourse on master-servant relations, one relating to relations between the shogun and his daimyō, and another to those between daimyō and their retainers.[10] From a dramatic perspective, kabuki scholar Watanabe Tamotsu distinguished the historical vendetta from *Chūshingura*, emphasizing that the popularity of the latter, especially in the character Ōboshi Yura-no-suke, was the product of successive great kabuki actors such as Sawamura Sōjūrō and Onoe Kikugorō, who defined their roles in ways that were utterly unlike history, but nevertheless phenomenally popular with audiences over time.[11]

In the 1980s, the vendetta entered a new, more reflective period, arguably beginning with Maruya Saiichi's *What Is Chūshingura?*, published in 1984. Rather than *bushidō* and utter loyalty in service to one's lord, Maruya suggested that at the core of the vendetta and its dramatic double, *Chūshingura*, was the Japanese belief that angry, vengeful spirits (*onryō*) must be pacified to preempt the havoc that they might otherwise wreak on humanity. Maruya saw dramatic performances as one form of ritual whereby vengeful spirits might be mollified. In effect, then, *Chūshingura* served as a "spiritual play" propitiating angry ghosts and thus securing spiritual and secular safety. Casting the vendetta play in a larger context, Maruya likened it to the European carnival celebration of the end of winter and the beginning of spring, often described in terms of the killing of the king of winter and welcoming of the king of spring. Although criticized harshly by some as little more than fiction, Maruya's book sparked a new round of *Chūshingura* studies that sought to go beyond the standard readings.[12]

The 1980s brought calls for internationalization within Japanese culture. Maruya's contextualization of the vendetta within a larger, more global spiritual context was arguably part of this trend. Similarly, Maurice Béjart's ballet, *The Kabuki*, based on *Kanadehon Chūshingura* and staged for the Tokyo Ballet, was another. Regardless of the controversy over Maruya's spiritual reading of the vendetta,

---

[10] Smith, "The Media and Politics in Japanese History," pp. 76–77.
[11] Miyazawa, *Kindai Nihon to Chūshingura*, pp. 237–239.
[12] Ibid., pp. 238–240. Also, Smith, "*Chūshingura* in the 1980s," pp. 203–205.

Béjart was apparently of similar mind, writing into his new dance rendition of it the appearance of Enya Hangan's (Asano Naganori's) ghost, in scene eight, guiding Ōboshi Yura-no-suke to take revenge. In scene nine, Enya's ghost appears again, this time to accept Kō-no-Moronao's head from the rōnin, and then disappearing. Suggested, of course, is that receipt of Kō's head calmed Enya's spiritual anger. Also implied is that, somehow, the ballet performance itself also had similar spiritual potency.

The Three novels from the 1980s revealed the seminal and yet troubling resilience of the vendetta. Morimura Seiichi, author of *The Devil's Gluttony* (1981), exposing Japan's biochemical experiments during World War II, authored several historical novels on the vendetta. In *Chūshingura*, published in 1986, Morimura recognized the appropriation of vendetta lore in pre-1945 Japan for the sake of veiling wartime atrocities, but nevertheless found in the rōnin incident expressions of political opposition to Tsunayoshi's oppressive regime. Distancing his book from the old ethical categories, Morimura did not dwell on collective praise for the rōnin as *chūshin gishi*, but instead portrayed them as unique human beings with their own desires, hopes, ambitions, and needs. In this way, Morimura's work reportedly established a very "human *Chūshingura*."[13]

The other two novels, however, focused on relatively unexplored dimensions of the vendetta. Inoue Hisashi's *A Treasury of Disloyal Retainers* and Kobayashi Nobuhiko's *The Two Sides of Chūshingura* examined the vendetta from the perspective of, first, those retainers who dropped out of the vendetta conspiracy, and second, Kira and his retainers.[14] The latter shift in focus from the Akō side toward that of Kira reflected, perhaps, the growing affluence and materialism of late Shōwa Japan, which in turn not only recalled the prosperous Genroku age, but also called into question the extreme self-

[13] Morimura Seiichi, *Chūshingura* (Tokyo: Asahi shinbunsha, 1986). Miyazawa, *Kindai Nihon to Chūshingura*, pp. 243–244. Morimura has authored other works on *Chūshingura*, including *Kira Chūshingura* (Tokyo: Kadokawa bunko, 2015).

[14] Inoue Hisashi, *Fuchūshingura* (Tokyo: Shūeisha, 1985). Kobayashi Nobuhiko, *Uraomote Chūshingura* (Tokyo: Shinchōsha, 1988). Miyazawa, *Kindai Nihon to Chūshingura*, pp. 244–248.

denying values of the vendetta. Somehow the newfound prosperity and material well-being of Japanese society left the Akō rōnin of history looking, once again, like bumpkin samurai, while Kira's excesses seemed more in keeping with the gilded opulence of Japan in the 1980s.

The 1990s: Liberation from Illusion?

According to historian Miyazawa Seiichi, Japan began to liberate itself from the illusion of the vendetta in the 1990s. As evidence, Miyazawa cites several iconoclastic explorations of the incident in fiction and drama that either contributed to or reflected its wane. One was Ikemiya Shōichirō's novel, *The Forty-Seven Assassins*, published in 1992. Ikemiya presents the rōnin as acting not out of a deep-seated sense of loyalty, nor in righteous opposition to a tyrannical regime, but rather as a group of cold-blooded terrorist-assassins intent simply on killing Kira.[15] This disturbing analysis cast the rōnin as everyman's worst nightmare, suddenly turning formerly righteous and heroic icons of cultural history into, once again perhaps, heinous criminals. By comparison, the eighteenth-century criticisms of Ogyū, Satō, and Dazai seemed mild.

Reflecting women's movements of the late 1990s, Yukawa Hiromitsu's *Yōzeiin: Asano Aguri, Chūshingura's Ringleader*, published in 1998, approached the vendetta from the perspective of Asano's wife, suggesting that she, Yōzeiin, rather than Ōishi, was the vendetta's mastermind. In addition to highlighting a woman's role in the vendetta, Yukawa's work was criticizing the hegemonic masculinity so characteristic of earlier vendetta narratives, as well as Japanese society historically. Clearly, the vendetta's old-fashioned machismo swag was under fire from recently empowered female cultural critics and producers, once again redefining the mysteries and ambiguities of the vendetta in ways that better suited their feminist ideological and aesthetic sensibilities. Gaku Shinya's *Kira's Say*, published in 1998, viewed the vendetta in sympathy with Kira, noting his legacy as a compassionate lord,

---

[15] Ikemiya Shōichirō, *Shijūshichinin no shikyaku* (Tokyo: Shinchōsha, 1992). Yukawa Hiromitsu, *Yōzeiin: Chūshingura no shubōsha Asano Aguri* (Tokyo: Shinchōsha, 1998). Gaku Shinya, *Kira no iibun* (Tokyo: KKS, 1998). Miyazawa, *Kindai Nihon to Chūshingura*, pp. 244–248.

and even suggested that moments before he was decapitated, Kira took his own life by drinking poison, meaning to establish his sincerity and his innocence through suicide. Sympathy with Kira similarly issued in part from a felt distance from the rustic martial ways of the rōnin, and an increasing proximity to the affluent grandeur of Kira and others of his ilk that, even in the late 1990s, still seemed fashionable in the age of "Japan as number one."

The 1997 opera *Chūshingura*, by composer Saegusa Shigeaki, rejected loyalty and political opposition as central themes of the vendetta, presenting the vengeance tale instead through romantic lore of the rōnin. Like the controversial Maruya, Saegusa also perceived a haunting spiritual dimension in the vendetta. At its opening, the townspeople exclaim:

> In order to put the samurai spirits to rest forever, please retell the story of the men who have died many times, and, many times, have come back to relive their lives. In the afterworld, where there is no beginning and no end, you can hear them faintly cry. A cry from the past: of victory, of anger, of sorrow and grief which echoes above the noise of the world.

Yet rather than be done with the rōnin, the opera concludes with the townspeople once again stating, "they have completed their mission. They're standing all again, and their names will go down in history forever. Call the story teller. The samurai are leaving. We must tie their souls to this world."[16] Thus, the opera seeks to pacify the samurai, but not to bury them. Rather, they are coveted as historical spirits integral to, at the very least, theatrical culture and its inherent spirituality in Japanese history.[17] Saegusa's suggestion, however, that the samurai spirits were increasingly faint presences reflected perhaps the extent to which, with time and a new cultural age, they seemed like a vanishing presence on the cultural horizon. Lest that process reach finality, the opera tries to lure the spirits of the rōnin back, longing to maintain their

---

[16] Saegusa Shigeaki et al., *Opera Chūshingura* (New York: Sony Classical, 1997).

[17] J. Thomas Rimer, "One Legacy of Madame Butterfly: *Chūshingura* as a Contemporary Opera," in Kevin J. Wetmore, ed., *Revenge Drama in European Renaissance and Japanese Theatre: From Hamlet to Madame Butterfly* (New York: Palgrave, 2008), p. 226. Miyazawa, *Kindai Nihon to Chūshingura*, pp. 249–250.

presence through stage performances invoking them for the sake of the vitality of Japanese culture, heritage, and identity.

Nevertheless, as Miyazawa and Henry Smith have suggested, the mystique has declined.[18] Miyazawa observes that material prosperity has brought a new aesthetic and historical sensibility that no longer prizes the self-sacrificing values integral to the rōnin vendetta. New social, political, and cultural forces such as feminism, ethnic and aboriginal movements, environmental movements, civic movements, and, of course, the peace movement, have advanced vitalistic, life-affirming, pacifistic ideals that are decidedly at odds with many of those intrinsic to the vendetta. In part, this became evident with NHK's last year-long drama series on the vendetta, *Genroku's Full Blossom*, broadcast in 1999. While NHK might have imagined, as seemed perennially true, that *Chūshingura*-anything would be a sure hit, the series was not the blockbuster many had expected. Recent interpretations of the rōnin as living, breathing human beings, rather than as ideal righteous samurai, along with explorations of the vendetta's spiritual nuances, and even suggestions that they were simply terrorist-assassins, have prompted many to question the impeccable integrity once attributed to them. Among intellectuals, the increasing prevalence of various forms of postmodern consciousness, questioning traditional narratives, ideologies, ethics, and paragons of virtue, has diminished the earlier high standing of the rōnin. Postmodernists today might, at best, agree with Fukuzawa in concluding that rōnin died like stubborn dogs, senselessly and needlessly.

Hello Kitty, Sailor Moon, and Girl Power

At another level, especially among young people, new cultural forms and values have appeared, cultivating an understanding and appreciation of more international if not universal values for the twenty-first century. Anime, manga, and especially the Internet rather than kabuki, opera, ballet, or even television and film are the defining media of emerging new generations. The new ethic and aesthetic of many young Japanese seems driven by decidedly different cultural forms

---

[18] Henry D. Smith, "The Capacity of Chūshingura," *Monumenta Nipponica*, vol. 58, No. 1 (Spring 2003), pp. 33–37.

such as the cute, nonviolent, and lovable Hello Kitty. Kitty's ubiquity resulted in Sanrio's 2006 release of the *Chūshingura* Hello Kitty cellphone strap series, featuring a tiny Hello Kitty on a lanyard, uniquely attired to represent every one of the forty-seven rōnin (including Terasaka), plus one for Asano Naganori and another for Kira Yoshinaka. In addition to the Ōishi-Kitty in the "forty-seven rōnin" set, there are two additional Ōishi-Kitty straps, one sold exclusively at the Sengakuji, and the other in Akō, so that the complete set includes fifty-one *Chūshingura* straps. Foreshadowing the Hello Kitty reinvention of the vendetta was the 2003 publication *The 47 Black Cats "Samurai Clash!"* by Akō-based designer Maekawa Masami. The work spins the vendetta playfully, with black cats, associated with good fortune, the counterpoint to Tsunayoshi's infatuation with dogs. The picture book claims to promote, in an admirable if ostensibly strained way, the cause of world peace and brotherhood.

As the vendetta and *Chūshingura* became the stuff of Hello Kitty aficionados, the traditional male chauvinist appeal of the historical events and the drama has been displaced. Also, the rōnin have been de-masculinized as cute kittens, again domesticated, dangling from backpacks and purses rather than revered in temples and shrines. Along more heroic lines, anime culture has created a succession of appealing and innovative female superstars. The most famous is Sailor Moon, the cute, Western-looking (blonde hair, blue eyes), early adolescent schoolgirl heroine who first won a following in the early 1990s in Takeuchi Naoko's comic series, then conquered a larger audience in anime renditions of the mid-1990s, and finally became an icon of popular culture, nationally and internationally, with the TV series *The Beautiful Young Warrior, Sailor Moon*. Prolific anime artist and producer Miyazaki Hayao added to the elevation of young female heroines as cultural icons with his popular film *Princess Mononoke* (1997), depicting yet another Western-looking (this time a brown-eyed brunette) young girl, San, the princess of the enchanted forest, prevailing over the forces of industry, pollution, and environmental degradation in a primordial struggle between good and evil in ancient, mythic Japan. With these heroic super girls affirming female power, vitality, and intuitive goodness rather than the suicidal ethic of macho rōnin violence, vendetta culture seemed increasingly dated and unenlightened.

Hollywood and the *47 Ronin*

The most recent reexamination of the vendetta came from Hollywood
with Universal Studios' *47 Ronin* starring Keanu Reeves and Sanada
Hiroyuki. Vaguely based on the historical vendetta rather than
Chūshingura, the film ended up being one of "Hollywood's biggest
box office bombs of 2013."[19] One reason was that the film was more
fantasy than faithful to the historical narrative to which it otherwise
alluded. The result for history buffs and Japanese culture groupies was
that the movie seemed confused and mistaken at every turn. Historical
fiction is fine, but those who enjoy it want their history to be recogniz-
able, and fiction, the spice. With *47 Ronin*, history became a receding
prompt for inverted flights of fantasy that must have left viewers wondering why Universal Studios even bothered with the reference to the
past if a science fiction vendetta were the real focus.

Also, the perennial hit throughout Japanese cultural history was
Chūshingura, the play. However, *47 Ronin* is distant from *Chūshingura*
on virtually all counts. Most conspicuously, the fictitious names and
identities – Enya, Kō, Ōboshi, etc. – were not used. Instead, the nomenclature – Asano, Kira, Tsunayoshi, etc. – suggests that the film tries to be
true to history. But then history ends up being so badly hallucinated that
47 Ronin essentially trips out with its narrative. Rather than being set in
the shogun's capital with Edo Castle as the main stage (and the implicit
appeal of Tokyo on the horizon), the drama unfolds in remote Akō,
deep in the, for some reason, dark hinterlands. Akō is in fact a beautiful
place, but what one sees in the film looks more like southwest China
under very dark storm clouds, not Japan.

Curiously, Asano is cast as a feeble old man, not the virile thirty-
five-year-old of history. The evil Kira is brimming with manly maturity,
not the sixty-year-old, aged master of court ceremonies. And where is
Genroku Japan, the cultural age superficially at odds with the vendetta
itself? Somehow, that dissonance is lost in the film, which suggests utter
consistency of historic age and hideous act. Most preposterously, the
film depicts shogun Tokugawa Tsunayoshi traveling from Edo to Akō,
slumming it to visit his lesser vassal, Asano, in an incredible reversal of

---

[19] Variety Staff, "Hollywood's Biggest Box Office Bombs of 2013," *Variety*
(December 26, 2013). Accessed May 7, 2017. http://variety.com/gallery/box-office-
disappointments-of-2013/#!1/the-lone-ranger-11/.

power relations. Audiences expect the grandeur of Edo, or at least nearby Kamakura, to make the vendetta all the more extraordinary. Having the attack and its vengeance play out in remote Akō ultimately marginalized both as the deeds of bumpkins. The big screen wanted, it seems, an against all odds metropolitan vendetta, not some darkly bucolic – as 47 *Ronin* presents pastoral Akō – rural retribution.

But for many viewers, these reversals might not have mattered. However, 47 *Ronin*'s most egregious and perhaps unforgivable mistake was its presumptuous upstaging of Ōishi Yoshio, the long-standing Yamato hero of the vendetta, with a foreign presence, Keanu Reeves, in the culturally gratuitous role of Kai. Admittedly, Kai is a "half-breed," or as Japanese would say, a *haafu*, i.e., part Japanese and part *gaijin* (foreigner), and so not thoroughly foreign, but neither a quintessential expression of the *Yamato damashii*, the distinctive spirit of the Japanese. As is well known, some Japanese unfortunately have issues with *haafu*, making Reeve's dominance in the film problematic there. Even with a December launch coinciding with the date of the vendetta, the film fared poorly in Japan. Reeve's role suggested that this quintessential Japanese narrative somehow needed a part-foreign presence to perfect the work of Ōishi and the rōnin. That suggestion was offensively Orientalist, reflecting American/Hollywood condescension bred by arrogance and ignorance. A cameo foreign presence might have worked, but one trying to upstage Ōishi, the all-time iconic Japanese hero, was simply outrageous, and so doomed to forfeit most of its Japanese audience forthwith.

Moreover, rather than delight audiences with Ōishi carousing in the pleasure quarters of Kyoto, 47 *Ronin* has him all but dehumanized by being thrown into a deep, dark, well-like pit for a solid year. In effect, one of the most popular moments in the whole narrative, set in Kyoto's geisha and tea house district, was simultaneously tossed into the trashcan. Finally, the handsome Reeves might attract Japanese females in some films, but a Japanese macho adventure based on the historical vendetta, as this one sought to be, was not one likely to attract large numbers of that audience regardless. The romanticized drama *Chūshingura* certainly would have, but 47 *Ronin* was no *Chūshingura*, nor was it straight history. Rather, it was an attempt by Hollywood to needlessly reinvent a Japanese tale in its own way and in its own image, seemingly without much of Japan or the Japanese hero.

Thinking that Keanu Reeves would suffice as a reasonable facsimile for the smarts of Ōishi and the rōnin band was Hollywood's costly mistake.

Postmodern Postmortem?

Controversies still envelop rōnin sites such as the Sengakuji where real estate developers appear eager to bury the historic Zen temple and its long-revered cemetery in the shadows of upscale high-rises, leaving the rōnin below forgotten as residents' gazes go seaward or toward the Tokyo skyline. Looking forward, however, there is no sense in indulging, prematurely, in a postmodern postmortem. Three centuries of cultural resilience are not easily laid to rest. Developments in popular culture and intellectual theory that have seemingly diminished the vendetta's vitality might soon become pregnant sources for its next reformulation. If the past is any indication, then whatever comes next will prompt a counterstatement, extending the contested, dialectical character of the incident in Japanese history. Most certainly, new presentations of the narrative will need to be cognizant of the indigenous springs from which the events unfolded. Otherwise, there will be no sense in calling it the forty-seven rōnin vendetta.

BIBLIOGRAPHY

Abe, Ryūichi. 1980. "Kimon gakuha shoka ryakuden to gakufū." In Nishi Junzō, ed., *Yamazaki Ansai gakuha*. Tokyo: Iwanami shoten, 1980.

Ada makura Chūshingura. 1857. Art Research Center Collection, Ritsumeikan University. www.dh-jac.net/db1/books/results-thum.php? f1=arcBK03-0138&f12=1&-sortField1=f8&-max=30&enter=portal#. Last accessed September 24, 2016.

Akō gishi jiten kankōkai, ed. 1972. *Akō gishi jiten*. Kobe: Akō gishi jiten kankōkai.

Akō shi bunka shinkō zaidan. 1999. *Akō gishi shiseki meguri*. Akō: Akō shi kyōiku kenkyūjo.

Akō shi sōmubu shishi hensanshitsu, ed. 1987–. *Chūshingura*. Seven volumes. Akō: Akō shi kenkyūjo.

Akutagawa, Ryūnosuke. 1917. "Aru hi no Ōishi Kura-no-suke." *Chūō kōron*, 32:9.

Alcock, Rutherford. 1863. *The Capital of the Tycoon: A Narrative of Three Year's Residence in Japan*, Vol. 2. New York: Harper and Brothers.

Analects. 1988. In *Lunyu yinde/Mengzi yinde*. Hong Ye et al., eds. Shanghai: Shanghai guji chubanshe.

Asami, Keisai. 1974. "Shijūroku shi ron." In Ishii Shirō, ed. *Kinsei buke shisō*. Tokyo: Iwanami shoten.

Atkinson, Brooks. "Theatre: More Kabuki, 'Chūshingura' Heads City Center Bill." *New York Times* (June 10, 1960).

"Visit by Kabuki: City Center Is Host to Troupe of Japanese." *New York Times* (June 12, 1960).

Austin, Michael. 2004. *Negotiating with Imperialism: The Unequal Treaties and the Culture of Japanese Diplomacy*. Cambridge, MA: Harvard University Press.

Bell, David. 1997. *Chūshingura and the Floating World: The Representation of Kanadehon Chūshingura in Ukiyo-e Prints*. London: Japan Library.

Benedict, Ruth. 1946. *The Chrysanthemum and the Sword*. New York: Houghton Mifflin Harcourt.

Bitō, Masahide. 2003. "The Akō Incident: 1701–1703." Henry D. Smith II, translator. *Monumenta Nipponica*, 58:2.

Bodart-Bailey, Beatrice. 2003. "Urbanisation and the Nature of the Tokugawa Hegemony." In Nicolas Fieve and Paul Waley, eds. *Japanese Capitals in Historical Perspective: Place, Power and Memory in Kyoto, Edo and Tokyo*. New York: Routledge.

2006. *The Dog Shogun: The Personality and Politics of Tokugawa Tsunayoshi*. Honolulu: University of Hawaii Press.

Bolitho, Harold. 1974. *Treasures among Men: The Fudai Daimyō of Tokugawa Japan*. New Haven, CT: Yale University Press.

Brandon, James R. 2009. *Kabuki's Forgotten War, 1931–1945*. Honolulu: University of Hawaii Press.

ed.1982. *Chūshingura: Studies in Kabuki and Puppet Plays*. Honolulu: University of Hawaii Press.

Chan, Wing-tsit, trans. 1986. *Neo-Confucian Terms Explained (The Pei-hsi tzu-i) by Ch'en Ch'un, 1159–1223*. New York: Columbia University Press.

Chen, Hongmeng. 1794. *Zhong chen ku*. Publisher unknown.

Chūō gishikai, eds. 1931. *Akō gishi shiryō*. Tokyo: Yūzankaku.

Clark, Hugh. 2015. "What Makes a Chinese God? Or, What Makes a God Chinese?" In Victor H. Mair and Liam Kelley, eds. *Imperial China and Its Southern Neighbors*. Singapore: Institute for Southeast Asian Studies.

Craig, Albert. 1961. *Chōshū and the Meiji Restoration*. Cambridge, MA: Harvard University Press.

Dazai, Shundai. "Akō shijūroku shi ron." In Ishii Shirō, ed., *Kinsei buke shisō*. Tokyo: Iwanami shoten.

De Bary, Wm. Theodore, Carol Gluck, and Arthur E. Tiedemann, eds. 2006. *Sources of Japanese Tradition, Volume Two: 1600–2000, Part One: 1600–1868*. New York: Columbia University Press.

Dickins, Frederick. 1880. *Chiushingura, or, The Loyal League: A Japanese Romance*. London: Allen and Co.

Dilworth, David, trans. 2012. *Fukuzawa Yukichi: An Encouragement of Learning*. New York: Columbia University Press.

Dousdebès, Albert, trans. 1886. *Tchou-Chin-Goura, ou Une Vengeance Japonaise*. Paris: Paul Ollendorff.

Earl, David M. 1964. *Emperor and Nation: Political Thinkers of the Tokugawa Period*. Seattle: University of Washington.

Fleming, William D. 2015. "Restaging the Forty-Seven Rōnin: Performance and Print in Late Eighteenth-Century Japan." *Eighteenth-Century Studies*, 48:4.

Foxwell, Chelsea. 2004. "The Double-Identity of *Chūshingura*: Theater and History in Nineteenth-Century Prints." *Impressions*, 26.

Fukumoto, Nichinan. 1909. *Genroku kaikyo roku*. Tokyo: Keiseisha.

1914. *Genroku kaikyo shinsō roku*. Tokyo: Tōadō shobō.

ed. 1921. *Gishi taikan*. Tokyo: Gishikai shuppanbu.

Fukuzawa, Yukichi. 1874. *Gakumon no susume*. Digital Gallery of Keio University Library. project.lib.keio.ac.jp/dg_kul/fukuzawa_vol.php? id=42. Last accessed September 24, 2016.

1958. "Fukuzawa zenshū shogen." *Fukuzawa Yukichi zenshū*. Tokyo: Iwanami shoten.

Gaku, Shinya. 1998. *Kira no iibun*. Tokyo: KKS.

Gekkai. 1910–1911. "Hakumyō waroku." In Nabeta Shōzan, ed. *Akō gijin sansho*, Vol. 3. Tokyo: Kokusho kankōkai.

Genroku Chūshingura no kai. 1999. *Genroku Chūshingura Dētafuairu*. Tokyo: Shinjinbutsu ōraisha.

Goi, Ranshū. "Baku Daizai Jun Akō shijūroku shi ron." In Ishii Shirō, ed. *Kinsei buke shisō*. Tokyo: Iwanami Shoten.

Hackett, Roger F. 1971. *Yamagata Aritomo in the Rise of Modern Japan, 1838–1922*. Cambridge, MA: Harvard University Press.

Haga, Yaichi. 1907. *Kokuminsei jūron*. Tokyo: Fuzanbō.

1912. *Nihonjin*. Tokyo: Bunkaidō shoten.

1915. *Sensō to kokuminsei*. Tokyo: Fuzanbō.

Hani, Gorō. 1929. "Ōishi Yoshio no baai." *Shinkō kagaku no hata no moto ni*.

Harper, Thomas. 2012. "The Kurisaki School of Sword Wound Surgery: From Sengoku to Genroku; Nagasaki to Edo (Via Manila)." In Anna Beerens and Mark Teeuwen, eds. *Unchartered Waters: Intellectual Life in the Edo Period: Essays in Honour of W. J. Boot*. Leiden: Leiden University Press.

Harper, Thomas J. and Henry D. Smith II, trans. 2002. "110 Manifesto." In *Sengakuji Akō gishi kinenkan shūzōhin mokuroku/Memorial Hall of Akō Loyal Retainers, Sengakuji Temple Catalogue of the Collection*. Tokyo: Sengakuji.

Hasegawa, Nyozekan. May 1931. "Yuibutsu shikan Akō gishi." *Chūō kōron*.

Hayashi, Hōkō. 1974. "Fukushū ron." In Ishii Shirō, ed. *Kinsei buke shisō*. Tokyo: Iwanami Shoten.

Hayashi, Razan. 1659. *Seiri jigi genkai*. Kyoto: Nakano Kozaemon.

Hearn, Lafcadio. 1905. "The Religion of Loyalty." In Lafcadio Hearn, ed. *Japan: An Attempt at Interpretation*. New York: Macmillan.

Hirao, Kojō. 1943. *Yamaga Sokō to Ōishi Yoshio*. Tokyo: Echigoya shobō.

Hori, Isao. 1959. *Yamaga Sokō*. Tokyo: Yoshikawa kōbunkan.

Horibe Taketsune hikki. 1974. In Ishii Shirō, ed. *Kinsei buke shisō*. Tokyo: Iwanami shoten.

Horiuchi Den'emon oboegaki. 1910–1911. In Nabeta Shōzan, ed. *Akō gijin sansho*, Vol. 1. Tokyo: Kokusho kankōkai.

Hurst, Cameron. 1990. "Death, Honor, and Loyalty: The Bushidō Ideal." *Philosophy East and West*, 40:4.

Hyōdō, Hiromi and Henry D. Smith II. 2006. "Singing Tales of the Gishi: *Naniwabushi* and the Forty-seven Rōnin in Late Meiji Japan." *Monumenta Nipponica*, 61:4.

Ikegami, Eiko. 1995. *The Taming of the Samurai: Honorific Individualism and the Making of Modern Japan*. Cambridge, MA: Harvard University Press.

Ikemiya, Shōichirō. 1992. *Shijūshichi nin no shikyaku*. Tokyo: Shinchōsha.

Imao, Tetsuya. 1987. *Kira no kubi: Chūshingura to imajinēshon*. Tokyo: Heibonsha.

Inoue, Hisashi. 1985. *Fuchūshingura*. Tokyo: Shūeisha.

Inoue, Tetsujirō. 1902. *Nihon kogakuha no tetsugaku*. Tokyo: Fuzanbō.

1941. *Senjinkun hongi*. Tokyo: Kōbundō shoten.

1942. *Bushidō no honshitsu*. Tokyo: Hakkōsha.

Inouye, Jukichi. 1894. *Chūshingura, or The Treasury of Loyal Retainers*. Tokyo: Nakanishi-ya.

Ishigami, Satoshi, ed. 1994. "Morishima Chūryō shū." In Takada Mamoru and Hara Michio, eds. *Sōsho Edo bunko*, Vol. 32. Tokyo: Kokusho kankōkai.

Ishii, Shirō, ed. 1974. *Kinsei buke shisō*. Tokyo: Iwanami shoten.

Izumi, Hideki. 1998. *Chūshingura hyakka*. Tokyo: Kōdansha.

Kaionji, Chūgorō. 1944. *Ōishi Yoshio*. Tokyo: Chūbunkaku.

Kajikawa shi hikki. 1910–1911. In *Akō gijin sansho*, Vol. 2. Tokyo: Kokusho kankōkai.

Kanai, Madoka, ed., 1985. *Dokai kōshūki*. Tokyo: Shinjinbutsu ōraisha.

Keene, Donald. "Classic Spectacular from Japan." *New York Times* (May 22, 1960).

trans. 1971. *Chūshingura*. New York: Columbia University Press.

1982. "Variations on a Theme: *Chūshingura*." In James Brandon, ed., *Chūshingura: Studies in Kabuki and the Puppet Theatre*. Honolulu: University of Hawaii Press.

Kobayashi, Nobuhiko. 1988. *Uraomote Chūshingura*. Tokyo: Shinchōsha.

Kojima, Yasunori. 2015. "Laughter Connects the Sacred (*sei*) and the Sexual (*sei*): The Blossoming of Parody in Edo Culture." In James E. Ketelaar,

Yasunori Kojima, and Peter Nosco, eds. *Values, Identity, and Equality in Eighteenth and Nineteenth Century Japan*. Leiden: E. J. Brill.

Kokushi meiga kankōkai, eds. 1935. *Yamatozakura*. Tokyo: Shōbunsha.

Kōseki kenmonki. 1910–1911. In Nabeta Shōzan, ed. *Akō gijin sansho*, Vol. 3. Tokyo: Kokusho kankōkai.

Kunaichō. 1968. *Meiji tennō ki*. Tokyo: Yoshikawa kōbunkan.

Kuroita, Katsumi, ed. 2003. *Tokugawa jikki*. Tokyo: Yoshikawa kōbunkan.

Laozi. 1978. Fukunaga Mitsuji, ed. Tokyo: Asahi shinbunsha.

Legge, James, trans. 1967. *Li Chi: Book of Rites*. Ch'u Chai and Winberg Chai, eds. New York: University Books.

Lequin, Frank, ed. 1990. *The Private Correspondence of Isaac Titsingh: Volume I (1785–1811)*. Japonica Neerlandica: Monographs of the Netherlands Association for Japanese Studies, 4. Amsterdam: J. C. Gieben.

Marcon, Federico and Henry D. Smith II. 2003. "A Chūshingura Palimpsest: Young Motoori Norinaga Hears the Story of the Akō Rōnin from a Buddhist Priest." *Monumenta Nipponica*, 58:4.

Marega, Mario, trans. 1948. *Il Ciuscingura, La vendetta dei 47 rōnin*. Bari: Gius. Laterza & Figli.

Maruya, Saiichi. 1984. *Chūshingura to wa nani ka*. Tokyo: Kōdansha.

Maruyama, Masao. 1963. Ivan Morris, ed. *Thought and Behavior in Modern Japanese Politics*. New York: Oxford University Press.

Masefield, John. 1915. *The Faithful: A Tragedy in Three Acts*. London: W. Heinemann.

Matsushima, Eiichi. 1964. *Chūshingura: Sono seiritsu to tenkai*. Tokyo: Iwanami.

McMullen, James. 2003. "Confucian Perspectives on the Akō Revenge: Law and Moral Agency." *Monumenta Nipponica*, 58:3.

Mengzi. 1988. In Hong Ye et al., eds. *Lunyu yinde/Mengzi yinde*. Shanghai: Shanghai Guji Chubanshe.

Mills, D. E. 1976. "Kataki-uchi: The Practice of Blood Revenge in Pre-modern Japan," *Modern Asian Studies*, 10:4.

Mitamura, Engyo. 1910. *Genroku kaikyo betsuroku*. Tokyo: Keiseisha.

Mitford, A. B. 1871. *Tales of Old Japan*. London: Macmillan and Co.

Miyazawa, Seiichi. 1999. *Akō rōshi: Tsumugidasareru Chūshingura*. Tokyo: Sanseidō.

———. 2001. *Kindai Nihon to Chūshingura gensō*. Tokyo: Aoki shoten.

Morimura, Seiichi. 1986. *Chūshingura*. Tokyo: Asahi shinbunsha.

Morishima, Chūryō. 1796. *Karadehon Chūshingura*. Waseda University Library. wul.waseda.ac.jp/kotenseki/html/he13/he13_01961_0151/index .html.

Motofuji, Frank T. 1972. "*Chūshingura* by Donald Keene." *Journal of Asian Studies*, 31:3.

Motoori, Norinaga and Federico Marcon, trans. 2003. "The Story of the Loyal Samurai of Akō." *Monumenta Nipponica*, 58:4.

Mueller, Jacqueline. 1986. "A Chronicle of Great Peace Played Out on a Chessboard: Chikamatsu Monzaemon's *Goban Taiheki*." *Harvard Journal of Asiatic Studies*, 46:1.

Murdoch, James. 1926. *A History of Japan, Vol. III: The Tokugawa Epoch, 1652–1868*. London: Kegan Paul, Trench, Trubner.

Muro, Kyūsō. 1974. "Akō gijin roku." In Ishii Shirō, ed., *Kinsei buke shisō*. Tokyo: Iwanami shoten.

Nabeta, Shōzan, ed. 1910–1911. *Akō gijin sansho*. Three volumes. Tokyo: Kokusho kankōkai.

Najita, Tetsuo. 1972. "Political Economism in the Thought of Dazai Shundai (1680–1747)." *Journal of Asian Studies*, 31:4.

Nakamura, Gihō. 1783. *Seiri jigi kōgi*. Unpublished manuscript.

Nihon oyobi Nihonjin, number 524. 1910. Tokyo: Seikyōsha.

Noguchi, Takehiko. 1994. *Chūshingura: Akō jiken, shijitsu no nikusei*. Tokyo: Chikuma shobō.

Ogyū, Sorai. 1911. "Sorai giritsusho." In Nabeta Shōzan, ed. *Akō gijin sansho*, Vol. 3. Tokyo: Kokusho Kankōkai.

   1974. "Shijūshichi shi no koto o ronzu." In Ishii Shirō, ed. *Kinsei buke shisō*. Tokyo: Iwanami shoten.

Okado hikki. 1910–1911. In Nabeta Shōzan, ed. *Akō gijin sansho*, Vol. 1. Tokyo: Kokusho kankōkai.

Osaragi, Jirō. 1986. *Akō rōshi*. Tokyo: Kōdansha.

Powell, Brian. 1984. "The Samurai Ethic in Mayama Seika's *Genroku Chūshingura*." *Modern Asian Studies*, 18:4.

   1990. *Kabuki in Modern Japan: Mayama Seika and His Plays*. New York: Macmillan.

Rimer, J. Thomas. 2008. "One Legacy of Madame Butterfly: *Chūshingura* as a Contemporary Opera." In Kevin J. Wetmore, ed. *Revenge Drama European Renaissance and Japanese Theatre: From Hamlet to Madame Butterfly*. New York: Palgrave.

Robinson, Basil William. 1961. *Kuniyoshi*. London: H. M. Stationery Office.

Rosen, Michael. 2015. "Carl Lumbly: 'Theatre is secular worship.'" *SFGate* .sfgate.com/ performance/article/Carl-Lumbly-Theater-is-secular-worship -6469120.php. Last accessed May 22, 2016.

Saitō, Gesshin and Hasegawa Settan. 1834. *Edo meisho zue*, Vol. 3. Tōto [Edo]: Suharayaihachi.

Saito, Shiuichiro and Edward Greey. 1880. *The Loyal Ronins: An Historical Romance, Translated from the Japanese of Tamenaga Shunsui.* New York: G. P. Putnam's Sons.

Satō, Hiroaki. 1995. *Legends of the Samurai.* Woodstock, NY: Overlook Press.

Satō, Naokata. 1974. "Shijūroku nin no hikki." In Ishii Shirō, ed. *Kinsei buke shisō.* Tokyo: Iwanami shoten.

Satō, Tadao. 1976. *Chūshingura: Iji no keifu.* Tokyo: Asahi shinbunsha.

Scherer, James A. B. 1938. *Japan Defies the World.* Indianapolis, IN: Bobbs-Merrill Press.

Screech, Timon, ed. 2006. "Introduction." In *Secret Memoirs of the Shoguns: Isaac Titsingh and Japan, 1779–1822.* London: Routledge.

Sekijō meiden. 1910–1911. Nabeta Shōzan, ed. *Akō gijin sansho,* Vol. 1. Tokyo: Kokusho kankōkai.

Shibusawa, Eiichi. *Shibusawa Eiichi zenshū.* Tokyo: Heibonsha, 1930.

Shigeno, Yasutsugu. 1889. *Akō gishi jitsuwa.* Tokyo: Taiseikan.

Shijūshichi shi: Genroku Akō jiken no zenbō. 1994. Tokyo: Gakushū kenkyūsha.

Shively, Donald H. 1982. "Tokugawa Plays on Forbidden Subjects." In James R. Brandon, ed. *Chūshingura: Studies in Kabuki and the Puppet Theatre.* Honolulu: University of Hawaii Press.

Sieffert, Réne and Michel Wassermann, trans. 1981. *Le mythe des quarante-sept rōnin. Kenkō-hōshi monomi-guruma par Chikamatsu Monzaemon; Goban Taihei par Chikamatsu Monzaemon; Le trésor des vassaux fidèles par Takéda Izumo; Fantômes à Yotsuya par Tsuruya Namboku.* Paris: Publications Orientalistes de France.

Sima, Qian. 1984. *Shiji.* Ogawa Tamaki, ed. Tokyo: Iwanami shoten.

Smith, Henry D. II 2003. "Part I: Theatre Texts and Color Woodblock Prints, 1–8," *Chūshingura On Stage and in Print.* columbia.edu/~hds2/chushingura/exhibition/pt1.html. Last accessed September 24, 2016.

——— 2003. "Part I: Theatre Texts and Color Woodblock Prints, 10–21," columbia.edu/~hds2/chushingura/exhibition/.

——— 2003. "The Capacity of Chūshingura." *Monumenta Nipponica,* 58:1.

——— 2004. "The Trouble with Terasaka: The Forty-Seventh Rōnin and the *Chūshingura* Imagination." *Nichibunken Japan Review,* 14.

——— 2006. "The Media and Politics of Japanese Popular History: The Case of the Akō Gishi." In James C. Baxter, ed. *Historical Consciousness, Historiography, and Modern Japanese Values.* Kyoto: International Research Center for Japanese Studies.

——— 2008. "*Chūshingura* in the 1980s." In Kevin J. Wetmore Jr., ed. *Revenge Drama in European Renaissance and Japanese Theatre.* New York: Palgrave.

Storry, Richard. 1956. *The Double Patriots: A Study of Japanese Nationalism*. Boston, MA: Houghton-Mifflin.

Tahara, Tsuguo. 1971. "Yamaga Sokō to bushidō." *Yamaga Sokō*. Tokyo: Chuō kōronsha.

1978. *Akō shijūroku shi ron: bakuhansei no seishin kōzō*. Tokyo: Yoshikawa Kōbunkan.

Taiunzan Kagakuji website. 2009–2016. kagakuji.jimdo.com/赤穂義士について. Last accessed September 24, 2016.

Takagi, Giken. 1943. *Ōishi Yoshio*. Tokyo: Dai Nippon yūbenkai.

Takanawa Sengakuji sanpai kinen gishi shijūshichi shi gachō. 1921. Tokyo: Tenshōdō shokyoku.

Takeda, Izumo and Shuzui Kenji. 1937. *Kanadehon Chūshingura*. Tokyo: Iwanami shoten.

Tamenaga, Shunsui. 1911. *Seishi jitsuden: Iroha bunko*. Tokyo: Yūhōdō shoten.

Tamura, Eitarō. 1964. *Akō rōshi: Sono rekishiteki haikei to ningensei*. Tokyo: Yūzankaku.

Titsingh, Isaac. 1822. *Illustrations of Japan: Consisting of Private Memoirs and Anecdotes of the Reigning Dynasty of the Djogouns, or Sovereigns of Japan*. London: R. Ackermann.

Tokugawa jikki. 1999. Kokushi taikei. Tokyo: Yoshikawa kōbunkan.

Tokutomi, Sohō. 1925. *Kinsei Nihon kokumin shi, Vol. 18, Genroku jidai, chū kan, Gishi hen*. Tokyo: Minyūsha.

Tsuda, Sōkichi. 1921. *Bungaku ni arawaretaru waga kokumin shisō no kenkyū*, Vol. 5. Tokyo: Rakuyōdō.

Tsuji, Tatsuya. 1991. "Politics in the Eighteenth Century." Translated by Harold Bolitho, in John Whitney Hall, ed. *The Cambridge History of Japan, Volume 4, Early Modern Japan*. Cambridge: Cambridge University Press.

Tsukahara, Jūshien. 1907. *Ōishi Yoshio*. Tokyo: Ryūbunkan.

Tucker, John A. 1998. *Itō Jinsai's Gomō Jigi and the Philosophical Definition of Early Modern Japan*. Leiden: E. J. Brill.

1999. "Rethinking the Akō Ronin Debate: The Religious Significance of *Chūshin gishi*." *Japanese Journal of Religious Studies*, 26:1–2.

2007. "Tokugawa Intellectual History and Prewar Ideology: The Case of Inoue Tetsujirō, Yamaga Sokō and the Forty-Seven Rōnin." In Joshua A. Fogel, ed., *Crossing the Yellow Sea: Sino-Japanese Cultural Contacts, 1600–1950*. Norwalk, CT: EastBridge.

Uchimura, J. K. 1886. "Moral Traits of the 'Yamato-Damashii' (Spirit of Japan)." *Methodist Review*, Vol. 68, Fifth Series, Vol. 2.

Uenaka, Shuzo. 1977. "Last Testament in Exile: Yamaga Sokō's *Haisho Zampitsu.*" *Monumenta Nipponica*, 32:2.

Ury, Marian. 1973. "Review: *Chūshingura* (*The Treasury of Loyal Retainers*) by Takeda Izumo, Miyoshi Shoraku, Namiki Senryu, Donald Keene." *Journal of the American Oriental Society*, 93:3.

Wikipedia. "Talk: Forty-seven Rōnin/HenryDSmith." 2004. en.wikipedia.org /wiki/Talk%3A Forty-seven_Ronin/HenryDSmith. Last accessed September 24, 2016.

Wilson, William Scott, trans. 2002. *Hagakure: The Book of the Samurai.* Tokyo: Kōdansha.

Yamaga, Sokō. 1979. "Haisho zanpitsu." In Tahara Tsuguo and Morimoto Junichiro, eds. *Yamaga Sokō.* Tokyo: Iwanami shoten.

Yamaji, Aizan. 1966. *Kirisutokyō hyōron/Nihon jinmin shi.* Tokyo: Iwanami shoten.

Yokoi, Yayū. 1974. "Yafudan." In Ishii Shirō, ed. *Kinsei buke shisō.* Tokyo: Iwanami shoten.

Yoshida, Shōin. 1978. "Saiyū nikki." In Yoshida Tsunekichi, Fujita Shōzō, and Nishida Taichirō, eds. *Yoshida Shōin.* Tokyo: Iwanami shoten.

Yukawa, Hiromitsu. 1998. *Yōzeiin: Chūshingura no shubōsha Asano Aguri.* Tokyo: Shinchōsha.

Zhuangzi. 1978. Fukunaga Mitsuji, ed. Tokyo: Asahi shinbunsha.

INDEX